# MEDITATIONS

ON THE

# MYSTERIES OF OUR HOLY FAITH.

HIC MAGNVS VOCABITVR QVI FECERIT, ET DOCVERIT
IHS
Venerabilis P. Ludovicus de Ponte
Soc. Iesu, Vallisoletanus, obijt magna cū
opinione Sanctitatis Vallisoleti in Collegio
S. Ambrosij decimo sexto Februarij Anno M.DC.
XXIV. Ætatis suæ Septuagesimo.

# MEDITATIONS

ON THE

# MYSTERIES OF OUR HOLY FAITH:

TOGETHER WITH

A TREATISE ON MENTAL PRAYER.

BY THE VEN. FATHER LOUIS DE PONTE, S. J.

BEING THE

TRANSLATION FROM THE ORIGINAL SPANISH BY JOHN HEIGHAM.

REVISED AND CORRECTED.

TO WHICH ARE ADDED

THE REV. F. C. BORGO'S

MEDITATIONS ON THE SACRED HEART.

TRANSLATED FROM THE ITALIAN.

IN SIX VOLS.—VOL. IV.

Permissu Superiorum.

SAINT LOUIS
LIBRI SANCTI PRESS
MMXXIII

NIHIL OBSTAT
George Porter, *SJ.*

IMPRIMATUR
✠ Henry Edward,
*Archbishop of Westminster*

*Originally published by*
*Richardson & Son, 1852*

*SECOND PRINTING*


info@librisanctipress.com

ISBN 979-8-8689-8525-6

# TABLE OF CONTENTS OF VOL. IV.

TO THE

# CHRISTIAN READER.

---

1. I could wish that I had an infinity of tongues, and all of fire, like those of the apostles, wherewith to publish through the whole world the infinite excellencies of our most High and most Sovereign God; and the most renowned mysteries which He has revealed to us, both of Himself and of His works; so that all infidels might with great certainty know and admit the truth and sovereignty of our holy faith, and all the faithful rejoice for their good fortune in having known and admitted it; and both the one and the other might be inflamed with the love of the infinite goodness of this great God, and encouraged perfectly to accomplish His most holy will. But since this is not afforded me, I have to this purpose endeavoured, in the three parts of this ensuing volume,* to point out, and to paint with the most lively colours that I possibly could, three of His principal views.

i. One shall be of the greatness of His divinity, that is to say, of His divine *being*, in unity of essence, and Trinity of Persons: of His eternity, goodness, charity, mercy, liberality, immensity, wisdom, and omnipotency, and of the most glorious works which have proceeded from Him; as the creation of the world, with all its or-

* In the original all the three parts are in one volume.

naments, the preservation and government of the same, with the innumerable natural and supernatural benefits which descend from His paternal providence for the profit of all men, but most especially for His elect, even to the enthroning of them in the most eminent thrones of His glory: all which is treated of in the *sixth* part.

ii. Another, which seems to go to the contrary extreme, is of *the extreme humiliations which the Son of the living God took upon Him in the sacred humanity*, which He united with His divine Person, "humbling Himself even to the death of the cross," with the innumerable ignominies which He endured in the course of His Passion, which is considered in the *fourth* part; in which Almighty God is so admirable and so incomprehensible for the infinite excellencies of His bounty and charity, which are intermixed with these degradations, that the Seraphim cover with their wings as well "the feet" as "the face"(1) of this Sovereign Lord, to signify that they confess themselves overcome with the incomprehensibility of these two extremes, and content themselves to publish with loud voices and grateful affection, the sanctity which shines in them.(2)

iii. The third view, which is as it were a mean between these two extremes, is of *the greatness of the most sacred humanity of our Lord Jesus Christ*, glorified in recompence of His humiliations, with infinite gifts, even to be placed at the right hand of God the Father, in the chiefest *goods* of His glory; which, although compared with those of the divinity, seem

(1) Is. vi. 2. (2) S. Bern. Ser. v. in hæc verba.

but little, yet in themselves are exceedingly great. And those which He gained by His merits, He distributes amongst men, to sanctify them in this life, desiring to lead them with Him to that Kingdom which He enjoys in the other; all which are treated in the *fifth part,* and are much more explained and declared by what is considered in the sixth, as will be seen there.

2. I only crave of the Christian reader to behold the three views painted and set forth in these three parts, in such wise that in reading, meditating, and contemplating them, he persuade himself that all which is said and written of Almighty God, and of His mysteries, is very little, and in a manner nothing in comparison of the infinity of things which remain to be said and written of Him; and yet, to understand perfectly even this little, he must love much; for, as he cannot understand Greek who never learned it, even so, says St. Bernard,(3) he cannot attain to the sublime feelings and effects of love, who knows not what it is to love: and when he shall love, then let him presently endeavour to transform himself, as the apostle says,(4) into a lively image of the perfection which he has meditated, first, conforming his life to the life of Christ, humbled and crucified; then to that of the same Lord exalted and placed on His throne; and lastly, to the image of His divinity, and to the exemplary virtues which shine there: endeavouring also to help all men with the favour of the divine grace to reform the image of their nature, and to conform it to this image, as will be declared in the ensuing meditatons.

(3) Serm. lxxix. in Cant. (4) 2 Cor. iii. 18.

# II.—FOR PROFICIENTS IN THE ILLUMINATIVE WAY.

## C.—MEDITATIONS UPON THE MYSTERIES OF THE PASSION OF JESUS CHRIST OUR LORD.

### INTRODUCTION—ON MENTAL PRAYER UPON THE PASSION OF OUR LORD JESUS CHRIST.

1. Notwithstanding that the meditations of the mysteries of the Passion of Jesus Christ our Lord belong, as has been declared in the introduction of this book, to the illuminative way, especially to its highest degree, which approaches nearest to the *unitive* way, nevertheless *they are exceedingly profitable for all sorts of persons*, by whatever way they walk, and in whatever degree of perfection they live: (1) forasmuch as sinners will find in them most effectual motives to purify themselves from all their sins; beginners, to mortify their passions; proficients, to increase in all kinds of virtue; and the perfect, to obtain union with Almighty God by fervent love.

2. For this cause, St. Bernard says, (2) that the Passion of Jesus Christ, even to this present day, makes the earth to *tremble*, *rends* the stones, *opens* the sepulchres, and rends "the veil of the Temple," dividing it "in two, from the top even to the bottom:" (3) for, as those who meditate the

(1) S. Bon. in stim. Div. Amoris, c. 1.
(2) Serm. in Ser. 4, majoris heb. (3) Mat. xxvii. 51, 52.

same seriously,—if they be earth, through their faults and affections to earthly things, *tremble* with the holy fear of Almighty God, and at the severe justice which He executed upon His own Son, moving themselves herewith, to forsake their *earthliness;*—if they be *stones*, by the hardness of their hearts, they become soft and tender, and rend themselves, as it were with the greatness of sorrow, as well for their own sins, as for the pains which Christ endured for them.—If they be sealed "sepulchres," by the shame which they have to discover their sins, they are "opened" by confession, to drive death from them, and to raise themselves again to newness of life.—And finally, that "*veil*" which made the division between God and us, is torn for all, that we may, as St. Paul says, (4) contemplate more manifestly the glory of our Lord, and the bottomless depth of His celestial secrets.

3. And not without cause did the veil rend itself "from the top" "to the bottom;" to signify that by the means of Christ crucified, we may contemplate the height of His divinity, and of His sovereign perfections: as also the depth and profundity of His humanity, and of His illustrious and resplendent virtues. So that sinners, who like "urchins," (5) are all thorny through their sins, may find an entrance into the cleft of this divine Rock, where, mournfully meditating for their sins, they will blunt the sharp points of their pricking thorns, and free themselves from all painful and remorseful prickings.—The more pure and more unspotted, like doves, may fly more high, and making their nests and abodes within "the clefts of" this "Rock, and in the hollow places of" this "wall," (6) will become much more pure and more beautiful.—And the perfect, who like to "harts," climb up the high mountains, meditating on Christ highly exalted from the earth,

(4) 2 Cor. iii. 18. (5) Ps. ciii. 18. (6) Cant. ii. 14.

will be drawn very forcibly to have their conversation above in heaven. And all, as St. Bernard says, may suck forth "honey out of" this "rock," and "oil" out of the hardest stone: (7) which, though it were hard in bearing injuries, and more hard in enduring scourges, and most hard of all in enduring the torments of the cross, yet is made to us a fountain both of "oil" and "honey," that heals our wounds, mollifies our hardnesses, strengthens our feebleness, and banquets our souls with the sweetness of His divine consolations.

4. And for this cause, with great reason Albertus Magnus says, (8) that the simple remembrance and devout meditation of the Passion of Jesus Christ, is much more profitable to a man, than to fast a whole year with bread and water, and to discipline himself every day, even to the shedding of his blood, and to recite every day the whole Psalter: because these exercises, although they are good and profitable, yet being only exterior works, if we take them alone, they are not so powerful to purify the soul from vices, and to enlighten it with verities and virtues, and to perfect it in the inflamed affections of divine love, as is the attentive and profound meditation of the Passion of Christ our Lord, which works all these effects within our souls, giving, moreover, spirit and life to penances and exterior actions, to the fervent exercise of which it carries us with courage and efficacy.

(7) Ser. de Pentec. Deut. xxxii. 13.

(8) Rosetum spirit. exercit. xxii. c. 1.

## Chap. I. On the end which we ought to have in meditating the Passion.

1. From this principle which has been proposed, is evidently deduced, that as the persons are different who meditate the Passion of Christ our Lord, so *the ends and scopes are also different which they desire* in meditating them, every one aiming at that affection and spiritual fruit, which is conformable to the state of his soul, and to the way by which he walks: that is to say, either to purge and *purify himself* from his sins and disordered passions; or to *adorn himself with heroic virtues;* or to *unite himself* to Almighty *God,* with fervent affections of love and charity, taking for a means to attain to all this, the affection of compassion, which opens the way to all the others.

2. For this reason it is to be presupposed, that *the Passion of Christ,* as St. Laurence Justinian says, *may serve for matter of joy or matter of sorrow,* because it may be considered in two different ways.

i. The one, inasmuch as it is a *most singular benefit of Almighty God:*—"In quo divinæ miserationis reseratur abyssus, cœlorum aperitur janua, charitatis latitudo ostenditur, et quantus sit homo apertissime demonstratur: vile enim esse non potest, quod Filii Dei sanguine comparatur;"—"In which the bottomless depth of the divine mercy is discovered, the gate of heaven is opened, the breadth of charity is manifested, and the esteem which Almighty God makes of man, is evidently declared; for that thing cannot be vile which was bought with the blood of the Son of God."(1) In this manner the medi-

(1) Lib. de Triump. agone Christi, c. 20.

tation of the Passion moves affections of joy and of gladness; as "Abraham rejoiced,"(2) when in the figure of the ram which he sacrificed instead of his son Isaac, he beheld in contemplation the death of Jesus Christ, rejoicing for the great good which the whole world was to receive by it. And Christ our Lord Himself, upon this motive, thinking on His Passion, called in the book of Canticles, this day upon which His mother the Synagogue "crowned" Him with a crown of thorns, in the day of His espousals, and in the day of the joy of His heart;"(3) and therefore He entered into Jerusalem with great signs of joy to receive this crown, and to celebrate on the bed-chamber of the cross "the espousals" with His Church. This sort of meditation is most proper to those who walk in the *unitive* way, considering the Passion, as other divine benefits, of which the sixth part treats.

ii. The *other* manner to meditate the Passion, of which we are principally to treat at present, is, inasmuch *as it was bitter, and very painful* to Christ our Lord; and that it was occasioned by our sins; and as it was a model of all virtues, especially of such as shine amidst the greatest adversities; and after this manner, it moves to sorrow and compassion of that Lord, who suffered so much for our sakes: even Christ Himself was broken, sad and heavy, with only thinking of it; and it is therefore reasonable that we should accompany Him in this His heaviness, lest He say of us, that of the psalm:—"I looked for one that would grieve together with me, but there was none; and for one that would comfort me, and I found none."(4)

**2.** But that it may be understood what sort of compassion this ought to be, and to what ends it is to be ordained, I premise, that Jesus Christ our Lord drank the

(2) Joan. viii. 56; S. Chrys. Hom. 54, in Joan.; Gen. xxii. 13.
(3) Cant. iii. 11. (4) Psal. lxviii. 21.

chalice of His Passion in two manners. The one was, *corporally*, by the hands of the cruel ministers and tormentors, when He was apprehended, scourged, crowned with thorns, and crucified. The other was, *spiritually*, in His mind by lively representation, and imagination of the same torments, and of the cause of them, which were our sins. Of both which His Majesty made mention, speaking to the sons of Zebedee, as has been noted in its place: for St. Matthew recounts that He said to them:—"Can you drink of the chalice that I shall drink?"(5) Where He spoke of the corporal drink which He was to taste of. And St. Mark relates it in the present tense, as if He were drinking it at that very time, saying:—"Can you drink of the chalice that I drink of, and be baptized with the Baptism wherewith I am baptized?"(6) Where He also declares the spiritual potion or drink, which He drank every day, although He drank the same with greater bitterness in the garden of Gethsemane, where, from the interior feeling of it, He was spiritually scourged, crowned with thorns, and crucified: and in both which manners of drinking this chalice, most excellent virtues shined, as we shall hereafter see. Hence follow the *ends* which we ought to have in these meditations, as also the *fruits* which we are to gather from them: which are to *unite*, *transform*, *and conform us to Christ*, afflicted and tormented in the two manners above-mentioned, drinking likewise in our manner, the chalice of His Passion in both ways.

i. First, procuring in meditation, to "let this mind be in" us, as St. Paul says, "which was also in Christ Jesus,"(7) *having the affections of compassion*, sorrow and sadness, in such a manner that we become "transformed" into Christ, sad, and afflicted for our sakes, and *spiritually*

(5) Mat. xx. 22. Med. 23 of the 3rd Part.
(6) Marc. x. 38. (7) Phil. ii. 5.

crucified with Him; in the same manner as the most holy Virgin felt the sorrows of her Son: for which cause Simeon said:—"that through her own soul a sword" should "pierce,"(8) not corporal but spiritual, of compassion and sorrow. This manner of feeling the Passion of Christ, is a special gift of the same Lord, who gives eyes to see His pains, and to deplore them; for which cause He said by Zachariah, that He would "pour out upon the house of David, and upon the inhabitants of Jerusalem, the spirit of grace and of prayer, and they shall look upon Him whom they have pierced, and they shall mourn for Him as one mourneth for an only son."(9) And although this passage is usually explained in another sense, and of other tears, which the incredulous Jews will have at the day of judgment; yet it may also be understood of those who receive from Almighty God the spirit of prayer, and in virtue of it, behold with the eyes of lively faith, Him "whom they have crucified by their sins,"(10) bitterly deploring His death. Here the disorder of some persons is apparent, who go to meditate the Passion, and desire therein tears and tenderness of heart, principally for their own pleasure, gust and consolation, which, although it seems to be spiritual, yet, as St. Bonaventure says, (11) is of self-love, and much disordered, for that it is great disorder to desire sweetness amidst the bitterness of Christ, and to desire comforts, meditating His discomforts, which ought not to be meditated, but that we may feel them, and to be partakers of them: although the bounty of our Lord is so great, that to discomfort ourselves with Him, is not one of the least comforts.

ii. The second end which we ought to aim at in these

(8) Luc. ii. 35. (9) Zach. xii. 10. Joan. xix. 37.
(10) Heb. vi. 6. (11) Stim. de Amor. c. 1, ad finem.

meditations, is also *to drink the cup of the Passion, corporally* conforming ourselves to Christ our Lord in the *selfsame sufferings*, taking strength and courage for this purpose, and making efficacious resolutions, imposing voluntarily upon ourselves some painful exercises, as fastings, disciplines, and other voluntary mortifications: supporting patiently and joyfully such as God shall vouchsafe to send, or suffer to befal us, believing, as St. Paul says, that to us "it is given" not only "to believe" in Christ, "but also to suffer for Him."(12) And so, imitating the same apostle, we ought to endeavour, when we meditate the Passion, to "bear always in our body the mortification of Jesus, (13) and "the marks" (14) of Jesus, which are the wounds and pains which afflict our flesh, as they afflicted His; so that in both manners every one may say,—"Christo crucifixus sum cruci." "With Christ I am nailed to the cross," (15) as well by compassion as by imitation, in suffering for Him, as He suffered for me.

3. Hence ensues the third principal end of these meditations, which is *to conform ourselves with Christ in the heroic virtues* which He practised, drinking His chalice as well spiritually as corporally—that is to say, in the love of Almighty God, and of men, in the zeal of the salvation of souls, in the purity of intention, and in the affection of obedience, humility, patience, poverty, and in the exterior works both of these and of other virtues, and particularly in the contempt of earthly things, and in the mortification of those affections which incite and stir us to the pursuit or retaining of them. So that being "armed," as St. Peter says, "with the same thought" (16) of that which Jesus Christ has endured, we become in all things like unto Him: and to this purpose the meditation of His

(12) Phil. i. 29. (13) 2 Cor. iv. 10. (14) Gal. vi. 17.
(15) Gal. ii. 19. (16) 1 Pet. iv. 1.

Passion serves us for an armour of proof, strong, bright, and beautiful, which arms us and covers us from head to foot, making us dreadful to the devils, terrible to the flesh, admirable to the world, grateful to the angels, and amiable to Almighty God.

## CHAP. II. ON THE DISPOSITIONS TO BE PROCURED IN MEDITATING THE PASSION.

1. To obtain the ends we propose in meditating the Passion, it is of great importance to *prepare ourselves* in the best manner we possibly can. For, notwithstanding that it is necessary, as the Holy Spirit says, "before prayer" to "prepare" the "soul," and not to approach to it "as a man that tempteth God," (1) expecting the dews of heaven, without any disposition to receive them, yet this is more especially important for that prayer and meditation, of which the subject is the sorrows and labours of Christ our Lord, for which He prepared Himself with great love, and requires that they be weighed and meditated with much fervour.

2. I may therefore imagine that He says to me that of Jeremias:—"Remember my poverty and transgression, the wormwood and the gall:" and that I answer Him, "I will be mindful and remember, and my soul shall languish within me. These things I will think over in my heart, therefore will I hope in Him."(2) That is to say, I will *call to mind very particularly, and with great fervour, Thy labours and afflictions*, feeling them so inwardly, that my soul shall languish for the greatness of grief and sorrow: and not content to have thought once only of all Thy pains, I will repeat them many times, and ruminate upon them

(1) Ecclus. xviii. 23. (2) Thren. iii. 19.

with great attention and affection, collecting from them great confidence.

3. The dispositions convenient to meditate these mysteries with more profit, St. Bonaventure succinctly declares, saying:—"Debet homo aggredi hoc tam nobile opus *humiliter, confidenter, instanter*, et *cum quantâ potest cordis sui munditiâ*"—"A man ought to take in hand this noble work, *humbly, confidently, earnestly*, and *with the greatest purity of heart* that he possibly can:"(3) where he puts down four principal virtues, which greatly dispose to receive from Almighty God the gifts and graces which He is wont to impart to those who exercise themselves in these meditations.

i. The first is, *humility of heart*, entering into meditation with shame and confusion for our offences; not only for this general reason, that "the just" in the beginning of his prayer, is "first accuser of himself,"(4) but in particular, because our sins are the cause of the torments of Christ, whom we behold and contemplate; as if a father were put into prison in a dungeon, bound with shackles and fetters, amongst thieves, suffering grievous sorrows and disgraces, not for his own, but for his son's offences—if such a son should enter to visit him, no doubt he would enter in with great humility, shame and confusion, for having caused his father these torments. And to this humility appertains to be clothed in mourning, that is to say, with exterior humility in apparel and dress, especially when the memory of the Passion is celebrated, or when it is seriously meditated; for if any one go to visit the afflicted, he goes not in wedding garments, but with garments of mourning, conforming himself to the afflicted; like as the friends of Job did, when they saw him full of ulcers, "sitting upon a dunghill."(5) It appertains also

(3) Stim. div. Amor. c. vi. (4) Prov. xviii. 17. Juxt. Sept. (5) Job. ii. 8.

to perfect humility, that a man acknowledge himself unworthy to assist at these mysteries, and to have a feeling of them, deeming it a special favour which Almighty God affords to His best beloved friends, as it was to share part of His sorrows to His three apostles in the garden: and to grant to His mother, St. John the Evangelist, and Mary Magdalen, to be present with Him on Mount Calvary when He was hanging upon the cross; and this especial grace is not given but to the humble, because the proud, as is said in the book of Job :—"shall fear Him, and all that seem to themselves to be wise shall not dare to behold Him:"(6) that is to say, it is not granted them to contemplate Almighty God, according to the greatness of His divinity, nor have the spirit to consider Him, according to the humiliations of His humanity.

ii. The second disposition is, great *confidence in the mercy of Christ* our Lord, that since He has vouchsafed to suffer so much for the love of us, He also will vouchsafe to grant us to suffer together with Him, so that from the meditation of His labours, we may draw the fruit for which they were ordained. And so coupling humility with confidence, I will request this grace of Him, alleging to Him three titles and reasons.—(a) The same Passion which He suffered.—(b) The compassion which He then had of sinners, making Himself their Advocate, and praying for them, that they might be capable of the fruit of His Passion.—(c) The liberality which He exercised towards one of them, namely, towards the good thief, who besought Him with humility and confidence, to "remember" him "when" He came "into" His "kingdom,"(7) and obtained more than he demanded, as shall be shown in its place. But I, says St. Laurence Justinian, after I shall have con-

(6) Job. xxxvii. 24. S. Greg. lib. 27, Mor. c. 27.
(7) Luc. xxiii. 42.

fessed myself a sinner like the thief, I will speak to my Lord nailed to the cross, and will say to Him with humility and confidence:—"Lord, remember me, not only that I may go into Thy Kingdom," "Sed ut doloribus compatiar tuis, tuæque communicem passioni;" "but also that I may have compassion on Thy sorrows, and may participate in Thy Passion:"(8) for well I know, that if I have part with Thee in suffering, I shall also have part with Thee in Thy Kingdom:(9) upon these considerations we ought to ground our confidence in Jesus Christ, which, says St. Bernard: "the greater it is, the more capable it makes us of divine favours, the vessel of the heart being emptied of itself by humility, the better to receive them."(10)

iii. The third disposition is, great *fervour and diligence in this work of* holy prayer; for it would be very shameful to meditate, faintly or coldly, that which Christ suffered with so great fervour. This fervour we must show in making our meditation very attentively, profoundly, and devoutly, driving out of the memory all distractions, out of the understanding dulness of discourse, that it may dive into the depth of the mysteries; and out of the will coldness in affections; endeavouring that they be very fervent, like those of Christ our Lord, making a generous determination to accompany Him; not sleeping like the three apostles in the garden, but watching as He watched, and praying with that agony, earnestness, and perseverance with which He prayed, spending in it some whole hours in imitation of Him.

iv. The fourth disposition is *purity of heart*, taking care to purge it, and to preserve it clean from all sin, so that entering pure into prayer I may abide in it with great

(8) Ser. de Pass. (9) Rom. viii. 17; 2 Tim. ii. 12.
(10) Ser. 32, in Cant.

confidence, without remorse, and well disposed to receive the gifts of Almighty God, and the fruits of His most precious blood: for no man of understanding will pour a precious liquor into a foul and defiled vessel. Wherefore, says S. Bernard, since the benediction is so ample, prepare pure vessels in which to receive it, devout souls, vigilant spirits, well-ordered affections, pure consciences, into which may be infused all such graces as are there communicated.(11)

These are the dispositions which one ought to bring with him to meditate these mysteries; but he that is without them, let him not for this reason, leave meditation;—for meditation will kindle the desire of them, as it likewise moves to other virtues, of which we are to speak presently.

## CHAP. III. DIFFERENT MANNERS OF MEDITATING THE PASSION.

1. To take away the irksomeness which our tepidity may find in often meditating the same thing in the same manner, it is well to know the divers ways that there are of meditating the Passion, besides those two which have been explained, of pondering the same as beneficial to us, or else as painful to Christ.

There are, then, other two very excellent methods, to which the rest are reduced after the manner of banquets, which are wont to be served in two ways;—i. the one, by *placing every dish apart by itself*, and having eaten of that, setting on another;—ii. the other, by setting on several dishes all together, and *taking a morsel of every one*, according to the appetite or necessity of him who is eating;—even so in

(11) Ser. in. Fer. quart. 4, Heb. penosæ.

this spiritual banquet of the *mysteries of the Passion*, there are *two manners of eating them spiritually.*

i. The first and most ordinary, is, meditating *every mystery apart by itself*, pondering in every one, that which is worthy of consideration, *according to the order of history;* especially fixing our eyes upon the four things which are noted in the introduction of the second part; that is to say,—(a) to behold the *persons* which are engaged, as well those of Christ our Lord and of His mother, and disciples, as also of His persecutors; pondering the qualities and conditions of every one.(1) (b) Moreover, to weigh the *words* they speak, (c) and the *works and actions* they do, learning out of those which Christ our Lord says and does what is profitable for us, and flying the evil which is said and done by His persecutors. (d) Finally, to behold *what Christ suffers*, pondering *how His divinity hides itself*, not destroying His enemies, but permitting them to torment His most sacred Humanity. Whence I will infer, what reason requires that I myself should do and suffer for the love of Him, who did and suffered so much for the love of me, entering upon this occasion into colloquies with God our Lord, in the manner which will be immediately declared.

ii. The second way of meditating these mysteries is, when, retaining them all in memory, we take for matter of meditation, *some particular pain or virtue of Christ our Lord,* pondering all the circumstances thereof, in all the passages of the Passion.

(a) If, for example, I desire to meditate the humility of Christ our Lord, I will weigh and ponder the acts of this virtue, which He practised in the whole course of His Passion. First, when He washed the feet of the apostles; secondly, when He was apprehended, and was for con-

(1) S. Ignat. in 1 exer. 3 hebd.

tempt trodden underneath the feet of His enemies, proceeding thus even to those which He exercised upon the cross. And if I desire to begin my contemplation of that virtue from the acts which He formerly exercised before His Passion, I may reflect on these acts of humility, which He practised in the time of His nativity, infancy, and preaching, drawing from them all motives to exercise this virtue thoroughly; forasmuch as in every mystery there shines some particularity, which appertains to its perfection. And in the same manner may be meditated the obedience, charity, or patience of the Saviour.

(b) In the same way may be taken for matter of meditation *any kind of particular pains, torment*, or *dishonour*, discoursing through the mysteries of the Passion, pondering only what concerns that pain in particular. As to meditate how many times He was with great ignominy stripped naked;—how many times He shed His precious blood;—the stations which He made during that time;—the disgraces which He endured with regard to His virtue or wisdom, endeavouring in every one of these, to take compassion on my Saviour, and to encourage myself to endure somewhat for Him in that very kind of suffering. And other times I may take for matter of meditation, the particular pain which Christ our Lord endured in some of His members or senses;—for example, to meditate the pains of His holy hands; being bound when He was taken prisoner;—afterwards at the pillar;—and lastly, when they were fastened to the cross; and so of the rest.

2. To these two manners of meditating the Passion, a third may be added, by applying *the interior senses* (2) *of the soul*, concerning each mystery, in the manner which has been explained in the twenty-sixth Meditation of the

(2) S. Tho. in Phil. ii. 5. "hoc sentite in vobis."

second part, by way of contemplation, without much discourse.

i. To *behold* with *the eyes* of the soul the exterior form of Christ our Lord, enough to move the hardest heart in the whole world to compassion. And also the interior of His soul on the one side, so surpassingly fair, and on the other side, so afflicted: both admiring and having compassion to see that "the brightness of" the "glory" of the Father, "and the figure of His substance,"(3) should be so disfigured for my sins.

ii. To *hear* interiorly the words of our Blessed Lord, so affable and so affectionate; the importunate clamours against Him; the fury of His enemies; the noise of the buffets, blows, whips, and hammers:—feeling in my heart what Jesus Christ felt in His.

iii. To *smell* with the interior smelling, as well the stink and obscenity of sin, which caused the death of this High Priest, as the sweetness of the sacrifice which He offered for them, and of the virtues which He exercised in this so devout oblation of His Passion; pondering how He appeased therewith the anger of His eternal Father; setting before us for a sign of reconciliation, not the rainbow which is formed in the clouds,(4) but His Son extended like a bow upon the cross, and raining blood for love of us.

iv. To *taste* the bitterness and gall of Christ our Lord, and so to feel bitterness and sorrow, as if I tasted them corporally;—as also to taste that sweetness of love with which He suffered them :—and that which Almighty God communicates to those who suffer something for His sake, marvelling to see so great sweetness mixed with so great bitterness.

v. To *touch* with the interior touch of the soul, those

(3) Heb. i. 3. (4) Gen. ix. 13.

dreadful instruments of the Passion of Christ our Lord;—as the rigour and severity of the cords, scourges, thorns, cross, and nails, feeling in my soul that which our Lord Jesus sensibly felt in His blessed body, and exciting the affections which are wont to arise from such feelings.

The practice of this manner of praying will be set down in the mysteries of the garden: and that of the other two manners will be seen in the ensuing meditation, which serves for a foundation and preamble to the others.

# MEDITATIONS

ON THE

# MYSTERIES OF THE WHOLE PASSION.

---

## I.—THE FUNDAMENTAL MEDITATION,

CONTAINING A SUMMARY OF THE THINGS TO BE CONSIDERED IN MEDITATING EACH MYSTERY OF OUR LORD'S PASSION.

That which is to be considered in every mystery of the Passion, may be reduced to six or seven principal points; that is to say,—i. *Who* the Person is that suffers those torments;—ii. *How many* and *how sharp* those torments are; —iii. *From what persons* He suffers them;—iv. *For whom;* —v. *For what cause;*—vi. *With what love* and affection;— and, vii. *The virtues which He exercised* in suffering, as also what sorrows His glorious Mother suffered with Him.

All this we will treat of in this meditation in general, that we may apply the same afterwards to every mystery in particular.

### POINT I.

OF THE PERSON THAT SUFFERED.

In the *person of Christ our Lord, who* suffered these torments, *three* things principally may be considered, which move very effectually to the affections of compassion, thanksgiving, love, and imitation.

1. The first is, *the innocence and sanctity of our Lord* who suffered, who was most innocent, without any spot of sin; most holy, with all kind of sanctity; full of all graces

and virtues; most wise and most discreet; in whom were "hid all the treasures of wisdom and knowledge" (1) of God, and of His Divine Spirit, without limit; whereby is to be seen, that what He suffered was without any fault of His, although that His enemies pretended Him to be wicked, and tormented Him as one guilty. How, then, shall I not take compassion to see suffering a Lord so innocent, so wise, and holy? If the centurion, and many others, who were present with Him upon Mount Calvary, smote their breasts for very sorrow, seeing Him suffer whom they regarded as "just," how shall not I smite my breast, considering that He who suffers is not an ordinary just man, but the Supreme of all the just, who never gave any culpable occasion of so great torments?

*Colloquy.*—O my heart, more hard than stone, how dost thou not rend in sunder for very sorrow, since they were rent, and shivered in pieces, when this living stone suffered, being the fountain of all grace, and the perfect pattern of all sanctity?

2. *His omnipotence and liberality* in doing good to all, and in being the universal benefactor of all, who "went about His whole life doing good," as St. Peter says, (2) "and healing all such that were oppressed by the Devil," gave sight to the blind, cleansed the lepers, cured the sick, and raised the dead; and more than this, did good also to the souls themselves, pardoning their sins, delivering them out of hell, opening to them the gates of heaven, imparting to them the light of His admirable doctrine, and the fire of charity, with the splendour of all virtue. Whence it follows, that He suffered torments and dishonours, not only without any fault but for that for which He deserved the greatest ease and sovereign honour. For which cause

(1) Col. ii. 3; Joan. iii. 34. (2) Act. x. 38.

St. Augustin says, that Christ our Lord lived in the world, "Mira faciens, et mala patiens, donec suspenderetur in ligno;" "Performing miracles, and patient of injuries, even to His crucifixion." (3)

*Colloquy.*—How then is it, O my soul, that thou art not altogether dissolved with sorrow, seeing this thy benefactor, and the benefactor of the whole world suffering; who, doing good and profiting all, received evil and hurt from all? Oh that I could obtain so much grace, that, doing good like my Lord, I might suffer some evil and torment for love of Him! I renounce all recompense of men for my good works, since my Redeemer received of them no other wages but grievous torments in payment of His.

3. I will consider thirdly, the infinite *charity* of our Lord, *in giving Himself to all*, and making Himself one with all; pondering how He is my Father, my master, my physician, my Redeemer, my pastor, my Creator, my benefactor, spouse of my soul, my God, and my all in all. And how a little before His Passion He made Himself my meat and my drink, to enter within me, and to make Himself one thing with me, for which cause I should consider His pains even as my own, to have compassion for them, and to feel them as if they were indeed my own, since He who suffers them is so much mine, and bears to me so great a love. If the son bewails the death of his father, the wife of her husband, and the friend of his beloved friend, how shall not I lament the death of such a Father, of such a husband, and of such a friend?

(To this purpose that will help us which will be proposed in the eighth point.)

(3) S. Aug. in Psal. xlix.

THE MULTITUDE AND GRIEVOUSNESS OF HIS TORMENTS.

POINT II.

The *multitude and grievousness of the torments* which Christ our Lord endured in His Passion, may in general be reduced to two kinds; 1. The one *exterior*, figured by baptism, (4) which wets the body exteriorly; 2. The other *interior*, figured by the drink of the chalice, which enters and pierces interiorly; for these two similes did our Lord use to explain them to us.

1. Beginning therefore with the *exterior* torments:—

i. First, we must discourse upon all those things which are *matter of corporal pain,* in which Christ our Lord suffered excessively.(5)

(a) In the *goods* and *necessary things* which He possessed, He was reduced to so great poverty, and so great nudity, that He died publicly, stark naked upon the cross, the soldiers taking His garments from Him, and dividing them amongst them.

(b) In His *honour* He suffered innumerable derisions and scornings, treated and used like a very thief, malefactor, and blasphemer against God: for which reason they blasphemed Him.

(c) In His *good name* He suffered many false accusations, by which they endeavoured to throw discredit on Him: so that, in matter of virtue and sanctity, He was despised and reputed a sinner, a Samaritan, possessed of the Devil, a seducer of the people, a glutton, a drunkard, and blasphemer; and consequently was held for a man reproved and condemned by God, which was the greatest disgrace that could be done Him; of which our Lord Himself complains in the person of David, saying,—" I am

(4) Marc. x. 38. (5) S. Thom. 3. p. q. xlvi., art, 5, 6, 7.

counted among them that go down to the pit. They have laid me in the lower pit, in the dark places, and in the shadow of death."(6)

(d) Moreover, in matter of *wisdom and knowledge*, He was despised and held for an idiot, without learning, a fool, mad, as imprudent, and a very dolt.

(e) In matter of *power and miracles* He was esteemed for an impostor and enchanter, and for a man who had correspondence with the Devil.(7)

(f) In *His own body* He suffered most grievous pains, as well because of their own nature they were most violent, as because He by complexion was most delicate, and therefore felt any pain and corporal hurt much more than other men.

(g) Lastly, He suffered in *His friends and alliances*, partly from most of them forsaking Him: and partly, on account of those who were present, He Himself felt the grief and disgrace which they endured, especially of His most holy mother.

*Colloquy.*—O most bountiful Redeemer, how well dost Thou pay our debts with Thine own pains, who, because all things in the world have been fuel to our covetousness, sensuality, and pride, wilt therefore suffer in all of them poverty, torment, and humiliation. Let them be to me for time to come instruments to serve Thee as they have hitherto been to offend Thee. O my soul, compare the excellencies of this Divine Person with the ignominies and pains which He endures, so as to confound thy pride and sensuality, learning to suffer in imitation of Him.

ii. Secondly, we may reflect upon *the subjects* of the pain, the *five senses of Christ* our Lord, pondering how

(6) Psal. lxxxvii. 5—7.
(7) Marc. iii. 21; Joan. vii. 15.

much He suffered in every one of them. (a) For, 1, His *eyes* were afflicted, beholding the mockings and the mouthings of His enemies, and the tears and sighings of His friends, and were also in a manner quite shut up with spittle, and with the drops of blood which ran down from His head, and with the scalding tears which He Himself shed. (b) His *ears* suffered, in hearing many, and most horrible blasphemies, the injuries, the false testimonies, and most malicious accusations of His enemies. (c) His *smelling* suffered, enduring the filthy savour of Mount Calvary, where He was crucified. (d) His *taste* suffered most cruel thirst, which was not assuaged, but tormented with gall and vinegar. (e) His *touch* suffered most intolerable pains of whips, thorns, and nails, which pierced His body.

*Colloquy.*—O senses of my sweet and beloved Jesus, worthy to be refreshed with all the delectable things upon the earth! How are ye thus afflicted with all the bitter and painful things of this life! O that my senses might conform themselves to those of my Lord, suffering the same pain, since the fault proceeded from them.

iii. We may consider *the seat* of the pain all the *members and principal parts of the body* of Christ our Lord, in which He suffered extreme pains and torments. His head was pierced with thorns, and smitten with a reed. His hair and beard torn off. His cheeks buffeted. His arms disjointed, so that the bones might be counted. His wrists rudely bound with rough cords. His hands and feet bored with nails. His shoulders and His whole body mangled with cruel scourges exceedingly. And as the lashes lighted upon the most sensible parts, they caused excessive agony.

*Colloquy.*—O most delicate body, with how great reason may it be said of Thee that "from the sole of the foot unto the top of the head there is no soundness"(8) in Thee! Thou art all full of stripes, ulcers, and of most terrible wounds and pains! Oh how much more reasonable were it that my body should be tormented in all its parts and senses, since in every part and in all its senses it has flowed with innumerable sins! Heal, O good Jesus, with the wounds of Thy body, the wounds of my soul, and through Thy corporal pains, deliver me from my spiritual evils. Amen.

2. There are the *interior pains* and afflictions of Christ our Lord, which accompanied these exterior ones, and were also as many, and as grievous of all sorts, as the most pure soul of our Saviour could possibly suffer without imperfection:—such as were interior derelictions of the Divinity;—suspension of sensible consolations of the heart;—vehement sadness of the will for the injuries committed against God, and for the perdition of men;—fears, sorrows, and terrible agonies, of which that sweat of blood was witness, as we shall see in the meditation of the garden:—finally, although the pains of the body were very terrible, yet those of the spirit were much greater: for in His interior He took to Himself as much pain as He Himself would have, who, as He loved much, so would He, that it should be much, for the greater good of those whom He loved so exceedingly.

*Colloquy.*—O sweet Redeemer, now I see with how great reason Isaiah calls Thee the "man of sorrows, and acquainted with infirmity,"(9) since Thou art encompassed with sorrow on every side, and environed with afflictions, the tempests of the bitter sea have drenched and tormented Thy body, and the waters

(8) Is. i. 6. (9) Is. liii. 5.

have "come in even into" Thy "soul."(10) Without, Thou art afflicted with the most painful baptism(11) of blood, and within with the exceeding bitter chalice of heaviness. Grant me, Lord, that I may be like Thee in all these pains, so that both my body and my spirit may be pleasing to Thee, that I may be made clean and unspotted.(12) Amen.

ON THE QUALITY OF THOSE WHO INFLICTED THEM.

POINT III.

1. In this point is to be considered, first, the *multitude and quality* of *those persons* who *conspired* against Christ our Lord, to despise Him, and torment Him in His Passion, pondering how there concurred to it kings,(13) judges, governors, high-priests, scribes, and Pharisees, who were the Religious of that time, courtiers, soldiers, Gentiles, and Jews; and even of His own disciples themselves, some there were who persecuted Him; king Herod, with his court, scorns Him.—Pilate the judge condemns Him.—Annas and Caiphas, both high-priests, reprove Him.—The scribes and Pharisees accuse Him.—The soldiers take Him and bind Him.—The tormentors whip Him, crown Him, and crucify Him.—The outcast of the people cry against Him, that He may be put to death.—One disciple sells Him;—another denies Him;—and all forsake Him.

To which may be added, that all these were *obliged to our blessed Lord by innumerable benefits, to love Him,* honour Him, and serve Him: forasmuch as, besides those general benefits which He communicated to all as God and Redeemer, He had besides done others peculiarly for that people;—teaching them His doctrine,—working in their presence many miracles,—healing their infirmities,

(10) Psal. lxviii. 1. (11) Luc. xii. 50.
(12) 2 Cor. vii. 1. (13) Psal. ii. 2.

and those of their children, servants, and friends,—and giving them meat in the desert miraculously, for which they would have made Him king, and received Him into their city with the greatest pomp that ever prince was received with upon earth.

All these, therefore, changed themselves, and turned against their God and Redeemer, and against their infinite benefactor, injuring, tormenting, and murdering Him, who had done them so great good, and whom a little before they judged worthy of the most sovereign honour, proclaiming Him the author of life.

*Colloquy.*—O sweet Jesus, King of kings, Judge of the living and the dead, high bishop and supreme priest, fountain of knowledge and of all sanctity, corner stone of the Gentiles and of the Jews, how art Thou persecuted by all earthly kings and judges, by the priests and the wise men of the earth, and by the people and nations of the world. I wonder not to see Thee persecuted by those who know Thee not; but what shall I say to see Thee persecuted by those who know Thee, and are bound to serve Thee on a thousand motives? Oh that I had never persecuted Thee with my sins! Permit me not, O Lord, to persecute Thee any more with them, but grant that I correspond faithfully with my services to Thy innumerable benefits. Amen.

2. Ponder the *cruelty and fierceness of His enemies and persecutors;* for, as they were proud, ambitious, covetous hypocrites, and egregious dissemblers, they were enemies of truth, of the master who taught it, and of that physician who desired to cure their mortal wounds. Moreover, they were possessed with passion, hatred, rancour, and envy against Christ, because He reprehended their vices, obscured their vain honours with the authority of

His wisdom, sanctity, and miracles; for which cause they desired to make away with Him, some from malice, to revenge their injuries; others through passion, fear, the favour of Cæsar, or of the people; others from ignorance, through not well understanding who He was; others through false zeal of religion, and of the commonwealth; which zeal, when it is joined with envy, enkindles cruelty, and makes men more fierce than the most wild and fiercest beasts.

*Colloquy.*—O most mild Lamb, with great reason dost Thou say, that many "dogs," "calves," and "fat bulls," "lions," and "unicorns," exceedingly fierce, have encompassed Thee: (14) for Thine enemies, like savage beasts, besiege Thee, and frighten Thee with their cries, tear Thee with their claws, bite Thee with their teeth, and push Thee hither and thither with their horns, dragging Thee from one tribunal to another, smiting Thee with such great cruelty, as if Thou wert not a man, but the picture of a man, "a worm, and the outcast of the people." Oh that I could deliver Thee from their infernal cruelty! But Thy charity gave not leave to Thy omnipotence, which could have done it, in order that amidst so many fierce and savage beasts, Thy sovereign virtues might the more appear.

3. The *principal persecutors* of Christ our Lord were the "*powers of*" *the infernal* "*darkness*,"(15) *which are the devils*, who abhorred Him excessively, because He drew them out of bodies, plucked souls out of their power, and destroyed their kingdom, which was the kingdom of sin. Wherefore, to revenge themselves on Him, they enkindled the fury of men to persecute Him.—Satan "put it into the heart of Judas"(16) to sell Him.—He

(14) Psal. xxi. 13, et seq. (15) Luc. xxii. 53.
(16) Joan. xiii. 2.

instructed the soldiers to contrive the mockeries with which they abused Him.—In the Jews he enkindled the fire of anger with which they burned.—And like as the leave which to his purpose was granted him, was not with that limitation, as when leave was given him to persecute Job, so he was not contented to cast Him "on a dunghill, full of sores, but further to take from Him His very life, with most terrible torments.

*Colloquy.*—O high priest Jesus,(17) what hast Thou to do with that infernal dog, that so great power is given to him over Thy sacred body? O insatiable love, which, not content to be tormented by men, wilt have them set on and goaded forward by the devils, to deliver me by these torments from those which they were to inflict upon me for my transgressions.

4. The pains of our most blessed Lord were yet augmented in *seeing, with the eyes of His most prudent soul* the rage of His enemies, not only by their works and outward signs as other men see, but *inasmuch as He pierced their very hearts, and saw clearly*(18) the enraged desires which they had to torment Him, which was a great deal more than what they manifested exteriorly: for although the torments which they gave Him were many and most grievous, yet they desired to give Him many more, and much more grievous, than they had been able.

*Colloquy.*—O most wise Jesus, Thy own knowledge augments Thy own sorrow, Thy love not becoming the colder for all this, because Thy heart was much more full of love towards Thy enemies to suffer for their good, than theirs was of hatred to seek Thy hurt. Replenish me, O Lord, with Thy inflamed charity, that I may imitate Thy invincible patience. Amen.

(17) Zach. iii. 1. (18) Jer. xi. 18.

ON THE PERSONS FOR WHOM, AND THE CAUSES FOR WHICH HE SUFFERED.

POINT IV.

1. *Christ our Saviour suffered all these contempts and sorrows for the sins of men*, past, present and to come, paying the debts of all with the price of His blood shed with so great sorrow and dishonour; whence we may gather certain particular *causes* of this so sovereign Passion.—i. To *defend the honour of His Father*, injured with so many offences, and to appease the just indignation which He had conceived against men, reconciling them to Him, and freeing them from their offences and from the pains, temporal and eternal, they had deserved for them.—ii. *To merit and obtain for them grace, charity, and all virtues*, together with the necessary and convenient means for their justification and perfection.—iii. And lastly, to *open to them the gates of heaven*, and to bring them into the glory of life eternal, removing all the impediments which might hinder them.

Hence it is, that, because the sins of men were not only infinite in number, but also infinitely enormous, as being committed against an infinite God, it was necessary that the Person should be of infinite excellence who should suffer for them, to discharge that infinite debt with any even justice. And although the least pain of Jesus Christ, and the very least drop of His precious blood had been sufficient for this, as being the blood of an infinite Person, yet would He suffer a multitude of torments, that so His "redemption" might be the more "plentiful," (19) and we men understand the infinite enormity of our sins; because, as S. Bernard says, (20) by considering the remedy, I see the greatness of my peril. O how grievous are the wounds for which it was necessary

(19) Ps. cxxix. 7. (20) Serm. 3, de Nat.

that Christ should be wounded! If the wounds had not been deadly, aye even to death eternal, never would the Son of God have died to remedy them. Our merciful Redeemer beheld the whole mystical body of mankind, wounded from the foot to the head with innumerable sins, and to cure him would have His body all wounded from the foot to the head with innumerable stripes, and His soul afflicted with most grievous sorrows, proportioning the medicine to the necessity of the wound.

To this purpose, for our inordinate desire of riches, Thou, O Lord, hangest naked upon the cross;—for the pride of the learned Thou art reputed for a fool;—for the vanity of those who presume they are holy Thou art scorned as a sinner;—for the haughtiness of the mighty Thou art treated as one feeble and miserable;—for the voluptuousness of the sensual Thou art laden with torments;—the pains of Thy five senses pay for the disorders of ours;—Thy head is crowned with thorns in chastisement for our ambition;—Thy tongue is afflicted with gall and vinegar for our gluttony;—Thy hands and feet are bored with nails in punishment of our evil works and pernicious steps;—Thy shoulders are furrowed with lashes for the thefts and mischiefs which we laid upon ours;—Thy back is charged with the burden of the cross because ours had cast off the burthen of Thy law.

*Colloquy.*—O most liberal Redeemer, whose redemption is so copious and abundant, that it is sufficient to remedy an infinite number of worlds, if there were so many, apply, I beseech Thee, this redemption to this one world which Thou hast created, that all enjoy the benefit of it, and be saved. Amen.

2. Christ our Lord suffered all these torments *for the very enemies who inflicted them,* and shed His precious blood to satisfy for the sins which His persecutors committed in

shedding it, and in proof of this He prayed for them upon the cross, and excused them to His Father. And His charity was so immense, that He offered His Passion to impart the same charity even to those who abhorred Him, —to honour those who dishonoured Him,—to give liberty to those who apprehended Him,—to give rest to those who afflicted Him,—and to give eternal life to those who inflicted upon Him a most cruel death.

*Colloquy.*—Blessed be Thy immense charity, O my Saviour, and glorified be Thy infinite mercy. Oh that Thy enemies knew of it; if they did, how confounded would they be for their ingratitude, and changed from foes into loving friends, would never cease to praise Thee, and to serve Thee with greater love than before they persecuted Thee with rancour. Open, O Lord, the eyes of those who persecute Thee at this present day, that, ceasing to persecute Thee, they may wholly employ themselves in serving Thee. Amen.

3. Consider with more exact attention how Christ our Lord suffered all these contempts and pains, *for all men in the world;* in such a manner that He suffered and offered them particularly for every one, and as if there had been but one alone in the whole world, whom He held present in His memory and in His heart, pondering on his sins, his miseries, and necessities, as if there had been no other to behold and remedy, save him alone, so that I may say that to myself what St. Paul said of himself, speaking of Christ our Lord:—"He who loved me, and delivered Himself for me." (21)

*Colloquy.*—O my soul, if thou hadst seen thyself in the heart of thy sweet Jesus, at the time when He was suffering these agonies! If thou understoodst the love and solicitude with which He offered them up for

(21) Gal. ii. 20.

thy sins, doubtless thou wouldst burst asunder with sorrow for having been the cause of His sorrows, and wouldst burn with love to see thyself so beloved in the midst of them. Deplore, then, now thy sins, for which He suffered so much, who loved thee so much, and love Him with all thy might who suffered so much for thee; and praise and glorify Him world without end, as if He had suffered them alone for thee. Amen.

THE LOVE AND AFFECTION WITH WHICH HE SUFFERED.

POINT V.

This point is the most tender, and which ought to serve as a sauce to give taste and spiritual relish to all our meditations on the Passion, considering the *greatness and immensity of the love with which our Lord endured* all these torments, because He did not endure them from any necessity or compulsion, but as the prophet Isaiah says, "He was offered because it was His own will," (22) because He was good and merciful, and desirous to please His Eternal Father, and to do good to all men, and to discover the infinite riches and treasures of the charity, mercy, and liberality of Almighty God towards His creatures. And as He loved His Eternal Father so much, and men for the love of Him, with the selfsame immense love, He suffered all that He suffered for them, embracing it with great delight and comfort for their good.

*Colloquy.*—Oh that I could find out and "comprehend" "what is the breadth and length and height and depth" of the charity of Jesus! Oh that I could enter into His inflamed heart, and see the furnace of infinite fire that burns there, and melt in those flames, that, issuing forth full of love, I might love as I am loved, and suffer with love for Him who suffered for me with so great love! From this interior love burst

(22) Is. liii. 7.

forth such exterior signs and demonstrations, as were sufficient to mollify a heart more frozen than ice itself, and harder than any marble.

1. The *first sign*, therefore, of *the love of labours* is, *to desire that they soon befall us;* to take delight in talking of them; to renew often the memory of them; to go with joy and gladness to the place where they are to be endured; to be sorry to see them deferred; and to rebuke those who seek to hinder them, calling them "Satan," and our adversaries. All this our sweet Jesus did, earnestly desiring to suffer, as we shall see hereafter; and for this reason, He said to His disciples:—"I have a baptism wherewith I am to be baptized; Oh, how am I straitened until it be accomplished!"(23)

*Colloquy.*—O my beloved, if this baptism were of water, I should not wonder that the expectation and delay were painful to Thee; but being a baptism of blood, and of blood drawn from Thy veins with terrible torments, how dost Thou desire it with such solicitude? Oh, who may give me such a hunger and desire to suffer tribulations, that I may recreate myself more in them than in rest itself.

2. But, because many boast of tribulations, and wish them greatly before they come, but being come, fly and abhor them; therefore there is another much more certain mark of love of afflictions, which is to *court them, and go, as it were, to meet them,* not to fly them, nor to hinder them, although one might do so; not to excuse oneself, not to recoil nor to speak in one's own defence, although provoked to do so, not to seek exemption, but promptly to offer oneself without resistance to all, whatever one's tormentors may do to one, with such a kind of meekness, that they be not afraid still to torment, after they have

(23) Luc. xii. 50.

inflicted many torments upon one. All this, and much more, Christ our Lord plainly discovered in His Passion; for He repaired to the garden where they were to apprehend Him:—He could have prayed His Father to have sent Him "legions of angels" to defend Him, and yet He would not:—He gave leave to His enemies, prostrated by His word upon the ground, to get up again and to apprehend Him:—He yielded His blessed face to buffets, and His body to whips without turning away His face, or shielding His body from any pain whatever:—He would work no miracles, to shelter Himself under Herod's protection; nor speak in His own defence, that Pilate might dismiss Him, although he provoked Him to it, and wondered at His silence;—finally, He accepted the unjust sentence, and embraced the cross, stretching Himself out upon it, and suffering Himself to be fastened to it with rude nails of iron, being already much more strongly nailed to it with the nails of love.

*Colloquy.*—O infinite love, and immense fire, which "many waters" of such immense tribulations could not "quench,"(24) but was enkindled the more with them! Enkindle in me, O Lord, this fire, and inflame me with this fervent love. Amen.

3. But the excessive love of Christ went yet further, to give greater signs of its excess, for not content with suffering what He did, He *desired to suffer infinitely more.* He saw how anxious His enemies were to invent new torments to afflict Him; and dilating so much the more His love, He not only desired to suffer the torments they laid upon Him, but was prepared to suffer all those which they *desired* to lay upon Him. Indeed, not contented with this, He was desirous and ready to suffer others incomparably greater, had it been necessary for our good.

(24) Cant. viii. 7.

*Colloquy.*—O infinite fire, which always burnest and never sayest, "enough," how shall I repay Thee this desire to suffer! Much do I owe Thee for the much Thou sufferedst for me; but much more do I owe Thee for that which Thou desiredst to suffer, had it been necessary for our redemption. If Thou receivedst five thousand stripes, Thou hadst the love to receive other five thousand millions, much more cruel. If Thy head was pierced with seventy-two thorns, Thy love was ready to suffer it to be pierced with seventy thousand of them.—If Thou wert nailed three hours to the cross with excessive pain, Thou wast prepared to be nailed millions of hours thereon, and that with many greater torments. More didst Thou desire to be tormented than Thine enemies could torment Thee: and more didst Thou love to suffer than all worldly men love repose.—O who will give me so insatiable a love, as never to be satisfied with suffering for Him who suffered so much for me with so insatiable a love?

A true testimony of this love is that which passed in the garden, where our Lord, foreseeing the torments of these tormentors, would of His own accord, give a beginning to His tribulations, with such signs of sorrow, that He sweat blood; as will be pondered in its place.

OF THE HEROIC VIRTUES EXERCISED BY HIM IN SUFFERING.

POINT VI.

Consider, first, how Christ our Lord exercised in His Passion *all the principal virtues of a Christian and perfect life*, and *every one of them in an heroic degree*—both as regards the *exterior* acts, and a great deal more regarding the *interior*, which accompanied the exterior.

1. The *causes* of this were:—

i. Because He was come to be an example and a *model*

of virtues, and therefore would at that time make an abridgment of all, and give singular example of them, as He said after He had washed the feet of His apostles. (25)—ii. Because by *His Passion we were to merit* and to gain all virtues, and therefore He would that the merits should be grounded in the *actual exercise* of all of them.—iii. *To repair* the *reputation* of virtues, which was much decayed and discredited with the world, especially those of which the end is to contemn all worldly things.

iv. That by His testament and last will confirmed by His own death, He might leave us for a *legacy the most excellent works* of all virtues; for, as He said in His last sermon:—"A new commandment I give unto you, that you love one another, as I have loved you."(26) So might He likewise say,—"A new commandment I give unto you, that you humble yourselves, as I have humbled myself, and that you obey and suffer, as I have obeyed and suffered."

*Colloquy.*—O sweet master, teach me, I beseech Thee, to exercise these virtues, imitating the example which Thou hast given me, to the end that with all my might I may sustain their reputation, to Thy honour and glory. Amen.

2. Ponder the *multitude* and *greatness* of these virtues, discoursing through those eight heroic acts which Christ our Lord, in the sermon on the mountain, called Beatitudes, and which He exercised in His Passion in an eminent degree.

i. First, He exercised *poverty of spirit*, renouncing all things, even to His very garment, remaining naked upon the cross. With this poverty He exercised *humility* comprised in it, treading under foot all the vain pomps and vanities of the world, and embracing all kinds of con-

(25) Joan. xiii. 15. (26) Joan. xiii. 34.

tempts, as has already been declared.—ii. He exercised most heroic *meekness*, in the midst of so many wild beasts which bit Him and tore Him, remaining like a lamb, without speaking, without defending or vexing Himself, and suffered all with such fortitude, as to seem as if insensible. —iii. He *mourned* most bitterly for our sins, with sorrow and sadness, even to the shedding, not only of tears through His eyes, but of blood through all the pores of His delicate body.—iv. He had an insatiable *hunger and thirst after justice*, not being able to satisfy Himself in doing good, and enduring evils to justify us, and to give us an example of sanctity, on which account He said upon the cross, "I thirst."—v. He showed most singular *mercy* towards such as were in misery, bestowing upon them whatever He had, goods, honour, blood, and life, to redress their miseries, His body for food to assuage their hunger, and His blood for drink to quench their thirst.—vi. He had a most eminent *purity of heart*, keeping Himself amidst such terrible occasions exempt from sin, even taking occasion by them to exercise admirable acts of virtue.—vii. He was a *peacemaker* in a most excellent manner, making peace between us and His eternal Father, obtaining for us true peace, and preserving it in Himself even with those with whom He had to wage such a terrible war.—viii. Finally, He showed Himself exceedingly *patient, suffering for justice* the greatest persecutions which ever were suffered, and with the greatest patience that ever any one had, on which account with great reason are due to Him all the rewards which belong to these virtues, which He also merited for such as should imitate Him in the practice of them.

*Colloquy.*—O sovereign master, if one had heard Thee speak on the first mountain, when Thou didst preach and teach these virtues, and had seen Thee suffer on the mount of Calvary, when Thou didst practise them, Thou wast the same, and hadst the same end on both mountains, speaking and working, teaching others to suffer, and suffering Thyself; give me grace, O Lord, to hear that which Thou hast taught me, and to exercise that which Thou didst exercise, conforming myself to Thee in all Thou didst, and in all Thou sufferedst. Amen.

3. These virtues of Christ our Lord may be pondered *every one apart*, running through the *degrees* and *properties* which every one contains. And because it would be over-tedious to give an example of every one, I will give an instance only in obedience, a virtue which embraces all the others, of which St. Paul said, that Christ our Lord "humbled Himself, becoming obedient unto death, *even to the death of the cross*," (27) and that being the Son of Almighty God, "He learned obedience by the things which He suffered," (28) which was most heroic.

i. Because He not only obeyed in things easy, but also *in things most difficult* and sharp, as was the death of the cross, with other painful things that went before it. —ii. Although the things were such, His obedience notwithstanding was most *entire*, without omitting one jot or tittle of all that the prophets had prophesied; and this St. John pondered when he said:—"Jesus, knowing that all things were now accomplished, that the Scripture might be fulfilled, He said, I thirst," (29) which was to say,—to the end that He might satisfy one of those penalties which were prophesied, and was yet unaccomplished, namely, that they were to give Him vinegar to drink when He was thirsty, He said, "I thirst."—iii. His obedience was most *prompt*, punctual, without delay, hesitation, reply, or excuse, to all that was commanded Him,

(27) Phil. ii. 8. (28) Heb. v. 8. (29) Joan. xix. 28.

although it were exceedingly painful, and on the part of the Jews and executioners most unjust.—iv. It was *general* and *humble*, for He subjected Himself to all sorts of evil and perverse men, understanding this to be the will of His heavenly Father, according to that which the prophet Isaiah said,—"The Lord hath opened my ears;" (30) that is to say, has commanded me to obey, and I have not gainsaid nor gone backwards, I have given my body to those who struck it, my cheeks to those who plucked me, I turned not my face away from those who injured me, and spat upon me.—v. It was an obedience *persevering even to death*, willing that first life should fail before obedience, and so He died obeying, and obeyed dying, and all with obedience of love, according to that which the same Lord said:—"That the world may know that I love the Father, and as the Father hath given me commandment, so do I—Arise, let us go hence to suffer." (31)

*Colloquy.*—I give Thee thanks, O most sweet Lord, for the heroic example which Thou hast given me of obedience; oh that I had the like strong, entire, prompt, punctual, persevering, and loving obedience, subjecting myself to every human creature for the love of Thee, that all the world may know that I love Thee, and that I accomplish Thy commandments, after the manner which Thou commandest. By Thy most holy obedience, I beg of Thee this obedience; command me, O my God, what it pleases Thee, so Thou give me this virtue to accomplish what Thou commandest me.

(After this manner may be made discourses about *humility*, *poverty*, *silence*, *modesty*, and other virtues.)

(30) Is. l. 5.    (31) Joan. xiv. 31.

OF THE SEVEN STATIONS MADE BY HIM IN HIS PASSION.

POINT VII.

1. The *stations* which Christ our Lord walked the night of His Passion, and the day following, may be reduced to *seven*, to meditate them in the seven days of the week, comprising in them the whole history of the Passion.—i. The first was with His disciples from the supper-room to the garden of Gethsemane, where He grew sad, prayed, and sweat blood.—ii. The second was from the garden, where He was apprehended, to the house of Annas, where He was examined, and received a cruel buffet on the face.—iii. The third was to the house of Caiphas, where He was spit upon, buffeted, and endured most grievous injuries and abuses all that night.—iv. The fourth was to the house of Pilate the president, where He was accused by the Jews, by the means of many false and suborned witnesses.—v. The fifth was to the palace of king Herod, where He was treated with scorn by him, and by his whole army.—vi. The sixth was at His return to the house of Pilate, where He was scourged, crowned with thorns, mocked, derided, and condemned to death.—vii. The seventh was from thence to the Mount of Calvary, bearing upon His shoulders the cross on which He was also crucified.

2. For these seven stations I ought, with holy David, to give thanks to God "seven times" a day, (32) glorifying Him for the judgments of His justice and mercy which shone in them, taking time to ruminate and consider at leisure,—i. *who* the Person is who walks these stations, and the *end* that He has in them;—ii. the *company* He leads;—iii. the *place whence* He departs, His manner of walking, *the place to which* He goes;—iv. *the things* which *He says*,

(32) Psal. cxviii. 164.

*does, and suffers*, drawing from all the spirit and profit for which they were ordained.

i. In *the Person* of Christ our Lord is to be considered *His infinite dignity*, as has been said, considering the paces and affections of spirit with which He accompanied the steps His body made, ordaining them to the sole glory of His eternal Father, to make satisfaction for our sins. And it may be that these stations were seven in chastisement of the evil steps which we have trod in the seven deadly sins, and to bruise the pride of the "red dragon having seven heads," (33) which held the world in tyranny, as also to tame the pride and rebellion of worldlings, and to give us all an example of humility and patience, according to that which is written, that "The ancient mountains were crushed to pieces, the hills of the world were bowed down by the journeys of His eternity," (34)—which is to say, that proud and haughty hearts, rebellious and perverse spirits, have humbled and subjected themselves by the ways and journeys this our Lord walked, and had traced out for that end from all eternity.

*Colloquy.*—O eternal God, and our Saviour, the Lamb sacrificed for us from the beginning of the world, enlighten the eyes of my soul, that I may consider these journeys and steps which Thou walkedst for our remedy, so that I may obtain the end for which Thou ordainedst them. Pardon, O Lord, by them, my evil steps, and direct them for the time to come according to Thy holy law, that "no iniquity have dominion over me."(35) O eternal Father, who numberest the steps of men,(36) as well of the evil to chastise them, as those of the good to reward them; behold the steps of Thy beloved Son, and by them I beseech Thee to direct mine, that in all things they may be conformable to His. Amen.

(33) Apoc. xii. 3. (34) Habac. iii. 6. (35) Psal. cxviii. 133. (36) Job. xiv. 16.

ii. Concerning *the company* which Christ our Lord led along with Him in these stations; sometimes He walked accompanied by His disciples, like as the shepherd walks in the midst of his sheep, as He did in the first station, from the supper-room to the garden, comforting them, exhorting them to watch and to pray, defending them from the wolves, who sought to persecute and destroy them;—but in the other stations He went environed with His enemies like a sheep amongst wolves, and like a lamb amongst lions and tigers, which with excessive cruelty and fierceness bit Him, tore Him, and afflicted Him with injuries, contempts, sorrows, and torments, leading Him tied and shackled, even as a sheep when he is led to the slaughter, without once opening His mouth to complain. Then did He personally accomplish in Himself that which He had said to His disciples:—"Behold, I send you therefore as lambs among wolves,"—"be ye wise as serpents, and simple as doves." (37) For in these stations, notwithstanding that the persecutions, calumnies, and treacheries of His enemies were very terrible, yet He always showed Himself mild as a lamb, without resisting them, simple and pure as a dove, without offending them, wiser than any serpent, for He was never deceived by them, but with admirable wisdom confounded them, sometimes holding His peace, sometimes speaking, according as the case required.

iii. Concerning the *places from which* He departed, the manner in which He walked, and *places to which* He went and ended His station,—all are to Him *places of affliction*, and of torment; leaving one, and entering into another, and almost always the latter more terrible than the former, passing from a lesser torment to a greater; all which journeys were made with great haste, by reason of the fury of His

(37) Luc. x. 3; Mat. x. 16.

enemies, who urged Him forward, as also for the greatness of the love with which He Himself desired to hasten, to conclude with expedition our redemption: so that we may say that of the Canticles:—"Behold He cometh leaping upon the mountains, and skipping over the hills."(38) The mountains and little hills are the tribunals and palaces of the high-priests, presidents, and kings, which this our Lord visited, not to enjoy those goods which there those worldlings enjoyed, but with great celerity like a hart pursued by dogs, passed through every one of them, being there torn, struck, and tormented, until, upon the mount of Calvary, He took His last rest, remaining all disjointed and dead upon the Cross.

iv. Lastly, in each of these places I will *build spiritually* certain *tabernacles*, such as Saint Peter would have built upon the mount of Thabor, there to remain with Christ transfigured in sorrows, weighing particularly what He *there says, does, and suffers for my sake.*—I will build a tabernacle in the garden of Gethsemane, and I will there abide with Christ, heavy and afflicted, watching and praying with Him, hearing the words which He speaks with His Father, and with His disciples; hearing likewise those which the angel spoke to Him when he comforted Him, and those which He returned in answer; and beholding the combat which He suffered within Himself, and His bloody sweat, His steps going and coming to His apostles to wake them, and to the place of prayer, to pray for Himself and them.—At one time I will beseech Him, as the disciple does his master, that He would teach me to watch and pray; at other times, as a friend, or faithful servant, I will comfort Him in His discomforts, taking compassion to see Him so discomforted, and bearing Him company in His solitude. And in the

(38) Cant. ii. 8.

selfsame abode I will behold how He goes to entertain His enemies, the words He says to them, the miracles He wrought upon them, and the torments He received at their hands, being taken, trampled upon, and manacled. And notwithstanding that all this was done hastily, yet I will ponder the same slowly, detaining myself in this abode and station, until my soul remain satisfied, instructed, and allured to the love and imitation of that which there she had beheld in her blessed Lord.

All this shall be drawn out of that which we shall say on the meditation of this mystery: and in the same manner we ought to proceed in the other mysteries.

### ON THE SORROWS FELT BY THE BLESSED VIRGIN, OUR LADY, OVER HIS PASSION.

### POINT VIII.

In these mysteries of the Passion we ought also to consider *the sorrows and afflictions of the blessed Virgin, our Lady,* to take compassion on her, for her great sufferings and those of her Son on this occasion, feeling what His glorious mother suffered. And as she is also our mother, and that our sins are the cause of her afflictions, it is with great reason that we feel them, and encourage ourselves also to imitate the excellent virtues she discovered in them.

The greatness of these sorrows is to be collected from two principal sources:—

1. From the great *love which she bore to Christ* our Lord: because, according to the measure of love, is the joy of the goods which the person beloved possesses, and the sorrow for the evils which he suffers. This love, therefore, and this sorrow, were excessive in the Blessed Virgin for many reasons.

i. Because *Christ* our Lord was *her natural Son,* whom

she loved with a love more tender and pure than all the mothers and fathers in the world love their children; as she alone was a mother without father, in whom was engrafted all the love both of a father and a mother. And as the conception of this Son was singular by the operation of the Holy Ghost, which is properly love; so the love was likewise singular, and consequently the sorrow which she suffered at His death was also most singular. So that she might justly say:—"O, all ye that pass by the way, attend and see if there be any sorrow like to my sorrow."(39)

ii. To this is to be added, that this son *was her first-born*, and *her only son*, whose life therefore was more dear, and His death more to be deplored. For the Sacred Scripture, to exaggerate the grief of anything, calls it "the mourning for the death of the only-begotten."(40) How deeply, then, did the Blessed Virgin deplore the death of this only-begotten, who at the same time was the Only-begotten of Almighty God, beholding Him crucified with so great pain and ignominy.

iii. The love of the Blessed Virgin was augmented more towards her Blessed Son on *account of the great likeness which existed between them;* likeness being the cause of love; and so we see that fathers are wont much more to love that son who most resembles them. Seeing, then, that the Blessed Virgin and her son were exactly alike in complexion and condition, in manners and virtues, were even two made one; hence it was, that the sorrow which pierced the one, pierced likewise the heart of the other.

iv. The fourth reason for loving Him, was, *the excellency of the sanctity and wisdom of her son;* as true charity loves those most who are the best, and approach nearer to

(39) Thren. i. 12. (40) Jer. vi. 26; Amos. viii. 10; Zach. xii. 10.

Almighty God.(41) And if it happen as well, that they be also connected with us by blood, the love augments so much the more; nature and grace uniting themselves to make it more perfect. For this respect sorrow increases, if we see one suffer who is most holy; and as we believe that he suffered innocently, this augments the more our sorrow. For if "the daughters of Jerusalem"(42) so bitterly lamented the torments of Christ, holding Him for innocent: how much more bitterly did she deplore them, who held Him for the Holy of holies, and for the very fountain of all holiness?

v. Because she acknowledged Him to be *her infinite benefactor*, of whom she had received innumerable and most excellent benefits; amongst which the rarest was, to have chosen her to be His mother. And as love is always grateful, so it wishes infinite good to its benefactor, in recompense of those goods which it has received from Him. What sorrow, then, did the Blessed Virgin feel, seeing Him to suffer such infinite evils, whom she desired should enjoy such infinite goods?

vi. Because, being her son, He also *was the Son of the living God*—God infinite, and therefore worthy to be loved with an infinite love, for His infinite goodness and beauty. And as the Virgin with a particular light knew this excellency of her son;—so she loved Him with her whole heart, with her whole soul, with her whole spirit, and with her whole forces, without omitting any of that singular love which she could offer Him. And according to this measure of love, her sorrow augmented, sorrowing with her whole heart,—with her whole soul—with her whole spirit,—and with all her forces to behold Him so despised and abhorred, who for infinite respects, deserved to be honoured and loved of all.

(41) S. Th. 2. 2. q. xxvi. art. 7 and 13. (42) Luc. xxiii. 28.

vii. Lastly, the Holy Ghost had poured into her heart the charity of Almighty God, *uniting her with Him with unitive love*, in such a manner that she was one spirit with Almighty God, and with her son; *so that she felt all the prosperities and adversities of her son, as if they had been her own;* and likewise deplored the afflictions of her son much more bitterly than if the same had been her own, because she loved Him more than she loved herself. And as the force of this love transported her out of herself, and set her in the heart of her son, so what He endured she endured, feeling in herself that which she saw her son suffer; and so might much better say than did S. Paul—"With Christ I am nailed to the cross: and I live now, not I, but Christ liveth in me,"(43) and I live in Christ.

2. With the greatness of this love was joined *the second source* of sorrow, that is to say,—the *lively apprehension which she had of the pains* of her son, with all the circumstances which have been related; for she had read the Holy Scriptures which recounted them, and penetrated into them with a heavenly light; and finding herself present at them, she not only pondered what He suffered without, but much more that which He endured within, of all which she framed to herself so lively a representation, that she transformed herself into the figure of that which her son suffered. This was the two-edged sword, sharpened with knowledge and love, which pierced, as Simeon said, not the body, but the soul of this most pure Virgin. And after this manner, she also drank the chalice of the Passion which Christ offered to the sons of Zebedee, and was baptised with the Baptism of pains, and submerged in the bitter sea of tribulations, in such a manner that we may say of her:—"Magna est velut mare contritio

(43) Gal. ii. 20.

tua;"—"Great as the sea is thy destruction,"(44) and marvellous the bitterness of thine affliction.

*Colloquy.*—O sovereign Virgin, who can express the bitterness which thou didst feel for these seven causes of love and of sorrow, which, like seven swords, pierced thy heart? Well might Thou say on this occasion;—"Call me not Noemi, (that is beautiful;) but call me Mara, (that is bitter,) because the Almighty hath quite filled me with bitterness."(45) Great favours did the Almighty do thee, in the day of His Incarnation, and great afflictions has the same Almighty given thee in the day of His Passion; and since the afflictions that He sends are reputed favours, beseech Him to manifest in me His almighty power, giving me feeling of what He suffered, with grace to imitate Him in them. Amen.

3. From these considerations I should gather that the highest disposition to feel the pains of the Passion of Christ our Lord, is *love*, which, as St. Bonaventure says, (46) the more enkindled it is, the greater will the sorrow and compassion be, and with the selfsame comparison love is augmented. Wherefore, of the seven titles and causes which have been related, I will take those which serve most to enlarge this fervent love, and to unite me with Christ, that He may make me partaker of His pains, and of the fruits which proceed from His precious example.

### OF THE HEROIC VIRTUES EXERCISED BY THE BLESSED VIRGIN OUR LADY IN HIS PASSION.

### POINT IX.

Lastly are to be considered those rare *virtues* which the Blessed Virgin exercised upon this occasion, that we may imitate her in them.

(44) Thren. ii. 13. (45) Ruth. i. 20. (46) Stim. Div. Amoris, c. 2.

1. The principal were four, in which many others are contained.

i. A most high *resignation of her will to the will of Almighty God*, in which she denied her own natural will, that she might conform it to the divine, saying that which her son said:—"Not what I will, but what Thou wilt." (47) And this resignation is so much the more heroic, as the labours are greater to which we expose ourselves through them.

ii. Most profound *humility* in not flying insults, but seeking and embracing them, rejoicing to manifest herself to be the mother of Him who publicly was oppressed with so many injuries, receiving a great part of them for her own share, as far as she could, and with this humility she stood by the cross of her blessed son, taking His Passion and death as suffered for her, for although she had no sins for which Christ need suffer death, yet was she by His merits preserved from them.

iii. Great *fortitude* and magnanimity, *joined with patience*, with which she approached the cross of her son, standing upright at its foot, nothing being able to remove her from His presence,—neither the cruelty of the persecutors, nor the asperity of the torments which she endured, but rather she desired that some occasion might be offered to suffer and die for the love of Him, who suffered and endured so much for the love of her.

iv. Most inflamed *charity and love of men*, even of the deadly enemies of her son, so that neither their blasphemies nor cruelties could move her to indignation, but rather to compassion and sorrow for the sins which they committed, and the evils which thereby they incurred, praying to Almighty God for them, and excusing them in

(47) Marc. xiv. 36.

the same manner that her son excused them, as shall be shown in its place.

2. In this manner did the Blessed Virgin join with her most bitter afflictions admirable acts of virtue, so that justly she might then have said that of the Canticles:—"I am black but beautiful, O ye daughters of Jerusalem, – do not consider me that I am brown, because the sun hath altered my colour." (48)

*Colloquy.*—Thou art black, indeed, O most holy Virgin, exteriorly, through the pains which thou sustainest; but most beautiful interiorly, for the virtues thou exercisest; the sun of justice has altered thy colour, because His sorrows are the cause of thine; and yet the selfsame sun makes thee beautiful, for His example gives splendour to thine, which thou showest in imitating His virtues. Beseech Him, therefore, O most pious mother, that He will illuminate and inflame my heart with the burning beams of His celestial light, that I may so meditate His bitter pains, as to have part in them, practising His blessed virtues. Amen.

*Conclusion.*—By what has been said in these nine points is declared in general what things are to be pondered more in particular in every mystery of the Passion, as well in the Person of Christ our Lord as of the Blessed Virgin His mother, taking them both for the principal matter of meditation and imitation, and the mother for our advocate, to obtain true feeling of what her son suffered. The practice of the whole will be given in the ensuing meditations.

(48) Cant. i. 4.

# MEDITATION II.

ON CHRIST'S ASCENDING TO JERUSALEM, WHEN HE DISCOVERED TO HIS DISCIPLES WHAT HE WAS TO SUFFER THERE, AND OF THE VARIOUS TIMES THAT HE MADE MENTION OF HIS PASSION TO THEM.

## POINT I.

Christ our Lord knowing that the time of His Passion approached, (1) and that in Jerusalem the Jews were plotting His death, would depart from the city of Ephrem, where He had recollected Himself with His apostles, and would go thither, in which journey He made extraordinary haste, for as St. Mark says:—"*Jesus went before them, and they were astonished*, and following Him, were afraid." (2)

Upon this point are to be pondered *the causes of this new* and unwonted *manner of going* in Christ our Lord so speedily, and the effects which it caused in His disciples.

1. The first cause was, *to declare the promptitude of will*, and the fervour of spirit with which He went to suffer; without any fear of the torments which awaited Him at Jerusalem, when going to do things of themselves easy and glorious, as to preach, to work miracles, heal the diseased, and the like, Christ our Lord used His *ordinary* pace, but to the painful and ignominious obedience of His Passion and death, He would use *extraordinary* haste, manifesting by His hasty pace the force of divine love. which is like fire, and to a prick or spur, that makes us hasten and run with fervour to that obedience which is most painful to the flesh, but most agreeable to Almighty God. The contrary to this self-love effects, which goes with feet of lead to the laborious exercises of virtue, and

(1) Mat. xx. 18; Marc. x. 33; Luc. xviii. 31; Joan. xi. 54.
(2) Marc. x. 32.

makes us to run with speed to all that is honourable and delightful. Hence I may conjecture how full I am of self-love, and how void and empty of divine.

*Colloquy.*—O most sweet Jesus, who, to suffer torments, ascendedst to Jerusalem with so great haste and fervour, as if it had been to receive the repose and hire of Thy labours; fill my heart, I beseech Thee, with that divine love which then forced Thee to make such haste; that, leaving my slow and idle pace, I may with fervour like Thine, offer myself to obey and to suffer all Thou shalt please to impose upon me. Amen.

2. The second cause why in this journey Christ our Lord would be the foremost, was *to signify that in matter of suffering* labours and afflictions, as well interior as exterior, *He Himself would go before all His apostles* (3) *and disciples*, and before all the martyrs and saints that ever were, or ever should be. Whereas, on the other hand, in working miracles, which is a thing of honour, He gave place even to His apostles and to other saints, contented that they should work greater miracles than Himself, according to that of St. John the Evangelist, saying:—"Amen, amen, I say to you, he that believeth in me, the works that I do, he also shall do, and greater than these shall he do." (4) But in matter of suffering none ever went before Him, or equalled Him, for He suffered more than Job, more than the beggar Lazarus, and more than the prophets, apostles, and martyrs, all of whom come behind Him, beholding Him as a most perfect pattern and example of suffering.

*Colloquy.*—O good Jesus, how contrary is Thy spirit to the spirit of the world; for it will go before

(3) S. Tho. 3, p. q. xlvi. art. 6. (4) Joan. xiv. 12.

all, in those things which respect honours and pleasures, but Thine in dishonours, torments, and afflictions. It desires to go before in the works of greatest glory, but Thine in the works of greatest ignominy. Give me, Lord, I beseech Thee, this spirit, of which Thou madest so great account, that I may contend to excel all others in this, that for Thy love I may be more contemned and afflicted than all others. Amen.

3. The third cause was, to *provoke His apostles*, both to admiration and to imitation, "Stupebant sequentes," for they were astonished, following Him, and hastening to overtake Him, each one contending to get before the other, and to approach nearer to Jesus, vanquishing the fear and timidity which withheld them, by the fire of love which they felt for Him, which also made them redouble their pace, urged by the same example of Christ our Lord. In which we are shown how we are to behold and meditate Jesus Christ in His holy Passion, admiring the things which He did and suffered, and labouring to imitate Him in them. When I behold Christ Jesus beaten with scourges, clad with purple, crowned with thorns, and bearing His cross, I will wonder to see that so great a Lord suffers with so great love things so painful, and I will draw near Him, as much as is possible for me, following Him in taking disciplines, wearing hair clothes, clothing myself in poor apparel, and carry my cross every day, hastening to go before others, and to follow Him, not "afar off," (5) as St. Peter followed Him the night on which He was apprehended, but near Him, beseeching this our Lord to help me to overcome such repugnances as divert me from following Him, and doing on my own part all that I can to overcome them.

(5) Mat. xxvi. 58.

POINT II.

Christ our Lord going in this manner, stood still awhile, until the twelve apostles came to Him, whom taking apart, He said to them secretly:—"Behold we go up to Jerusalem, and *all things shall be accomplished which were written by the prophets concerning the Son of Man.* For He shall be delivered to the Gentiles, and shall be mocked, and scourged, and spit upon, and after they have scourged Him they will put Him to death, and the third day He shall rise again." (6)

1. This now was the third time Christ our Lord discovered His Passion to His apostles, for twice before He had done the same, although not so distinctly as at this time—after St. Peter had confessed Him for "the Son of the living God,"—when He healed the lunatic that was possessed by a devil, to the great admiration and astonishment of all that were present, as St. Luke observes. (7)

2. Upon all which we are to ponder the *reasons why* Christ our Lord would so often *discover to His apostles* the labours of His Passion and His death on such occasions, making choice of those which serve most for our own spiritual profit.

i. The first was, *that all might understand how present* each one *ought always to have this holy Passion in His memory*, taking continually its bitterness, and drinking incessantly this chalice so painful, so that when He ate, or drank, or preached, or conferred, or wrought miracles, or other marvellous works, He had the same always present; even in His most glorious transfiguration, speaking with Moses and Elias of the "decease that He should accomplish in Jerusalem," (8) He talked of it as of a thing in

(6) Luc. xviii. 31.
(7) Mat. xvi. 16, 17, 22; Marc. viii. 31, and ix. 31; Luc. ix. 22.
(8) Luc. ix. 31.

which He greatly delighted, though in truth it was most bitter; all this He did, to move me by His example, that I also have the same Passion always present before my eyes, and delight in thinking of it, and oftentimes to talk of it, so that it may be to me as bread, which is eaten with all other meats.

*Colloquy.*—O sweet Jesus, how is it that I am not delighted to think of that of which Thou thoughtest, and to talk of that of which Thou talkedst? This is my desire, O my beloved, to make "a bundle of myrrh"(9) of Thy excessive sorrows, and to place it always before my eyes, and between my breasts, that I may continually remember them, have compassion on Thee, and love Thee much more than my own self. Never will I cast them behind me, but ever keep them betwixt my breasts, as a thing most grateful to me, and which I greatly desire to embrace; nor will I take Thy sufferings in a confused bulk altogether, but remember and recount each one by itself, as long as I walk the way of this mortal life, comforting myself with their most pleasing odour, until I attain to life eternal.

ii. The second cause was, to *confirm His disciples in the faith* and belief *of these His contumelies*, as things harder to be believed than His excellencies, that they might arm themselves with great constancy to undergo them; for which cause, when He saw Himself highly honoured amongst His disciples, by reason of the confession of St. Peter, and again amongst the people, for the greatness of His miracles, He discovered to them His Passion, remembering what the Wise man says:—"In the day of good things be not unmindful of the day of evils," (10) preparing them in the one day for the other. "Behold, I go up to Jerusa-

(9) Cant. i. 12. (10) Ecclus. xi. 27.

lem," where I am to be delivered up to death, with great contumelies and ignominies, and seeing you also go up with me, prepare yourselves to suffer somewhat with me, lest otherwise you come to fail in the faith and love which you bear me.

*Colloquy.*—O sovereign master, whither Thou ascendest, thither also will I ascend, for, to suffer with Thee is not to descend, but to ascend and to profit. And so long as I see myself in Thy company, I have no cause to fear, because Thy succour is most certain. With Thee, therefore, will I suffer in the earthly Jerusalem, that I may reign with Thee in the heavenly.

3. Of these words of Jesus Christ our Lord I will make my profit in my labours, imagining that He says to me:—"Behold we go up to Jerusalem," first to suffer, and afterwards to reign; neither goest thou alone, but I go with thee to assist thee; I go before, do thou follow after me, to imitate me, that, suffering with me thou mayest likewise reign with me, world without end. Amen.

POINT III.

Then immediately the Evangelists added:—"*And they understood none of these things*, and this word was hid from them, and they understood not the things that were said." And they were afraid to ask Him of this word. "And they were troubled exceedingly." (11)

1. *Not all that hear* the Passion preached, or read it, or hear others talk of it, *understand, penetrate, or truly feel it*, as neither at that time the apostles themselves understood or penetrated it, for that they were as yet imperfect. For, truly to feel, and effectually to penetrate its hidden mysteries, fruits, and excellencies, is the especial gift of Al-

(11) Luc. xviii. 34; Mat. xvii. 22.

mighty God, which He imparts to His best friends when it pleases Him, and therefore I will humbly beg the same of Him, saying:—

*Colloquy.*—O my Redeemer, my understanding is much obscured, and the mysteries of Thy passion are concealed and hidden from me; give me, I humbly beseech Thee, true understanding and feeling of them, since Thou commandest me by Thine apostle, to feel in myself that which Thou dost suffer.(12)

2. The *reasons why* the apostles understood not, nor penetrated those things which were spoken to them of the Passion, were, because *they held as base*, and *feared* exceedingly *contempts* and ignominies, and much esteemed and loved honour and dignities; for which cause, when Christ spoke to them of His contempts and ignominies, they were exceedingly sad, and greatly depressed in mind, holding it as a thing most unworthy that He should ever permit such things to befal Him. Hence also it proceeds when I meditate the same Passion, that I am dry or without any feeling or taste for it, because I come with a disposition contrary to these mysteries; and, therefore, truly to feel them, I ought to lay aside that vain fear of contempts and tribulations, of self-love, honours, and dignities, endeavouring to make great account and estimation of all that which affords me matter of suffering afflictions and contempts, whereby to accomplish the will of Almighty God.

3. To have a greater and more effectual feeling of this truth, it will help much to ponder on this occasion *what happened to Christ our Lord with St. Peter*, who had scarcely finished confessing Him to be the Son of the living God by revelation, which he had received from the Father of heaven, but he presently discovered his own grossness and stupidity, for hearing his master speak of His Passion,

(12) Phil. ii. 5.

he esteemed it so basely, that he took upon himself to reprehend Him for it, saying:—"Lord, be it *far from Thee, that shall not be unto Thee.*" (13) But Christ our Lord looking upon the other apostles rebuked him, and answered him very sharply, saying:—"Go behind me, Satan, thou art a scandal unto me, because thou savourest not of the things that are of God, but the things that are of men;" as if He had said more evidently,—"Thou who hast honoured me, confessing me the Son of the living God, art now become Satan, and my enemy, in that thou opposest thyself to my Passion, seeking by all means in thy power to avert me from it, contrary to the will of my Father, who wills that I suffer it; all which proceeds from thee, because thou wantest true heavenly wisdom, to know and to savour those things which are ordained of Almighty God, and hast only a human and earthly wisdom, to know and savour the things which are of men, and which they prize and make account of. Go, therefore, after me, and follow me, for I may not follow thy fond and erroneous judgment, but thou must humbly follow mine, which is assured."

Hence I may see how *greatly Christ our Lord esteemed His death and Passion*, as being ordained by the will of the eternal Father, for the good of the whole world, and the great account which He wills that we also make of all the contempts and contumelies which He endured for this cause, so that whosoever should attempt to divert us from it we should hold as Satan, and a stone of scandal and offence to us, and not go after him, but endeavour to draw him after us, that following us he may likewise feel that which we feel, and notwithstanding that under the pretext of pious zeal he should oppose us, even although he be a

(13) Mat. xvi. 22, 23.

saint, and very highly illuminated of God in other things, and other ways our friend and dear to us, yet ought we to repel him from us, as here we see Christ repelled St. Peter from him.

*Colloquy.*—O Sovereign master, who prizest and valuest so highly Thy Passion, by reason of the celestial wisdom with which Thou didst behold the causes of it, take from me all earthly wisdom, and endue me with heavenly, to the end that I may also highly esteem Thy pains, and those which Thou desirest that I suffer for the love of Thee. I will not, O my Redeemer, induce Thee nor draw Thee to follow my judgment and my desire, because it is erroneous judgment and earthly desire, but after Thee will I go, Thee will I follow, prizing what Thou prizest, loving what Thou lovest, and abhorring what Thou abhorrest; and since Thou givest me such a desire, give me grace also to execute the same. Amen.

---

## MEDITATION III.

### ON CHRIST'S ENTRANCE WITH PALMS INTO JERUSALEM.(1)

#### POINT I.

Christ our Lord, five days before His death, would enter into Jerusalem, where He was to be crucified, *with great signs of joy and extraordinary exterior pomp;* according as the Hebrews were accustomed to bring the Paschal lamb into their houses five days before they sacrificed it.(2)

This entrance our Saviour ordained for certain mysterious causes, all full of love.

i. *To manifest the desire He had of suffering*, and the contentment with which He embraced the sufferings which awaited Him in Jerusalem, entering upon them

(1) Mat. xxi; Marc. xi; Luc. xix; Joan. xii. (2) Exod. xii. 6.

with as much joy as if He were going to a marriage; for the zeal of the glory of Almighty God, and of accomplishing the will of His eternal Father, for the salvation of men, wrought in Him this great contentment to endure all those sufferings, which He held as present in His memory, as if at that instant He had been undergoing them. And it is this example that causes martyrs to go as joyfully to prison as to a wedding, and lie as joyfully upon burning gridirons, as upon beds strewed with flowers.

*Colloquy.*—O blessed Jesus, I blush in Thy presence for the repugnance which I feel in myself to suffer troubles for the love of Thee; help me, my joy, that I may rejoice to suffer something for Thee, as Thou rejoicedst when Thou wast to suffer for me. Amen.

ii. To *give us to understand that when in the garden of Gethsemane*, and during His Passion, He suffered fears, heaviness, grief, and agonies, *all this happened principally in the interior part of His soul*, whose natural inclination is to avoid the sorrows of the body; notwithstanding He supported them willingly, and with great contentment of the superior part of the spirit, forasmuch as the will of the eternal Father shone in them, and in this He persevered even to death;—teaching us by this example, that the most perfect patience consists in offering oneself with great contentment of spirit to suffer, not only exterior pain, but also interior afflictions. And to this must I aspire, saying with the apostle:—"Gladly, therefore, will I glory in my infirmities," and "please myself in reproaches, in necessities, in persecutions, in distresses for Christ."(3)

*Colloquy.*—Gladly, O my Saviour, will I embrace

(3) 2 Cor. xii. 9.

the afflictions and agonies of the flesh, and renounce all its sensible contentments, accepting them to imitate Thee with joy of spirit. Amen.

iii. *To show that all the injuries, calumnies, and persecutions* which He had received in Jerusalem, the sundry times He had been there, *were not sufficient to extinguish the love and charity which He bore it*, and the desire He had of visiting it, teaching it and doing it all the good that He was able; and moreover He assured it, that neither the contumelies and sorrows which at that present He was there to suffer should any way cool His charity, nor in any way hinder His receiving it into His favour and friendship, if it would. O immense charity of Jesus Christ, O vehement fire of inflamed love, which neither many waters, nor floods of tribulations could extinguish. The self same charity remains in Him to this present day, for although I admit into my soul some mortal sin, although with the same sin I crucify Him anew in my soul,(4) and trample His precious blood under my feet, and consequently drive Him from me ignominiously, He visits my soul with His holy grace, and refuses not to return the second time, and to enter within my gates with great alacrity, that in visiting me He may again favourably impart His grace to me; and if yet again I return to crucify, trample, and to expel Him from me, He returns the third time with the same contentment as at first.

*Colloquy.*—O blessed be such excessive charity and let the angels thank Him for the same a thousand times. Come, come Thy majesty, O my Redeemer, to this ungrateful city of my soul, since Thou hast so great desire to visit it, for I now firmly purpose never more to drive Thee forth, but to entertain Thee hereafter with such reverence and obedience, as such

(4) Hebr. vi. 6.

a charity of right deserves: and because I am a man inconstant and mutable, let Thy grace assist me, that I may continue constant. Amen.

iv. *That we might understand, that to suffer contempts* and contumelies to accomplish the will of Almighty God, and for virtue's sake, *is a thing most glorious* and honourable in the eyes of God, of His angels, and of just men; and that, therefore, we are to undertake them, and to enter into them, not only with joy, but as marks of honour, as one that highly prizes them, and honours himself by the means of them, not being ashamed, nor blushing at them. But God forbid, as S. Peter says, that I suffer "as a murderer, or a thief, or a railer, or a coveter of other men's goods,"(5) that is, in punishment of such crimes, for of these I might worthily be ashamed, but to suffer as a Christian, for justice sake, would be honour to me, as it was to my Lord.

v. But the charity of Jesus passed yet further, and His desire to suffer; for He would enter into Jerusalem with so great honour and so many attendants *that the contempts* and ignominies which He was afterwards to undergo, *might be so much the greater*, as it happens to them who fall from some great honour and worldly dignity, according to that which David said:—"Being exalted, I have been humbled and troubled."(6) And His Father says by the prophet Isaiah:—"My servant shall be exalted, and extolled, and shall be exceeding high. As many have been astonished at thee, so shall His visage be inglorious among men, and His form among the sons of men."(7) Thus our good Jesus always fled the exterior honour of men; and if at this present He sought it, or accepted it, He did it that His dishonour might afterwards be so much the greater, ordaining this honour to suffer more ignominy.

(5) 1 Pet. iv. 15. (6) Psal. lxxxvii. 16. (7) Is. lii. 13.

*Colloquy.*—I render Thee thanks, O most sweet Jesus, for that insatiable hunger which Thou hadst to suffer injuries. For the love of Thee, I beg that I become not slack in it, even when I am honoured. Amen.

POINT II.

Secondly, is to be considered, the *preparation* which Christ our Lord made in this entrance. For He "sent two disciples, saying to them, Go ye into the town that is over against you, and immediately you shall find an ass tied, and a colt with her; loose them and bring them to me; and if any man shall say anything to you, say ye that the Lord hath need of them, and forthwith he will let them go." And the disciples going, did as Jesus commanded them, and they "laid their garments upon" the colt, "and made" Jesus "sit thereon."(8)

1. This King of heaven, to give some proof of His royalty, being always accustomed to walk on foot throughout all Galilee and Judea, yet at this time would not *enter into Jerusalem on foot;* yet neither mounted on a steed, or mule covered with rich and costly ornaments, but *upon a common ass, covered with the poor garments of His disciples;* by this fact trampling under foot the pomp of the world, and manifesting His poverty, humility, and meekness, by which, as by the ensigns of His Kingdom, He was to be acknowledged in the world, its Mesiah and Saviour, as had been foretold by the prophet Zachariah, when he said:—"Ecce Rex tuus veniet tibi, justus et Salvator, ipse pauper et ascendens super asinam."—"Rejoice greatly, O daughter of Sion.—Behold thy King will come to thee, the just, and Saviour, He is poor, and riding upon an ass."(9) By this example I will learn to abhor the pomp of the world, and to embrace the poverty, meekness, and humility of Jesus Christ; for if these be the marks of my

(8) Mat. xxi. 2; Marc. xi. 2; Luc. xix. 35. (9) Zach. ix. 9.

King and of my Lord, it is reason that they be also of those who glory in being His vassals, and with them am I to prepare and adorn myself to go to receive Him, since to me also is said:—" Ecce Rex tuus venit tibi."—" Behold thy King cometh unto thee." O would that I understood aright who this my King is, and in what manner He comes to me! Thou, O my Saviour, art my King—King of kings, King of men, King of angels, and of heaven and earth, a King by nature,—Son of the eternal Father, and of all things created absolute monarch; and yet Thou comest from heaven for me, for my salvation, for my consolation, for my remedy, for my example, for my defence, and my protection.

*Colloquy.*—O my King. and my beloved, " Thou to me, and I to Thee." Behold me from henceforth dedicated to Thee, to Thy service, honour, and glory; to obey Thee, to love Thee, to adore Thee, and to be entirely Thine, since Thou art entirely and wholly mine. And since Thou comest to me poor, meek, and humble, I likewise will go to meet Thee with poverty, meekness, and humility, wearing the same livery which Thou didst wear. Amen.

2. I will ponder, secondly, the *peculiarities* which lie *hid* in this holy mystery.—i. He sent "*two* disciples" to fetch the ass, and not one alone, to keep His wonted custom, which was, to send His disciples in company, and two by two, united in charity.—ii. He commanded that they "*loose*" *the beasts*, and bring them to Him: to signify, that the apostolical office is, to unloose sinners, and such as lead a bestial life, and who are bound with the ropes of their sins,(10) and to bring them to Christ, that He may sit upon them, and may rule them, as one rules the beast on which he sits.—iii. He wills that if any one

(10) Prov. v. 22.

should attempt to hinder them, *they should* "*say that the Lord hath need of*" *them;* insinuating hereby, that as there would not be wanting such as would hinder their office of converting and unloosing the souls of sinners, so those hindrances should cease in the name of the same Lord who sent them for them, for that He has need of them for His glory.

*Colloquy.*—O Almighty Word, which so stops the mouths, and binds the hands of those who attempt to hinder the commandment of our Lord! O King of glory, what need hast Thou of so vile and abject a beast, as is a sinner? "Who, when he was in honour, did not understand; he is compared to senseless beasts, and is become like unto them."(11) I wretch am he that have need of Thee, not Thou of me. I, for my sins, am made as a beast before Thee, and am bound with the cords of my passions. Command, Lord, that I be let loose, and that I be presented to Thee, for it will be a comfort to me to bear the burthen of Thy law, and Thee also, my Lord, for my guide. Suffer not that the world, the flesh, or the Devil hinder this unloosing, but say to them with Thy word, that Thou hast need of this Thy servant, that they may immediately set me free, to serve Thee as I desire. Amen.

### POINT III.

As Christ our Lord went forward, sitting upon this humble ass, suddenly, by inspiration from heaven, there came to meet Him "*a very great multitude*, some of whom spread their garments in the way; and others cut down boughs from the trees, and strewed them in the way;" others from the city of Jerusalem came forth to meet Him, bearing palms in their hands in sign of victory, and all with unspeakable joy praised God, and cried out, say-

(11) Psal. xlviii. 13.

ing: "Hosanna to the Son of David, blessed is he that cometh in the name of the Lord, Hosanna in the highest."(12)

1. In this wonderful occurrence, which was altogether the effect of the inspiration of the Holy Ghost, how truly the eternal Father honours His Son with true honours and true praises. For even as when at His first entrance into the world, being born in poverty, in the stable of Bethlehem, He sent an army of angels to solemnize His entrance, singing:—"Glory to God in the highest, and on earth peace to men of good will."(13) So now entering into Jerusalem poor and meek upon an ass, the same eternal Father raised up an army of men, and of innocent children, to solemnize His entrance, with the selfsame spirit as did the angels, saying:—"Heaven hath peace with us who inhabit and dwell in earth, and glory be to God in the highest, blessed is He that cometh in the name of our Lord." There the angels asked peace in earth from men to God: and here these Hebrews ask peace in heaven, from God to men.

*Colloquy.*—O eternal Father, I give Thee thanks for the honour which Thou didst bestow on Thine only-begotten Son, when, to accomplish Thy will, He went to undergo contempts and ignominies. O most sacred Spirit, I give Thee thanks that Thou inspiredst into that crowd of people this form of praise, redounding to the glory of my Redeemer. I rejoice, O my Redeemer, to see that all bless and praise Thee, and I also with the selfsame spirit bless and praise Thee, saying,—"Hosanna filio David."—"Blessed is He that cometh in the name of the Lord."

These words the Church uses in the mass at the end of the preface, in memory of the coming of Christ our Lord

(12) Mat. xxi. 8; Luc. xix. 38. (13) Luc. ii. 14.

in the most holy Sacrament of the Altar; with which words, and with which spirit crying out, I also will say:—"Blessed is He who cometh from heaven into this sacrament for our salvation: let peace from heaven come with Him, and glory be given to God in the highest."

2. I will ponder the devotion of that crowd of people, who, in sign of reverence, stripped themselves of their own garments, "and strewed them in the way," that Christ our Lord might tread upon them, thinking themselves happy, that He would vouchsafe to touch their garments. And with this spirit will I cast all that I have at the feet of Jesus, that He dispose of them as He shall please.

*Colloquy.*—Behold, my Redeemer, I humbly cast at Thy feet not only my substance, but also my honour, myself wholly, and whatsoever may bring me contentment; tread and trample upon me, O Lord, and dispose of me in whatever way Thou wilt: triumph over me, because I have been Thine enemy, and I myself am well content to carry in my own hands the palm of this Thy victory, and will gladly publish it to the whole world; for, to render myself vanquished to Thee, is indeed Thy victory, but my commodity, and is also my victory in virtue of Thine.

POINT IV.

Jesus Christ, entering into the city, "some of the Pharisees from amongst the multitude, said to Him, Master rebuke Thy disciples, and command them to hold their peace." To whom He said:—"I say to you, that *if these shall hold their peace, the stones will cry out.*"(14)

1. Here is to be pondered, *the sin of him who is envious*, who takes to heart the glory of his neighbour, and condemns for evil that which is good, and calls that

(14) Luc. xix. 39.

passion which is the inspiration of Almighty God, and therefore wishes him to be reprehended. For which reason such an envious person makes himself unworthy, that God should inspire and move him, as He moved these simple people, to employ himself in the praise of Jesus Christ.

2. The *force of divine inspiration*, which so changed the hearts of men, instructed the ignorant, and moved them to glorify Almighty God with so great fervour, leaving the proud and presumptuous Pharisees in their tepidity, which these ensuing words witness:—"I say to you, that if these shall hold their peace, the stones will cry out;" as if He had said:—"These will not cease to speak, seeing that Almighty God, with vehement force, has inspired and moved them to it; for if they should hold their peace, God would raise up others, though they were as hard as stones, which should cry out and promulgate what they speak; for God is powerful to do all things, even of stones to raise up children to Abraham:"(15) and although these should "hold their peace now, within a little while, viz. in my Passion, the very stones will indeed cry out, rending themselves asunder with great clamour, thus proclaiming me to be Almighty God."

*Colloquy.*—O sweet Jesus, mollify the hardness of the hearts of the Jews and Gentiles, that Thy divine Spirit may enter into them, and acknowledging Thee for the true Messiah, they may cry out, and say, "Blessed be He who" hath come "in the name of our Lord" to save us. Save them all, O my Saviour, and be not unmindful of my heart, harder than stone, but soften it, move it, and make it tender and supple with the spirit of devotion, whenever I pray to Thee, that I may ever laud Thee, and ever love Thee, world without end. Amen.

(15) Mat. iii 9.

# MEDITATION IV.

ON THE TEARS SHED BY CHRIST WHEN BEHOLDING THE CITY OF JERUSALEM, AND ON THAT WHICH HAPPENED TO HIM ON THAT DAY.

## POINT I.

Jesus Christ going on His journey, accompanied and applauded by all the people, as before said, "when He drew near, seeing the city, He wept over it." (1)

Here consider the *motive and occasion of these tears of Christ*, as having some particular and hidden mystery, which His tears had not at other times. Now we know He wept on four different occasions:—i. When He was an infant *lying in a manger*, which was no marvel, since it is natural for infants when they are newly born, as the Wise man says:—"The first voice which I uttered was crying, as all others do:"(2)—ii. He wept *when He raised Lazarus*, for St. John says:—"And Jesus wept;"(3) nor was this any wonder, since Jesus saw Mary Magdalen weep, and the Jews also who came with her, for it becomes the just to "rejoice with them that rejoice, to weep with them that weep:"(4)—iii. He wept also *upon the cross*, as the apostle St. Paul says:—"Who in the days of His flesh, with a strong cry and tears, offering up prayers and supplications to Him that was able to save Him from death, was heard for His reverence." (5) Neither was this any great marvel, since He was so full of pains and sorrows, contemned by all, and as it were forsaken by His own Father.—iv. But the real wonder is, that He wept *on this occasion*, even when He saw Himself in so great honour, triumph, and

(1) Luc. xix. 41. (2) Sap. vii. 3. (3) Joan. xi. 35.
(4) Rom. xii. 15. (5) Heb. v. 7.

glory, and when all pronounced a thousand songs of praise for joy.

The causes of His weeping were the four following:—

1. The first was, *to show how little account He made of worldly glory*, and how little contentment all that honour gave to His heart, since in the midst of all those praises and rejoicings, and when all sung triumphs to Him, He shed tears. O how far was He from laughing, or from taking any complacency in those prosperities, who watered them with tears and sighs.

2. The second and chief cause was, *His infinite charity*, whence proceeded the internal joy He felt in His mind on entering Jerusalem to suffer there, because of the incomparable good that would thence result to His elect; and from the same charity that shedding forth of tears proceeded, considering the evils which would arise to the reprobate by His death.

3. Nor does St. Luke only say that He wept, but that "*He wept over the city*," to make us to understand that He wept not for Himself, for the pains which He was shortly to suffer, but forgetful of them, He wept for that unfortunate city of Jerusalem, and for the sins it would commit in killing Him, and for the calamities which on this account would befal it, all which He set before Him at the time that He now beheld it.

*Colloquy.*—O sweet Jesus, how happy were he who could accompany Thee in these tears, and forgetting his own pains, could with charity deplore the sins of his neighbours, and the just punishments which they are to suffer for them! Oh how great an evil is that to be esteemed, which moved Christ amidst such praises and triumphs, to shed tears! O my soul, how dost Thou not tremble with fear at so great an evil, which causes God himself to weep for compassion!

4. It is probable that, as Christ our Lord, beholding the city of Jerusalem, in which there were some good but many wicked persons, *deplored the sins of the wicked,* and the destruction which for their sakes was to befal it;—He also at the same time represented to Himself the city *of this world* and the earthly Jerusalem, in which the sinners and the just are mixed together; and, beholding the sins of the wicked, and the *chastisements* which for this cause were to *come upon them,* He wept also over them; and I am yet further to think that He then wept also for my sins, which He likewise had present before Him.

*Colloquy.*—O my Redeemer, how sorry am I that I have been, and am, the cause of these Thy tears; I desire as much as lies in me to wipe them away, by taking away the cause of them, which is my sins. I am he who ought to weep, because I am he who have sinned; help me, therefore, O Lord, to weep so long that I may at length deserve to be comforted. Amen.

POINT II.

1. Secondly, *the words themselves* are to be pondered which Christ our Lord spoke when He wept; first, He said:—"If thou also hadst known, and that in this thy day, the things that are to thy peace; but *now they are hidden from thine eyes;*" (6) that is to say, "O Jerusalem, if thou knewest that which I know of thee, thou doubtless wouldst weep, as I do, and if thou knewest what I offer to thee for thy peace and prosperity, as this company which comes with me knows, doubtless thou also wouldst burst forth into my praises, and with ineffable joy wouldst receive that good which enters in at thy gates.—And if thou knewest this thy day, this 'good day,' (7) which shines upon thy house by means of my coming, doubtless thou wouldst admit it, and wouldst not let it depart from

(6) Luc. xix. 42. (7) Ecclus. xiv. 14.

thee; but now all this is hidden from thee for thy sins; and for this cause thou neither weepest nor seekest it, nor coming to thee, dost receive it.

Hence I will gather, that the beginning of my remedy consists in the lively and profound *knowledge* of two things,—*of my miseries*, and of *the remedy of them*, which is Jesus Christ our Lord, who offers me means most fit for this purpose, which are, to believe, love, and obey Him. And particularly, it is important for me to know the *means which He offers me* for the peace of my soul, in that state or rank which I hold in the Church or in Religion; and on the contrary, the origin of my ruin is, the ignorance and the little regard which I make of these things, which although they are before my eyes, I neither know nor observe them.

*Colloquy.*—O good Jesus, now I plainly see with how great reason Thou deplorest our blindness, since we so little regard the good which Thou offerest us, notwithstanding it is worthy of infinite esteem. Take from me, and from all men, O Lord, I beseech Thee, this veil of ignorance, that we may see and weep; for the eye which sees not weeps not; and if it saw, it would forthwith weep.

2. He *foretold at this time the evils and chastisements* which were *to come* upon that city, saying:—"The days shall come upon thee, and thine enemies shall cast a trench about thee, and compass thee round, and straiten thee on every side, and beat thee flat to the ground, and thy children who are in thee; and they shall not leave in thee a stone upon a stone, because thou hast not known the time of thy visitation;" (8) that is to say, because thou knowest not this day upon which God visits thee, and comes to save thee.

(8) Luc. xix. 43.

Hence I will infer, that if the present Jerusalem, that is, the city and souls of the faithful, do not acknowledge this gracious visitation of Almighty God, and the manifold occasions which Christ offers for their salvation and perfection, she will be chastised with most horrible punishments; and consequently, since scarcely there is any one day in which God does not in prayer, or out of prayer, visit me with His divine inspirations,(9) inciting me to serve Him, if I know not this time of His visitation, I also am justly to be chastised.

*Colloquy.*—Wherefore, O my soul, open thine eyes to know this happy time, and be not more slothful than "the kite, the turtle, and the swallow, and the stork,"(10) which know the times of their coming; behold diligently the times when God visits thee every day, since He comes for thy profit; and if thou admit Him not, or deny Him entrance, it will doubtless turn to thy eternal loss.

3. If Christ our Lord so greatly deplored the temporal chastisement of that city, for the love which He bore it, how much more bitterly would He weep for *the eternal chastisement it was to receive* in the other life, when He will come to visit it, not with the visitation of mercy, but of exact justice, in the last and dreadful day of reckoning?

*Colloquy.*—O good Jesus, with how great affection didst Thou deplore the perdition of the unfortunate people of this perverse Jerusalem, foreseeing how they were to be encompassed and entrenched, not so much by the Romans, as by the devils: beaten flat, not only to the ground, but even to the very bottom of hell, tormented in all their powers, with grief and eternal disorder, leaving no stone upon another, nor any part

(9) Job. vii. 18. (10) Jer. viii. 7.

which was not filled with confusion. There they lament with everlasting lamentations, because they neither wept nor lamented in this life, nor profited by the tears which Thou didst shed for them, nor received that fatherly advice which Thou didst give them. Open, O Lord, I beseech Thee, the eyes of all sinners, that we may fear that visitation which Thou art to make in the hour of death, preparing us for it with lamentations for our sins, lest otherwise we fall into those everlasting lamentations. Amen.

POINT III.

Thirdly is to be considered, that as soon as Christ our Lord had entered into the city of Jerusalem, He went to the Temple, to give thanks to His eternal Father, according to His custom:—"And there came to Him the blind and the lame...*and He healed them*...and the chief priests and the scribes seeing...the children crying in the Temple, and saying: *Hosanna to the Son of David*, were moved with indignation. And said to Him: Hearest Thou what these say? And Jesus said to them: Yea, have you never read: *Out of the mouths of infants and of sucklings Thou hast perfected praise?*" (11)

1. Here consider on the one side the *bounty and liberality of Christ* our Lord, in doing good to all, both blind and lame, as many as came to Him, by this proving who He was; and also the efficacy of divine inspiration which moved *the tongues even of those little children*, to sound forth the praises and glories of Jesus Christ, testifying His greatness by their prayers.—And on the other side, *the malice of the Pharisees*, who drew poison out of all these praises, for being full of envy, neither did the meekness of Christ soften them, nor the greatness of His works, no

(11) Mat. xxi. 14; Psal. viii. 3.

the praises of the children who could scarcely speak, move them to break forth into His praises.

*Colloquy.*—O eternal God, deliver me, I beseech Thee, from this blindness and hardness of heart, that I may never draw harm from that which Thou hast ordained for my profit. And make me, likewise, a little infant in sincerity and purity, that so my mouth may become a worthy instrument of Thy praises, whereby many others also may take occasion to glorify Thee, world without end. Amen.

2. Christ our Lord having employed the whole of that day in labouring, preaching, and working miracles, it growing late, He looked around upon all, to see if there were any amongst them who would invite Him to his house, or give Him a lodging, and seeing that there was none who made any such proffer, for fear of the Pharisees, He *returned fasting with His disciples to Bethania,* (12) which was two thousand paces distant from Jerusalem. In which is to be remarked the infinite liberality and mercy of Almighty God towards men, and how sparing and ungrateful men are towards Almighty God, and how little trust is to be placed in them, since they so soon forsook, for human fear, Him whom they had received on that very day with such exultation. Their punishment, therefore, Christ our Lord prophesied to them the next day in the morning, in cursing the fig-tree upon which He found no fruit. For as St. Matthew said:—"In the morning returning into the city, and seeing a certain fig-tree by the wayside, He came to it, and found nothing on it but leaves only, and He saith to it: May no fruit grow on thee henceforward for ever, and immediately the fig-tree withered away." (13)

(12) Marc. xi. 11. (13) Mat. xxi. 18.

*Colloquy.*—O most just judge, how justly wilt Thou pour forth Thy vengeance upon the wicked in the day of judgment, since when Thou wast hungry they gave Thee not to eat, and when a stranger, they harboured Thee not! O my soul, omit not for human fear to invite and harbour Jesus Christ, so that He exclude thee not from His Kingdom; and cease not to do good to thy neighbours, although thou receivest no recompense from them. Accompany thy Lord as the apostles did in this His so honourable entrance into Jerusalem, and in His so ignominious going forth from it, serving Him both in honour and dishonour, that so He may receive thee into His perpetual company. Amen.

---

## MEDITATION V.

### ON CHRIST'S SUPPER IN BETHANIA.

Notwithstanding that this supper took place six days before that of the Paschal Lamb, and one day before the entrance of Christ our Lord into Jerusalem, with the branches of palms, as S. John relates; yet S. Matthew and S. Mark,(1) recount it after that entrance, on account of Judas having taken occasion at that supper to sell Christ, and I for the same reason will observe and follow their order.

#### POINT I.

Christ our Lord, having been invited to Bethania, and sitting at table, Mary, the sister of Lazarus, came with an alabaster box containing "a pound of ointment of spikenard, of great price, and anointed the feet of Jesus, and wiped His feet with her hair," and "poured it on His

(1) Mat. xxvi.; Marc. xiv; Joan. xii.

head;" "and the house was filled with the odour of the ointment."(2)

1. Mary *twice* anointed Christ our Lord. First, *at her conversion*, to obtain pardon of her sins, as has already been treated of in the third part, meditation twenty-five. —Secondly, *at this supper*, as a mark of her gratitude for the raising again of her brother Lazarus, of which she would make a public demonstration, prostrating herself at the feet of Christ, and washing them, as is believed, with tears of love, as she did the first time with tears of sorrow, then did she wipe them with the fairest towel which she had, her hair, and anointed them with a very precious ointment; and getting new confidence, she emboldened herself to anoint His head, breaking the box of alabaster; for although there was a whole "pound" of it, yet nothing should be left, which should not be shed upon the head or feet of Jesus Christ. O how attentive, and how contented was our Saviour, beholding this of His servant; but much more attentively pondering the devotion and inward affection with which she performed it, wishing that there were many in His Church who would imitate her in this. And I, to imitate the spirit of these two anointings, ought to take care with all possible fervour to pay to God our Lord the two debts which I owe Him; one for my sins, the other for His benefits; and this by the more fervour of spirit and gratitude, by giving demonstration of it by my works, bestowing upon Him the best and most precious things I have.

2. I will principally offer to Him an ample vessel of "alabaster," full of spiritual "ointment," with which to anoint Him. This vessel or box of alabaster *is my heart and my body*, which I am to break with the exercises of mortification and penance, with sorrow and contrition for

(2) Joan. xii. 3; Mat. xxvi. 6.

my sins, breaking my will and my inordinate appetites. The unction must be with a faithful ointment, and with pure spikenard, (3) that is, with manifold affections, and most excellent works of humility and charity, with fidelity and purity of intention in doing them, so that my charity may proceed, as the apostle says, "from a pure heart, and a good conscience, and an unfeigned faith."(4) With this ointment I ought spiritually to anoint Christ, first His feet, and afterwards His head; because first I ought to meditate upon the humiliations and ignominies of His humanity, figured by the feet, endeavouring to imitate and embrace them by undertaking works of penance and mortification, and after to ascend to meditate the excellencies of His divinity, figured by the head, rejoicing for them both, and thanking Him for the benefits which come to us from them.

*Colloquy.*—O most sweet Jesus, true God and true man, since I have received from Thy holy hand whatever good I have in this frail and broken vessel, I wholly offer it to Thee; yes, though the box must be broken in pieces, if Thy service shall require it.

3. As all "*the house was filled with the*" fragrant "odour" of the ointment which Mary Magdalen poured forth,—even so the universal Church, and *every Religious house, is edified* and comforted with *the like glorious exercises of virtue.* For this cause I will endeavour to stir myself up to the exercise of them, that so I may be made, as the apostle says, "a good odour of Christ" (5) in every place, and to procure also, by my example, that others with whom I live be incited to do the same.

POINT I.

Judas Iscariot, seeing what Mary Magdalen had done,

(3) S. Ber. ser. 42 in Cant. (4) 1 Tim. i. 5.
(5) 2 Cor. ii. 15.

said:—"Why *was not this ointment sold for three hundred pence*, and given to the poor? Now he said this, not because he cared for the poor, but because he was a thief, and having the purse, carried the things that were put therein," *and some others of the disciples also had* "*indignation* within themselves, and said:—*Why was this waste* of ointment made? and they murmured against her." (6)

1. There will *never be wanting some who will judge rashly*, and murmur against the good works of the just,—some from a bad intention, like Judas,—others through ignorance or good zeal, although indiscreet, like the disciples who murmured against this action of Mary Magdalen, condemning her as prodigal, as if she had been casting away an ointment so precious upon an occasion even ungrateful to Christ Himself, as they suppose that pleasure was which He received from the odour of that ointment;—as also that she was indiscreet, since with the price of that ointment she might have succoured a number of poor; and secretly this murmuring redounded also against the master Himself, who permitted it. But all of them erred in their judgments, not pondering that spirit which moved this holy woman to perform this work, nor that which moved Christ to accept it, and therefore, because of their own little devotion, or because they judged the work superficially, they both condemned the work and murmured against the woman who wrought it.

2. Hence I will learn *never rashly to judge evil of any, nor interpret for the worse* the actions which may be good of their own nature, and much less to murmur at them, but to leave all such things to the judgment of Almighty God, who is the true and upright judge; for otherwise I may easily err and sin against my neighbour, and against the Holy Ghost also, who moved them to the work

(6) Joan. xii. 5; Marc. xiv. 10.

against which I murmur, which injury He Himself knows how to revenge. For which cause Christ our Lord commanded, saying:—"Judge not, and you shall not be judged; condemn not, and you shall not be condemned." (7) Nor will the outward show of piety, with which I seek to cloak my rash judgments and murmurings, excuse me; for many times with this cloak perverse intentions are covered, as Judas covered the desire he had to steal the money which might have been made of the ointment, under the colour of giving it in alms to the poor.

3. It is very probable that this murmuring took its first beginning from Judas, and by his bad example induced the other disciples to murmur also, which shows *how pernicious one bad example is*, and how one wicked companion draws after him and perverts many good. For, as the house of Bethania was filled with the "good odour," which proceeded from the good work which Mary did, even so was it filled and infected with the evil savour which issued forth of the pestiferous mouth of wicked Judas, troubling the other disciples, and infecting them with the baneful contagion of the vice of murmuring.

POINT III.

"And Jesus knowing it, said to them: *Why do you trouble this woman?* for she hath wrought a good work upon me; for the poor you have always with you, but me you have not always. For she, in pouring this ointment upon my body, hath done it for my burial. Amen, I say to you, *wheresoever this Gospel shall be preached* in the whole world, *that also which she hath done shall be told* for a memory of her." (8)

Here is to be considered the *heroic virtues* which Christ our Lord showed on this occasion.

(7) Luc. vi. 37. (8) Mat. xxvi. 10.

1. The first was, His great *fidelity in defending His servant Magdalen*, she remaining silent, as He had already done twice before; (9) for it is the property of our Lord to defend the honour of them, who for His sake are oppressed with murmurings and detractions, they of their own humility forbearing to excuse themselves, or to plead in their justification, but wholly committing themselves to His divine providence. It is, therefore, great wisdom and prudence in such like cases patiently to hold my peace, because Almighty God both knows and can excuse me, and defend my honour, much better than I myself am able to do, as Christ our Lord defended Mary Magdalen much better than she could defend herself, for if she had excused or defended herself, perhaps it would not have so well succeeded with her, nor been brought to so favourable a termination, nor had the issue been what she desired.

2. The second virtue was, *great benignity and gentleness* in correcting Judas and His disciples; for, although He saw His whole college disturbed, yet was He not moved nor angry at it, but with meekness rescued them from the error into which they had fallen, and dissolved their false apprehensions, approving that work, and attributing it to the divine instinct of the Holy Ghost which moved this woman to anoint with that ointment His body whilst alive, with which she could not anoint Him when dead. This in truth came to pass,—for when she went to anoint Him after His death, He then was raised again to life.

*Colloquy.*—O most wise master, teach me, I beseech Thee, how to correct others "in the spirit of meekness,"(10) so that I may with meekness cure their maladies, and not make them become worse by my indignation.

(9) Luc. vii. 44; x. 42. (10) Gal. vi. 1.

3. The third virtue was, great *charity and liberality*, with great signs of that providence which He uses in converting all things which happen to those who love Him, to their greater good, for if Mary Magdalen had not been murmured against in this good work, neither would the work have been published nor she rewarded with so great honour;—nor would our loving Saviour suffer murmurings against the just if He could not, and would not, draw from these murmurings greater good, profit, and advantage to them,—and for this cause He promised that this work should be published throughout the whole world, wherever His Gospel should be preached, to honour her who had so honoured Him, which came, indeed, to pass, for all faithful Christians believe that this work was most holy, and wrought by the inspiration of the Holy Ghost, and therefore we all commend her who wrought it.

*Colloquy.*—O my Redeemer, in accomplishment of this Thy promise, I rejoice in the devotion of this Thy servant, and thank her for the service and honour which she did Thee, but much more do I extol Thy bounty in so liberally rewarding so little a service done Thee, and the little which we suffer for Thee; for while a few men murmur at this deed, it is Thy will that millions magnify it. Do not, O my soul, serve any other Lord than Christ, since He is so liberal in honouring those who honour Him, and in rewarding those who serve Him.

# MEDITATION VI.

### ON JUDAS' SELLING CHRIST FOR THIRTY PIECES OF SILVER, THE CHIEF PRIESTS' DECREE TO KILL HIM.

"Satan entered into Judas, who was surnamed Iscariot, one of the twelve, and he went and discoursed with the chief priests and the magistrates," "and said to them: What will you give me, and I will deliver Him unto you? But they appointed him thirty pieces of silver. And from thenceforth *he sought opportunity to betray Him.*" (1)

*The first part* of the Passion of Christ our Lord, and the first of all His injuries was, *to be sold by Judas to His enemies;* and this was one of the greatest ignominies which He sustained, and which He afterwards most of all dwelt on, when at supper with His disciples.

Therefore, here are to be considered all *the circumstances* which concurred in this sale; that is to say,—i. *who He is* that is sold,—and *why He suffers Himself* to be sold;—ii. *who* he is *that sells* Him,—and upon *what motive and occasion;*—iii. who *persuaded* him to do so,—for *what cause,*—and *under what colour;*—iv. *to whom* he sold Him, by what occasion, *for what end;*—v. for what price, and in what manner;—vi. and lastly, what followed of this sale: because each of these particulars augments the greatness of the injury.

#### POINT I.

He *who is* injuriously *sold is Jesus Christ* the Son of the living God, Lord of all things created, whose property is to be inestimable, because His value is infinite;—who of His immense charity, descended from heaven, that He

(1) Luc. xxii. 3; Mat. xxvi. 15.

might ransom us with the price of His blood, and in this recover for us the goods of grace, and of glory which we had lost;—and employed His whole life, imparting to men innumerable benefits, to free them from the bondage of the Devil, to whom of their own accord they had sold themselves through their sin, according to that of the prophet Isaiah, saying:—"You were sold gratis, and you shall be redeemed without money."(2) This sovereign Lord, therefore, and so great a benefactor of all men, is sold by treason, and as if He were a slave.

This ignominious sale *He permitted, chiefly for two causes.*

i. *To satisfy* by this means, *for the injury which I have done* to Almighty God, in selling my own soul to the Devil through my own sin.

*Colloquy.*—O merciful Redeemer, I confess that I have given up, and, like another Achab, (3) sold and delivered myself to innumerable sins, for which I have deserved that Thou shouldst command me to be sold, and all that I have, like the servant who owed ten thousand talents.(4) But since Thou wouldst vouchsafe to be sold to pay my debts, pardon them for Thy mercies sake, and suffer me not, I beseech Thee, to fall any more into them. Amen.

ii. To *give us example of rare humility:* for, as for the love of us, He took upon Himself the form of a servant and of a slave: so would He humble Himself to the vilest and basest extremity of slaves, which is, to be sold for money.

*Colloquy.*—O sweet Jesus, how many inventions dost Thou seek to humble Thyself, to heal my pride by Thy humility? Heal it, O Lord, once more, since

(2) Is. lii. 3. (3) 3 Reg. xxi, 20. (4) Mat. xviii. 25.

Thou so greatly desirest it, that I may imitate this Thy humility as I desire. Amen.

POINT II.

1. The injury done to Christ our Lord increased in this, that *he who sold Him was* not some professed or open enemy, *but His disciple*, and yet, not one of those who commonly followed Him,—nor of the seventy-two disciples who were more familiar with Him, but *one of the twelve*, whom He had named for His special apostle, and one to whom He had imparted extraordinary favours and benefits, discovering to him His secrets, and giving him power to expel devils and to work miracles.

2. The *principal motive* which moved Judas to work this treason was *covetousness*, for, from this root his iniquity took its rise, and so went forward, until it reached the height of impiety, thus accomplishing what St. Paul said:—"That desire of money is the root of all evil, which some coveting, have erred from the faith, and have entangled themselves in many sorrows." (5) Judas was inclined to the love of money, and to possess things in propriety, and suffering himself to be vanquished by this passion in little and trifling things, (6) came to fall into others more enormous; for, having entrusted to him the care of the alms which were given to his master, he began to steal some part of them, and to employ them after his own fancy in frivolous things, for his own profit.

In this manner he began to violate the vow of holy poverty, (if it be true that the apostles had then made this vow,) and came to lose the grace of God, and when Mary Magdalen anointed the feet of Christ our Lord, he murmured against so holy a work, and even against Christ Himself for allowing it. *Upon which occasion he so ab-*

(5) 1 Tim. vi. 10. (6) Ecclus. xix. 1.

*horred Him in his heart*, and arrived at such a height of wickedness as to sell Him, so to repair the loss of that which he should have stolen if the ointment with which His feet were anointed had been sold for three hundred pieces of silver. Thus, therefore, covetousness engendered theft, violation of his vow, murmuring, scandal, abhorring his master, and treacherously selling Him to His enemies; whence appears the extreme malice in which a man falls when he is forsaken by Almighty God, and suffers himself to be led away by his perverse passions, since we see Judas fall from the worthiest and highest estate that was in the Church of God, to fall into the deepest profundity of detestable wickedness that ever was. This Christ our Lord Himself pondered with great feeling, when He said to His apostles:—"Have not I chosen you twelve, and one of you is a devil;"(7) as if He had said, "I being properly He, who of my mere grace have chosen you to be apostles, one of you has converted himself into a devil, and is become, through his own default, my open adversary."

3. For this consideration I will conceive a *great fear and apprehension of the judgments of God*, for, as the glorious St. Bernard says, (8) in no place are pilgrims in perfect security, not in heaven itself, since Lucifer fell from thence,—nor in paradise, since Adam was driven thence,—and much less in this world, since Judas perished in the school of our Saviour. Which, however, is not said that a man ought not to choose the most secure place, but, that after any one has chosen it, he become not careless from false security, nor cease to implore the mercy of God to protect and defend him with His holy hand.

*Colloquy.*—O my soul, although thou standest at

(7) Joan. vi. 71. (8) Serm. de Lig. Fœn. et Stip.

this present upon thy feet, yet fear and take heed that thou fallest not, for if he fell who was an apostle of Christ, and conversed with Him familiarly, hearing His sermons, seeing His examples, and enjoying His miracles, how fearest not thou to fall, thou I say, who enjoyest nothing of all this? O holy master, protect with Thy hand Thy poor disciple, lest he fall into the miseries of this false apostle. Amen.

POINT III.

*He who persuaded Judas* to commit this wicked deed *was*, as the Evangelist St. John says, *Satan*, (9) who did it partly to rob Judas of his soul, partly for the hatred he bore Christ our Lord, whom he desired to deprive of His life, and withdraw from His protection that disciple.

1. In this fact consider that the perdition of Judas, although it began by his yielding to *his own depraved inclinations*, yet increased much by *the subtle endeavour of the Devil*, who every moment fed and favoured that inclination, and so entered into his soul,—for a passion not mortified is like a domestic enemy, who opens the gate of the heart to the Devil, that, entering in, he may precipitate it into the abyss of all iniquity, for so long as that passion reigns he is in peaceable possession of our heart, and quietly enjoys it. Hence I will learn how pernicious a thing it is to leave one only passion unmortified in me, for of that Satan makes a snare (10) with which to ensnare me, and to draw me where he pleases, like the fowler, who if he have the eagle fast by one claw only, can easily afterwards break her wings, and wring her neck.

*Colloquy.*—O most powerful Saviour, who camest into this world that Thou mightest cast forth of our souls the strong-armed man, who peaceably possessed

(9) Joan. xiii. 2. (10) S. Doroth. Ser. 11.

them; show Thyself to be stronger than he, so expelling him from my soul, that he never more presume to enter into it.(11) Amen.

2. Consider, secondly, the crafty and plausible *reason* with which this subtle serpent caught and deceived this miserable man, colouring his malice *after this manner:*—"Thy master says that He is to die at this Paschal feast, and the Jews earnestly desire His death, and study how to bring this business about: since, therefore, the matter is come to this pass, and that thy master wills it, *thou wilt do Him but little hurt if thou sellest Him,* thou wilt even accomplish His desire, *and wilt at the same time effect thine own, recovering the money* which thou losedst through the wasteful effusion of the ointment." This reason it was which convinced Judas, passion having blinded his mind, and making him easily believe whatever the Devil whispered to him, and suggested in favour of his design, though most unjust. Hence I will learn not to give credit to such thoughts as favour my passionate heart, persuading myself that they proceed from the infernal serpent, whose office it is to deceive us as he deceived Eve, proposing to us that which pleases and is delightful to us, colouring the evil with the false appearance of good.

### POINT IV.

Fourthly are to be considered the *persons to whom* Christ our Lord was sold, and *the end for which* they buy Him.

1. Those who bought Him were the *chief priests, with other scribes and Pharisees, and the elders of the people,* at the same time that they consulted together to kill Christ, for *the envy* and rage which they bore Him; the traitor, therefore, sold Him, not to His mother, who would have

(11) Luc. xi. 22.

redeemed Him the second time, as she redeemed Him in the Temple, that she might treat Him tenderly;—nor did he sell Him to the disciples, or to other friends, who would have bought Him to set Him at liberty, and have accepted Him for their Lord,—but he sold Him to *the greatest enemies* that He had, who bought Him to take His life from Him, by most exquisite and cruel torments. Oh, diabolical cruelty of the seller! Oh, infernal fury of the buyers! It is evident that Satan was the broker in this bargain, which was directed for such an end.

*Colloquy.*—O most meek lamb, what wonderful injury dost Thou suffer, whilst Thou art sold to be sacrificed, and that by the hands of such cruel tormentors! O Saviour of the world, this day art Thou sold, as was the patriarch Joseph by his own brethren,(12) although for a different end: for he was sold to the Midian merchants, so to save him from death; but Thou art sold, that Thou mayest suffer a cruel death;—he with his life saved Egypt;—and Thou with Thy death hast saved the world. Save me, Lord, for Thy mercy's sake, and since Thou hast bought me with Thy precious blood, suffer me not, I beseech Thee, to sell myself for the base price of sin.

2. How greatly was Christ our Lord disgraced in the opinion of the people, on account of this sale, and the great patience with which He supported it, when, though far absent, He beheld it; for it is to be believed that Judas himself, to excuse so base a deed as selling his own master, *spoke ill of Him* to those of the council, saying that he forsook His school because he observed that He was a *breaker of the law*, an enemy of the ancient customs, a great eater and drinker in banquets, favourable to Himself, and over prodigal, permitting a woman to anoint His head and His feet with a certain ointment, which might have been sold

(12) Gen. xxxvii. 28.

for three hundred pence,—all which things were heard by that council with great applause and satisfaction, without alleging anything at all in behalf of Christ.

*Colloquy.*—O sweet master, will no man be found to stop the mouth of this false murmurer, nor answer a word for Thy innocence, as Thou didst answer for that of Mary Magdalen? Oh, with what great reason dost Thou complain by the mouth of Thy prophet, saying,—"If mine enemy had reviled me, I would verily have borne with it."(13) And if he that hated me had spoken great things against me, I would perhaps have hid myself from him:—but Thou, O Judas, "a man of one mind, my guide, and my familiar, and so my own, that Thou didst take sweet meats together with me in the house of God," in which "we walked with" one "consent;" how is it that thou hast betrayed me?" Great, O my Lord, was this injury, but yet much greater was Thy patience; for more didst Thou feel the fault of the offender than the wrong done to Thyself.

By this example, masters, prelates, and princes may take comfort, when, without their fault, their disciples, or subjects, speak ill of them.

3. It was a great disgrace to Christ our Lord, in the eyes of those men and of the people, that there should issue forth *from His own school* so covetous and abominable a disciple as to sell his own master, with such evident arguments and demonstrations, that he abhorred and detested Him, whence His enemies took occasion to say, The disciple is like his master.

*Colloquy.*—O heavenly master, suffer not, I beseech Thee, that by my evil life I dishonour Thee, nor that by reason of me Thy name be blasphemed amongst the nations.(14) Let us all, dear Lord, be Thy disciples,

(13) Psal. liv. 13. (14) Is. lii. 5.

such as Thou Thyself, our only master, (15) art, that we may all be a glory to Thee. Amen.

POINT V.

1. *The price for which Christ our Lord was sold was thirty pieces of silver*, a price most vile, since Joseph was sold by his own brethren (16) for the same price, and it was the sum at which the Jews usually valued their slaves, (17) when any one had chanced to kill them. This much increased the injury of our Saviour Christ, for by this appeared the base estimation that was made of Him, as well by him that sold Him as by those that bought Him.

2. But yet much more injury was done Him in *the manner of the bargain*, for this wretched disciple, covetous of some little money, *wholly referred the price to the will of the buyers*, saying:—" *What will you give me*, and I will deliver Him unto you?" As if he had said, "You cannot offer me so little but that it shall suffice to make me betray Him into your hands." Hereupon, they partly seeing the covetousness of the seller, partly from the base account they made of Christ, and the hatred which they bore Him, at the first word offered the ordinary price appointed by the law to be given for slaves, which was thirty pieces of silver, which yet they gave not in the way in which the like price was given for slaves,—in satisfaction for their death,—but that they might have Christ to inflict a most cruel death upon Him.

*Colloquy.*—O Saviour of the world, how much greater is the value Thou dost set on sinners than that which they set on Thee. They sell Thee for thirty pieces of silver, and Thou buyest them with Thy precious blood:—they put in the will of their flesh, as the price of this sale, and Thou puttest in the will of

(15) Rom. ii. 21. (16) Gen. xxxvii. 28. (17) Exod. xxi. 32.

Thy Father, as the price of this purchase. O eternal Father, Creator of all things, behold at what price Thy Son is prized! O Son of the living God, with what reason dost Thou complain by Thy prophet, saying, "A handsome price that I was prized at by them:"(18) but since Thou hast taken the form of a slave, it is not much if Thou undergo the ignominy of a slave, and art sold for the price of slaves. I give Thee thanks for this first injury which Thou receivedst in Thy Passion, in gratitude for which I offer myself to Thee as Thy slave for ever, with desire never to depart from Thy holy service.

3. Hence I will derive great *shame and confusion*, remembering how often I have sold Christ our Lord for a more base price than thirty pieces of silver,—that is to say, for some *sensual delight* of the flesh, for some *point of honour*, or for some *little gain* of temporal things, thus delivering Him so many times into the hands of His enemies,—(that is, of sins,)—and crucifying Him anew within my heart. For which cause I may imagine Christ to say to me that which the prophet Zacharias writes:—"If it be good in your eyes, bring hither my wages," for the benefits which I have done you, "and if not, be quiet," because I will not compel you; to which so just petition, that which I answer by my works, is to have sold Him for so vile a price, that He says to me:—"A handsome price that I was prized at by thee!" (19) O my soul, how is it that thou dost not hide thyself from shame, hearing these words of thy Redeemer!

*Colloquy.*—O my Redeemer, how justly mayest Thou take away from me the staff of Thy government, and cut asunder the thread of my life, since I so little benefit myself by it! Pardon, dear Lord, I

(18) Zach. xi. 13. (19) Ibid. ver. 12.

beseech Thee, my former injuries, and assist me to prize Thee hereafter as Thou deservest, so that Thou mayest not say to me in derision, "A handsome price that I am prized at by thee."

POINT VI.

Consider *that which happened after this sale*, as well to Judas himself as to the chief priests.

1. For first, Judas having now agreed on the price, "*spopondit*," promised to accomplish what he had undertaken, and, therefore, with great solicitude *sought for an opportunity to betray Him*, that so he might at once possess the money the Jews had promised him. Accordingly he returned to the college of the apostles, and into the company of Christ, cunningly cloaking and dissembling his sin, for, having now lost his faith, he supposed that Christ was ignorant of what had passed; but Christ our Lord admitted him with the same signs and tokens of love, as if He had been utterly ignorant of his treachery, showing in this the greatest love of His enemies, without either reprehending or disgracing him, or yet discovering his conspiracy, perhaps saying to him:—"My good friend, thou art welcome, where hast thou been? and what hast thou done?" to which he falsely and fraudulently returning answer, was not once so much as rebuked by Him, but as if He had believed him, held His peace with great silence.

*Colloquy.*—O most meek pastor, and most sweet father, what didst Thou feel in Thy holy heart, when Thou sawest this wolf enter in amongst Thy sheep, disguised and covered with a sheep's skin, not to take away any of them, but to the intent that he might take and seize upon his own shepherd, and deliver him to death? He dissembles that he be not known for a wolf, though Thou knowest him well, yet appearest not to know him;—he comes from the place where he treated of delivering Thee to death,—and Thou receivedst him with as great love as if he came to give Thee life. O immense charity! O infinite meekness! make me, sweet Lord, I beseech Thee, as meek as a lamb, that with the aspect of this Thy love, I may gladly suffer for Thy sake the outrages of all the wolves of this world. Amen.

2. The chief priests remained most contented and glad, and *forthwith changed the design* which they had before the coming of Judas, for they had decreed not to kill Christ "on the festival day, lest, perhaps, there should be a tumult amongst the people;" (20) but after Judas had made this agreement with them, they judged it not expedient to lose the opportunity, and therefore resolved to put Him to death whenever Judas should deliver Him, without making now any more account of the tumult of the people. Hence is to be seen, on the one side, the rage and fury of these cruel enemies, and their restless envy to destroy Christ, and on the other, how wonderfully the wisdom and providence of Almighty God appears, in bringing things to their preordained ends,—which was, that Christ should die on that festival day, that the true Lamb of God should be sacrificed at the same time, when that figurative lamb was to be offered.

*Colloquy.*—O most innocent lamb, Christ Jesus, with how great reason may we call Thee the Paschal lamb, since Thou reputest it a feast and a Passover to die, to deliver us from death, and to be sacrificed to give us life. And if Thine enemies make such haste to murder Thee, that they will not wait till the solemn feast be past, yet much more haste dost Thou make to die for them, than they do to put Thee to death. Blessed be this Thine infinite charity, in virtue of which I beseech Thee to inflame my heart with so

(20) Mat. xxvi. 5.

great fervour, that I may repute it a Paschal feast to suffer for the love of Thee. Amen.

3. From what has been said in this meditation, I will deduce two *principal causes for which Christ our Lord suffered Judas to remain so long in His school*, expecting his repentance.

i. That we may understand that in *all congregations, though very religious, some will become impious*, without any fault at all of those that govern them, as it came to pass in this selected by Christ Himself, in which, notwithstanding, a Judas was found. For this cause St. Augustin says:—"Ad quamcumque professionem te converteris, para te pati fictos"—"Of what profession of life soever thou shalt make election, prepare thyself to suffer from dissemblers;" (21) for if thou dost not first attend to these words, and prepare to suffer, thou shalt find that which thou didst not expect, and shalt either fail in thy vocation, or feel disheartened and perplexed in it.

ii. That He might take occasion *to exercise for our example most heroic acts of meekness*, patience, charity, and other virtues, which cannot be exercised but amongst enemies, and in particular, to give an example to prelates and superiors how to support and bear with their evil subjects, although they cause them to suffer much; for as St. Bernard says, evil subjects, as they make the charge of government more grievous, so they make it more meritorious —"Et in quantum gravaris, in tantum lucraris"—"The greater the charge, the greater the gain." (22)

(21) Ser. 1, in Psal. xxxvi. (22) Epist. xxxvii.

## MEDITATION VII.

ON THE LAST SUPPER IN WHICH CHRIST ATE THE LEGAL LAMB WITH HIS APOSTLES; AND HIS PREVIOUS LEAVETAKING OF HIS HOLY MOTHER.

### POINT I.

The first day of the azymes being come, on which, according to the law, "it was necessary that the Pasch should be killed," Jesus "sent Peter and John" from Bethania to Jerusalem, "saying: Go, and prepare for us the Pasch, that we may eat: But they said, Where wilt Thou that we prepare? And He said to them: Behold, as you go into the city there shall meet you a man, carrying a pitcher of water, follow him into the house where he entereth in; and you shall say to the good man of the house," "*My time is near at hand, with thee I make the Pasch with my disciples;* And he will show you a large dining-room furnished, and *there prepare ye for us*" (1) that which is necessary for the Pasch.

1. Here consider *the great solicitude of Christ* our Lord, concerning the *observation of the law*, since He would go to Jerusalem, where it was necessary to eat the lamb, knowing that there He was to be apprehended, crucified, and that this journey would cost Him His life, thus making Himself obedient even unto death. I will also consider that it is proper to those who are perfectly obedient, to prepare beforehand such things as are necessary to perform their obedience without impediment; for even so Christ would prepare beforehand that which was necessary for this purpose, giving us example of His obedience, diligence, and providence in the execution of it, for the greater confusion of my disobedience, carelessness, and

(1) Luc. xxii. 7; Marc. xiv. 13; Mat. xxvi. 18.

negligence in the observation of His holy law, in things which I may fulfil with little labour, and which will cost me but little to keep.

*Colloquy.*—O my soul, remember that which the Wise man says,—"Prepare thy work without, and diligently till thy ground, that afterwards thou mayest build thy house;"(2) for thou canst not well cultivate the field of thy soul by mortifications, nor build up the house of thy conscience with virtues, if first thou prepare not that which is necessary for perfecting it.

2. Christ our Lord *chose two apostles* most dear to Him, and for their faith, love, and obedience, the most remarkable among the rest, namely, *Peter* and *John*, to prepare a house and lodging, to help their Lord, by their dexterity and diligence, in providing what was necessary for the sacrifice of the Paschal lamb,—to teach us by this the care we ought to take in preparing our souls with all that is necessary to celebrate the sacrifice and eating of that most pure lamb of the new law, which is given us to eat in that most holy Sacrament of the Altar. To which preparation first belongs the virtue of *faith*, figured by *St. Peter*, and next that of *charity*, figured by glorious *St. John*, both of them fervent, and accompanied with most perfect obedience.

*Colloquy.*—O lamb of God, who "takest away the sins of the world," it is most just that we receive Thee with great preparation, cleansing and adorning the hall and chamber in which Thou art spiritually to be sacrificed and eaten. Send, dear Lord, from heaven to this poor soul of mine, liveliness of faith and fervour of charity, with promptitude of obedience, to enlarge, adorn, and prepare it as is befitting for this celestial

(2) Prov. xxiv. 27.

banquet; for unless Thou send me this assistance, never shall I be able to prepare myself as I ought.

3. I will ponder the *brief and courteous salutation* which He sent to the master of that house, saying:—"The master saith, my time is at hand, with thee I make my Pasch with my disciples;" which message and words were so effectual, that immediately the master of that house, touched and inspired with the Holy Ghost, offered the best room in his house for Christ our Lord to celebrate His Passover in, and would himself serve Him, with all that he had immediately to effect.

*Colloquy.*—O sovereign master and my Redeemer, whose words are so effectual, as immediately to effect what they command, say to my soul,—"My time is at hand, and in thy house I desire to celebrate my pasch with my disciples." O most happy time in which my Redeemer applies to me the fruit of His Passion, and entering into my soul, celebrates His pasch, which is the passing from earthly to heavenly things. Come, O sweet master, with the sweet company of Thy virtues, and together with them, celebrate within my soul this celestial pasch and banquet: for which I offer Thee not only the best room that is in my house, but the whole house, since the whole is Thine, and would to God it were a great deal better than it is, that so it might please Thee to dwell in it perpetually.

POINT II.

Christ our Lord, before He set out from Bethania, *would take leave of His most holy mother*, and tell her that the hour of His Passion and death was now at hand, which so many years past He had expected, to finish the redemption of the world, according as His eternal Father had commanded Him. And the better to prepare her, it is to be believed that in the most tender, and yet most manful manner, He recounted to her all that was to befal Him saying:—"Mother, I go to Jerusalem to sacrifice and eat the Paschal lamb, and to institute that Sacrifice and Sacrament, which was represented by it, and forthwith I shall be apprehended by my enemies in the garden of Gethsemane as a thief; from thence I shall be led pinioned and bound to the house of Caiphas, where I shall pass the whole night in grievous contumelies and torments; and then, as soon as it is day, I shall be brought before the tribunal of Pilate, by whose command I shall be cruelly scourged, crowned with thorns, scorned, adjudged to die the death of the cross, and, laden with it, I shall go forth from his consistory to the mount of Calvary, were I shall be crucified between two thieves, and after three hours shall give up the ghost. All this is decreed by my eternal Father, and is required for the redemption of the world; I, therefore, for this cause, greatly desire to embrace this occasion, since it suffices that it is my Father's will that I accept it, for thus ought all those who love my Father to conform themselves to His will."

2. When *the Virgin heard these and other like words*, which her most holy son related to her, *her blessed soul was pierced with most painful agony*, for every word of these was a sword which passed through her holy heart; but she lifting up her eyes to heaven, and directing her speech to the eternal Father, said to Him:—"Father, if it be possible, suffer not Thy Son and mine to drink this bitter chalice of His Passion, yet not my will, but Thine be fulfilled." And turning to her son, she might say to Him,—"Son, since it pleases Thee to drink this chalice, permit me also to drink it entirely with Thee, assisting at Thy torments, yet not as I will, but as Thou wilt." After this manner did the Blessed Virgin feel an extreme inward

grief, preserving, nevertheless, within her soul a most singular resignation to the will of Almighty God.

3. Christ our Lord, who well knew the faith and invincible courage of His mother, *might have recommended* her, in this His short absence, *to gather together the dispersed flock of His apostles* and disciples, and confirm them in the faith of His resurrection, and animate and comfort them. For which reason it is to be believed that He related to her some of these many reasons which He made use of to His disciples in that last sermon which He made to them after supper.

*Colloquy.*—O sovereign Virgin, what a doleful day was this to thee, drinking off as it were at one draught the whole chalice of the Passion, which there thy son related to thee! Now the "sword"(3) which Simeon prophesied began to pierce thy soul with excessive sorrow: and if it be so sharp-pointed now, prepare thy heart against to-morrow, when it shall be whetted much more sharply. Oh that it had happened to me to have been in thy company, that I might have tasted one only drop of this chalice, and that the point, at the least, of this sword of sorrow might have touched my soul! Obtain for me, O my Lady, favour from heaven, that I may so meditate both thine and thy son's pains, that I may be made partaker of them. Amen.

POINT III.

On Thursday night Christ went forth from Bethania with His apostles, and coming to Jerusalem, to the place appointed, sat down with them, and said to them:—"*With desire I have desired to eat this Pasch with you;*" that is to say, this Paschal lamb, "before I suffer."(4)

1. Here consider the different *countenances* and *gestures* of those who went this journey, from Bethania to Jerusa-

(3) Luc. ii. 35. (4) Luc. xxii. 15.

lem. For Christ our *Lord* went *rejoicing*, because He knew that He went to die, according to the decree of His eternal Father.—*Judas* also went *rejoicing*, because He saw the time approach, and the occasion of delivering Him whom he had sold, and of receiving the price which was promised him.—But the *other apostles walked sorrowfully*, remembering what He had said to them two days before:—"After two days shall be the Pasch, and the Son of Man shall be delivered up to be crucified."(5)

*Colloquy.*—O Son of Man, true God and true man, why leadest Thou in Thy company him that will deliver Thee to be crucified? Behold how this wolf will come to trouble all the flock, and since Thou hast laboured so much in gathering it, chase him away who will disperse it. Oh what sweet conferences held Christ our Lord with His disciples, to moderate the sorrows of their souls, and to ease the labour the way! Happy he who walks with Jesus, not hypocritically, like Judas, but in truth and simplicity, like the other disciples; for in His sweet and blessed company, he shall find solace in his sorrows.

2. *The cordial charity and affability of Christ* our Lord, which He expressed in those tender words:—"With a desire I have desired to eat this Paschal lamb with you." As if He had said, "It is now long since I earnestly wished and desired this day, to manfest to you how much I love you, eating with you, not only this legal lamb, but another much more excellent and much more precious, which I intend to give you before I suffer."

*Colloquy.*—O most sweet and loving master, Thy bitter Passion being so nigh at hand, Thou sayest that with a burning desire Thou hast desired this banquet before Thou beginnest it, how shall I requite Thee

(5) Mat. xxvi. 2.

for these desires, but in conceiving such like desires to serve Thee? And since Thou, Lord, desirest so much to eat this last Pasch with me, I also desire earnestly to eat it with Thee. O King of heaven, who standest at the door of our heart knocking,(6) desiring vehemently that Thy voice be heard, and that the gate may be opened, that entering into us, Thou mayest sup with us, and we with Thee; come, Lord, into my house, for I open the gate to Thee, and with an exceeding desire, desire Thy coming, that I may be partaker of this Thy supper. Amen.

POINT IV.

1. Christ our Lord ate this Paschal lamb, *observing all the ceremonies of the law*, and contemplating, with great feeling of heart, that which they signified. For, beholding that lamb upon the table, dead, flayed, and roasted with fire,(7) He represented to Himself how He was to be extended upon the table of the cross, dead, flayed with whips, and scorched and burned with the fire of torments. —Beholding how it was cut in pieces, without breaking the bones, He beheld Himself all disjointed, without breaking any of His bones, as happened to the thieves.—Beholding also the haste with which they ate the lamb, there occurred to Him the fury of His enemies, rushing upon Him to torment and destroy Him.—Tasting also of the bitter lettice, He called to mind the galls and other bitternesses, which they were then preparing for Him.—And beholding the staff which He held in His hand, He called to mind the cross which He was to embrace, and to which He was to be fastened with rude nails.

*Colloquy.*—O sweet Jesus, how bitter was this meat, mingled with such sorrowful representations! With such sauce, O Lord, do I ever desire to season

(6) Apoc. iii. 20. (7) Exod. xii. 9.

my meat, mindful of the torments which Thou sustainedst for me, and of the gall and vinegar which Thou drankest for me. Amen.

2. Finally, the legal supper being ended, it is to be believed that Christ our Lord *rendered thanks to His eternal Father, for having at last put an end to this figure* and representation; and that He offered Himself to suffer whatsoever was shadowed in that supper, in order fully to accomplish His divine pleasure, saying furthermore: "O my Father, I know well that 'sacrifice and oblation Thou didst not desire,'(8) nor requirest the holocaust of this law for sin, for none of these things fully please Thee, and therefore hast Thou sent me into this world, giving me 'a body,' apt to be sacrificed: and, forasmuch as the hour of this sacrifice is now at hand, 'behold I come,' O my God, 'to do Thy will,'(9) for, as Thou hast appointed me, so I will."

*Colloquy.*—I give Thee thanks, O Only-begotten Son of God, for this new oblation of Thyself, which Thou offerest to Thine eternal Father, and with it I also offer myself to fulfil Thy will; command me, Lord, what Thou wilt, helping me with Thy grace duly to accomplish what Thou commandest. Amen.

---

## MEDITATION VIII.

### ON HIS WASHING THE DISCIPLES' FEET.

#### POINT I.

"Jesus, knowing that His hour was come, that He should pass out of this world to the Father, having loved His own who were in the world, *He loved them unto the end.*"(1)

Upon this point, which is the introduction which the

(8) Psal. xxxix. 7. (9) Heb. x. 6. (1) Joan. xiii. 1.

glorious apostle S. John makes, to the mysteries which immediately follow, are to be considered, the *properties of the love of Christ* our Lord *towards His disciples*, and to all those who then lived, or who shall hereafter live in the whole world.

1. Here is to be presupposed, that that *Lord* had *three* families or households of creatures belonging to Him:—one of angels in Heaven;—another of holy souls in Limbo; and a third of His disciples in the world. And although these last were intermixed with many other evil persons, who were none of His because they were evil, and even had as yet certain faults and imperfections, nevertheless He loved them with a tender and fatherly affection, because they were His; that is to say, His sons, His friends, and His faithful servants.

2. Hence follow the properties of this love:

i. That He loved them *as His own peculiar and proper good*, and consequently even *as Himself*, after some sort, even *more* than Himself, since approaching to death, as forgetful of Himself and of His labours, He wholly bestowed Himself to relieve them, losing His life to save theirs, taking upon Him the sins and miseries of His elect as His own, and discharging their debts by His death.

*Colloquy.*—O beloved of my soul, if Thou lovest me as Thine, I say to Thee, that I love Thee as mine, for as I am Thine, so Thou art mine. I am Thy creature, Thy slave, and Thy son; but Thou art my Creator, and my Redeemer, my Lord, and my Father. I therefore will love Thee not as myself, but above myself, and above all things created, and to be created, for that Thou art worthy to be beloved more than all things whatsoever.

ii. He loved them *with a most steadfast and constant love* even to the end; for He loved them whilst He lived in this life, and even unto the end of His life; and likewise loved them even to the end also of their lives, and ever will love all His, even to the consummation of the world.

*Colloquy.*—O constant love of Jesus Christ, whose fire neither the waters of immense tribulations, nor the floods of innumerable torments, could extinguish! Oh how often have I with my sins, as much as lay in me, gone about to quench this fire!(2) But He always prevailed, ever doing good to him who served Him evilly, casting "hot coals upon his head,"(3) who daily multiplied more offences. Cease not, O my Saviour, to love me to the end, that so I may love Thee also without end. Amen.

iii. He loved them with an *excessive love*, and without limit, and to that highest degree that love can arrive, doing and suffering for them all that He could, and was convenient to do and suffer, and desired to do much more without end, had it been necessary for their remedy.

*Colloquy.*—O my beloved, I also desire to love Thee, as the precept of love commands, that is, with my "whole heart," with my "whole soul," and with my "whole strength,"(4) without any kind of bound or limit, aspiring if I may to that perfection, to which the love of a creature towards his Creator may aspire. I desire to love Thee more than the angels and the Seraphim love Thee, and if it were possible for me to have an infinite love, with it would I love Thee without being ever weary, didst Thou but assist me to increase in Thy love, until by love I attained to the end prescribed by Thee, because Thou art worthy to be beloved without end.

iv. He loved them *for an end*;—that is to say, for that end for which they were ordained, which is, to love and

(2) Cant. viii. 7. (3) Prov. xxv. 22. (4) Deut. vi. 5.

serve Him in this mortal life, and to enjoy Him in the life eternal. He loved them not to the end to give them riches, honours, or temporal commodities;—for this was not His end,—but that He might give them all the means of His grace, whereby they might obtain the end of glory. He also loved them for Himself, who is both the beginning and the ending of all things, to unite them with Himself by the union of love, that in Him they might finally rest as in their end.

*Colloquy.*—O my beloved, would to God that I might love Thee for the end for which Thou lovedst me! I love Thee not, O my Lord, that Thou mayest enrich me with temporal goods, but I love Thee because Thou lovest me, that Thou mayest impart to me spiritual goods, with which I may increase in Thy holy love, and unite myself to Thee without end, who art my last end, and supreme blessedness. Amen.

POINT II.

"When supper was done, (the Devil having now put into the heart of Judas Iscariot, the son of Simon, to betray Him,) knowing that the Father had given Him all things into His hands, and that He came from God, and goeth to God, He riseth from supper, and layeth aside His garment, and having taken a towel, girded Himself. And after that, He putteth water into a basin, and *began to wash the feet of the disciples*, and to wipe them with the towel wherewith He was girded."(5)

Upon this passage is to be considered:—1. *the excellency of the Person* that does this work:—2. the *manner in which* He does it, as that He does it only by Himself:—3. and *the mystery of the Incarnation* and Passion which He represented to us.

1. First, therefore, make a pause upon that which St.

(5) Joan. xiii. 2.

John dwells on in this place,—the *excellency of the Person* that humbled Himself to so base a work, as was that of washing the feet of His disciples: for the greater He is who humbles Himself, so much the more is His humility to be admired; and the humility is so much the more heroic, as the person is more excellent by whom it is exercised.

To this purpose I will behold in Christ our Lord what He is in Himself as He is God,—and what He does here as He is man.—As He is God, He is *in heaven environed round about with innumerable* angels, who, lying prostrate before His feet, adore Him;—as He is man, he is present here in a poor chamber, and in the midst of poor fishermen, Himself prostrate at their feet, to wash them —As He is God, "*He is clothed with beauty;* the Lord is clothed with strength,"(6) and with His hands hath created all things ;—as He is man, He puts off His garments,—girds Himself with a towel,—and with His hands washes the feet of His own creatures.

But in particular, our Lord, who here humbles Himself, is *infinitely wise*, from whom nothing is concealed, neither His own excellency, nor His disciple's iniquity who sold Him, nor the basenesses and timorousness of those others who were before Him.—He is likewise *infinitely mighty*, because His eternal Father has put all things into His hand and power, communicating to Him, as He is God, His omnipotency in virtue of His divine generation;—and as He is man, for the hypostatical union with the Word eternal—He also is the *natural Son of Almighty God*, of whom He was begotten from all eternity, and came into the world to redeem it, and after death, to return to God, to sit on His throne upon the right hand of the Father. Knowing all which most perfectly He

(6) Psal. xcii. 1.

would notwithstanding humble Himself to this work; so that He did not humble Himself, as though He were ignorant who He was, nor constrained to it by any other, nor that He Himself was basely descended, or had a base intention, or proposed to Himself any abject end,—but only because He would Himself, and for the love of us, take on Himself the form of a servant, perfectly accomplishing the counsel of the Wise man, who says,—"The greater thou art, the more humble thyself in all things."(7)

*Colloquy.*—O infinite humility, which so greatly shinest in a person of such infinite dignity, to confound the pride of my infinite baseness! If Jesus, infinitely wise and powerful, became so humble, how shall I, being so notoriously ignorant and feeble, become so proud? If the Son of God, who came from God, and who returns again to God, abased Himself, "taking the form of a servant,"(8) how shall I, that am the son of wrath and slave of the Devil, who am made of dust, and shall return to the same dust, presume to raise up myself, and to seek to be served like a lord? O humble Jesus, deliver me from the spirit of pride, and ground my heart in profound humility, who for so many respects am bound to humble myself.

2. The humility of our high Lord was *loving* and *diligent*, doing all this work by *Himself alone*, without the help of any other, in sign and token of His love. For He *Himself* put off "His garment," "girded Himself," "put water into the *basin*," *bore* it to the place where the disciples sat, prostrated Himself, and "washed," not their hands, but their dirty feet: and so *Himself* lovingly "wiped them with the towel wherewith He was girded," pleasing and contenting Himself to do all these things in His

(7) Ecclus. iii. 20. (8) Phil. ii. 7.

own person;—teaching me this to exercise the works of humility and charity in my own person, rejoicing more to do them myself, than to command them to be done by others, and performing every humble work without any mixture of boasting.

*Colloquy.*—O most loving master, who, without speaking, criest out aloud:—"Learn of me, because I am meek and humble of heart;"(9) grant me this Thy meekness and loving gentleness, that I may find grace before Thee, whom the prayer of the humble and meek have always pleased. Amen.

3. But if the humility of this outward work be so great, much greater is the humility and the *care which it represents*, and which He exercised towards us all; for being the Son of Almighty God, for our sakes He *emptied Himself, taking the form of a servant*,"(10) despoiled Himself of the garments of the greatness of His glories, and girded Himself with mortal and passible flesh, and was subject to many penalties; and upon the mount of Calvary consented to be stripped of His garments with great ignominy,—and there shed forth, instead of water, all the most precious blood within His veins, pouring it into the sacraments which He ordained, by it to wash us from our sins; and that we might remain clean, He willed that the most pure towel of His sacred Humanity, with which He was girded, should remain, in exterior show, foul, bespotted, and defiled.

*Colloquy.*—O eternal God, what shall I render Thee, for the favours which Thou hast done me? I desire to despoil myself of all temporal greatness, and to gird myself with the rigour of penance, and to shed my blood for the love of Thee, undergoing those pains which Thou dost undergo for my offences: and after

(9) Mat. xi. 29. (10) Phil. ii. 7.

I have done all this, I will still, notwithstanding, say, that I am an unprofitable servant,(11) for not having done the least part of that which my blessed Lord has done for me.

POINT III.

The third point shall be, to consider *what passed between Christ our* Lord, and *St. Peter, when He came to wash his feet,* and the mutual words and speeches that passed between them.

1. Peter, standing astonished at the humility of His master, said,—" Domine tu mihi lavas pedes?"—" *Lord, dost Thou wash my feet?*"(12) In which words he discovered a lively faith of the excellency of Christ our Lord, and of his own baseness, and of the baseness of that work, to which Christ his master humbled Himself. And from the interior consideration of all this, with great admiration and astonishment of affection, burst forth into these words: "Lord, dost thou wash my feet?"—" Thou who art infinite God, Creator of heaven and earth, Lord of Angels, and of Seraphim, stoopest to me, Thy servant, Thy slave, a vile sinner; and with those hands which give sight to the blind, health to the sick, and life to the dead, wilt wash, not my head, or my hands, but my loathsome and abominable feet. I, Lord, ought to serve Thee, and to wash Thy feet; nor do I esteem myself worthy to do this work, and wilt Thou wash my feet?" Hence I will learn to think highly of Jesus Christ, and very basely of myself, and making comparison of that which a God so high does to a man so low, I will draw acts of admiration, of thanksgiving, and of imitation.

2. To these words of St. Peter, which proceed from great fervour, Christ our Lord made answer with words, instructing him in that which was most fit, saying:

(11) Luc. xvii. 10. (12) Joan. xiii. 6.

"*What I do thou knowest not now, but thou shalt know hereafter.*"(13) As if He had said, "That which I now do contains a mystery which thou understandest not, but afterwards I will disclose it to thee; for the present *suffer thyself to be governed by me.*" Peter answered, "Thou shalt never wash my feet." Christ replied: "If I wash thee not, thou shalt not have part with me." How greatly any disobedience and rebellion offends Christ, or any little insinuation of our own judgment, notwithstanding it be hidden under the cloak of humility and reverence; since this vice alone sufficed to cause Christ to use to Peter that fearful threatening, saying:—"Thou shalt have no part with me." That is to say: "Thou shalt no more be my disciple, nor will I suffer thee any more in my school and company, nor admit thee to the inheritance of my Kingdom!" Whence I will learn *never to resist the will of God,* nor of my superiors, under any pretext of apparent virtue, but to surrender my judgment upon the first admonition, and upon the first correction of love, before the second of threats and chastisements fall upon me. For although I were as intimate with Christ as was St. Peter, and as highly favoured of the eternal Father as he was, the favour endures no longer than the obedience endures, and failing in it by my pertinacity, the favour also presently fails.

*Colloquy.*—O good Jesus, mirror of all perfection and obedience, suffer me not to be deceived by my own judgment, preferring it before Thine, nor under any pretext of humility, to follow my own, leaving Thine, lest so terrible a threatening fall upon me, that I shall "have no part with" Thee. Amen.

3. How necessary it is for me *that Christ* our Lord *wash me,* and cleanse me of *my sins,* because, unless He wash

(13) Joan. xiii. 8.

me, I shall "have no part with" Him. And for this cause Christ said not: "if I wash not *thy feet*," but, "if I wash *thee not*, thou shalt have no part with me."

*Colloquy.*—O Saviour of the world, I confess that I am foul and defiled with innumerable sins, of which I cannot "wash" myself, for to sin is mine, but to pardon them is Thine; wherefore "wash me yet more from my iniquity, and cleanse me from my sin;"(14) and after Thou hast once washed me, wash me yet once more, that I may have a greater part with Thee, with more security never to lose it.

POINT IV.

Consider, fourthly, *the effect which this threatening* of Christ's *wrought* in the heart of St Peter, and the answer which Christ returned him.

1. For, first, to this threatening St. Peter answered:—"Lord, not only my feet, but also my hands and my head." In which words he discovered the great love which he bore to Christ our Lord, and the great account which he made to be always with Him, and the grief which he conceived at being separated from Him. And therefore he said:—"Lord, if to have part with Thee, it be needful that Thou wash me, wash not only my feet, but also my hands and my head."

Hence I will learn to *submit myself to Almighty God*, and my superiors, for fear lest I separate myself from Him: for this fear is not servile, as that of slaves, but a filial fear, and the fear of such as are very just; for this is to give myself to God, and not to want God. And for this cause Christ our Lord said not to St. Peter: "If I wash thee not, I will cast thee into hell;" but, "if I wash thee not, thou shalt *have no part* with me," as he that desired

(14) Psal. l. 4.

to be obeyed with a chaste, not with a base or servile fear.

2. To this reply of St. Peter, Christ our Lord answered, saying:—"He that is washed, needeth not but to wash his feet, but is clean wholly; and you are clean, but not all. For He knew who he was that would betray Him."(15) In which words He would teach us, that he who is washed by baptism and penance from deadly sins, although he be supposed to be wholly "clean," because he has that cleanness which is necessary for him to be in the grace and friendship of Almighty God, nevertheless needs to wash his feet from earthly affections and from lighter faults, which stick to them, by conversing and dealing in earthly affairs. This is also necessary to have part with Christ, in this sense, that we shall not enter into heaven till we be cleansed also from these offences, of which Christ Himself must also cleanse us.

Hence I will gather *how great an evil one venial sin is*, as St. Bernard weighs,(16) and how much it ought to be abhorred for two reasons.—i. Because it is not pardoned, but at the expense of the blood of Christ, in virtue of which we are warned from these spots.—ii. Because it is impossible to have "part with" Christ in heaven, until we are washed, either in this life, or in the other, with the fire of purgatory. And because the bath of purgatory is most bitter, as we have said in the last meditation of the first part, it will be great wisdom, since every day I defile myself with these venial sins, to wash myself often in the sweet baths which Christ hath left in His holy Church.

3. Lastly, I will consider the *cause why Christ our Lord said*:—"You are clean, but not all;" wishing by these words to admonish Judas secretly that he was unclean, and that he stood in need of being washed, under pain never

(15) Joan. xiii. 10. (16) Serm. in Cœn. Dom.

more to have part with Him. And by the way He also admonishes me that I look diligently if I be clean from grievous sins, for amongst many clean there are some unclean, and perhaps I am one of them, and although it be no more than one, yet can it not be hid from Christ, who sees and discerns marvellously well who are clean and who are not.

POINT V.

Christ our Lord, prosecuting this work of humility and charity, *would likewise perform the same to Judas himself*, and coming with the basin to the place where he was, prostrating Himself at his feet, He washed them and wiped them with the towel, as He had done the others, and even with greater signs of charity and love, in order to mollify him. And it is to be believed that He spoke to his heart, saying:—"Oh, Judas, my disciple and apostle, what have I done to thee, that so thou dost abhor me and determine to sell me? If thou hast any quarrel against me, behold thou hast me here at thy feet, do with me what thou wilt, so that thou neither commit any sin, nor cast away thyself for ever. He who washes the feet of thy body desires to wash the spots off thy soul; refuse not that I wash thee, for otherwise thou shalt never 'have part with' me, and if thou have not part with me, thy part shall be with hypocrites and dissemblers, in that miserable lake where shall be perpetual 'weeping and gnashing of teeth.'" (17) It is also to be believed that He shed tears forth of His eyes for the hardness and misery of that wretched soul, and mingled them with the water in the basin, so to wash his feet also with them, but nothing availed, because his heart was hardened and possessed of Satan. Yet this example ought to teach me to profit thereby to love my enemies, doing them all the

(17) Mat. xxv. 30.

good that I am able, to reduce them to the true frienship, first of God, and then of myself, for the love of God.

From the hardness, also, of Judas, I should learn to take example by other men's harms, remembering what the Wise man says:—"The wicked man, when he is come into the depths of sin, He contemneth," (18) and that "no man can correct him whom" God "hath despised," because he first has despised God.

*Colloquy.*—O my soul, contemplate with attention the two examples which thou hast before thee; one of the greatest charity, another of the greatest hardness that ever was in the whole world; for, could any charity ascend higher than to abase God Himself to wash the feet of a traitor who conspired to sell Him? And whither could the malice and hardness of a traitor's heart extend farther than not to be mollified with the immense charity of Him who laid Himself prostrate at his feet? O God of my soul, turn my heart of stone into "a heart of flesh,"(19) that so I may feel Thy divine inspirations, and also embrace Thy loving examples. Amen.

POINT VI.

Having finished washing their feet, Christ our Lord put off the towel with which He was girded, considering in them the spots of others' sins, which were to be the cause that His most holy humanity was to be dyed with His own blood, which was to be shed to deliver us. "Then, after He had washed their feet, and taken His garments, being sat down again He said to them: Know you what I have done to you? You call me master and Lord, and you say well, for so I am. If, then, I, being your Lord and master, have washed your feet, you also ought to wash one another's feet, for I have given you an example, that as I have done

(18) Prov. xviii. 3; Ecclus. vii. 14. (19) Ezech. xxxvi. 26.

to you, so you do also....If you know these things, you shall be blessed if you do them. I speak not of you all, I know whom I have chosen." (20)

1. Here is to be considered, first, *what that demand of Christ* our Lord *meant* :—"Know you what I have done to you?" that is to say, understand you the mystery contained in this, and the end for which I do it? Here He gives us to understand, that all those who see His exterior works do not understand the secret and spirit of them.

*Colloquy.*—O celestial master, illuminate my eyes with Thy supernatural light, that I may with a lively faith believe, understand, and penetrate the things which Thou hast done for us, that I may draw fruit from all of them, to Thy honour and glory. Amen.

2. I will consider the *force of that argument which* Christ used:—"If I, being your Lord and master, have washed your feet, you also ought to wash one another's feet;" that is to say, that you exercise one to another the works of humility and charity, since I have employed my whole life in giving you example of this virtue, that after my example you also may exercise yourselves in them.

3. Finally, I will ponder those last words:—"If you know these things, you shall be blessed if you do them;" where He teaches us, that it is not enough to know the examples of the virtues which He gave us, unless we also put them into execution, nor that he is blessed, or elected for heaven, who knows them, only to know them, unless he also imitate them, for Judas, who was there present, knew them well, but did not imitate them, and, therefore, became one of the reprobate.

*Colloquy.*—O my blessedness, since Thou hast done me so great a favour, as to let me know what Thou

(20) Joan. xiii. 12.

hast done for me, let it please Thee that I execute all that which Thou commandest me. I confess, O Lord, that I do not that which I do know, nor act according to what I understand, for which cause I deserve to be "beaten with many stripes,"(21) like the servant who knew the will of his lord, and did not according to it. Pardon me, dear Lord, my past errors, and move me to the amendment of them, that so I may be of the number of Thine elect, and may come to be blessed, enjoying Thee for ever. Amen.

---

## (2.) MEDITATIONS ON THE MOST HOLY SACRAMENT OF THE EUCHARIST.

Having ended the washing of the apostles' feet, and concluded the discourse which He had with them, to declare the mystery enclosed therein, He would give to them other greater signs and proofs of the love He bore them, and other more singular tokens that "He loved them to the end," not only to the end of His life, but even until the end of the world; and for this cause He would institute a most excellent Sacrament, in which He would remain with them truly and really, "even to the consummation of the world," (1) making them a solemn and continual banquet, in which He would give them His own body to eat, and His own blood to drink, and that after a most marvellous, sweet, and delightful manner, as will be seen in the ensuing meditations.

(21) Luc. xii. 47. (1) Mat. xxviii. 20.

## MEDITATION IX.

### OF CHRIST'S ACTIONS AND DISCOURSE PREVIOUS TO HIS INSTITUTION OF THE MOST HOLY SACRAMENT, REPRESENTING TO US THE DISPOSITION WHICH THOSE ARE TO HAVE WHO APPROACH TO RECEIVE IT.

#### POINT I.

Consider *the causes* why this washing of feet *preceded the institution of this sovereign Sacrament.*

1. The first was, to *teach us the great purity and cleanness which those ought to have who come to receive* and participate of this banquet, not contenting themselves with being clean and exempt from mortal, but, as far as they can, even from venial sins, washing their feet from the dust which cleaves to them by means of earthly affections; for Christ being purity itself, it is reason that we receive Him with the greatest purity it is possible for us, washing ourselves with the sacrament of Confession, and with the water of tears, beseeching our Lord that He vouchsafe so to wash us and purify us, that we may worthily receive Him. To this purpose I should imagine that our Lord says to me that which He said to St. Peter:—"If I wash thee not, thou shalt have no part with me" (2) in this banquet, because thou wilt not receive those fruits and contentments which those receive who approach washed and pure.

*Colloquy.*—O God of my soul, if this be so, wash "my head, my hands, and feet;" wash my thoughts, my works, and affections; that coming to this banquet washed, pure, and clean, I may be partaker of its fruits. Amen.

2. The second cause was, that *it was a custom when one person entertained another*, to wash his feet, in sign of

(2) Joan. xiii. 8.

humility and charity, and for this reason it was, that Christ our Lord complained of the Pharisee, that entering into his house to eat, he gave Him not water for His feet. (3) By the practice of which laudable custom our Lord would signify, that those who are to be present at this banquet ought, in imitation of Him, to exercise themselves in great affections of humility and charity, which are the two best dispositions which they can bring to this blessed banquet, humbling themselves before Almighty God and before men, and loving God with their whole heart, and all men for God, performing towards them works of piety, with reverence and charity.

*Colloquy.*—O my soul, if thou desirest to enjoy the banquet of Christ, learn first the lesson which He taught thee, when He said, "Know you what I have done to you?" Follow, therefore, His example, that this His Sacrament may be profitable to thee.

POINT II.

Next are to be considered *the causes why the supper of the Paschal lamb preceded the mysterious supper*, in which this divine Sacrament was ordained and received, which were *two principal*, in which the *figure* and the *thing figured* might agree in conformity.

1. The first cause was, *to give us to understand* that as that lamb was sacrificed in thanksgiving for the benefit which God had done to His people, in delivering them from the captivity of Pharao, and with its blood sprinkling the doors of the houses of the Hebrews, that the angel of God, who slew all the firstborn of Egypt, might not hurt them, (4) and with its flesh fortifying those who were to undertake that journey, that nourished by it they might begin and prosecute it;—even so *this lamb of God*, whose flesh and blood is in this Blessed Sacrament, is *sacrificed in*

(3) Luc. vii. 44. (4) Exod. xii. 29.

*the holy Mass*, in memory and gratitude of the sovereign benefit which Christ our Lord imparted to us, in *delivering us from the captivity of the Devil*, by means of His Passion and death; (5) in whose blood, and in virtue of whom, we are delivered from the death of sin, as also from eternal death, and are sustained and comforted with His precious flesh, to depart forth of the servitude of Egypt, and to begin with new fervour the journey of virtue, prosecuting it till we arrive to life eternal.

*Colloquy*.—O lamb of God, "slain from the beginning of the world,"(6) not in Thy holy humanity, but in the figures of it, beginning even from the creation of the world to impart the graces and gifts which Thou wast to purchase with Thy death: what shall I give Thee for the innumerable benefits which Thou hast purchased for me with this Thy precious death? I have nothing, O my Lord, more precious to give Thee, than to offer Thee this sacrifice of Thyself, and to receive the "chalice of salvation"(7) with praises of Thy holy name. Deliver me, O most immaculate lamb, from the servitude of the Devil, that so the firstborn in the house of my soul die not, that is to say, my free will: comfort me also, that I may walk through the desert of this life, until I finally arrive at the rest of glory. Amen.

2. The second cause was, *to teach us* in the eating of the legal lamb, *the dispositions which are required in us to eat this divine lamb*, figured in that other.—i. For it is to be eaten with "the loins girded" with chastity, mortifying all the sensual delights of the flesh, because this lamb, as He is most chaste, so is He chiefly delighted with virginal purity.—ii. We must have "*shoes*" on our feet, a watch-

(5) S. Tho. 3, p. q. lxxiii. art. 6.
(6) Apoc. xiii. 8. (7) Psalm. cxv. 13.

ful custody of the heart, and of all our affections, that they be not defiled nor polluted with the touch of earthly things.—iii. "*Holding staves in our hands,*" (8) placing our confidence in the cross of Christ our Lord, and in His government and protection, performing works agreeable and pleasing in His sight.—iv. It must be eaten "in haste" with haste of spiritual fervour, shaking off all slowness and slothfulness of mind, eating this lamb, not with sloth, loathing, or want of relish, but with hunger, and with great desire to eat.—v. With "*unleavened bread*" *and* "*with wild lettuce;*" that is, with purity of soul, without corruption of sin, and with the exercises of mortification bitter to the flesh.—vi. Nothing of it must be eaten "*raw,*" nor boiled in water, but "*roasted with fire;*" for it is not to be eaten without having first considered what this meat is, and that not with a cold and raw consideration, but with such meditation as causes the fire of love to burn in the heart.

Pondering these six things, *I will reflect upon myself* with blushes and confusion, for that cold disposition with which I eat this celestial lamb, and will endeavour for the time to come to have a more exact and perfect disposition, saying that of the apostle:—"For Christ our Pasch is sacrificed for us, therefore let us feast, not with the old leaven, nor with the leaven of malice, but with the unleavened bread of sincerity and truth." (9)

POINT III.

The third point shall be, to recal to memory those affectionate words which we have related Christ our Lord to have spoken to His apostles at the beginning of the supper, and may be He spoke them at the beginning of this sacramental supper:—"*With desire I have desired to eat this*

(8) Exod. xii. 11. (9) 1 Cor. v. 8.

*Pasch with you before I suffer.* For I say to you, that from this time I will not eat it, till it be fulfilled in the Kingdom of God." (10)

In these words He makes known to us *two things*, which admirably dispose us worthily to receive this holy Sacrament.

1. That we ought to approach *with a very great and vehement desire*, as He vehemently desired to eat this supper with His disciples, for so precious a lamb deserves to be eaten with a very vehement hunger and desire, arising from the consideration of our own great necessity, and of His excellency and dignity, for no necessity can be greater than ours, nor any meat more excellent than His, and consequently no hunger ought to be like the hunger for it.

2. That *we ought to eat this lamb every time as if it were the very last*, and as one who never were to eat it more unless in heaven, for, therefore it is called the "Viaticum," as being received by those who are about to pass to the other life. And if I communicate with this affection, my communion will be both devout and profitable to me, calling to mind what the Wise man says:—"When thou shalt sit to eat with a prince, attend diligently what is set before thee, and put a knife to thy throat;" (11) that is to say, eat this meat offered thee by the Prince of heaven, as if thou now hadst the knife sticking in thy throat, and wert upon the point of giving up the ghost, and eat it, having first mortified the inordinate affections of the flesh, and as thou wouldst mortify them if thou knewest for certain that this were to be thy last meal.

*Colloquy.*—O King of heaven, since it is Thy will that I sit with Thee at this celestial table, give me force to cut off entirely all affections which may make me unworthy, preparing myself for this banquet, as

(10) Luc. xxii. 15. (11) Prov. xxiii. 1.

one that is ready presently to pass to eternity, where I shall enjoy Thee for ever and ever. Amen.

---

## MEDITATION X.

### OF THE TIME, PLACE, AND COMPANY, CHOSEN BY HIM FOR INSTITUTING THE BLESSED SACRAMENT.

#### POINT I.

Consider first, the *reasons why* our Lord would institute this most holy Sacrament, *the night before His Passion*, and the cause of His death; seeing that He might have deferred its institution till after His resurrection.

1. The first cause was, *the more to manifest the greatness of the love He bare us*, since, even then, when men were contriving to take away His life by most exquisite torments and disgraces, He ordained a celestial banquet which should give them life; together with admirable favours and delights, of which were to participate a great number even of those who then were actually plotting and contriving His death. In this He teaches us, that as the injuries and persecutions of the wicked were not able to quench or extinguish His charity, nor make Him desist from providing this banquet for His elect; so no crosses, no disgraces, nor torments ought to be able to divert the elect from His holy service, or to withhold them from this most holy banquet, and to reap its most copious fruit. Hence it is that S. Paul cries out, saying:—"Quis ergo separabit nos a charitate Christi? tribulatio? an angustia?" &c.—"Who then shalt separate us from the love of Christ? tribulation or distress?"(1) &c. As well from that which He bears us, as from that which, assisted with His grace, we ought to render Him. What shall be able to

(1) Rom. viii. 35.

make a divorce and separation between these two charities and friendships? shall tribulation? or anguish, or persecution, or the sword? "Certus sum enim, quia neque mors, neque vita," &c. "For I am sure that neither death, nor life"—"nor any other creature, shall be able to separate us from the love of God which is in Christ Jesus our Lord."

*Colloquy.*—O sweet Jesus, I am most assured that no persecutions or torments whatsoever shall ever be able to extinguish Thy charity, seeing that even in the midst of them Thou hast given for a pledge of Thy love Thy sacred body for meat, and Thy precious blood for drink; for which charity I beseech Thee to grant me another charity, so inflamed and so fervent, that no persecution be ever able to quench it. Amen.

2. To *manifest to us the hearty desire He had* of remaining *for ever with us*, not only as God, but also *as man.*(2) Insomuch that intending to withdraw Himself from us as regards the corporal, visible, and ordinary presence of His humanity, He contrived a means to remain present with us in another manner, yet so as to be with us at all times, and for ever, until the ending of the world, under the forms of this Blessed Sacrament. And although it had been sufficient to have instituted it a little before His ascending to heaven, He would nevertheless ordain it before His Passion, that He might leave registered even in His mortal life, this manner of abiding with mortal men, for the love of whom He had instituted this Sacrament. And, moreover, to manifest hereby His infinite charity, that even when men would, through envy and rancour, cast Him out of the world, He contrived to leave Himself with them in the world, after another manner, full of piety and of love.

(2) S. Tho. 3, p. q. lxxiii. art. 9.

*Colloquy.*—O beloved of my heart, if Thou so much desirest to be always with me, I ought much more to desire to be always with Thee, beholding Thee present in every place, as Thou art God, and in this holy Sacrament, as Thou art Man. Oh that I could be continually present in the Church when this divine mystery is celebrated, and where this divine Sacrament is offered up, to enjoy the presence of it? But not being able to do that which I desire, I will do what I am able by endeavouring as often as possible to be present at it, both in body and soul, and always with my heart and affection.

3. *That the world might never want a memory of His most sacred Passion,*(3) and some sacrifice ordained to appease and glorify Almighty God; forasmuch, therefore, as in this supper, and by His Passion, the memory of the Paschal lamb, together with the sacrifices of the old law ceased, He would at the same time institute this divine Sacrament and Sacrifice, to serve us for a memory and representation of His Passion, by which the fruit and virtue of it might be applied to us. And although, as we said before, it had sufficed to have instituted it after His resurrection, yet would He not, but preferred that it should be done before His Passion; because the nature of vehement love is rather to hasten the benefit that it intends to bestow upon the beloved object than to defer it. That He might also by this oblige us the more to have a tender memory of Himself, because those things which fathers commend to their children at the time of their death, are wont to make a deeper impression in their memory.

*Colloquy.*—O most loving Father, seeing that at that hour it pleased Thee to leave so lively a memory

(3) Luc. xxii. 19.

of Thy Passion and death, "I will be mindful and remember, and my soul shall languish within me,"(4) even to the last gasp of my life. "If I forget Thee, let my right hand be forgotten, and let my tongue cleave to my jaw, if I do not remember Thee."(5)

POINT II.

Consider *the place* which our Lord chose for the institution of this Sacrament, together with the mysteries contained in it.

For, first, He chose "a *large dining room furnished*,"(6) offered to Him with a hearty good will, by a man whose name is not mentioned, and which our Lord accepted of, accommodated, and made use of for several of His mysterious works. For,—i. besides the eating of the Paschal lamb in it, and the institution of this holy Sacrament, the *apostles after* the Passion, together with the *Blessed Virgin, retired themselves* into the same place.(7)—ii. Our Lord *there appeared to them after His resurrection.*—iii. There also they *assemble themselves* to make their prayers, *expecting the coming of the Holy Ghost*, who in the same place descended upon them in tongues of fire.—iv. From this place did *the apostles issue forth*, to go and preach the law of the Gospel.(8)

And although this hall be principally the figure of the Catholic Church, in which only, and not out of it, it is lawful to eat this holy lamb and receive the gifts and graces which proceed from it; yet is it also a figure of the devout soul, into which Christ our Lord enters and makes His abode, by the means of this divine Sacrament. Which soul ought to be *large*, and very spacious for the reception of celestial gifts,—ample, by the latitude of charity and

(4) Thren. iii. 20. (5) Psal. cxxxvi. 5.
(6) Marc. xiv. 15; Luc. xxii. 12.
(7) Joan. xx. 19. (8) Act. i. 13; ii. 3.

love of God and our neighbour,—*long*, by the longanimity of hope,—and strewed, and furnished with all sorts of virtues, which are the hangings and ornaments of that living abode which God inhabits; for, as the heavens are tapestried with stars, so ought the soul to be well furnished and adorned with holy virtues.

*Colloquy.*—O eternal God, seeing it is Thy gracious pleasure to come and enter into this poor habitation of my soul, behold how little it is, how narrow and poor, without any ornament or decking at all; enlarge it, I beseech Thee, with Thy gifts, replenish it with charity, dilate it with confidence, adorn it with Thy virtues; "Inclina cœlos tuos, et descende;" "Bow down Thy" starry "heavens,"(9) and engrave in me a lively figure of them, to the end that I may be made a worthy habitation for Thee. Amen.

The mystery of the two disciples, who went to prepare this hall, also serves to this purpose, as has been declared in the seventh meditation.

2. *How much does our Lord esteem a good and prompt will of receiving Him*, making no account of the greatness, or magnificence of the world; and for this cause He suppressed the name of the man that lent Him his house, to show by this that He neither makes any account nor cares much whether he be rich or poor, noble or ignoble, wise or ignorant, that is to receive Him into his soul; provided that he offer Him that which he has with a right good heart and devout will, inspired into him by Almighty God, man consenting to it.

3. When He enters into a soul that receives Him worthily, He *appropriates and takes her to Him for His own;* and makes her a place of prayer, discovers to her His high mysteries, communicates to her the gifts of the

(9) Psal. cxliii. 5.

Holy Ghost, and finally makes her issue forth, to publish His greatness, and to assist her neighbour.

*Colloquy.*—Blessed is that soul whose happy lot it is to be made the receptacle of Jesus Christ, in which He takes pleasure to inhabit, and therein to work His holy mysteries. Come, dear Lord, into the habitation of my heart, and take it for Thine, for I will not henceforth that it be any longer mine.

POINT III.

Consider the *company of persons* which our Lord chose, to institute in their presence this holy Sacrament, and to make them participant of the same, namely, His apostles, amongst whom it is the more certain opinion, as S. Thomas holds,(10) that Judas was present, who was not as yet gone out of the hall to work his treason. Consider, therefore, the difference that there was between the eleven apostles and this traitor; for the other eleven were there present both in body and spirit, with due attention and reverence, beholding and understanding what our Saviour did, and receiving this divine meat with singular devotion, receiving it very differently from ordinary food. Whereas Judas was present there in body only, his spirit being wholly plunged in his wicked intentions, insomuch that he took no heed at all, nor understood what our Lord did, so that he swallowed down this bread of life without distinguishing between this and ordinary bread: and therefore did not profit but greatly hurt himself by receiving it; for presently he went forth from thence to betray his master, and in the end died most miserably, according to the doctrine of S. Paul:—"Whosoever shall eat this bread or drink the chalice of the Lord unworthily, shall be guilty of the body and of the blood of our Lord,"(11) no

(10) D. Tho. 3, p. q. lxxxi. art. 2. (11) 1 Cor. xi. 27.

less than if he should betray Him to His enemies. And for this cause, many fall sick, become every day weaker and weaker, and die amongst you disastrously.

Therefore, fearing to do such an injury to a body so venerable, I ought to endeavour to assist at this banquet in the same manner as the apostles did, by being present both in body and in spirit, with due attention, reverence and devotion, ruminating and pondering with myself what our Lord does here for me, as also what I ought to do in receiving Him, withdrawing my heart, not only from evil things, but also from all other affairs whatever; attentive, as the Wise man says, to "consider diligently what that is set before" me.(12)

---

## MEDITATION XI.

ON THE MIRACULOUS CONVERSION WROUGHT BY CHRIST OF BREAD INTO HIS BODY, AND OF THE MANNER IN WHICH HIMSELF AND HIS APOSTLES COMMUNICATED.

### POINT I.

Consider first, that our Lord, sitting at the table, took into His blessed hands one of those loaves which were there placed and pronouncing these words:—"Hoc est corpus meum"(1)—"This is my body," in virtue of them, changed the substance of bread into His most sacred body: so that what was before the utterance of these words true bread, directly the words were finished, was converted into His true body, covered only with the exterior species or accidents of bread.

Upon this truth of our faith I ought to ponder, first, the infinite wonders which our Lord manifested in this work, especially His infinite *wisdom*, *omnipotency*, *bounty*, *and charity*.

(12) Prov. xxiii. 1.

(1) Mat. xxvi. 26; Marc. xiv. 22; Luc. xxii. 18; 1 Cor. xi. 24.

1. He manifests His *wisdom* in inventing such an ineffable means of *communicating Himself to men*, and giving them the food of life, which means certainly could not have been found out but by the infinite knowledge of God alone. And even as in the works of the Incarnation, the wisdom of God marvellously appeared, in finding out a means of uniting together two such extremes, as God and man, in the unity of one Person for our remedy;—so in this mystery of the Eucharist the same wisdom no less appears in having invented a means of joining together God made man, with the forms of bread and wine, in a sacrament for our sustenance. Hence will I draw affections of admiration, joy, and thanksgiving, rejoicing with myself that I have a God so wise, praising Him for the inventions of His wisdom, and forcing my judgment by acts of faith to believe that which He invented by it, for it is no great marvel if He who is so infinitely wise can do that which I can no way comprehend.

*Colloquy.*—O most wise Jesus, in whom are hid all the treasures of the knowledge and wisdom of Almighty God, give me, I beseech Thee, some little parcel of this wisdom, that I may know and esteem this favour, and give Thee thanks for it as I ought. Amen.

2. *The omnipotency* of Christ our Lord here appears in this, that with one only word, and in a moment, He works infinite miracles, as well in the bread as in His body itself, linking and uniting them together for our sustenance; for in an instant He changed and converted the substance of bread into His blessed body, there remaining nothing but the bare accidents of bread with which to cover the body; which also He disposes in such a manner, that it is whole and entire in every little particle of the Host; so that He is, "Totus in toto, et totus in qualibet parte:"—

*all in the whole, and all in every part*, without dividing the body, although the Host be divided, which thing I am to believe entirely with a lively faith; for, to believe He *can* do this, it suffices that He is omnipotent;—and to believe that indeed He *has* done this, it suffices that He has *said* it.

*Colloquy.*—O the greatness of the omnipotency of Jesus Christ! what is this Thou dost, O most mighty Saviour; to sustain a miserable worm Thou dost alter the whole order of nature, framing Thy body after a new and stupendous manner, thereby to accommodate it to the weakness and incapacity of Thy slave! Blessed be Thy omnipotency, by which I beseech Thee to vouchsafe to alter me into a new man, that I may enjoy the fruit of it. Amen.

3. The *infinite bounty and charity* of our Lord is here discovered with the greatest arguments that could be given for our sustentation. For, as the eternal Father manifested His exceeding bounty and charity in giving to the world the most precious thing He had to save it, namely, His Son,(2) with whom He likewise gave us all things, the more fully to complete our redemption, even so did the Son of God discover His excessive bounty and charity in giving the most precious and dearest thing He had for our sustenance, namely, Himself, and His sacred body, together with all whatsoever it contained (3) As if a king having a rich coffer full of treasures of gold and silver, of pearls and jewels of infinite value, should say to some one about him, "Take this coffer for thyself," in giving him the coffer, gives him likewise together with the same all that is contained in it:—even so our sovereign King, in giving us His body and His most holy flesh, also gives us His blood, His soul, His divinity, together with all the

(2) Joan. iii. 16. (3) Rom. viii. 32.

treasures of His merits and satisfactions, that we should enjoy them as our own, desirous to be always with us, and to be our companion, our banquet and our constant delight.

*Colloquy.*—O my best beloved, how shall I prove my gratitude for such a bounty and charity, as in this Blessed Sacrament Thou dost manifest to us? Thou, Lord, givest me the best thing Thou hast, I therefore will give Thee the best thing I have; Thou dost give me Thyself, together with all that depends thereon, and I here offer Thee myself, with all that is mine, my body, my soul, my blood, and my life;—in a word, all that I can or may any way have, I offer and consecrate to Thy service; assist me, dear Lord, to accomplish this my desire, in gratitude for the much which I owe Thee, for so inestimable a benefit. Amen.

4. Christ our Lord discovers in this *the most fervent zeal which He has of our salvation*, in inventing such a means to apply to us by Himself the fruits of His Passion,—insomuch that He might then justly say:—" Zelus Domus tuæ comedit me;"—" The zeal of Thy house hath eaten me."(4) For it hath not only eaten and consumed my honour, my goods, and my life, but it has made me myself small, or become food, and even suffer myself to be eaten, to give health and life to those that inhabit my house.

*Colloquy.*—O sweet Jesus, I give Thee humble thanks for the burning zeal that Thou hast for Thy Father's house, which is Thy Church: and as my soul is also Thy house, for the nourishment of which Thou hast made Thyself meat; grant me, I beseech Thee, such a fervent zeal of Thy glory, that to maintain the same I would suffer myself to be eaten, and even to be torn and pulled in pieces. Amen.

(4) Psal. lxviii. 10.

POINT II.

Consider the great mysteries that are contained in those words which our Lord spake when He consecrated the bread. St. Luke reports that He said:—"*Hoc est corpus meum quod pro vobis datur.*"—"This is my body, which is given for you."(5)

1. He does not say:—"This is *a figure* or *a representation* of my body;" but,—"This is my body," real and true;—thereby to declare the real presence of His most holy body, as also to give us most excellent proofs and arguments of His mercy and paternal providence towards us;(6) for, to feed and sanctify us spiritually it had been sufficient that this Sacrament had consisted of pure bread, as being only representative of Christ our Lord; in the same manner as in Baptism pure and simple water washes and sanctifies us; but the infinite charity of our Lord did not content itself herewith, but would that His own body, and His own person, should be in this Blessed Sacrament, and should sanctify us, to declare to us the great love He bore us, and His anxiety to feed and cherish us. For that which a man does himself, he does with greater love, greater compassion, greater diligence, and providence, just as the mother that greatly esteems and loves her child, will not permit that any other nurse than herself, give it suck, nor that it be nourished with any other milk than with her own, but she herself nurses and nourishes it with the milk of her own breasts, which she most carefully and tenderly offers to it, having a motherly care and compassion of her child's necessities.(7)

*Colloquy.*—O most tender Father, O mother and nurse most compassionate! Why do I not melt and dissolve myself to serve Thee with love, doing for

(5) Luc. xxii. 19; 1 Cor. xi. 24.
(6) S. Th. 3, p. q. lxxviii. art. 2. (7) Ose. xi. 3.

Thee what Thou dost for me? I will not content myself for time to come to observe that which Thou commandest for the accomplishment of Thy precepts, but I will also most exactly follow Thy holy counsels.

2. He does not say:—"This is a *piece or part* of my body, or of my flesh;" but,—"This is *my body*," whole, perfect, and entire. For although the least particle of this flesh had been sufficient to have sanctified us, yet would He put there His whole body entirely, His head, His eyes, His ears, His mouth, His tongue, His breast, His heart, His hands, and His feet, to signify that with His sacred members He would sanctify every member of him that should receive Him, and so entirely heal the whole man. With His eyes He will sanctify my eyes;—with His heart my heart;—and with His hands my hands;—like Eliseus the prophet, who, to raise to life the dead child, contracted and shrunk himself up, joining his eyes, his mouth, and his hands, to the eyes, mouth, and hands of the child, and by this means gave it life. In like manner, when I receive this Blessed Sacrament, I will speak to Him, and discourse upon His sacred members, saying:

*Colloquy.*—O sweet Jesus, seeing that to give life to my soul Thou hast so shrunk up Thyself in this Blessed Sacrament, sanctify, I beseech Thee, with Thy eyes and ears, my eyes and ears in such a manner that I only see and hear what shall be pleasing to Thee; with Thy tongue purify mine, that it speak not anything that may offend Thee; with Thy hands and feet fortify mine, that I may execute Thy holy will. O my best beloved, open the eyes of Thy mercy, and look upon me, and illuminate mine, that I may know Thee, and with a lively faith believe in Thee. Open Thy ears, and hearken to my prayers, sobs, and groanings, making mine open also, that I may hear Thy word, and obey Thy holy law. Open

Thy mouth, and Thy most blessed tongue, and speak somewhat to my heart, whereby my mouth may be opened to bless Thee, and my tongue never cease to magnify Thee. Open, O my Lord, Thy breast, and enlarge Thy heart to harbour me within, that it may burn and wholly inflame me with the fire of Thy love. Stretch forth Thy hands, and touch me with them, that mine may be sanctified in the works they do. By the steps of Thy most holy feet, I beseech Thee, that Thou direct my steps conformably to Thine, and that my whole body may be a lively portraiture and resemblance of the sanctity and purity which shone in Thine. Amen.

3. Ponder these words:—"Hoc est corpus meum, quod provobis tradetur."—"This is my body, which shall be delivered for you."(8) Which words teach us that there is the *same body which was to be sold, delivered,* and *put to death* for us: and that the self-same body that was delivered up to death, delivered itself to be eaten: both the one and the other, proceeding from one and the self-same love He bore us. I will also consider, in this most holy body, the five wounds that He received in His Passion, which are the marks of His death, and of our life; by which I will beseech Him to revive and sanctify me, and vouchsafe to hide me within them, saying to Him:

*Colloquy.*—O most holy body of my Lord and Saviour, pierced upon the cross with nails, and with a lance, receiving thereby five cruel wounds, and now in heaven, and also in this most holy Sacrament, with the selfsame wounds, most bright and most resplendent: I adore Thee, I praise and glorify Thee, and beseech Thee, that by the same sacred wounds Thou wilt vouchsafe to heal mine, and with Thy holy grace, to convert into beauty and splendour the foulness and ignominy which by my fault I am fallen into.

(8) 1 Cor. xi. 8,

POINT III.

Our Lord communicated all His apostles; in which consider the *exceeding devotion with which they received* and ate this most blessed bread.

1. For, at the same instant God wrought another miracle of His omnipotency in the hearts and understandings of these rude fishermen and imperfect disciples, illuminating them with an extraordinary light, that with a lively faith they might most assuredly believe, that that which was under the form of bread, was indeed the true body of their master; insomuch that they received it with the love and reverence which they bore Him, and ravished in admiration at this new miracle, on the one side they trembled out of a regardful respect, and on the other side their hearts leaped for joy that they were to put Him into their bowels.

*Colloquy.*—O sacred apostles, beseech your master and mine that He vouchsafe to give me that holy fear and love with which you communicated, that I may receive Him with the same profit with which you then received Him. Amen.

2. Consider the *great sweetness* and *affections that the apostles felt in this first communion*, which no doubt were so excellent, that they from that time acknowledged the infinite dignity and excellency of this divine meat, proving by experience how far this divine bread differed from that which they had eaten but a little before. Only that unfortunate wretch, Judas, found in this food no taste nor savour, because he ate it without either faith, reverence, or any manner of attention; all which, that I may the better conceive, I may piously discourse upon the eleven apostles, pondering with myself the manner in which each of them then communicated. St. Peter, therefore, reviving

and quickening his faith, might perhaps say to that which was contained in this bread:—"Tu es Christus filius Dei vivi,"—"Thou art Christ, the Son of the living God." And it may be that our Lord might answer him:—"Beatus es Simon, Bar-jona," &c. "Blessed art thou, Simon Bar-jona, because flesh and blood have not revealed this to thee, but my Father who is in heaven."(9) And when our Lord gave him the consecrated bread, with the same lively faith, full of reverence, he might say within himself:—"Exi a me Domine quia homo peccator sum."—"Depart from me, because I am a sinful man, O Lord."(10) Yet, for obedience, did he take it and eat it. I may likewise consider in St. John, how he did revive his affections of love, beholding his master, not only join him to Himself, but also enter into his very breast; and therefore he remained so absorbed with the ecstasy of the excessive love, that this mystical supper being ended, he reclined upon the breast of our Saviour, where he fell into a most sweet slumber of contemplation.

O that I could have a faith and reverence like that of St. Peter's, and a love and charity like that of St. John's, to receive my Lord as they received Him! O how well did Christ our Lord recompense the pains they had taken in preparing the supper of the lamb; for on them doubtless, as on those who were the most fervent and best beloved, did He bestow a better portion.

*Colloquy.*—Obtain for me, O glorious apostles, that spirit with which you communicated, that I may likewise participate of the same sweetness, that you tasted in it. Amen.

(In this manner may I reason upon the rest of the apostles, according to the devotion that I may imagine to have been in every one of them.)

(9) Mat. xvi. 17. (10) Luc. v. 8.

POINT IV.

Our Lord, as the common opinion of holy men is,(11) taking into His hands a piece of this most holy bread, *communicated Himself*, both to encourage His apostles to eat, as also to give them an example of that reverence, modesty, and devotion, with which they were to receive Him. Because He would in everything instruct us, first by example rather than by precept, and by works rather than by words. And so as He would receive Baptism, so would He likewise receive the holy communion. O what reverence and great devotion did He show exteriorly, when this morsel approached near to His mouth, beholding the divinity which was united to the bread He received! O how did His most holy soul even leap within Him at the new and unaccustomed joy it felt when He ate and received Himself, by reason of the contentment He felt in having instituted so admirable a Sacrament.

*Colloquy.*—O sweet Jesus, that I could receive Thee with that love and reverence with which Thou then receivedst Thyself, imitating Thee as far as I may. Dear Lord, I offer Thee Thine own, in place of that which is wanting in me, and by the same I beseech Thee to give me as great a portion of it as is possible, considering that all this of right is due to so excellent a majesty.

---

## MEDITATION XII.

### ON THE CONVERSION OF THE WINE INTO CHRIST'S BLOOD AND OF THE UNSPEAKABLE TREASURES WHICH LIE HID IN IT.

POINT I.

After the consecration and communion of bread, our Lord took into His hands a *cup* of wine and said:—" *This is*

(11) S. Th. 3, p. q. lxxxi. art. 5.

*the chalice of my blood, of the new Testament*, which shall be shed for you, and for many, unto remission of sins."(1) By virtue of which words, the wine was converted into His precious blood.

1. In this I will consider the infinite *charity, liberality, and omnipotency* of Christ our Lord,(2) which appeared in this, that He would put into this chalice *all His blood*, not reserving so much as one only drop, and this for our comfort and consolation; for, without all doubt, it had been sufficient for our sanctification, that there had been no more quantity of blood in the chalice, than there was of wine, or one only drop of His blood, yet would He shed into that chalice all the blood of His veins, of His head, of His heart, of His arms, and of His whole body, giving it all to us liberally, and without limitation, declaring to us, by this argument, His love and liberality; as also to invite me hereby to employ, if need were, every drop of my blood in His holy service.

2. But His charity and liberality goes *yet further*, since He not only gives us His blood, but also bestows upon us *the most precious vessel in which it is contained*, no otherwise than if a prince should offer us some excellent wine to drink out of a cup of gold, set with precious stones, and should at the same time say to us, "take the wine, and the cup also;" for even so our Lord Jesus Christ both gives us His precious blood, and the vessel in which it is contained, which are His veins, His flesh, and His *most holy body*, His *soul*, and *His divinity*, that all may be made our meat and drink.

*Colloquy.*—O immense charity, O most holy prodigality, how shall not I, dear Lord, give Thee all that

(1) Mat. xxvi. 28; Luc. xxii. 20; Marc. xiv. 24.
(2) S. Th. 3, p. q. lxxxvii. art. 3.

I have, seeing that Thou dost give me, and that after so admirable a manner, all that Thou hast!

3. This word "*my*," likewise is not void of great mystery; of my own blood, not the blood of *another body*. In this He manifests to us that His charity is far different from that of kings and princes of the earth, who drink the blood of their vassals and subjects, make havoc of it, and with it defend their dominions, and conquer those of other men; but Christ our Lord gives to drink to His subjects of His *own* precious blood; for He is very frank and liberal of it, and gains them treasures and kingdoms by means of it.

*Colloquy.*—O sovereign King, not a tyrant, but a Father, and a most loving and tender Father, who gives life and sustenance to Thy subjects and children, by nourishing them with the blood of Thy own veins, to the end we may all be of Thy royal blood, making us "genus electum, regale Sacerdotium, gens sancta," "a chosen generation, a kingly priesthood, a holy nation."(3) Oh that all Christian people knew their race and blood, by it to prize and value themselves accordingly, imitating Thy holy and generous virtues.

POINT II.

1. Our Lord called this chalice of His blood His "New Testament." First, to declare by this the excellence of the New Testament above the Old, which consisted of nothing but the blood of beasts, inasmuch as they represented, and were a figure of, the blood of Christ; but the New Testament, in the very blood of our Lord Jesus, in which it was founded, established, and confirmed. I will, therefore, represent to my consideration, how our Lord, the night of His Passion, made His last will and

(3) 1 Pet. ii. 9.

testament, conveying many legacies and promises of infinite value: they comprehend all the treasures of grace, and of glory, which God imparts to His elect.

2. In this testament He *promises us the pardon of our sins*, and consequently of the eternal pains which we had deserved for them, promising us the grace of adoption of the children of God, together with charity, and all the virtues and gifts of the Holy Ghost, and of the inheritance of the Kingdom of heaven, which is eternal beatitude, and that He will hear our prayers, that He will assist us in our afflictions, and help us in all our actions; of all which legacies and promises His blood is the assurance, the gage, the pledge, the evidence of the *writ of privilege*, by which we must obtain that which our Lord Jesus has purchased for us, and that which He hath promised and bequeathed to us in His Testament; having, therefore, this privilege with us, it ought to be to us an occasion and motive of great affections of love and confidence, of joy and assurance of our salvation. When, therefore, we hear Mass, or communicate, we ought boldly and with great confidence to offer to the eternal Father this blood for the obtaining of all that has been said, saying to Him:—

*Colloquy.*—O eternal Father, I here present to Thee the most precious blood of this chalice, as an authentic charter of the testament of Thy Son, by which He promised me that Thou shouldst give me whatsoever I demand of Thee; and seeing that Thou art the executor of this His will, accomplish in me, I beseech Thee, His testament, in granting me that which I require. Amen.

3. Our Lord Jesus also *left* us in this His last testament *most excellent counsels* and admonitions, as the new commandment of loving one another, the observation of His precepts, and all that belongs to the works of humility,

patience, and Christian perfection, for to all this is the blood available, which is contained in this chalice, and by it we obtain force for the accomplishing of it, endeavouring, as the proverb says, to "have blood in our eyes," that is to say, ever to show ourselves valiant and resolute in His divine service.

POINT III.

Consider, thirdly, that which Christ our Lord said to His apostles concerning His blood, viz:—"*Which shall be shed for you, and for many, unto remission of sins.*"

1. *It* "*shall be shed for you,*" which He shed as well to move them to compassion and grief, as to great love and thankfulness, as if He had said:—"Behold, I here give you the very same blood which with great pains and torments I am to shed, not for any respect or profit of my own, but for *yours*, and for your salvation; take, then, compassion of me, who so liberally pour it out for your sakes, and love me, seeing that I so dearly love you." And, as He said these words, "Pro vobis," "for you," speaking to many, so might He likewise have said the same to every one in particular, "Hic est sanguis," &c.—"This is my blood which I shed for *thee*." And so may I imagine with myself that He says the same to me.

*Colloquy.*—O most loving Redeemer, who hast so painfully poured out Thy precious blood for me, and dost bestow it on me in this Blessed Sacrament with so great love, give me grace, I beseech Thee, that I may have compassion of Thy pains, and answer to this Thy love, by my loyal services.

2. He says:—"Qui pro multis effundetur"—"Which shall be shed *for many;*" that is to say, *for all men in the world, Quoad sufficientiam*, as to the sufficiency;—and also *for many, Quoad efficaciam*,—as to the efficacy and

fruit they draw from it; and it is put into this chalice for all those for whom it has been shed. Of this He makes mention that we might understand His great liberality, since there is no man in the world, be he ever so wretched, for whom He has not shed His blood, and whom He does not invite to partake of its fruit, be he but a very slave, and the scum and refuse of the earth.

*Colloquy.*—O most liberal Saviour, seeing that one only drop of Thy precious blood suffices for the whole world, apply, I beseech Thee, the value of it to "many," to the end that "many" may enjoy its fruit. Amen.

3. He adds:—"Qui effundetur in remissionem *peccatorum*"—"Which shall be shed *unto remission of sins,*" without limiting either the number or the enormity of them, since there is no number of sins so huge, nor any sin so enormous and abominable, which cannot be pardoned in this blood: even the sins of those tyrants and tormentors themselves, who with more than devilish cruelty shed it, might by this blood have been pardoned, it having been shed likewise for them, and, if they themselves had wished it, they might easily have obtained pardon.

*Colloquy.*—O most precious blood of the lamb Jesus, in virtue of which we may all wash, and make white our garments, cleansing our souls from the spots of sin, wash, whiten, cleanse, and beautify my soul, by blotting out the blemishes of sin, covering them with the virtues of Thy divine grace. Amen.

This word also, effundetur, "shall be shed," must be considered, which represents to us, that it will issue out of His body, not drop by drop, distilling thence sparingly, but that it will gush forth in great abundance, and from every part of His body, as we shall declare in the meditation following.

4. The fourth point may be concerning the manner how our Lord Jesus, together with His apostles, drank this chalice, pondering what we have said before about the bread.

---

## MEDITATION XIII.

### ON THE SACRAMENTAL SPECIES OF BREAD AND WINE, AND OF THAT WHICH IS REPRESENTED TO US BY IT.

This meditation, and the next following, may serve when we hear mass, taking some certain points out of the same, to exercise acts of devotion concerning that mystery which is represented.

#### POINT I.

First, consider the *causes* of our Lord's instituting this Sacrament in *two distinct and different forms or species*, of bread and wine, putting in the one principally His body, and in the other His blood, supposing that the body is truly with the blood, and the blood with the body inseparable.

Of this there are *two principal causes.*

1. The first, to signify that the banquet which He made us *was a most complete banquet*, for, as in earthly banquets both meat and drink are set upon the table, so would He also that there should be in this heavenly banquet, notwithstanding that through His power and infinite excellency the one is joined to the other, and that the least portion or parcel of the same banquet both satisfies our hunger and quenches our thirst; for which I am to give Him infinite thanks, rejoicing within myself to see Him so perfect in all His works.

2. The second cause and more important was, to signify that all His most precious *blood was entirely separated*

*from his body* in His Passion, shedding it for our sins with most grievous pains and torments; when, therefore, hearing Mass, I shall see first the host alone elevated by the priest, and then the chalice, I ought to call to my remembrance this painful separation, revolving with myself that into this chalice is poured all the blood that our blessed Lord shed on the night and day of His Passion five several times, namely, by sweat in the garden, by whips at the pillar, by the thorns, by the nails, and by the lance on the cross; and so discoursing through every one of them, I may make to our Lord colloquies of demands, accompanied with affections of love, of thanksgiving, and of compunction for my sins, in the following manner:—

*Colloquy.*—O most precious blood of my Lord Jesus, which was shed in the garden of Gethsemane, by the pores of His body, with excessive heaviness and agony of His soul; I rejoice to see thee gathered together, and put into this chalice, to be adored by all the faithful. I adore and glorify thee as much as I am able, and beseech thee that thou wilt vouchsafe to deliver me from those eternal heavinesses and agonies, which I have deserved for my sins, since for them it was that thou wast shed. Amen.

*Colloquy.*—O most precious chalice, full of that blood of my Lord Jesus that streamed down from His shoulders, all torn with whips and scourges, and also with the same that issued from His head, when it was pierced with most sharp thorns, inebriate me, I beseech thee, with the divine liquor of this most precious blood, that I may be wholly converted into the love of Him, that shed it for the love of me. Amen.

*Colloquy.*—O most loving Jesus, who hast placed in this chalice the blood which Thou didst shed upon the cross, issuing from the holes which the nails made in Thy hands and feet, and from the wound with which the lance was made in Thy side. What shall I render Thee, O my Lord, for so great a benefit, but only to offer to Thee the selfsame blood in this "chalice of" my "salvation,"(1) glorifying thereby Thy holy name? Amen.

POINT II.

Consider, secondly, the *causes* why Christ our Lord would that the conversion of the bread and wine into His body and blood should be *made invisibly*, the visible accidents of bread and wine still remaining to cover them, seeing that He could easily, if He had pleased, have made some visible change, or else have put there some exterior sign, that might have manifested the interior majesty which is there enclosed.

1. The first cause was on the part of our Lord Himself, *to humble Himself* and to give us a rare and continual *example of humility*, as also of most heroic patience; for even as, in the Incarnation, He who was the Son of God "debased Himself, taking the form of a servant," covering the majesty of His divinity with the baseness of His humanity, on account of which He was by many unknown, contemned and evil-treated, as if He had been but a mere man;—even so in this Sacrament, He who was jointly true God and true Man, would humble Himself, by taking sacramentally this exterior figure of bread and wine, and would under it cover the excellency both of His divinity and humanity, which thing is in like manner the cause, that many not knowing Him contemn Him, and evil treat Him, and oftentimes tread Him under foot, as if He were but mere bread and mere wine, all which He suffers with great patience, without once showing any sign of revenge, in order that we may learn the same from His example.

(1) Psal. cxv. 13.

*Colloquy.*—O most humble and most patient Lord, I give Thee thanks for the rare humility and patience which here Thou didst exercise for our example; assist me, O Lord, to follow Thy example, hiding that which may give among men any occasion of vain honour, and patiently enduring whatsoever contempt or injury I may receive at their hands. Illuminate our eyes with the light of Thy holy faith, that we may believe and reverence the infinite majesty that lies hid under this veil; for, the more Thou dost vouchsafe to humble Thyself for the love of us, the more reasonable is it that we should exalt Thee, and magnify Thee for ever and ever. Amen.

2. The second cause was, that we on our parts *might have a new and continual exercise of a generous faith*, by renouncing and denying all our senses, together with the reasonings which our understanding draws from them, captivating and submitting it to that which faith dictates to us; and hence it is, that in the words of the consecration of the chalice, our Lord calls this sacrament "Mysterium fidei," "a mystery of faith," as a name peculiarly, and by a certain excellency, proper to this sacrament. And truly one of the greatest miracles that our Lord worked that night, was, as we have said before, so suddenly to change the hearts and understandings of the apostles, as to make them firmly believe that the same thing which He held in His hands, by the pronouncing of the words, "This is my body," presently ceased to be bread, and became wholly converted into the body of Him who spoke the words; when, therefore, I communicate or hear Mass, or do but enter into the Church, it is an admirable way of quickening and reviving in me the acts of faith, to exercise my senses in this manner.

*Colloquy.*—I believe, O Lord, that although my

eyes see the colour and figure of bread, yet is it no more bare bread, but Thyself. O Son of the living God, "brightness of" the Father's "glory, and the figure of His substance."(2)—"Dilectus meus, candidus et rubicundus, electus ex millibus."—"My beloved white and ruddy chosen out of thousands."(3) I believe, my God, that although with my sense of smelling I smell the odour of bread and wine, yet under the same Thou art there hidden, true Jacob, the odour of whom resembles the odour of a field covered over with ears of corn, "which the Lord has blessed."(4) I believe, likewise, that although my taste savours bread, and that my touch feels the qualities of bread, nevertheless there is no more any earthly bread, but Thou Thyself, "the living bread,"(5) who camest down from heaven, the fountain of all sweetness and delight. O most sweet Saviour, illuminate my understanding in the same manner that Thou didst illuminate that of Thine apostles, that I may know and understand with a lively faith the infinite beauty that is enclosed therein, and that I may be comforted with the most sweet odour of Thy virtues, and sustained and recreated with the pleasing sweetness of their delights.

3. A third cause of this may also be pondered, which was *to animate our confidence*, and to give us a courage and boldness to touch Him, receive, and eat Him, for if He were not thus covered and veiled, who would be so hardy as to approach Him; so that the same love that moved Him to remain here with us, also caused Him to remain thus dignified, in order that we might enjoy Him with a more excellent and indissoluble union, at such time as we receive Him within us.

*Colloquy.*—O blessed be such a love, that, forgetful of His own greatness, accommodates Himself to our

(2) Hebr. i. 3. (3) Cant. v. 10. (4) Gen. xxvii. 27. (5) Joan. vi. 51.

weakness, lest otherwise such poor worms should have stood affrighted, or fled away from so great a majesty.

POINT III.

Consider the *causes* why our Lord Jesus would remain with us *under the forms of bread and wine*, rather than under any visible thing, applying the same to our spiritual profit.

1. The first cause was, to *unite and join Himself to us*, not only spiritually as He is God, but also corporally as *He is man*, and that with the closest union that possibly could be, for there is nothing that so much unites itself to man, as the meat and drink he takes, which does not barely cleave to the exterior only, but entering at the mouth, penetrates further to his very bowels, and there is united and incorporated with them; and even as true love has the force to unite him that loves with the thing that is loved,—so our most loving Jesus would not content Himself with remaining near to us, or about us, but He would also enter into us, and with this sacramental union cause the spiritual union of perfect love.

*Colloquy.*—O most loving Jesus, how dost Thou not abhor to enter into the bowels of so corrupt and putrefied a body as mine? what is the cause of this but only the excess of Thy love, which lays aside all greatness, that it may unite itself to our baseness; unite me, then, loving Lord, to Thee with perfect union of charity, in such a manner that I may never be separated from Thee for all eternity. Amen.

2. The second cause was, *to signify that He works within our souls all the effects which bread and wine are wont to work within our bodies*, because by His presence, and through the grace which He communicates to us in this divine Sacrament, He nourishes, conserves, and augments

our spiritual life, He fortifies and exhilarates the heart, He resists and refrigerates the perverse and pernicious heat of self-love, and repairs the damages we receive thereby; in a word, He makes us like Himself, by imprinting in us His virtues and properties. Hence it is that He says:—"Qui manducat me, ipse vivet propter me"—"He that eateth me, the same also shall live by me." (6) By these considerations I will excite in myself a hearty hunger and desire of this holy Sacrament, weighing well with myself how much it concerns my soul to receive it often, as it is requisite for the sustenance of my body that I eat often.

*Colloquy.*—O celestial food, O bread of angels! "O panem quotidianum," "O daily bread!" O that I could so eat Thee every day, that I might by means of Thee live a life celestial and divine; "O vinum germinans virgines," "O wine springing forth virgins,"(7) and cheering "the heart of man," come, I beseech Thee, and purify my soul with Thy virginal purity, and make me glad, and inebriate me with the force of Thy divine love. Amen.

3. The third cause was, to signify that as bread is made of many grains of wheat, ground and made into one mass, and wine of many grapes, trodden together in the wine press,—even so *this divine food and drink requires hearts united together in true charity*, and it is instituted to cause this union of many faithful in one spirit, whence it is that it is called Communio, the Communion, that is a community and union of many amongst themselves, and of all with Jesus Christ, of whose spirit all participate. And, if to attain to this union and community, it be needful that I suffer myself to be ground upon the mill, trodden upon, and bruised in pieces, by mortifying all that which is in

(6) Joan. vi. 58. (7) Zach. ix. 17; Psal. ciii. 15.

me of the old man, I will offer myself to it right willingly, in order that I may taste the sweetness of this divine meat, and unite myself to Jesus Christ.

*Colloquy.*—O most sweet Jesus, who didst unite Thy blessed body to the forms of bread that had first been ground; and Thy precious blood to the accidents of wine, that had been trodden upon, and past the press; I here offer myself to be ground and bruised, trodden upon, and even reduced into dust for the preserving of Thy love, and of union and concord with my brethren, that Thou, O my God, vouchsafe to unite Thyself to me in this life by abundant grace, and after this life in the perpetual union of Thy eternal glory. Amen.

---

## MEDITATION XIV.

### OF SIX MYSTICAL THINGS DONE AND SAID BY OUR LORD IN HIS CONSECRATION OF THE BREAD AND WINE.

#### POINT I.

Consider how our Lord Jesus Christ, with an exterior gesture, grave, modest, and devout, sufficient to cause reverence and admiration in His disciples, took from the table, "*in His holy and venerable hands,*"(1) a loaf of bread, and though He might have consecrated it as it stood upon the table, yet would *He hold it in both His hands,* to signify thereby that the conversion of this bread into His body was a work of His omnipotence and liberality, and one of His meritorious works, all which are signified by the hands.

1. First, it was a work of *His omnipotence* as He was God, and of the excellent power that He had as He was man, given to Him by His Father, "who had given Him

(1) Vide Canon. Missæ, "Qui pridie," &c.

all things into His hands," with which He wrought this stupendous conversion, insomuch that He held Himself wholly and entire in His own hands, and He Himself not moving from the place where He was, He gave Himself whole and entire into the hands of His disciples, that they might eat Him.

*Colloquy.*—O the greatness of the power of Almighty God; "O change of the right hand of the highest!"(2) I rejoice, my dear Saviour, that Thy hands are so powerful; change me, I beseech Thee, wholly by their virtue, and let Thy right hand in such a manner transform me, that I may receive the virtue of this most sovereign bread. Amen.

2. Secondly, He here showed a work of *His infinite liberality*, for as the prophet David says:—"All expect of Thee that Thou give them food in season...When Thou openest Thy hand they shall all be filled with" (3) bounty and benediction, for so liberally does He give us this heavenly meat, and opens both His hands that He may replenish us with His benedictions and His virtues. What greater liberality can there be than to give Himself to us wholly and entirely, without reserving anything to Himself, that He may be our ransom, our food, and our companion, and that gratis and freely, without any profit to Himself, but only because He is good and liberal of Himself? With this consideration I will humbly crave of our Lord that He will vouchsafe to let me kiss and reverence these His powerful and liberal hands, in thanksgiving for the favours He has shown me, glorifying Him for all the wonders that He has wrought by them.

3. This work was of His hands, *that by His merits, and by the labour of His hands*, and in the sweat of His brows,

(2) Psal. lxxvii. 11. (3) Psal. ciii. 27, and cxliv. 15

He earned this bread that He has given us. Besides, His will is, that this bread be the meat, not of the idle and the lazy, but of such as live by the labour of their hands; and for this cause, as the Psalmist says, "blessed," disposing themselves to eat of this heavenly bread, by the exercise of good works, and after eating it, prosecuting the labour of their hands in His holy service.(4)

*Colloquy.*—O celestial Adam, who, in imitation of the terrestrial, hast laboured in Thy sweat to earn the bread that Thou wast afterwards to give to Thy children; I praise and glorify Thee that it has pleased Thee to bestow on me freely part of that which Thou hast so dearly bought, and which has cost Thee so much to earn. It is most reasonable, dear Lord, that I also travel and labour with my hands, lest I be found unworthy to eat this divine bread, for it is written, that "if any man will not work, neither let him eat." (5)

POINT II.

1. Christ our Lord, holding the bread in His holy hands, *lifted up His eyes to heaven*, to signify(6) that the bread that He meant to give them was not bread of earth, but the bread of heaven, the bread of angels, supersubstantial bread, given by His eternal Father, in accomplishment of that which He had promised in a sermon, when He said:—"Moses gave you not bread from heaven, but my Father giveth you the true bread from heaven. I am the living bread which came down from heaven."(7) He lifted up, therefore, His eyes to heaven, with the intention of moving His disciples, and all of us, to elevate our hearts to heaven, with great affections of hope, of prayer, and of purity, hoping to receive this meat from the hands

(4) Psal. cxxvii. 2. (5) 2 Thess. iii. 10.
(6) S. Tho. 3, p. q. lxxxiii. art. 4, ad. 2.
(7) Joan. vi. 7, 32, 51.

of our celestial Father who is in heaven, and craving it of Him with a devout and affectionate prayer;—finally disposing ourselves to it with the purity of a celestial life, accomplishing in this what the Church says in the preface of the holy mass: "Sursum corda," "lift up your hearts;" to which we answer: "Habemus ad Dominum," "we have already lifted them up to our Lord."

*Colloquy.*—O our Father who art in heaven, lift up, we beseech Thee, our hearts there where Thou art, and give us this day this supersubstantial bread, that came down from heaven, to give to the world a life celestial. Amen.

2. After this, "Gratias egit," "*He gave thanks*" to His eternal Father for so inestimable a favour as it pleased Him, by His hands, to impart to the world, in giving and bestowing upon it, for nourishment and food, such a kind of bread; teaching us by this that this divine bread ought to be eaten by us with great affection and thanksgiving, both before and after receiving it. And for this cause it is called "Eucharistia," which signifies "Thanksgiving." O what fervent and most hearty thanks did Christ our Lord give in that hour! For, if He gave thanks for the barley loaves with which he fed five thousand men in the desert, how much greater and more hearty thanks did He give for this bread of heaven, which He gives to all men in the desert of this world? For, according to the measure of the benefit, the affection of gratitude increases; and considering that I am no way able to render Him due thanks in that measure to which I am bound, I will offer to Him those same which He Himself gave to His Father, and I will receive the eternal sacrament that He has instituted for this effect.

3. This done, "Benedixit," "*He blessed the bread;*" so

that He not only blessed His eternal Father with a blessing of praise and thanksgiving, but He also blessed the bread itself with the blessing of prayer, able to effect that which He blessed it for. For we bless a thing with desire and prayer only, desiring some good thing, and craving at God's hands that He would vouchsafe to confer the same; but Christ our Lord blessed the bread, not only in demanding of His Father the conversion and transubstantiation which He intended to make, but at the same time communicating to it divine virtues, and imprinting in it so great a good and excellence, as to change it into His own blessed body, and to make it the beginning and cause of all spiritual benedictions which, by His means, descend from heaven for our salvation.

*Colloquy.*—O efficacy of the benediction of our Lord Jesus, bless me, my sweet Saviour, I beseech Thee, for Thy blessing, or "*well saying*," is also "*well doing*," that being blessed by Thee, I may come to eat of this most blessed bread, and be made partaker of those benedictions, which by it Thou dost bestow upon us. Amen.

4. This done, the fourth mysterious action was, that "*He broke*" the bread, for it was not without great mystery that He took into His hands a whole loaf, and then divided it, and gave to His apostles.—i. To signify that all of them were to eat of *one and the same bread*, and to drink of one and the same drink; and that, therefore, all of them were to be united in one and the same love, because they were all to be one among themselves.—ii. To give us to understand that this bread *might be divided*, and notwithstanding that which lay hid within it, *remain entire*, for His whole body was in each part of it, and in every morsel He gave to His disciples, there was as much in the whole loaf.—iii. To signify that this divine bread ought

not to be eaten whole, and as it were at one morsel, but divided and *parted by meditation*, seriously ruminating that which lies hid in it, namely the true flesh of Jesus Christ, His most precious blood, His most holy soul, His divinity, together with all His merit,—for devoutly to ponder every one of these apart, is spiritually to divide this bread, the better to eat it.

*Colloquy.*—O my Redeemer, forasmuch as I am such a weakling, that I am not able to divide this bread, nor yet can eat it, unless it be divided; divide it for me, I beseech Thee, with Thy blessed hand, that I may with profit eat, tasting very particularly, that which is contained and hidden it. Amen.

POINT III.

After our Lord had broken the bread, He gave it to His disciples, saying: "Take ye and eat, this is my body."

1. In this consider these words, "*He gave it to His disciples.*"(8) O precious gift, in which He gave to them all He was, and all He had, and that of His mere grace only, because He loves to give as a friend.

*Colloquy.*—O infinite charity! O immense bounty! Which does not here will itself to be for itself, but to give itself to us. O most liberal giver, give Thyself, I beseech Thee, to me, seeing that I am also Thy disciple; and although I no way merit such a gift, yet know I well that Thou dost not give it because we merit it, but because Thou art good, and art delighted to give us a gift so great, that it surpasses all kind of merits.

2. The apostles had such an esteem of this blessed bread, and bore so great a reverence to it, on account of the internal light of a lively faith, that our Lord had com-

(0) Mat. xxvi. 20.

municated to them, that if He had not said to them these words:—" Accipite et comedite omnes;"—" Take and eat you all of this," they had never dared to have taken the same into their hands, much less to have tasted of it. This was, therefore, the reason that He commanded them, saying:—" Take this bread, which I do not give you only to kiss and adore, or to elevate it above your heads, or to keep it by you as a precious relic for your consolation, but in order that you may eat it, and be sustained by it. 'Comedite ex eo omnes.'—' Eat of it, therefore, every one of you,' and let not any one excuse himself, under pretence of humility; for I give it to you all that are my true disciples, and not only to those that are present, but to those also who shall succeed you, until the ending of the world."

*Colloquy.*—O dearly beloved of my soul, seeing that Thou dost command me to eat of this divine meat, I will take it, and will adore it, and then I will eat it, to obey Thee, as also, in order that I may enjoy Thy sweet presence, hoping that Thou wilt vouchsafe to supply my unworthiness with the abundance of Thy infinite mercy and liberality. Amen.

---

## MEDITATION XV.

OF THE POWER GIVEN BY CHRIST TO HIS APOSTLES TO DO THE SAME THAT HE HAD DONE; AND OF THE POWER HAD BY PRIESTS AT THIS DAY, OF CONSECRATING THE SACRIFICE OF THE BODY AND BLOOD OF OUR LORD.

### POINT I.

Consider how our Lord, after He had instituted this most blessed Sacrament, said to His apostles:—" *Hoc facite in meam commemorationem.*"—" Do this for a commemoration of me." In which words it appears that He gave them power to do the very same that He had done, converting the bread into His body, and the wine into His precious blood, commanding them, and all priests, that should succeed them in priestly dignity, to do the same, and in the manner that He had done.(1)

1. Upon this so friendly a command consider, first, the infinite charity of Christ our Lord, in that *He would give power over His true body and blood*, not to the angels of heaven, *but to men living here on earth*, so that they, representing His very person, might truly say upon the bread, "Hoc est Corpus meum,"—"This is my body;" and in virtue of these words, convert the bread into the body of Christ, in the manner that the same Lord converted it, with such multitude of miracles, that they exceed those miracles of giving sight to the blind, health to the sick, and life to the dead.

*Colloquy.*—O most loving Jesus, what couldst Thou do more for men than to give them a power which far exceeds the dignity of angels? Thou hadst made man "a little less than the angels,"(2) appointing him over the works of Thy hands; and now Thou dost exalt him higher than they, in giving him power to draw from heaven Thy body and blood into their own hands. Let all Thy creatures bless Thee, O Lord, for this infinite favour, and let my soul for ever sing Thy praises. Amen.

2. But there is yet much more to be considered in the infinite liberality of this divine Lord, who *would not restrain or limit this power* to a certain number of *persons*, nor to certain determinate *times*, to the end that all might enjoy the fruit of this Sacrament in great abundance. For He might have ordained that there should be but one

(1) S. Tho. 3, p. q. lxxxi. art. 1, et in supplem. q. iv; Luc. xxii. 19, 1 Cor. xi. 25, &c.

(2) Psal. viii. 6.

priest in the whole world, or else but one in every province, or in every town but one. Likewise that the priests, unless they were most holy, should not have power to consecrate, or else that this Sacrament, like to that of the Paschal lamb,(3) should not be celebrated but in one certain place, and that but once every year: yet none of all these restrictions would our blessed Saviour's liberality admit, but He would give full faculty that there might be many priests, and that they, though never so wicked, should be able to consecrate at all times, in all places, and every day, in every church or oratory of the least village or hamlet that was in the world.

*Colloquy.*—O liberality of our Lord, without all measure! Didst Thou not, O Saviour, know our nature and condition, who, though a thing be precious if it be not also rare, do not make any great estimation of it? Wherefore then wouldst Thou that there should be so many priests, and that all of them should have full power to celebrate so often this divine Sacrament? But Thy love, dear Lord, is without bound and measure, which patiently suffers that bad men abuse Thy gifts and graces, that Thou mayest do good to the good, who will make good use of them. Oh that we were all so liberal in serving Thee without bound or measure, as Thou art liberal to gratify us without bound or measure.

3. Besides all this, much more worthy to be pondered, is the infinite humility and obedience which our Lord shows at the voice and word of priests. For, from this instant has He obliged Himself, even unto the end of the world, to *come down, at the voice of the priest, as often as he consecrates,* without delay or hesitation, at what time, and in what place soever he shall perform the same, even

(3) Exod. xii. 46.

though the priest should be ever so wicked, and also consecrate to a damnable end, even were it with intention to tread Him under his feet, or else to cast Him into the fire, and all this in favour, and for the good of the elect.

*Colloquy.*—O vast and immense ocean of the charity of our Lord Jesus! Is it possible that God should obey "the voice of a man,"(4) and that not of a holy man, such as Joshua was, but even the voice of as vile a traitor as was Judas, that He should suffer Himself to be handled with hands so imbued in blood; and that Almighty God should submit Himself to so many, and so great indignities? O dear Lord, how great a friend art Thou to humility and obedience, seeing that Thou wouldst every day give to us such singular and so rare examples of it! By this example I am to learn to obey my superiors in every lawful thing they shall command me, though they themselves be perverse, and of depraved intentions, fulfilling their commandments with an obedience punctual, prompt, and persevering until death, never wearied in obeying, after the example of Christ, who is never wearied in accomplishing that which once He promised.

POINT II.

In the selfsame words, "Hoc facite," "Do this," our Lord wills and *commands* His apostles, and the priests of His church, to *offer the same sacrifice that He here instituted*, of His precious body and blood, under the accidents of bread and wine, in place of the sacrifices of the old law; pondering also the excellency of this sacrifice, and the goods which come from it.

1. First, then, a sacrifice is an *oblation* which man makes *to Almighty God* of *anything that is pleasing to Him*, thereby to reverence and honour Him, in protestation of

(4) Jos. x. 14.

His infinite excellency and majesty. Now then, what thing can we offer to the eternal Father more precious, or that can be more pleasing to Him, than His own dear Son, true God and true man, of whom He has said:—"Hic est filius meus dilectus in quo mihi complacui."—"This is my beloved Son, in whom I am well pleased."(5)

*Colloquy.*—O how much are we bound to Thee, Saviour of the world, for having given us for a sacrament and sacrifice the best and dearest thing that Thou couldst possibly give us; no other than Thine own self: and besides, in order that the oblation, though otherwise most precious, should not be rejected on account of the unworthiness of him that offers it, Thou Thyself wouldst be the principal offerer, as being an eternal "priest according to the order of Melchisedech,"(6) Thyself offering this celestial bread and wine by the hands of earthly priests!

2. That this sacrifice is "*eminenter*," that is, by an eminent and superexcellent prerogative, effectual in three things, for which all sacrifices are ordained,—namely, in *satisfaction for our sins;—in thanksgiving for benefits received;*—and for *obtaining at the hands of Almighty God*, such good things as we desire, whether temporal or eternal. For these ends, therefore, I will hear Mass, setting up all the sails of confidence to the uttermost, considering that in this Sacrifice there is sufficient ground and foundation for all this, hoping, by the means of this Sacrifice, to appease the wrath of the eternal Father, to pay the debts of my sins, and to obtain such gifts and graces as I shall demand of Him. And by charity will I also extend all this to the good of my neighbours, as well living as departed, and in purgatory, this being sufficient for them all, speaking myself, the better to stir up and quicken my

(5) Mat. iii. 17. (6) Psal. cix. 4; Heb. vii. 17.

confidence, in this manner:—"What sins can there be found so enormous, for which, by virtue of this divine Sacrifice of the body and blood of our Lord, offered upon the cross for all sinners, pardon may not be obtained?"—And what pains due to our most grievous faults will not be acquitted by such payment as this, offering the same satisfactions that our Lord Jesus offered to pay and satisfy for the same?—Finally, what good thing can there be demanded at the merciful hands of Almighty God, that I shall not obtain by the means of such an oblation, in which He Himself is so sovereignly delighted?

*Colloquy.*—O eternal Father, if the oblation of the innocent Abel was so grateful to Thee, that his brother Cain, of mere envy, unjustly slew him for it, how much more grateful will the oblation of Thy innocent Son Jesus be to Thee, who was unjustly slain through the envy of his brethren, the Hebrew people, He offering His life to redeem us from death? Accept, O most merciful Father, this holy Sacrifice in remission of my sins; accept it also in thanksgiving for the innumerable benefits which I have received from Thy most liberal hand; and by it vouchsafe, I beseech Thee, to give me here the abundance of Thy graces, and hereafter life everlasting. Amen.

POINT III.

1. In those same words our Saviour likewise charged His apostles to do the same *in remembrance of Him*, and especially in memory of His death and Passion. In which I may ponder how Christ our Lord offered for our sakes two Sacrifices,—the one bloody upon the cross,—the other unbloody at His last supper, which He would have to be the representation of the other: thereby to testify to us the great desire He has that we should be mindful of Him, and of His most sacred Passion, in consideration of the

profit that we reap by it; for this was the occasion for which He instituted this Sacrament and Sacrifice, in which He Himself remains, that He might the better stir us up to remembrance of Him, and at the same time move us to the exercise of the three acts of thanksgiving; which are, —to acknowledge and esteem the benefit,—to praise and extol the benefactor,—and to render Him service for the same.

2. To this effect ponder how Christ, when at any time He imparted any notable benefit to His people, likewise *ordained some kind of thanksgiving to be returned for the same*, —a thing that much imports us; for if we expect to receive at His hands new benefits, it is reasonable that we show ourselves thankful for those received. And as this benefit of the Passion, together with the gifts and graces that result from it, could not be sufficiently or worthily acknowledged by men, He would supply our default by making Himself our oblation, that so we might offer the same to Himself in thanksgiving for the great gifts, benefits, and graces which He has bestowed upon us. And as this oblation itself is a new benefit to us, there remains no better means of showing ourselves grateful to Him for it than by renewing its memory, by endeavouring to be present every day at this venerable Sacrifice, and spiritually to receive this divine Sacrament, and sometimes also sacramentally, as we have said in the first part, the thirty-third and thirty-fourth meditations.

*Colloquy.*—O most sweet Saviour, seeing that Thou dost vouchsafe to remain with us, to excite and revive our memory by Thy presence, grant me, I beseech Thee, that I be ever mindful of Thee, as Thou art mindful of me, and that I may incessantly praise Thee for the innumerable benefits that I have received of Thee. Amen.

3. Our Lord wills also that we celebrate this mystery, in *memory of the heroic virtues* which He practised during His life and at His death;—of all which virtues this venerable Sacrament is a lively portraiture. For, as He came into the world, not only to redeem us, but also to show us examples of all virtue, so He comes into this Sacrament to sanctify us, and also to renew the memory of the same examples, which being both present and perpetual, very much move us to imitate them. And so I may imagine with myself that He says to me from hence, as He did to His apostles:—"I have given you an example, that as I have done to you, so do you also."(7) "Learn of me, because I am meek and humble of heart."(8) These virtues are charity, mercy, liberality, humility, patience, with perseverance in all these virtues until the end of the world, as we have already considered in this meditation, and in the preceding, and shall more largely in the sixth part, in order that we may fully declare all that concerns this sovereign benefit. The imitation of these virtues ought to be one of the principal fruits that we are to draw from these meditations, humbly beseeching our Lord that He will vouchsafe to assist us with His holy grace to put them in execution.

*Colloquy.*—O God of virtues, who "hast made a remembrance"(9) of them, by giving Thyself in "food to them that fear" Thee; grant, I beseech Thee, that I may meditate upon them, and so participate in these sacred mysteries, that I may imitate Thy resplendent examples. Amen.

(7) Joan. xiii. 13. (8) Mat. xi. 29. (9) Psal. cx. 4.

# MEDITATION XVI.

ON OUR LORD'S DISCOURSE AT SUPPER, TELLING TO HIS APOSTLES THAT ONE OF THEM SHOULD BETRAY HIM; AND JUDAS' DEPARTURE FOR THAT PURPOSE.

POINT I.

Our Lord being at the table with His twelve apostles' became suddenly troubled in spirit, and said with gr ea feeling and grief:—"Amen, I say unto you, that one of you" who sits with me at the table, and "who dippeth his hand with me in the dish, he shall betray me.—The Son of man indeed goeth as it is written of Him, but woe be to that man by whom the Son of man shall be betrayed. It were better for him if that man had never been born."(1)

1. Concerning this point, ponder, first, *the cause of this trouble*, and inward grief of our Lord Jesus; which was, to see Judas amongst the rest of the apostles, a man perverse, incorrigible, and reprobate of Almighty God; who, though he were but one, was notwithstanding sufficient to trouble and afflict our Saviour, and to poison the satisfaction He felt in being with so many good men and His elect;—not that He abhorred the person of Judas, but because He had his sin in an extreme abomination, particularly his detestable ingratitude, after having received so many benefits at His hands; this His divine majesty would declare with words of great weight and import, saying:—"Unus ex vobis," "one of you," whom I have chosen for an apostle, to whom I have discovered my secrets, and have given power to work miracles, whose feet I have washed, and to whom I have given my body to eat, and my blood to drink, who has eaten with me from

(1) Mat. xxvi. 21; Marc. xiv. 18; Luc. xxii. 21; Joan. xiii. 21.

the same dish, and drunk with me in the same cup, "Tradet me,"—this same man shall betray me to death.

*Colloquy.*—O good Jesus, no wonder Thou art troubled in spirit, and dost of Thy own accord admit this trouble and sadness, considering that this detestable crime gives Thee sufficient cause. I am most heartily sorry for the cause I have given to Thy afflictions, by my great ingratitude, of which I purpose by Thy holy assistance, to amend myself.

2. Consider secondly, *two reasons* that moved our Lord to speak in this manner, in the presence of His apostles.

i. The first was, to make them all know that *He was God, who knew well the heart of every one*, and what they plotted against Him. And this His knowledge was one of the circumstances that most augmented His afflictions and torments: according to that of the Wise man, saying: "He that addeth knowledge, addeth also labour,"(2) which knowledge He used not as an instrument to revenge Himself of His enemies, but that by means of it He might suffer the more for them.

ii. The second reason, and that a very particular one, was, the great *compassion that He had for Judas*, being most desirous by the arguments He used here, which were very forcible and efficacious for converting a sinner, to reclaim him, and to draw him again to His grace and favour. Of which the first was, by declaring to him that He perfectly beheld his most secret thoughts, together with his wicked practices and intentions, and consequently that He was his God, and his judge, from whom nothing could be hid.—The second, by overthrowing his false foundation upon which he had built and grounded his sin; for, as we observed before, Judas thought to excuse his malice with this device, that as our Lord was to die

(2) Eccles. i. 18.

by the hands of the Jews, it was no great matter to sell Him to them, to get a piece of money by it. To this thought and internal reasoning, our Lord makes answer in these words:—True it is indeed, "the Son of man goeth as it is written of Him; but woe be to that man by whom the Son of man shall be betrayed." As if He had said:—"The decree of my Father that I must die, does not any way force thee to betray me, thou hast free liberty not to do it, and it is thy fault in seeking to effect it."—The third was, thundering against him terrible *threats*, saying: "It were better for him if that man had never been born,"(3) rather than to commit so grievous a sin, for which sin he will be condemned to eternal fire, where he will wish that he had not, nor ever had any being, that so he might escape the torments, but this will not be granted him.

These three reasons, therefore, ought to make me *tremble at every mortal sin*, considering that it cannot be hid from God, nor attributed to any other cause, than to my own perverse will; and lastly, that this evil is so grievous, that it had been better not to have had any being at all, than for doing it to be damned everlastingly.

POINT II.

Consider next, *what happened to the other apostles* upon this sentence of our Saviour, and what our Saviour did in this case.

1. All the apostles became presently exceedingly heavy, and began to ask our Lord, one by one,—"*Nunquid ego sum Domine?*"—"*Is it I, Lord?*"(4) Where we may see how good souls fear to offend, even where there is no cause at all of fear. For by reason of the great love they bear to Almighty God, they are so averse from all sin,

(3) Mat. xxvi. 25. (4) Mat. xxvi. 22.

that they are frightened to see its very shadow, and to understand that the least sign or trace of it should be amongst them.

*Colloquy.*—Oh that I had the love of Jesus so deeply engraven in my heart, that the very apprehension alone of offending His majesty might make me tremble. Amen.

2. Our Lord, with His accustomed charity and providence, *would not tax this traitor publicly*, who was yet unknown, lest He should have given occasion to the other apostles of anger and indignation against him; teaching us by this example, to conceal the sins of our neighbour, although they are upon the very point of being punished by some other means; as also to take away all occasion of discord and sedition from amongst the community in which we live. This treason He declared only to two persons;—the one was Judas himself, who with a brazen impudence, that he might the better hide and cover his sin, did as the rest had done, asking whether it were he that our Saviour meant. "Nunquid ego sum Rabbi?"—"Is it I, Rabbi?" To whom our Lord, without either change in His countenance or any the least motion of passion, or indignation at this traitor, answered him softly in his ear, lest the rest might have understood Him: "Tu dixisti." "Thou hast said it."(5) It is even thyself that I speak of, who art to betray me, but thou hast yet time to repent thee if thou wilt, and I will pardon thee.—The other person to whom our Saviour revealed this treason, was His well-beloved S. John, who was then leaning upon His breast, that he might be a witness of the charity He used towards Judas. "Ille est," says He, "cui ego intinctum panem porrexero."—"He it is to whom I shall reach

(5) Ibid. 25.

bread dipped," which, moreover, He gave to Judas with great signs, as it may be presumed, of love, and even as a mother does to her child, or one dear friend to another, to show by this how far the charity of our Lord Jesus extends itself, who having been troubled and grieved by the treason of this man, did not yet cease to cherish and use him very kindly, endeavouring thereby to win him over and draw him from his wicked design.

*Colloquy.*—I humbly thank Thee, my most loving Saviour, who art never weary of heaping coals of fire (6) upon the head of him that abhors Thee, alluring him with this delicious morsel, to the end Thou mightest bend and mollify his obdurate heart.

POINT III.

The wretched miscreant, Judas, *took this "morsel,"* remaining, notwithstanding, still obstinate in his devilish resolution, as if he had said to our Lord:—"Thou dost but lose Thy labour in using me thus kindly, for I am fully resolved for all this, to sell and betray Thee, and to recover the money that I lost for Thy sake." In chastisement of which obstinacy, two fearful punishments fell upon him.

1. The first punishment was, to permit that "after the morsel *Satan should enter into him.*"(7) Twice, therefore, did the Devil enter into Judas, as appears in the Gospel. First, to persuade him to sell Christ our Lord, to which he assented, as has been said;—secondly, to make him promptly execute the same, urging him to go out of that hall to put in execution the execrable treason he had determined upon: and this happened to him even as he took that morsel of bread. By which we see, how dangerous it is to abuse the graces of Almighty God, and the signs of

(6) Prov. xxv. 22. (7) Joan. xiii. 27.

love that He shows to us; and consequently how dangerous it is to receive in a bad state the bread of life, dipped in the most precious blood contained in Christ's body, and given to us in sign of the perfect love which Christ bears us; for, in punishment of this extreme presumption and ingratitude "after the morsel," the Devil enters and possesses the receiver's heart, instigating him to other innumerable and abominable sins.

2. The second punishment was, that our *Lord Jesus said to him*:—"*Quod facis, fac citius.*"—"*That which thou doest, do it quickly.*" By these words *abandoning him*, as it were, and withdrawing from him His holy grace, permitting him to accomplish his damnable design. As if He had said:—"Hitherto have I retained thee in my company and in this room, doing to thee many kindnesses and favours, that thou shouldst repent thee of thy sin; but, seeing thou wilt not, I leave thee to thyself, and permit thee to go and put thy design in execution. Seeing, therefore, that thou art resolved to do it, 'Fac citius;' dispatch it quickly, for I am more desirous to die than thou art to deliver me to death."

*Colloquy.*—O immense charity of Jesus, O devilish obstinacy of Judas! For how greatly soever Judas desired to sell Jesus, yet much more did Jesus desire to be sold, and to be delivered to death to save Judas. But when obstinate Malice resists Charity, her sister Justice enters to revenge the injury, and sentences him to be abandoned, who through rebellion will not be cured, according to that of the prophet Jeremy, "We would have cured Babylon, but she is not healed; let us forsake her."(8) Wherefore, O my soul, sing to thy God mercy and judgment, so that if His mercy does not allure thee to that which is good, His judg-

(8) Jer. li. 9.

ment may divert thee from that which is evil, and the fear of a just judge, extort that which the love of a merciful Father cannot obtain. Amen.

### POINT IV.

Judas having now this permission and license, presently went out of the room; then our Lord said to His apostles: —" Nunc clarificatus est filius hominis," &c.—" Now is the Son of man glorified, and God is glorified in Him," (9) and He will by and by glorify Him. By these words He intended to teach us two things of great consolation.

1. The first, that by the departure of Judas He remained glorified, because His college and flock remained now pure and holy, even as it will be at the day of judgment, when He will come to judge in great glory, separating the wicked from the good and elected. As, therefore, Christ was troubled and grieved to see Judas in the company of His elect, so was He glad, and gloried to see him separated from them.

*Colloquy.*—O that I were so happy as that Jesus Christ might glory to have me in His holy company; permit not, good Lord, that my sins ever rise to so great a heap, that Thou shouldst esteem it an honour to Thee to chase and expel me from Thy company.

2. The second was, that with the departure of Judas He made a beginning of His Passion, by which He was glorified, for He reputed it His glory to die for the glory of His Father; and God was glorified in Him, and did glorify Him with miracles in His Passion, and soon after with the glory of His resurrection, by which we may see with what eyes Christ our Lord beheld His ignominies, seeing that He called them His glory, as also with what

(9) Joan. xiii. 31.

eyes God beholds the ignominies of His elect, since He glorifies Himself in them, and by the occasion of them glorifies and honours His elect with a surpassing glory, to teach me by this to glory in suffering for Christ, since Christ is glorified in what I suffer, who also will glorify me for what I suffer.

*Colloquy.*—Wherefore, O my soul, "glory" with the apostle in the "tribulations," and in the "cross of Christ,"(10) considering that from them, and by them, Christ is glorified; to whom be all honour and glory, for ever and ever. Amen.

---

## MEDITATION XVII.

ON THE CONTENTION AMONG THE APOSTLES CONCERNING SUPERIORITY, OUR LORD'S REPREHENSION OF THEM, AND HIS ADMONITION TO THEM OF THE SCANDAL WHICH THEY SHOULD TAKE IN HIM THAT NIGHT, AND PREDICTION TO PETER OF HIS DENIAL.

### POINT I.

Our Lord having told His apostles that He was then "glorified," and that His Father would glorify Him, there arose suddenly "*a strife amongst them, as to which of them should seem to be the greater.*" (1)

1. In this we may see the vivacity and *activity of this passion of honour*, which is ready upon every slight occasion to break out and show itself; for those who but a very little before were overwhelmed by the news that one of them should betray their master, now enter into contention as to which of them shall be most intimate with Him, and who greatest and most honoured. This contention our Lord presently cut short, telling them, first, that in His school they were to proceed in another manner than

(10) 2 Cor. xii.; Gal. vi. 14. (1) Luc. xxii. 24.

in the world, and among the kings of the nations, for whoever must be greatest among them ought to endeavour to be as the least, and he that desired to have the precedence was to be made to serve the rest, in the same manner as He Himself was among them, that is, serving them with humility, as we have already noted in the twenty-third meditation of the third part.

2. Then to encourage them to this, He added:—"*You are they who have continued with me in my temptations*" and tribulations; go on, therefore, and continue in the same, and do not aim at nor hunt after pre-eminencies and superiorities, for I dispose and ordain by my Testament, to give my Kingdom as my Father has given it to me; that is to say, I ordain that you enter into my Kingdom by humiliations and tribulations, as I myself enter by them.

*Colloquy.*—O sweet Jesus, I accept of the legacy of Thy Kingdom, with this condition of perseverance in tribulations for Thy holy service; give me, therefore, I beseech Thee, the gift of perseverance, lest otherwise I lose the crown that is promised to the same. Amen.

3. Hence I will learn, that if I were to enter into contention with anybody, it should not be for any point of pre-eminency, but rather *for matter of humiliation*, desiring even the lowest place, and to submit myself to all, for this is the way to become the greatest in the Kingdom of Christ.

POINT II.

Consider other sorrowful news which our Lord imparted to His apostles, saying:—"*All you shall be scandalized in me this night.* For it is written, *I will strike the shepherd, and the sheep of the flock shall be dispersed;* but after I shall be risen again, I will go before you into Galilee." (2)

(2) Mat. xxvi. 31; Marc. xiv. 27; Zach. xiii. 7.

As if He would say:—"You, my apostles, whom I have so affected and favoured, shall be so much scandalized to see what will come to pass this night concerning me, that you will forsake me, and will either lose your faith or remain very doubtful and staggering in it, but do not despair for this, for I shall rise again, and gather you together in Galilee."

1. This He said to them partly to humble them and to lay the smoke of their ambition, admonishing them beforehand of the frailty and imbecility they were to fall into; partly, also, to preserve them from despair, and lest they should have been utterly overwhelmed through grief and discouragement, promising them that He would visit them. These two points shall teach me to live in fear that I be not scandalized, nor forsake my Lord Jesus, and if at any time I have forsaken Him, yet not to despair, seeing that He shows Himself so ready and gentle to receive me again.

2. To this St. Peter made answer:—"*Although all shall be scandalized in Thee, I will never be scandalized;*" on the contrary,......I am ready to go to prison, and to "die with Thee." (3) In these words we may see that fervour without humility is the cause of many errors, for St. Peter committed here *three.*

i. The first was, to contradict Christ, or not to give credit to what He said;—ii. The second was, to presume to himself more than all the rest, preferring himself before them;—iii. The third was, to promise himself more force than indeed he had, and to vaunt it. Hence it came that the rest of the apostles, that they might not seem inferior to St. Peter, and be taxed with cowardice, said all the same, that they were likewise ready to follow our Lord, even to death; in which, if they had spoken with humili-

(3) Mat. xxvi. 33; Luc. xxvii. 33; Joan. xiii. 37.

ty, beseeching their master to assist them, they had not erred, but that which proceeded from presumption was no way pleasing to Christ our Lord, who might well have answered them with that of the prophet:—"We have heard the pride of Moab, he is exceeding proud; I know, saith the Lord, his boasting, and that the strength thereof is not according to it, neither hath it endeavoured to do according as it was able," (4) which saying was even literally fulfilled in the apostles.

3. But our Saviour, letting alone the rest of the apostles, turned Himself towards St. Peter, and said to him:—"Amen, I say to thee, *the cock shall not crow till thou deny me thrice*;"(5) which was as much as to say, "Thou that presumest of thyself more than the rest, wilt be this night scandalized more than all the rest, renouncing and abjuring me thrice in that time." Where it seems that our Lord permitted these three denials in St. Peter, in punishment of the three errors which he had committed in those words he spoke, as we shall see hereafter. This shall admonish me not to presume anything of myself, not to prefer myself before others, but, on the contrary, fearing with humility my own frailty, I will beseech our Lord that He does not withdraw His holy hand from me, seeing that I am one, who although all be not scandalized, yet unless He assist and favour me I shall be scandalized.

*Colloquy.*—Behold, O my God, my great weakness, and have compassion of it, for unless Thou assistest me in each occasion of scandal that shall assail me, I shall be sure to fall, and to offend Thee.

POINT III.

Consider another warning which our Lord gave St. Peter, and by the way to the rest of the apostles also, saying:—"Simon, Simon, behold *Satan hath desired to have*

(4) Jer. xlviii. 29. (5) Joan. xiii. 38.

*you, that he may sift you as wheat;* but I have prayed for thee, that thy faith fail not, and thou being once converted, confirm thy brethren." (6)

In these words are contained *three instructions* of great moment.

1. That Satan their adversary had demanded license to tempt them, without which license he could not have done it, no more than he was able to tempt Job, (7) or so much as enter into a herd of swine (8) to hurt and injure them; moreover that he had obtained this leave, because it was convenient that it should be so, for although the Devil intended to trouble them, and scatter them, as he that sifts wheat most narrowly, yet, notwithstanding, our Lord intended to turn this temptation to His own glory, making them by this means more humble hereafter, and more like wheat when it is well purged, and has no more chaff or cockle in it. This thing ought to comfort me when I am tempted, making me imagine with myself that the temptation is the sieve, in which, though the Devil furiously tosses me up and down, not with any intention to cleanse or purify me, but quite to overthrow me, yet God's holy protection is wont to encompass the sieve, and to preserve him that is sifted, and so holds the Devil's hand, that instead of overturning him he purifies and perfects him, which protection will never be wanting to me, if with humility and confidence I have recourse to the mercy of Almighty God.

2. The second instruction was, that He had prayed for St. Peter, lest his faith should fail or be lost, giving him by this to understand that it had without all doubt perished, and that Satan had prevailed against him, and utterly overthrown him, but for His prayer and protection.

(6) Luc. xxii. 31. (7) Job. i. 12. (8) Matt. viii. 31.

*Colloquy.*—O most sweet Jesus, I beseech Thy divine Majesty, that if at any time Thou shalt give leave to Satan to sift me like wheat, Thou wilt vouchsafe to be my advocate and protector, for fear either my faith should fail me, or my charity should diminish: but convert, O Lord, the temptation to my good, (9) that the affliction may serve to purify me in the sieve, separating from me all that shall be found bad or earthly. Amen.

3. The third instruction was in these words:—"And thou being once converted, confirm thy brethren." In which words the mercy of our Lord, with which He tempered His former rigour, declares itself; for, as He had revealed to him that He would deny Him thrice, so did He reveal to him that he should be converted, lest seeing himself overthrown, he might fall into despair; moreover, in this He exhorts him to show himself grateful for the favour which he was to receive in his conversion, by helping to convert and confirm his brethren. Where we may note the charity of our Lord towards those that are His, for He did not say to him, "when thou art converted look that thou thankest me heartily in that I have prayed for thee," but "Confirma fratres"—"Confirm thy brethren" in their faith and confidence, take care of them, and assist them in that in which thou thyself hast been assisted, in doing this thou shalt in some sort satisfy me for all that I have done for thee.

---

## MEDITATION XVIII.

### ON THE SERMON WHICH OUR LORD MADE TO HIS DISCIPLES AFTER SUPPER.

The supper being ended, our Lord made to His apostles a most devout and *sublime sermon*, in which He exercised

(9) 1 Cor. x. 13.

admirably the three principal offices which He held, of master,—comforter,—and advocate;—as *master* He exhorted them to heroic acts of virtues,—as *comforter* He made them great promises tending to their consolation,—and as *advocate* prayed to the eternal Father for them; as will be pondered in this ensuing meditation.

POINT I.

1. Beginning with the love of God, which is the first and chiefest commandment, our Lord exhorted His apostles in this sermon to the love of Himself, adducing to this effect great and weighty reasons, amongst which He said to them:—"*As my Father hath loved me, I also have loved you: Abide in my love.*" (1) Which is to say, I do not love you with a common and ordinary love, but with the selfsame love with which my Father loveth me, imparting to you gratis many of those gifts which my Father hath imparted to me; and this is the reason why I admonish you to persist and abide in my love, endeavouring on your parts to preserve this love which I bear you, that I may not, through your default, cease to love you, endeavouring to love me as I love you, for love is not repaid but with love, and love makes to be beloved.

*Colloquy.*—O most sweet love, with what more loving words couldst Thou exaggerate and declare the excess of the love Thou bearest us, than in saying that Thou lovest us with the same love that Thy Father loveth Thee? And with what more forcible reasons couldst Thou move us to love Thee than in declaring to us the greatness of Thine own love? Oh that I could love Thee with the like love, seeing Thou desirest to be loved with such a love!

2. He told them that this *love principally discovers itself in obedience, and in keeping His commandments,* for which

(1) Joan. xv. 9.

He gave them many reasons, saying:—"*If you love me keep my commandments*...He that hath my commandments and keepeth them, he it is that loveth me, and he that loveth me shall be loved of my Father: and I will love him, and manifest myself to him."—"If any love me, he will keep my word, and my Father will love him; and we will come to him, and will make abode with him." (2) In this discourse He teaches us that the true love of God is not idle, nor does it live at its own liberty, but that it labours to accomplish the will of Almighty God, in which three great goods are contained;—i. First, "*to be loved by the eternal Father*," with particular signs of His love and affection; for, if to be loved and favoured by kings and princes of the earth be esteemed for so great a good, with how much greater reason ought we to esteem being loved and favoured by the King of heaven, seeing that nothing can be wanting to those that are the favourites of such a King.—ii. The second is, that the Father and the Son, and being consequently the Holy Ghost, "*will come to him," and will make their abode within his soul*, governing it, cherishing, and fostering it with a particular care.—iii. The third is, that Jesus Christ "*will manifest Himself* to him," as well in this life by the clear light of faith with the grace of contemplation, as in the other by the beatific vision, where God shall be seen face to face.

*Colloquy.*—O happy are they that love Jesus Christ, fulfilling His commandments, whereby they shall receive so great a good! O my soul, love in obeying, and obey in loving, that thou mayest so purify thyself by this obedience of charity, that thou mayest see Him whom thou lovest, and rejoice in beholding Him for ever and ever. Amen.

3. He proposed Himself for an example and pattern of

(2) Joan. xiv. 15, 21, 23.

all that He had spoken, saying:—"*If you keep my commandments* you shall abide in my love, as I also have kept my Father's commandments, and do abide in His love," (3) as well in the love that He beareth me, as in that which I bear Him; so that the observance of God's commandments preserve in us our love to God, and also God's love towards us all, after the example of our Lord Jesus, considering that He has observed His Father's commandments, even to the laying down of His life, for the fulfilling of them.

*Colloquy.*—O my well-beloved, I desire to accomplish the will of Thy Father in the same manner as Thou hast accomplished it, loving Him as Thou hast loved Him, to the end I may be loved by Him, as Thou hast been, and that I may love Thee as I am loved by Thee; since, therefore, Thou commandest me to love Thee, give me what Thou commandest, that I may love Thee as Thou desirest.

(Of this point we will treat more largely in the sixth part of this work.)

POINT II.

With the precept of the love of God is joined the commandment *of the love of our neighbour*, to which our Lord exhorted His apostles *three several times* in this sermon with very grave and effectual words.

1. *First*, He said to them:—"*A new commandment* I give to you, that *you love one another*, as I have loved you. By this shall all men know that you are my disciples, *if you have love one for another*." (4) He calls this commandment new because He renewed it, being in a manner abolished and out of use, re-establishing it in its former perfection, as the foundation of the new law, which is

(3) Joan. xv. 10. (4) Joan. xiii. 34.

altogether a law of love, and by which we are made like the new Adam, are renewed in spirit, and attain the new dignity of being the sons of God, by the adoption of Jesus Christ, and because He Himself gives us a new commandment and example of love. The old law of love commanded, "thou shalt love thy neighbour as thyself;"—the new commands, that we should love him as Christ has loved us,—that is to say, with that purity and fervour, and with that intention that He loved us, willing and procuring for our neighbours, as He did principally, spiritual goods, although with the loss of our own temporal commodities; and that we might have this love in more esteem and reputation, He said that it shall be the mark and sign by which His disciples shall be known; as if He would say, —The disciples of Moses are known by the observations of the ceremonies of the law,—those of St. John Baptist by corporal fasting and austerities,—those of the Pharisees by their habits and exterior ceremonies,—those of the philosophers by their sharp and witty sentences,—but the disciples of my school shall be known by their mutual love, for although besides these there are sundry other signs of Christ's disciples, as are faith, prophecy, miracles, and other good and laudable works, nevertheless, there is no sign so certain and assured as is this of *love*, which may be found in all, and without which the rest are imperfect. Hence it is that the Wise man says:—"The sons of wisdom are the Church" or congregation "of the just, whose nature and condition is obedience and love;" (5) for, as the nations of the world are known by their language, by their habit, or by their laws, and other exterior signs, so the nation of the children of the Wisdom Incarnate, which is Jesus Christ, are known by obedience, and by the love of God, and the love of one another.

(5) Ecclus. iii. 1.

*Colloquy.*—O most sweet master, give me, I beseech Thee, the mark of those that pass their course in Thy holy school, that this do not serve me for a bare mark only to be known by, but that by the same Thou mayest also be glorified, seeing that the learning of the disciple is the glory of his master.

2. The *second time* that our Saviour exhorted them to this love was, when He said to them:—"*This is my commandment, that you love one another,* as I have loved you. Greater love than this no man hath, that a man lay down his life for his friends." (6) In which words the commandment of love, which before He had called "new," He now calls *His*, for although the other commandments are also His, this, notwithstanding, is His by excellency—is His because He grounds His law upon it, and rejoices to observe it most perfectly, and because He esteems it more than the rest, and by it makes men become His,—His children,—His friends,—and His faithful servants, and by it He imparts to them all that He has, that is to say, His grace, and the inheritance of His glory, and even His own self; in a word, this precept is His own, because He makes Himself the example of this love, whose chief and principal perfection is, to expose, when need so requires, our life for our friends, that is to say, for those whom we love.

*Colloquy.*—O infinite lover, who hast given Thy life for us all, inasmuch as Thou lovest all, and although they were Thine enemies,(7) yet didst offer it for them, that Thou mightest win them to be Thy friends; give me, I beseech Thee, a love as perfect as this, for there is no reason why I should love my life, so base and miserable, more than Thou hast loved Thine, so precious and admirable.

3. *The third time* He said to them :—"*These things I com-*

(6) Joan. xv. 12. (7) Rom. v. 10.

*mand you that you love one another.*"(8) In which words He gives clearly to understand that all that He has ordained in His law, and all the rest of the commandments, are contained in this commandment of love; and this is the reason that He says to them:—"I recommend this thing; that you love one another, for if you love one another you will fulfil the whole law,(9) of which the precepts are nothing but love." He repeats this commandment thrice, to the end that it might take the deeper root in their hearts, and all three times He calls it a commandment; but when He persuaded them to love Him, He used not this word of "commandment;" as if He had said:—"That you love me, it will not be needful to say that I *command* you to do it, for the love which I bear you, and the good which I have done you, must sufficiently provoke you, but that you love your neighbour; this I expressly command you, once, twice, and thrice, lest you become cold and careless in this love."

POINT III.

In this same sermon, our Lord also exhorted His apostles three several times *to the exercise of prayer*, declaring to them the confidence, and other conditions which ought to accompany this holy exercise.

1. First, He said to them:—"He that believeth in me, the works that I do he also shall do, and greater than these shall he do. Because I go to the Father, and *whatsoever you shall ask in my name that will I do*, that the Father may be glorified in the Son. *If you shall ask me anything in my name, that I will do.*"(10) In these words He teaches us, that prayer, joined with a lively faith, and an assured confidence in His word, is powerful to obtain of the eternal Father and of Christ Himself, strength and

(8) Joan. xv. 17. (9) Rom. xiii. 10. (10) Joan. xiv. 12.

force to *do marvellous works*, and like those which He Himself did whilst He was in this world, as well works of virtue and sanctity, as also miracles, and that greater if need be than were His own. And to assure us of this so much the better, He repeats the same thing twice, and affirms that it is the glory of His Father to grant the same for His Son's sake, thereby to show that they will both of them accomplish it most willingly.

2. Secondly, He said to them:—"If you abide in me, and my words abide in you; *you shall ask what thing soever you will, and it shall be done unto you.*"(11) In these words He teaches us the wonderful efficacy, force, and connexion which prayer has, together with union with Christ by love and obedience to His word, for He puts into the hands of the will, thus united with Jesus Christ, both to will and to demand; and our Saviour obliges Himself to grant that which shall be demanded of Him. Which, however, is only to be understood in case that, moved by the instinct of this divine union, we will and demand that which is agreeable to it, and never will anything but that which shall be pleasing to God, nor ever demand anything but what shall be agreeable to His Majesty, as having now no more our own will, but assuming the will of Almighty God for our own. And hence it is that S. Thomas says, that "the prayer of those who pray in this manner is always heard."(12)

*Colloquy.*—O God of my soul, grant me, I beseech Thee, that I be always united to Thee, and that Thy words and precepts be always imprinted in me, loving them, and fulfilling them with a hearty affection; for I am most assured that if I love Thee, and obey Thee, conforming my desires to the law of love, I may demand whatsoever I will, and Thou wilt give me

(11) Joan. xv. 7. (12) S. Tho. 3, p. q. xxi., art. 4.

whatsoever I shall demand,(13) since Thou dost delight to please those who please Thee, and to fulfil the will of those who always fulfil Thine.

3. Thirdly, He said to them with this asseveration:—"*Amen, Amen*, I say to you, *if you ask the Father anything in my name He will give it you.* Hitherto you have not asked anything in my name: *Ask and you shall receive*, that your joy may be full."(14) In these words He makes them a solemn promise, and with great assurance, that He will give them all that they shall demand in His name, and exhorts them to make trial thereof, that their own experience may show them the truth of it, and that so they may thoroughly rejoice to see it accomplished.

4. And that we may the better comprehend the excellence of this promise, we must consider *these ensuing circumstances;*—i. *who it* is that *makes* it;—ii. *to whom* it is made;—iii. *who it* is that is *to execute it;*—*to whom we* are to *have recourse;*—iv. *how;*—v. for what things;—vi. and *in what manner.*

i. *He who makes this promise is the Son of the living God*, whose name is faithful, and true; truth itself, and the infinite wisdom, who can neither be deceived nor deceive;—who knows what to promise and what He can and will fulfil, and what is expedient, and therefore His promise is on every side most assured.

ii. Those *to whom* this promise is made, are *the disciples of Christ*, who were then present with Him in this chamber, Judas having already gone out; that is to say, it is made only to those who believe in Jesus Christ, hope in Him, and who desire to serve and obey Him as His disciples, but not to rebellious and obstinate sinners, who withdraw themselves from His school and obedience. And in this sense the man that was born blind in the Gospel, said,

(13) Psal. cxliv. 19. (14) Joan. xvi. 23.

"that God doth not hear sinners."(15) And the Wise man says: "He that turneth away his ears from hearing the law, his prayer shall be an abomination."(16) Nevertheless, if they are sinners, but desire to be no longer such, rather seeking to render themselves disciples of Christ, such as these have also part in this promise, whenever they shall ask to be received in His school; for our heavenly Father gives His good Spirit to him that demands it, to withdraw himself from evil; yet more especially do they enjoy it who "abide in" Christ, and whose "words abide in" them, as we have said before.

iii. "*He who is to accomplish* this promise, or to whom we are to have recourse, *is* "*the Father*," that is to say, this Lord who by excellency deserves this name; who is a Father, loving, careful, and powerful to give His children whatever they shall demand of Him, far better than all the fathers of the earth, for He gives without losing anything, without diminishing anything of His treasures, and much delights to give to all; for this cause our Lord says in the Gospel:—"If you then being evil, know how to give good gifts to your children, how much more will your Father from heaven, give the good Spirit to them that ask Him?"(17) It belongs also to the same Son of God to accomplish this promise, who has so much loved us as to die for us, and who is so liberal a friend and so desirous to give, that He gives Himself for us, and enjoins us on account of the great desire He has of giving to us, to demand of Him what we will. Finally, the *Holy Ghost* will also accomplish this promise, who is one God with the other two, and who, as the apostle says, "asketh for us,"(18) and also inspires us to demand, by reason of the great desire He has to give to us.

(15) Joan. ix. 31. (16) Prov. xxviii. 9. (17) Luc. xi. 13. (18) Rom. viii. 16.

iv. The *titles and privileges by which* we are to demand, are *the name of Jesus Christ,*—that is to say, the bounty of Jesus Christ, and all His virtues and merits, the labours of His life and death, the services He has done to His Father, and for His glory and honour, and to the end that His name be highly glorified; so that I ought not to demand in my own name, nor trusting in my own virtue, nor merits, nor in the glory of my name, but setting all this aside, and distrusting in myself, I must wholly rely upon our Lord Jesus, and direct that which I shall demand to His greater glory.

v. The *things comprehended in this promise, are all things which are decent and convenient to the bounty of the Father*, who is to give them,(19) and to the name and virtue of the Son by whom we are to demand them, and also to the necessity of him who demands them, for the good either of his own soul, or of the souls of others, for whom he requires them,—and that without any restriction or limitation, seeing that He that has made the promise, has not put any limit; whence it follows, that as God will be liberal in giving, I ought not to be niggardly in demanding, but so to ask as one that asks of a most liberal Lord, and to ask, as our Lord says, "Ut gaudium vestrum sit plenum," "that" our "joy may be full," that is to say,—not to demand principally earthly things, which cannot afford us a complete joy and contentment; but to demand heavenly things, and that not sparingly, but in such abundance, that they may satisfy our joy, and give full content to our desire, both in this life and in the life eternal.

vi. *The manner in which* we are to demand, is, *with a great faith* and confidence in the bounty and liberality of Him who promises, who will give that which we demand

(19) S. Basil de Const. Monast. c. 2.

of Him, and in the merits of the Mediator in whose name we demand. This is that faith of which our Lord speaks in S. Mark, when He says: "Habete fidem Dei,"—"Have the faith of God,"(20) that is, a faith exceeding great, a faith worthy of God, a faith most sublime, which, leaving all the baseness of the earth, has its anchors above in heaven, hoping to obtain at the hands of Almighty God, all whatsoever He has promised, it being founded in His word, and in that which He Himself is.(21) This is that faith which He compares in another place "to a grain of mustard seed,"(22) of which we have already spoken in the 3rd part of the forty-sixth meditation. To this faith must be joined a great *perseverance* even to the time that our joy be accomplished,—that is to say, until we shall perceive by experience that we are heard, and that we enjoy the thing demanded, receiving with the gift a perfect contentment.

*Colloquy.*—O Redeemer of the world, who art so liberal in promising, and so faithful in accomplishing what Thou dost promise, I give Thee thanks for this Thy liberality and fidelity, which in all things Thou makest apparent, and I beseech Thee that Thou wilt vouchsafe to give me the grace to demand what Thou biddest me demand, and in that manner in which Thou wouldst have it demanded, that so receiving what I demand my joy may be full, rejoicing not only in Thy gifts, but much more in Thyself, who art the giver; for my joy will never be complete, unless I enjoy Thee, who art my chief and sovereign joy, world without end. Amen.

The remainder of this promise shall be pondered in the fifth part of this work.

POINT IV.

Our Lord employed the greatest part of His sermon in

(20) Marc. xi. 22. (21) Jac. i. 6. (22) Mat. xvii. 19.

*encouraging His apostles*, and in comforting them in their present troubles, as also in those which they were shortly after to endure in the world, *alleging reasons to this end*, of which I will set down some, though not in the same order as He spake them, to serve us for helps to meditate, and for motives both to comfort and encourage us to suffer patiently such persecutions and afflictions as may befal us.

1. The first reason was, the example of that which our Lord Himself suffered:—"Remember my word that I said to you: The servant is not greater than his lord. If *they have persecuted me they will also persecute you.*"(23) "They will put you out of the synagogues; yea, the hour cometh that whosoever killeth you, will think that he doth service to God. And these things they will do to you; because they have not known the Father, nor me."(24)

*Colloquy.*—O happy afflictions, of which Christ is the cause, and by which we are made like to our Lord Jesus. I will not, dear Lord, be privileged nor exempted from these afflictions, for being Thy servant, it will be a very great honour to me to walk by the same way that my Lord walked.

2. The second reason was, that *to be persecuted is a mark that they are not of the rank of the reprobate* of the world, and consequently that they are of the fold of Christ and of His elect. "If the world," says He, "hate you, know ye that it hated me before you. If you had been of the world, the world would love his own. But *because you are not of the world, but* I have chosen you out of the world, *therefore the world hateth you.*"(25)

*Colloquy.*—O good Jesus, I will be of Thy com-

(23) Joan. xv. 20. (24) Ibid. xvi. 2. (25) Ibid. xv. 18, 19.

pany, and not of the faction of the world, and if the world hates me and persecutes me, I will rejoice at it, for Thou wilt protect me, because the world vexes and molests me for Thy sake.

3. The third reason was, *because these troubles and afflictions* will be by and by converted into joys, in the same manner as a woman, "when she is in labour, hath sorrow, because her hour is come: but when she hath brought forth the child, she remembereth no more the anguish for joy that a man is born into the world;"(26) even so in like manner shall you be sad and discomforted for my absence and for my death, but soon after I will rise again, as he that is newly born into the world, and will turn your tears into joy;—you shall feel great pains like those which women feel in time of travail, in preaching my law, and in doing that which I command you, for which great persecutions will be raised against you; yet nevertheless, the self-same thing which was the occasion of your former heaviness, will after cause in you such joy and contentment, that you will no more remember the heaviness past, by reason of the fruit which you will gather from it; the pain will not last long, and the joy will be such and so permanent, that none shall be able to take it from you.

*Colloquy.*—O my soul, do not covet the joy of the world, which is wont to end in mourning, but rather "count it all joy,"(27) to suffer heaviness and sorrow for Christ, which soon shall be converted into joy; love tribulations, and thou wilt find in them consolation.

4. The fourth reason was, that *in heaven there are eternal mansions*, in which our Lord Jesus will lodge all those who suffer for Him; "Let not your heart be troubled. You believe in God, believe also in me. *In my Father's*

(26) Ibid. xvi. 20. (27) Jac. i. 2.

*house there are many mansions.* If not, I would have told you; that I go to prepare a place for you, and if I shall go and prepare a place for you, I will come again and will take you to myself, that where I am, you also may be. And whither I go you know, and the way you know."(28)

*Colloquy.*—O my soul, do not trouble thyself, and do not afflict thyself at thy travails, for the mansion of this world is but a temporary one, and our Lord Jesus will come and fetch thee at the hour of thy death, to recompense thee for all that thou hast suffered in thy life, placing thee with unspeakable joy in His eternal habitations.

5. The fifth reason was, that in the midst of the travails and afflictions of this life, He *Himself comes to visit and to help us*, for so does He say: "*I will not leave you orphans*,"(29) for I will defend you, let not your heart be troubled for fear, seeing that I have said that I am to depart, and to come again to you. "A little while, and now you shall not see me: and again a little while, *and you shall see me*, because I go to the Father;"(30) at which your heart shall rejoice, and nobody shall be able to take from you that joy which I will give you.

*Colloquy.*—O most loving Father, who dost never leave Thy children orphans, not even when they think Thee to be absent from them, for indeed Thou art never so absent, but that Thou still hast regard to their good; I desire that I may not trouble nor afflict myself in my crosses, seeing that Thou art so soon to come to visit me, and to comfort me in them. Give me, dear Lord, that inward joy, of which neither the Devil, nor the world, nor any creature whatsoever else shall ever be able to deprive me, for possessing this joy all tribulations will be pleasing to me.

(28) Joan. xiv. 1. (29) Ibid. 18. (30) Ibid. xvi. 16.

6. The *sixth* reason was, that, although they were afflicted with adversities, yet *they are beloved of the eternal Father.* "I say not to you that I will ask the Father for you, *for the Father Himself loveth you,* because you have loved me, and have believed that I came out from God."(31) As if He had said,—"Be not troubled, fear not, and do not lose your confidence, nor be discouraged in the midst of the crosses and afflictions which you shall suffer for my sake; for these are the pledges of the love of my Father towards you, for the love which you have showed in suffering for my sake; and if my Father love you, He will, assure yourselves, defend and comfort you, for a Father so loving and powerful can never fail to comfort His children."

*Colloquy.*—O most loving Father, I will desire no other consolation in this world but to know that Thou lovest me, for if Thou lovest me, nothing can be wanting to me, Thou who knowest not how to love, and to be lacking to him whom Thou lovest.

7. The *seventh* reason of consolation is, the great assurance and *confidence we have of remaining victorious over all our enemies* that persecute us. "In the world," says our Lord, "you shall have distress; but have confidence, *I have overcome the world.*"(32) –That is, "I have overcome the Devil, the prince of the world. I have overcome the fury of persecutions and crosses, I have overcome death and sin, and in virtue of my victory, you ought assuredly to hope that you will likewise overcome, considering that I have already overcome them for you, and that it is I that yet fight in you, in order that you may overcome."

*Colloquy.*—I yield Thee thanks, O eternal Father, for that Thou hast given us the victory, "through our

(31) Ibid. 26. (32) Ibid. 33.

Lord Jesus Christ,"(33) and seeing that both the victory and the glory is Thine, I can no way doubt nor distrust, but that I may easily obtain the victory.

Our Lord further alleges other reasons of this consolation, grounded upon the coming of the Holy Ghost, which we will reserve for the fifth part of this work, in the meditations of that matter.(34)

---

## MEDITATION XIX.

### ON THE PRAYER WHICH OUR LORD MADE TO HIS FATHER AT THE END OF THE SERMON AFTER SUPPER.

This prayer of our Lord is a most lively and most perfect example of all such things as ought to be in a fervent and excellent prayer(1)—both with regard to the *persons for whom* we ought to pray, and *the things we are to demand*,—the *patronage and titles* which are to be alleged for obtaining them, or the order we ought to observe in all these. We will therefore reduce this prayer to three points, as it consists of three parts.—i. For, first, Christ, as He was man, prayed *for Himself*, and for His own necessities.—ii. Secondly, *for His apostles*, who were there present, and were under His charge.—iii. Thirdly, *for all the elect*, and for all the faithful who were to be to the end of the world, according to the rule that is required in a well ordered charity; all which we ought to observe in the selfsame form and manner our Lord observed them.

#### POINT I.

1. Our Lord Jesus, standing up in the presence of His apostles, lifted up His eyes to heaven, and with a loud and clear voice prayed to His Father *for Himself*, saying,—

(33) 1 Cor. xv. 57. (34) Med. xvii. 22.

(1) S. Tho. 3, p. q. xxi., art. 3.

"Father, the hour is come, *glorify Thy Son*, that Thy Son may glorify Thee."(2)

i. Consider here both the *internal* and the *external reverence* with which our Lord prayed, the *devotion* which He showed, lifting up His eyes to Heaven, the sounding voice, the sweet, pleasing, and penetrating words which He pronounced, to instruct the apostles, by His example, how they were to pray, and comfort them by the care He showed for them.

ii. *What He demanded* in this prayer, namely, that He might *be glorified* at the time of His Passion by miracles, which might sufficiently manifest, that although He suffered things so ignominious, yet that He was the Son of God;—moreover, that He might be likewise glorified with the splendour and glory of His resurrection and ascension into heaven;—as also that He might be glorified in the world, and acknowledged by men to be Son of God. And to show that He did not desire this for His own glory, He added, "I crave this, O Father," "ut filius tuus clarificet te," to the end "that Thy Son may glorify Thee;" —that is, "that my glory may redound to Thine, so that after Thou shalt have glorified me, I may likewise glorify Thee, and publish Thy glory to my disciples, and by them to all the world."

2. This prayer of our Lord I will endeavour to use in divers manners,—beseeching of the eternal Father that He would glorify His Son throughout the world;—amongst the *infidels*, giving them light to believe in Him, and to glorify Him as His Son, and that in doing this the Father Himself may be glorified, and with this spirit I will often say:—"Father, glorify Thy Son," that Thy Son may glorify Thee "throughout the world." At other times I will appropriate this prayer to myself, demanding

(2) Joan. xvii. 1—4.

of the eternal Father that He would glorify me, a miserable wretch, and His unworthy son, with the glory of His grace, and with excellent acts of virtue, yet not for my own honour, but for His glory, and to the end that I may glorify and publish His greatness; and in this sense, demanding for myself, I will say, "Father, glorify Thy son, that Thy son may glorify Thee." And it is no arrogance to use this manner of prayer; for since God will have me call Him Father, I may, by the same reason, well call myself His son; but if I have not courage enough to say this, I will, instead of "son," say "servant," or "slave," saying:

*Colloquy.*—O my God, glorify Thy servant, that Thy servant may glorify Thee. Father, love this Thy slave, to the end Thy slave may love Thee. Amen.

3. Our Lord added to this prayer *the reasons* of that which He demanded, saying:—"*I have glorified Thee upon the earth: I have finished the work* which Thou gavest me to do: and now glorify Thou me, O Father, with Thyself, with the glory which I had, before the world was, with Thee." As if He had said:—"I have reason to ask this at Thy hands, for I have always promoted Thy glory here upon earth, and have obeyed Thy will, performing all that Thou hast commanded me; there is, therefore, good reason that Thou shouldst glorify me with the glory and recompense which Thou hast assigned to me in Thine eternal predestination."

4. Hence I will note two things:—

i. That such as are perfect, when they demand anything of God, *may*, as we have declared before, *allege humbly to* Him *the services* which they have done Him in seeking His glory, and obeying His holy will; for if their consciences yield them assured testimony of this, they may confidently press and urge Him.

*Colloquy.*—O most loving Father, oh that I could truly say to Thee, that I had always glorified Thee upon earth, and had accomplished that work which Thou hast committed to my charge! But, alas! I have lived quite otherwise, seeking my own glory, with the contempt of Thine, and have transgressed Thy will to accomplish my own. Wherefore I beseech Thee, not in the quality of a faithful servant, but as a poor miscreant, that Thou wouldst vouchsafe to glorify me with Thy grace, that henceforward I may glorify Thee upon earth, and accomplish all that Thou hast commanded me. Amen.

ii. The second is, that *prayer is a means to purchase* those things which God has ordained in His eternal predestination, so that we ought not to be defective in continual prayer, because it may be, that by the means of it, we shall receive that which God has predestinated for our salvation; wherefore we ought urgently to importune Him, not for the glory of this world before men, but for that glory with Him for which He has designed us.(3)

POINT II.

Moreover, consider the prayer which our Lord *made for His apostles.*

1. In this He first declared *for whom* He prayed, saying to His Father:—"I pray not for the world, but *for them whom Thou hast given me:* because they are Thine."(4) He calls "the world" the multitude of the reprobates, rebels to God, and to His law, who, by their own faults, render themselves unworthy that our Lord Jesus should pray for them, as concerning the efficacy of His prayer,

(3) S. Th. ii. 2, q. lxxxiii. art. 2. S Greg. 1, Dial., c. 2.
(4) Joan. xvii. 10.

which hath no effect in them. And therefore He says, that He prays *for the apostles*, the elected of His Father. "Quia tui sunt," says He, "*because they are Thine,*" Thy friends, Thy faithful servants, Thy chosen, whom Thou dost keep under Thy protection. This is a most fit title to allege in our prayers to God, saying to Him:—

*Colloquy.*—O heavenly Father, favour, I beseech Thee, those whom Thou hast committed to me, and vouchsafe to assist all faithful people, because they are Thine; my God, have a care of my body and my soul, of all my senses, and my faculties, which Thou hast given me, because they are Thine. Preserve and nourish the desires and good purposes which Thou hast inspired into me, because they are Thine, for who is he that will not have a care of that which is his own? "Tuus sum ego, salvum me fac,"—"I am Thine, save Thou me;"(5) my soul is Thine, save it, my understanding is Thine, illuminate it; my will is Thine, govern it. Do not permit, O Lord, that I be of the world's party, for whom Thou dost not pray, for if Thou dost exclude me out of Thy prayer, I shall likewise be excluded out of Thy Kingdom.

2. After this our Lord demanded for His apostles *three excellent things.*

i. The first was in these words:—"*Holy Father, keep them in Thy name* whom Thou hast given me; *that they may be one,* as we also are."(6) In which words He craves of His heavenly Father that He would have care of them, that He would preserve them, giving them the union of charity, both among themselves, and with Almighty God; and that not an ordinary union, but a most perfect union, that should resemble that which the Father and the Son have in the unity of essence. Insomuch that as those two who make but one God, have one and the same

(5) Psal. cxviii. 94. (6) Joan. xvii. 11.

understanding, will, and action;—even so ought the faithful to conform themselves wholly to the understanding of God, and to His holy will, working only that which God would that they should work,—that so all agreeing in this union with God, they should also remain united among themselves.

ii. The second thing that He demands for them is, that God *would deliver them from all that shall be contrary to this divine union*, saying:—"I pray not that Thou shouldst take them out of the world, but *that Thou shouldst keep them from evil*:"(7) that is to say, "forasmuch as they are to endure great persecutions and afflictions in the world, Father, I do not desire that Thou shouldst take them out of the world, because it is necessary that they remain in it, but that Thou deliver them from evil, that is to say, from the sin of disunion, from discord and dissension, from the Devil and from everlasting evil, so that they live in the world without being hurt or corrupted with its evils."

iii. The third thing that He demanded for them is, *the plenitude of all virtues*, saying:—"*Sanctify them in truth*...for them do I sanctify myself; that they also may be sanctified in truth;"(8) as if He had said:—"Do not only deliver them from evil, but 'sanctify them' with the abundance of true virtue, exempt from all fiction and hypocrisy, according to the truth which I have preached to them, seeing that I have consecrated myself, and offered myself in a holy sacrifice and host to make them holy." By which we may see that our Lord wills that we demand in our prayers things that are excellent and worthy of God, alleging two principal titles for the obtaining them; the one, the glory and majesty of His holy name;—the other, the sanc-

(7) Ibid. 15. (8) Ibid. 19.

tity of the Sacrifice which He Himself has offered for us upon the cross.

*Colloquy.*—O sovereign Father, hearken, I beseech Thee, to the prayer of Thy only Son, and by virtue of this prayer preserve me from that "evil," with which the world is infected, and "sanctify me" with a true sanctity, that I may enjoy the union which Thou hast with Him, and be united with Thee in perfect charity. Amen.

POINT III.

Lastly, we must consider the prayer which He made *for all the rest of the faithful*, in demanding for them the goods of grace and life everlasting.

1. First, then, He says:—"And not for them only do I pray, but *for them also that through their word shall believe in me*, that they all may be one, as Thou, Father, in me, and I in Thee; that they also may be one in us, that the world may believe that Thou hast sent me."(9) Whence it appears, that He prayed for *all those who live in His Church at this present time*, and consequently that He prayed for me; for He had all, and every one of us, as present there with Him, as those who were in that dining room; and He demanded for all this union of perfect charity between God and us, in the same manner as I have said before; which prayer was so effectual and so forcible, that it was sufficient to convert the whole world, and to make the infidels believe that Jesus Christ was God, by considering that He had disciples so united together in holy charity.

*Colloquy.*—O most sweet Jesus, how careful and zealous art Thou of the good of Thy elect, who prayest for them, even before they are born, and demandest so rich gifts for them! O most loving Father, hearken,

(9) Ibid. 20.

I beseech Thee, to this prayer which Thy only Son offers Thee in my behalf, and make me participate of the sovereign union which Thou hast with Him. Grant also, I beseech Thee, this union among all Religious persons, that those of the world may learn by this that Thy only Son dwells in them. Grant the same also to all the rest of the faithful, that the infidels, admiring this wonderful union, may receive Thy holy law. And as Thy Son offers to us the light of His grace, that we may become consummate in one,—that is to say, complete and perfect in this grace, which is to be one thing; grant, I beseech Thee, to all the just, who are made partakers of this light, that they may arrive at its utmost height; that so the splendour of its glory may be dilated over all the world. Amen.

2. The second thing which He demanded for them was, that where He was *they might also be.* "Father, I will, that where I am, *they also,* whom Thou hast given me, *may be with me;* that they may see my glory, which Thou hast given me."(10)—Which is to say; "Father, I do not demand only the union of charity for my faithful friends, and their perfection in this life, but that after it they be with me in heaven where I am, and enjoy my company, that they may see the glory which Thou hast given me, as well in that I am God, as in that I am man, and that by this vision they be made blessed for ever."

*Colloquy.*—O most sweet lover, with what efficacy didst Thou pray when Thou saidst this,—seeing that speaking to Thy Father, Thou didst interpose Thy sovereign authority and equality, saying, "Pater volo, ut ubi ego sum, et illi sint." "Father, I will that where I am, there my disciples be also!" Who is able to contradict and resist this Thy will; for whatsoever Thou

(10) Ibid. 24.

wilt efficaciously, will infallibly be accomplished. Oh that I were where Thou art! True it is that Thou art in every place, both where the good and the bad are; but all are not with Thee where Thou art, enjoying Thy sweet and blessed company.(11) Grant, I beseech Thee, that I may be always where Thou art, seeing Thee in this life, by clear faith, and afterwards by a clear vision in Thy glory. Amen.

---

## MEDITATION XX.

### ON OUR LORD'S GOING OUT OF THE SUPPER CHAMBER TO THE GARDEN OF GETHSEMANE, AND OF HIS INWARD HEAVINESS AND AGONY.

#### POINT I.

After the supper and sermon were ended, and the accustomed hymn had been said, in sign of thanksgiving, our Lord went forth from the place where He had supped with the eleven apostles, and passed over the brook of Cedron, to go into a field on the mount of Olives, called Gethsemane, where there was a garden, into which He entered, as it had been His custom to do many times before.(1)

Upon this point ponder, first, the *causes of our Lord's departing* out of the supper chamber to go to the garden.

1. The first cause was, to observe His devout custom of *withdrawing Himself into some solitary place*, to make His prayer, after He had accomplished the office of preaching. And it is very worthy of consideration, to note the magnanimity and integrity of our Lord, who, for no afflictions nor perils, would omit any of His good customs; for so we see here that He preached, He said the ordinary hymn after supper, and afterward went into a solitary place to pray, as if He had no thought at all of any affliction that

(11) S. Dion. c. 3, de Divin. Nomi.
(1) Mat. xxvi. 30; Joan. xviii. 1; Luc. xxii. 39.

was to follow: which example may make me blush at my own tepidity, and that at every little occasion I leave off my laudable customs, especially of prayer, though I ought to do quite the contrary; and at such times as I shall find myself most oppressed with grief and affliction, then soonest of all to have recourse to prayer.

2. The second cause was, that *His apprehension should not take place in the supping chamber*, and in the house of another man, but in *solitude*, and in the country, where it might be done more commodiously, and without any inconvenience to His host. And to show that He did not fly, He went to a place which was very well known to the traitor, who was to betray Him, as that He offered Himself voluntarily both to prison and to death, rather drawn by the chains of love and obedience, than of iron, as the words which He spoke to His disciples after the sermon and supper, sufficiently testify. "But that the world may know that I love the Father; and as the Father hath given me commandment, so do I. Arise, let us go hence."(2)

*Colloquy.*—O sweet Jesus, give me those affections of love and obedience, that I may offer myself freely to endure afflictions without flying from them, following Thee with love, and accompanying Thee with obedience.

3. The third cause was, to *signify*, that as the perdition of the world began through the liberty which Adam ambitioned in a garden;—so the salvation of the world should begin *by the apprehension of Christ in another garden*, planted in the valley of Olives; for, indeed, all that happened in this place, was to us an immense flood of mercy, although to Him a violent stream of sadness and afflictions. And although when He passed the brook of

(2) Joan. xiv. 31.

Cedron, He reflected upon the streams of dolours which were breaking in upon His soul, yet notwithstanding He went on with His apostles most cheerfully, and showed them extraordinary signs of love and kindness.

*Colloquy.*—O my Saviour, give me leave to associate myself to Thee, and pass over the torrents of pains and torments in Thy company, since I will repute all to be to me a valley of olives and of mercies.

POINT II.

Being now come to the place appointed, He left the rest of His apostles, all except Peter, James, and John; and "*He began to grow sorrowful, and to be sad.*"(3)

1. Our Lord would enter upon His Passion by *two most terrible things*, which rendered it most painful to Him.

i. The first was, voluntarily *to deprive Himself of all sensible comfort,* insomuch that, although at other times He had accustomed Himself to take pleasure in suffering, and to show signs of the joy He took in it; yet then did He utterly deprive Himself of it in the inferior part of His soul, and shut the gate against all sensible consolations which might have come to Him from the superior part.

ii. The second thing was, voluntarily to *admit the contrary affections*, viz., of fear and heaviness, giving free leave to His appetites, to produce with all vehemence these painful affections; for, whereas it was in His power either to admit or reject them, or to take no more of them than He would Himself, yet to the end His Passion might be the more bitter, He admitted them in great abundance. For, sensible consolation blunts and abates the fury of pains and afflictions, as many holy martyrs have experienced, but when there is also joined with these a heaviness and

(3) Matt. xxvi. 37.

grief, their pains, no doubt, must be the more terrible; and then to suffer with patience is much more glorious, for then a man suffers without the help of sensible succour, and the unsavoury and bitter meat of tribulation is swallowed down without any sauce to make it pleasant, purely for the love of God.

*Colloquy.*—O sweet Jesus, I give Thee thanks for this beginning that Thou didst give to Thy pains, in admitting all that might any way increase and exasperate them; grant, I beseech Thee, that for the love of Thee I may deprive myself of all sensible satisfactions, offering myself to drink the cup of Thy Passion, pure and unsweetened, as Thou vouchsafest to drink it. Amen.

2. Consider the *multitude and grievousness of these inward afflictions* of our Lord, which the Evangelist calls by the name of "fear," "grief," "sorrow," and "agony."

i. The fear was of His torments and terrible death, of which He had so lively an apprehension, that He in a manner touched them with His finger, which fear or apprehension is sometimes more bitter and insupportable than is death itself, and causes a certain interior trembling or fright, which is called "agony," of which we shall speak hereafter. This fear assaults our Lord like an army of innumerable soldiers, by framing in His imagination as many fears as He was to endure torments; for He then felt the fear of His apprehension, the injuries of that night, the whips, the crown of thorns, the cross and nails, even to the very wound of the lance, which He was to receive after His death, by all these fears and agonies that He might afflict Himself so much the more, and that He might show His strength in resisting them, He suffered Himself voluntarily to be wholly seized on, without making any manner of resistance, any more than He had done at the beginning, when He first admitted them into His soul.

*Colloquy.*—O most valiant warrior, with how far greater reason mightest Thou then have said, than did David: "My heart is troubled within me; and the fear of death is fallen upon me. Fear and trembling are come upon me; and darkness hath covered me."(4) But yet for all this Thou hast not desired "wings like a dove," as David did, to "fly" from this, for that Thou hast taken to Thee even fear itself, whereby to overcome the same.

ii. His "grief" was a certain distaste and aversion of all things in the world, finding nothing in the earth that would give Him contentment, consolation, or ease of His pains, nay, His life itself was tedious to Him as it was to Job, (5) seeing Himself environed about with so many evils and perils, and by this means He satisfied for the distaste which I feel in the works of virtue, as also the distaste I have to suffer anything that is bitter or unpleasant to me.

iii. His "sorrow" was a *heaviness*, and an inward affliction for the evils and torments which He saw to be nigh at hand, as being contrary to the natural inclination of His flesh; and as the torments were many, and very terrible, the apprehension of them was very lively, and so much the more because He knew them, according to the divine decree, to be inevitable; for this reason did He feel the greatest heaviness and sorrow that ever was, or possibly can be in this life, which heaviness assailed Him like a strong troop of furious soldiers, as if He then beheld Himself scorned, contemned, spit upon, abandoned, and persecuted.

(4) Psal. liv. 5. (5) Job x. 1.

*Colloquy.*—O joy of angels, wherefore dost Thou submit Thyself to so great heaviness? Thou wilt needs convert Thy joys into pains, to the end Thou mayest turn my pains into joys; let all the angels bless Thee for this Thy great charity, that Thou dost choose for Thyself sorrow, to replenish me with gladness. Grant me, dear Lord, such force in Thy service, that neither fear terrify me, nor tediousness overwhelm me, nor sorrow consume me. Amen.

3. In all this consider, that even as the infinite charity of our Lord Jesus shows itself in His desiring to die, and rejoicing to suffer for our good, even so *does it now clearly shine* and declare itself in this—that He voluntarily takes upon Himself these painful afflictions, in order that He may endure the inward labours and afflictions which His elect suffer, and may *make Himself like His brethren* in those things which are natural to them, sin excepted, so to be an example to us of patience, and how to support our own, if at any time we shall see ourselves reduced to the state in which Job was when he said:—"Factus sum mihimetipsi gravis"—"I am become burdensome to myself." (6)

POINT III.

Consider yet *other causes* which our Lord added, to move and excite Himself to this inward sorrow and affliction, in which are represented the motives that I may use in order to conceive a just sorrow, which St. Paul calls: —"Tristitiam secundum Deum"—"Sorrow that is according to God." (7)

1. The first was, a remembrance and lively apprehension *of the sins of all the men in the world*, past, present, and to come, all which He had then present before His eyes, with a most evident knowledge of them, deeply pondering with

(6) Job. vii. 20. (7) 2 Cor. vii. 10.

Himself three weighty and terrible circumstances contained in them, namely, their multitude without number,—their enormity almost infinite, on account of the injury which is done by them to Almighty God, and the grievous harm that they bring to men, condemning and sending them to the most terrible torments of hell;—all this caused in Him a wonderful sorrow and heaviness, which He voluntarily took to Himself,—the one to supply the defect of that sorrow which men are wont to have for their sins, and so by this His inward grief to satisfy for the same,—the other, to deliver them from the eternal sorrow which their sins deserved.

In considering and examining this point, I will imagine myself to be included *within the heart and memory* of our Lord, and there I will observe how He beholds all my sins and tepidity, and how for them He is extremely grieved and afflicted, on which account I will in like manner afflict myself, considering those three circumstances above mentioned, viz., their multitude,—their enormity,—and the eternal pain which I have deserved for them, and I will endeavour to detest sin, seeing that it is so great an evil, that the sole consideration of it was sufficient to cause in Christ such a sadness.

*Colloquy.*—O eternal Father, I offer to Thee this grief and sorrow of Thine only Son, in satisfaction for my manifold and enormous sins, and I am heartily sorry that I have committed them; but because this sorrow is not so great as it ought to be, I join it with that of Thy Son Jesus, by whose sorrow I beseech Thee that Thou wilt vouchsafe to augment mine, that so I may with this pain pay the debt due for my faults. O my sweet Saviour, I give Thee humble thanks for the sorrow which Thou hadst for my sins; oh that I had never committed them, nor caused Thee so great pain by means of them! Dear Lord, blot them out of my soul, that so there remain no longer anything there, that may put Thee to pain and sadness.

2. The second cause of His sorrow was, *the consideration of the little profit which the greater part of men would make of His Incarnation, Passion, and death*, of His sacraments and sacrifices, of His doctrine, and the examples of His life, in all which He considered the intolerable and unspeakable ingratitude of men, their blindness, hardness, and rebellion, in rejecting the benefits which He, at His so great expense, offered them, for which reason many would be finally damned. He was also much afflicted at the slothfulness and tepidity of many, in not making use of these so efficacious means, for their soul's benefit and perfection. In this regard I will imagine myself to be also one of those that so afflicted my Saviour by my tepidities, not making that estimation which I ought of His bitter Passion and death, for which I will also afflict myself, and be grieved with Him, beseeching Him that He will take from me that which may cause Him such pain.

3. The third cause of this sorrow was, the consideration of all the *crosses and afflictions which the elect and just were to suffer for His sake*, all which were then present to Him, feeling them as if He Himself had endured them, for He had them united to Him with a love and charity most cordial, so much so, that whoever touched the least of them touched "the apple of" His "eye,"(8) for they were far nearer united to His heart than is the apple of the eye to the eye. There He felt the afflictions of the apostles and martyrs, the persecutions of the doctors and ministers of the gospel, the temptations suffered by confessors and virgins, the sorrows and discomforts of the just afflicted. He had likewise before His eyes my tribulations and temptations, my fears and sorrows, for which He was

(8) Zach. ii. 8.

afflicted, taking compassion on me, and desiring by this affection of compassion to endure that which I endure, thus obliging me, with the same affection of compassion, to suffer that which He has suffered.

*Colloquy.*—O most pious and most clement Jesus, what is this that Thou dost to grieve and afflict Thyself? Art not Thou content with the consideration of Thine own pains, but that Thou wilt also afflict Thyself for those of others, as much as for Thine own? It had been enough, dear Lord, that Thou hadst been sorry for my sins, rejoicing with Thyself, notwithstanding for the pains that I justly suffer for them, but because Thy immense charity is without all limits, it will needs have an inward feeling of my sins, and of my pains, thereby to deliver me from them. Grant me, dear Lord, that I may be grieved for Thy sufferings, as Thou art afflicted and grieved for mine, for indeed Thine are truly mine, inasmuch as Thou hast suffered them for my sake.

4. To these general causes of our Lord's sorrow, others which are more particular may be added, which are, the *perdition of the Hebrew nation*, whom He had chosen for His own people,—together with the extreme ingratitude which they showed in putting Him to death. Moreover, I may imagine that our Lord was afflicted by the lively feeling which He had of the *defect of different Christian kingdoms* from Christianity, who were to forsake and lose the faith.

5. Also for the *damnation and perdition of Judas*, whom the Devil had, as it were, violently torn from His college, imagining with myself that even as a man feels intolerable pain, when one of the members joined to his body is cut off, so did our Lord feel in His heart all the subtle causes and cunning shifts with which Satan cut off or plucked from His mystical body, any living part or member, and

that no less than if he had rent His very bowels, to tear and pluck from thence him that was lodged in them.

*Colloquy.*—O good Jesus, how dost Thou all at once and by heaps, endure these kind of torments in having present before Thy eyes, so many falls of the just, whom the Devil did as it were trail and draw after him! Dear Lord, have, I beseech Thee, compassion on me, and do not suffer that I be at any time separated from Thee. Amen.

6. He was also grieved for *the scandal of His disciples*, and for the *affliction of His doleful mother*, which He had present before Him. Finally, that being true which the Wise man says:—"Qui addit scientiam, addit et laborem" —"He that addeth knowledge addeth also labour." (9) Our Lord, then, must needs have redoubled His sorrows by the great knowledge and lively apprehension of all that could cause them in Him.

*Colloquy.*—"O Deus scientiarum Domine," O God and Lord "of all knowledge,"(10) give me a true knowledge of Thy sorrows and afflictions, that I may have a large share in them. Amen.

POINT IV.

Consider that our Lord, being retired from the rest of His disciples, declared to Peter, James, and John, His affliction, saying to them with a countenance greatly changed:—"My soul is sorrowful, even unto death: stay you here and watch with me." (11)

1. First consider these *words* of our Lord, together with their signification. "My soul," He says, "is sorrowful," with that sorrowfulness which those are wont to endure that labour in the pangs of death, it being sufficient to deprive me of my life, were it not that I had reserved

(9) Eccles. i. 18. (10) 1 Reg. ii. (11) Mat. xxvi. 38.

it for a more cruel death, and this will last as long as my life lasts, without any intermission or release at all, even until the instant of my death, and will banish from me all kind of consolation during the time that I shall yet live in this mortal life.

*Colloquy.*—O sweet Saviour, how is it that these words do not pierce my heart, and that they do not wound it with a mortal wound, beholding Thee to be afflicted with a mortal heaviness, by my occasion? O most holy Virgin, if thou shouldst have understood these words, what a sword of grief would have pierced thy soul, which was so united with the soul of thy son, thus overwhelmed with grief. O mortal sin, how extremely heavy art thou, since thou causest in our Lord Jesus so mortal a heaviness!

2. Secondly, *the motives* that moved our Lord to use this speech to His apostles, are to be considered.—i. The one was, that this His sorrow being interior, it was necessary that *He should manifest exteriorly* how grievous was its weight and burden, that we may thereby know how much He endured for us, acknowledge the benefit, and our obligation to Him, and animate ourselves to imitate Him in the same. So being afterwards upon the cross, He said:—"Sitio"—"I thirst," to declare by this the secret and inward labours and afflictions He endured for our sakes.—iii. The other motive was, to *show that He was man*, and that He submitted Himself to fears and sorrows as man, comforting Himself with His well-beloved disciples, in discovering to them His afflictions, that they might have compassion of Him, and comfort Him as man; and therefore He said to them:—"Vigilate mecum"—"Watch with me," and keep me company.

*Colloquy.*—O comfort of the discomforted! who has reduced Thee to this state, to beg comfort of

Thine own creatures? My sins have done this, and the desire which Thou hast to procure me comfort, which Thou hast purchased with the price of Thine own discomforts.

I may also from hence gather, that it is not against the perfection of patience, for any one to recount His discomforts to his confessor or spiritual father, and to his faithful friends, who can comfort him in Christ with true comfort.

3. Consider for what reason our Lord declared this His sorrow and affliction to *those three apostles*, rather than to the rest, which was, in order that those who had been *witnesses of the glory* which He had in His *Transfiguration*, might also testify the sorrow and agony which He endured in His Passion, and that, comparing the one with the other, they might acknowledge and witness to the world how much we are bound to Him, who, for the love of us deprived His body of such glory, and now afflicted it with so violent an agony;—moreover, to make us understand, that if God imparts consolations to His elect during this life, it is to prepare and to *encourage them to great labours and crosses*,—and that if it be reputed a favour to be with our Lord in the mount Thabor, beholding Him glorified, and there participating in the joys of His glory, it is to be deemed no less a favour to be with the same Christ in the garden, to see Him there sad and afflicted, and to participate in His sorrows and afflictions, and that this favour is not communicated to all, but only to such as are His peculiar favourites.

*Colloquy.*—I believe it to be so, my sweet Saviour, and desire the same thing at Thy hands, beseeching Thee to show me so much favour, as that I may be one of that "little flock," to whom Thou impartest Thy afflictions, and a most sensible and tender feeling of them. Amen.

# MEDITATION XXI.

## ON THE PRAYER THAT OUR LORD MADE IN THE GARDEN.

### POINT I.

Our Lord Jesus being sorrowful and grievously afflicted, as we have said, and perceiving that His apostles were heavy also, He counselled them to pray, saying to them: "*Watch ye, and pray, that ye enter not into temptation;*" (1) and taking the same counsel for Himself, He retired from them about a stone's throw.

1. Our Lord here teaches us, both by His word and example, that *the remedy of our afflictions is not to speak of them, and to tell them to men*, who are not able to afford us any inward comfort, but to *open them to God in holy prayer*, to whom we ought to have recourse as to our principal and chief comforter, who is able either to take quite away or else to moderate our sorrows, according as shall be most expedient for us. (2) I will, therefore, learn by this example in my afflictions, not to put my chief consolation in man, nor immoderately to seek after earthly consolations, but first and principally, as the apostle St. James says, (3) to crave it at God's hands, and to expect it from Him, after the example of the prophet David, who said:—"My soul refused to be comforted, I remembered God, and was delighted." (4)

2. Our Lord also by this admonishes us, that *prayer is a most assured remedy against imminent perils and temptations*, and that, therefore, when we are closest beset and environed with them, then ought we most of all to pray

(1) Mat. xxvi. 41; Luc. xxii. 41.
(2) S. Tho. 3, p. q. xxi. per totam maxime art. 4.
(3) Jac. v. 13. (4) Psal. lxxvi. 4.

with the greatest fervour. Our Lord does not say, "pray that you be not *tempted*," but "pray that ye *enter not into* temptation," and that so you be not overwhelmed and drowned in it, for it is often requisite that we should be tempted and afflicted, but prayer hinders us from fainting under it, or else helps us so as to rise again, if by frailty we have fallen, being assisted by the grace which God will give us to this end, lest we should utterly perish in them; and, therefore, as temptations are very ordinary and daily, I will devoutly recite the last petition of our Lord's prayer:—"Et ne nos inducas in tentationem, sed libera nos a malo"—"And lead us not into temptation, but deliver us from evil. Amen."

3. This word:—"*Vigilate mecum*"—"*Watch ye with me*," that is, in my company, and in the same manner that I watch, in imitation of me,—gives us to understand, that *He watches with those that watch*, and prays with those that pray; those, likewise, that watch and pray do the same with Him, they having Him for their master, their companion, and coadjutor; being, therefore, in such good company, how can I do otherwise than take pleasure in praying?

*Colloquy.*—Assist me, O most sweet Jesus, to watch always with Thee, by employing the day in labour, and the night in prayer, spending both day and night in obeying Him, who has always watched, prayed, and laboured for the love of me. Amen.

4. Consider that *act of mortification* which our Lord practised in *retiring from the company of His apostles*, to make His prayer, for in great sorrows and afflictions nature desires to be in the company of friends, in order to receive consolation from them; but our Lord overcame that inclination by His spiritual strength, which thing the Evangelist

well notes in saying:—"Et ipse *avulsus est* ab eis, quantum jactus est lapidis"—"And He was withdrawn" or plucked "away from them a stone's throw;" (5) that is, He overcame by the force of the spirit that inclination which according to the flesh He had to remain with those persons whom naturally He loved best, separating Himself from them to pray apart, that so His prayer might be the more attentive.

*Colloquy.*—O my God, grant me that I may wean myself from the milk, and pluck myself away from the breast of human consolations, so that I may apply myself wholly to prayer, there to know Thy holy will, and to put it in execution. Amen.

POINT II.

Our Lord being come to the place of prayer, He kneeled down, and fell prostrate with His face upon the earth, where remaining in that manner, He said:—"My Father, if it be possible, *let this chalice pass from me. Nevertheless, not as I will, but as Thou wilt.*" (6) As if He had said: "Father, if it be a thing that may be done without violating the decree of Thy justice, that the cup of my Passion may pass me without drinking it, grant it me, I beseech Thee; yet, nevertheless, do not that which my natural will, following her own inclination, wills, but that which shall please Thee best, for I will prefer Thy will before my own."

*Colloquy.*—O profound prayer! O excellent resignation! O master of prayer and of obedience: what high lessons dost Thou dictate to me of these two virtues! open, I beseech Thee, my eyes, that I may see them, and my ears to understand and accomplish them. Amen.

(5) Luc. xxii. 41. (6) Mat. xxvi. 39.

1. There are four things very remarkable in this prayer which I will examine for my spiritual profit.

i. That it was a prayer made *apart and retired from company*, taking away all occasions of diverting His mind from speaking with God, "alone with Him alone," surmounting the difficulties of natural propensity, as we have said a little before.

ii. The second is, a profound *reverence* and *humility*, both interior and exterior, which proceeded from the most excellent esteem which our Lord Jesus had of the divine majesty, and from the knowledge of the baseness of His humanity, as He was a creature, and of the necessity in which He was; for that at other times when He prayed He stood upon His feet, but now at this time, being in great affliction of spirit, He prayed upon His knees, His face prostrate upon the earth.

iii. The third was, a great *confidence and love*, which He declared in this word:—"My Father,"—for at other times when He prayed He called Him simply "Father," but at this time He adds "*My* Father," giving signs and arguments of augmenting the confidence and love, by which He was His Father, after a particular and singular manner, namely, not by adoption, but by nature.

iv. A great *abnegation of His own will*, with a resignation to the divine will, for as the pains were terrible, and the natural inclination to avoid them very strong, as also the internal agony extreme and excessive, to resign Himself at this time to that which God should dispose concerning Him, against His own inclination, was certainly an act of heroic virtue.

Considering all this, I *ought to confound myself for the want of these virtues*, and to beseech our Lord Jesus that He would vouchsafe to impart them to me, and when I shall at any time find myself in any affliction whatsoever,

I will also repeat the same prayer, and that, if it were possible, with the same spirit with which our Lord uttered it, saying:—"O Father, if it be possible, remove from me this bitter chalice, which so afflicts me; nevertheless, do not in this my will, but rather do Thine own."

2. There is another thing worth noting in this prayer of our Lord, namely, that it *was long*, for we must not think that it lasted no longer than whilst He uttered those short words, but that it endured, at the least, the space of *an hour*, as may be gathered by that which He said to St. Peter:—"What, could you not watch one hour with me?" (7) Our Lord spent all that time in thinking on those things which might cause in Him a reverence, a confidence, a love, and resignation, together with other affections which He exercised in this His prayer. He also caused to pass through His memory every parcel and part of His chalice, resigning Himself in all to the will of His Father, saying:—"Father, if it be possible, let this chalice" of grief and agony "pass from me; nevertheless, not as I will, but as Thou wilt;" let this chalice of my apprehension pass, let this chalice of my scourging pass, and so of the rest, nevertheless, in all this let not my will be done, "but Thine."

3. It is also probable, that during this hour's space He said this prayer *in these other senses* also, which are related by holy saints, as in that which St. Catherine of Sienna knew by revelation, namely, that our Lord Jesus, desirous to suffer for the absolute accomplishing of the redemption of the world, requested that if it were possible this drink of His chalice might speedily pass and be drunk off. In this request He was heard, for that within a few hours after the process of His Passion was concluded; and He

(7) Mat. xxvi. 40.

might also make it in other senses, as we shall speak of by and by.

In imitation, therefore, of this, I will employ a whole hour or more in retired prayer, and that although the theme or matter of prayer be but some short sentence, yet the variety of consideration and affections may much enlarge it, as St. Francis did, who spent a whole night in prayer, not saying any other thing than this:—"Deus meus et omnia"—"My God and my all;" or as St. Augustine, when he spoke with God by prayer, in these words only:—"Quis sum ego, et quis es tu?"—"Who am I, O my God, and who art Thou?"

POINT III.

This first prayer being now ended, our Lord returned to His disciples, to see whether they watched or no, as He had enjoined them, and finding them asleep, He awakened them, and said to them in a sweet manner, but especially to St. Peter, who vaunted himself to be the most fervent:—"What, could you not watch one hour with me? watch ye, and pray, that ye enter not into temptation. The spirit, indeed, is willing, but the flesh weak."(8)

1. Ponder upon this point the great *charity, solicitude, and care which Christ our Lord had of His disciples,* seeing that even in the midst of so great afflictions He interrupted His own prayer to come to visit and encourage them, and although He found them fast asleep, yet was He not for all that angry with them, but gently reprehended them, admonishing them of the danger they were in, repeating that which He had said to them before, that they should pray, lest otherwise they entered into temptation, for though the spirit be prompt, yet if the flesh, which is feeble, be not assisted by prayer, it will be easily overcome. From

(8) Ibid, 40, 41.

all this I will gather admonitions and counsels of perfection, by endeavouring in such a manner to apply myself to prayer and recollection, that I be not found defective in the care of those persons and affairs which are committed in charge to me, as also not to reprehend over sharply, but with a gentle spirit, and with loving reasons, those who offend rather through frailty than wilful malice.

2. Consider in the disciples the *slothfulness of men in the affairs of their own salvation,*—a thing, nevertheless, that our Lord undertook here so seriously, and with such great care. In the persons of these sleepers I will behold myself to sleep and snore in that which is profitable to me, imagining with myself that I hear our Lord reprehend me with the same words with which He reprehended His disciples, saying:—"Sic! non potuistis una hora vigilare mecum?"—"For shame! canst thou not watch one hour with me?"

*Colloquy.*—O Lord, how justly do I merit to be blamed, since I sleep when Thou dost watch, not being able to watch one hour, no, nor yet half an hour, as I ought, being carried away and overcome by my frailty, but, dear Lord, as Thou seest well how feeble my flesh is, strengthen my feebleness, I beseech Thee, in such a manner, that I may never be weary of watching in Thy company. Amen.

3. Consider the *difference between the perfect and those that are imperfect;* for in these heaviness is the cause of sleep and dejection of mind, and makes prayer irksome to them, and in discontinuing the same they came easily to fall into temptation, as the apostles did, who abandoned our Lord Jesus; but heaviness in the perfect unites and animates them to prayer, and makes them more prompt in it, and the more their sadness increases, so much the more do they redouble their fervour and devotion in prayer, as

we see it here increased in our Lord, and therefore they are so far from yielding to temptation, that they gather more strength and courage to resist it.

*Colloquy.*—O most bountiful God, "non amoveas orationem, et misericordiam tuam a me"—"Remove not prayer and Thy mercies from me," and permit not that I abandon prayer, for if I forsake it not, Thy mercy will never forsake me.(9)

POINT IV.

Our Lord returned again to prayer, and repeated the same words as before, but with greater fervour and vehemence, for it is probable that He then used those words which are in St. Mark:—"Abba Father, all things are possible to Thee, remove this chalice from me, but not what I will, but what Thou wilt." (10)

1. Consider here the great affection *of confidence and love*, declared as well in the repetition of the word "Abba Father," as in the confession of His omnipotence, on which this prayer is founded, *praising Him first before He would demand* that which He desired, as if He had said:—"Thou canst not refuse to hear me for want of love, for Thou art my Father, and twice my Father; neither canst Thou refuse me for want of power, for all things are possible to Thee." I may also make use of this prayer in my perils and afflictions, and compose to myself another like this, saying to Him:—

*Colloquy.*—"Abba Father, all things are possible to Thee," deliver me from this temptation which I endure, grant me this virtue which I demand, succour me in the calamity into which I have fallen, but yet let Thy will be done in this, and not mine.

2. Our Lord spent a long while in this prayer, and it is

(9) S. Aug. in Psal. lxv. 20. (10) Marc. xiv. 36.

very probable that during this time He prayed for all mankind, whose Redeemer He was, desiring on His part, as Redeemer of all, that all should be saved, and that His Passion might be profitable to all, and the fruit of such great pains and torments might not perish. And in this sense, together with that we have spoken of before, we may believe that He uttered those words which we have related, saying:—"Father, all things are possible to Thee." If it be possible, let not this chalice of my Passion rest in me alone, but let it pass from me to every man, that they may all receive the profit of it; nevertheless, let "not my will" be done to the prejudice of Thine; and this petition of our Saviour was very conformable to His great charity, which request I may also make, beseeching the eternal Father that the chalice of the Passion of His Son may be effectually transferred from Him to all the world, submitting, nevertheless, my judgment to His eternal decree and ordination.

In this consideration I may imagine our Lord Jesus as if He were present, and that He prays His Father that the chalice of His Passion may pass from Him to me, in communicating to me the fruit of it, as I myself also will beseech Him that He will apply the same to me, saying:—

*Colloquy.*—O eternal Father, seeing that Thy Son Himself has drunk this bitter chalice, which is even to give life to the whole world, sufficient to a thousand worlds, show, I beseech Thee, Thy charity and Thy omnipotence in transferring the fruit and utility of it to many, to the glory of Him who has drunk it for them, let it pass to me also, and replenish me with its bitterness, and with the graces and gifts which He has obtained by it.

3. To this purpose we may also consider what St. Matthew reports that our Saviour said in this His second

prayer:—viz.:—"*My Father, if this chalice may not pass away, but I must drink it, Thy will be done.*"(11) As if He would say, "if this chalice of my Passion cannot pass to the elect, and be profitable to them, unless I drink it, I am well content to drink it, for their sakes."

*Colloquy.*—I give Thee humble thanks, most loving Redeemer, for the estimation that Thou makest of me, in offering to drink a chalice so bitter for my sake. It is very necessary, dear Lord, that this chalice pass first by Thee, that passing by Thee, it lose its bitterness, that so when it passes by me, it may be the more easy for me to drink. If Thou hadst not drunk of it first, who is he that would have had the courage to have drunk of it, but since Thou hast drunk it, who will not take pleasure in drinking it. Let it pass, let it pass, dear Lord, from Thee to me, for all afflictions whatsoever suffered for Thee, will hereafter be most sweet to me.

POINT V.

Our Lord, having now finished His second prayer, returned again to His apostles with the same charity and sweetness as before, and finding them again asleep, He had compassion on their weakness, and let them alone, and so returned to make His prayer, "*the third time* repeating the selfsame words," saying:—"Father, if Thou wilt, remove this chalice from me; yet not my will, but Thine, be done."(12) Which prayer was fully as long as the former, for as the same Evangelist adds:—"*Et factus in agonia, prolixius orabat;*" "*being in an agony,*" and an intolerable anguish of mind, "*He prayed the longer.*"(13)

1. Our Lord, notwithstanding that He knew well that His apostles were asleep, *would nevertheless* go visit them, to declare in this manner the care He had of them:—par-

(11) Mat. xxvi. 42. (12) Marc. xiv.; Mat. xxvi. 44.
(13) Luc. xxii. 43.

ticularly I will consider the great anxiety which our Lord felt when He saw Himself deprived of all consolation, the place remote and solitary,—the night obscure, His disciples heavy with sleep,—His blessed mother absent—His heavenly Father seeming to stop His ears, and not to answer Him,—His divinity and the superior part of His soul giving full scope to the inferior part to suffer, fulfilling that which the Psalmist says:—"I looked for one that would grieve together with me, but there was none; and for one that would comfort me, and I found none."(14) And it is likely that He then also used these other words of the same prophet:—"God, my God look upon me! why hast Thou forsaken me? My God, I shall cry by day, and Thou wilt not hear: and by night, and it shall not be reputed as folly in me."(15)

2. Hence proceeded the *perseverance of our Lord in His prayer*, without either impatiently complaining that He was not heard, or through tediousness desisting from prayer, but on the contrary, He persisted, and repeated twice or thrice the self-same thing, augmenting by this His fervour; to instruct me by this number of three, which signifies perfection and constancy,(16) that I ought to pray instantly, and with perseverance, without either complaining that God does not hear me, or that He defers to grant me my request, nor ought I, on that account, to cease praying any longer. For if our Lord Jesus Himself, who merited to have been heard even at the first word, does not receive any answer, till He had prayed three several times, ought I to find fault, or be offended, if I am made to expect a while, who do not deserve to be heard at all? Now, if this His deferring and putting off was not to His detriment, no more will it be to mine; and if

(14) Psal. lxviii. 21. (15) Psal. xxi. 2. (16) 2 Cor. xii. 8.

I persevere,(17) I shall, without doubt, be heard in a time that will be most salutary for me, assuring myself, that though I do not deserve it as a friend, yet I shall obtain it in the quality of an importunate person.

3. The eternal Father so long deferred to hearken to the prayer of our Lord Jesus, *that He might make us know* thereby the great necessity we had of the Passion and death of His Son, seeing He would not give Him any answer at that time, when He craved so instantly that if it were possible He might be exempted from the same Passion, which certainly obliges me so much the more to love Him, seeing that He so much esteemed my good.

*Colloquy.*—O merciful Father, wherefore dost Thou love slaves so much, that for their sakes Thou afflictest Thine own Son? Wherefore dost Thou seem to be deaf to His request, refusing to grant Him His desire, for the sake of those who never accomplish Thy desire? If Thou fulfillest the will of those that fear Thee, and dost presently grant them their requests, why then dost Thou not accomplish the will of Him that so exceedingly loves Thee? He crying out aloud to Thee, why dost Thou not answer, "Here I am,"(18) what dost Thou require of me? Thy charity, O my God, together with that of Thy Son, is the only cause of this, for Thou refusest to hear Him, and He is as willing not to be heard by Thee, esteeming more our good than His own life. Grant me, O Lord, this conformity to Thy will in whatsoever Thou shalt ordain; for, although Thy deferring to hearken to me may proceed from my fault, yet this delay shall not be to my loss, by reason of the great love which Thou bearest to Thy dear Son, to whom be honour and glory for ever and ever. Amen.

(17) Luc. xi. 8. (18) Is. lviii. 9.

# MEDITATION XXII.

ON THE APPEARANCE OF THE ANGEL TO CHRIST, AND OF HIS BLOODY SWEAT.

POINT I.

Christ our Lord being in His prayer, "*there appeared to Him an angel from heaven, strengthening Him.*"(1)

1. First, consider concerning this point.—i. Who it was that sent this angel.—ii. What angel it was.—iii. And in what manner he strengthened and comforted our Lord.

i. It was the *eternal Father that sent him*, who, beholding His Son in such great affliction, and as it were universally abandoned, and yet for all this not ceasing to persevere in His prayer; to show His fatherly providence, and care He had of Him, and that He did not contemn this His prayer, He sent Him this messenger from heaven, to comfort Him in His name, even as He had done before, when after His victory obtained over the Devil in the desert, He sent His angels to carry Him meat.(2) In which thing He gives us to understand the fatherly care He has of those that pray, in sending to them timely consolation, by the means of some invisible angels, which are His holy inspirations; and that if He defer this, it is not because He contemns or neglects us, but only remits it to some more fit and convenient time.

*Colloquy.*—O heavenly Father, I give Thee humble thanks for the care Thou hadst in sending consolation to Thy discomforted Son, by whom, I beseech Thee, that Thou forsake me not in my afflictions, but that Thou vouchsafe to send me in due time such strength

(1) Luc. xxii. 43. (2) Mat. iv. 11.

and consolation, as shall be requisite to bear and support them. Amen.

ii. As for the angel, *it is probable that it was the angel Gabriel,* who had the charge of the mystery of the Word Incarnate,(3) not in quality of an angel keeper, but as *minister* and *executor* of that which concerned the mystery of the redemption; and although there came but one angel alone, which was sufficient for the proposed end,—namely, for the comforting of our Lord Jesus; yet if it had been needful to have had "twelve legions of angels," His prayer was of force to have obtained them of His Father, as He Himself not long after insinuated. This thing represents to us that the office of angels is to assist those that pray, to comfort and encourage them, and to present their prayers to Almighty God, and to bring back to us His favour in return; besides that by our prayer we, as it were, oblige even all of them, if need be, to come to succour and assist us.

iii. The angel, therefore, presenting himself in a visible form before our Lord, made *his speech to Him very respectfully, and with a countenance full of compassion,* alleging reasons sufficient to comfort Him and to fortify Him in His affliction: as, that it was the will and the decree of the Eternal Father that He should die, and drink of that chalice: that it was necessary for the salvation of the whole world:—that by this the just detained in Limbo might be released, that heaven might be repeopled, and that all prophecies might be fulfilled; telling Him besides, that His pains should not endure long, but that they should be presently seconded with the glory of the Resurrection, and with the eternal rest and repose of His flesh. These reasons, amongst many others, might the angel allege, all which our Lord hearkened to very humbly, testifying, that as

(3) S. Tho. 1, p. q. cxiii. art. 4, ad. 1.

man, He stood in need of the consolation of His own creatures; and although He knew well all that the angel did, or could say to Him, yet He took pleasure in hearing him, and received comfort and strength from his discourse.

*Colloquy.*—O my sweet Saviour, how comes it to pass that Thou, who art the consolation and the fortitude of angels, hast reduced Thyself to that necessity, as to be comforted of them? This is, no doubt, an act of Thy charity, for which I infinitely thank Thee, and humbly beseech Thee to assist me, that I may ever benefit from such consolations and admonitions, which either my good angel-guardian, or Thou Thyself, who art the Angel of the great Counsel, shalt at any time impart to me.

2. I will also, from this example, learn *humbly to submit myself to receive consolations from whomsoever it be,* though far inferior to me in wisdom and discretion, even though I shall know before much more than he can tell me; for it happens many times that God comforts great ones by the means of little ones, and gives by them a new feeling and understanding of those truths which before they had studied and contemplated. This thing likewise admonishes me, that I should endeavour, in my crosses and afflictions, to collect reasons of comfort, rather divine and heavenly, than human and earthly, and also give ear to those which the Holy Ghost, the common Comforter of all, is wont to inspire into the hearts of such as are afflicted.

POINT II.

Our Lord having heard the reasons of the angel, fell into such "an agony, that He prayed "longer" than He had done before, "and *His sweat became as drops of blood trickling down upon the ground.*"(4)

Upon this most touching point consider the *causes of*

(4) Luc. xxii. 43.

*His sweat*, so extraordinary and prodigious, which expressed the greatness of the internal affliction that the most blessed soul of our Lord then endured.

1. Consider, therefore, to this effect, how *there arose within Him a terrible combat between fear*, dread of death, and horror of torments on the one side, and *zeal for the glory of God, and of man's salvation* on the other: the imagination, by a lively apprehension of excruciating pains, did, as it were, waken and stir up the passions of fear, grief, and inward anguish; but reason approving and admitting of death for the motives before alleged, revived and quickened the affections of zeal and love, making resistance to their contrary passions. In this combat the agony was so great, that the very blood burst forth, and dispersed itself in a sweat over all His body in such abundance, that it ran down to the ground.

*Colloquy.*—O worthy champion, what need hadst Thou thus to strive against fears and griefs, with such a zeal, seeing that all these are subject to Thy will? Is it perhaps to make a trial beforehand, and to dispose Thyself to the combat, which is in preparation for Thee, by those cruel murderers and tormentors? Or wilt Thou with Thy mind and imagination run the race of Thy approaching Passion, before Thou dost really enter into it? Or is it to give me an example to wrestle and fight against my passions, resisting them courageously, even to the shedding of my blood, for the conquering and overcoming them? Howsoever it be, I give Thee humble thanks for the same, even from the bottom of my heart, and beseech Thee that Thou wilt vouchsafe to prevent me with Thy grace, so that I may wrestle courageously with them. Amen.

The manner of combating against my passions, in imitation of our Lord Jesus in this place, ought to be by *setting distinctly and particularly before my eyes every thing* that either causes fear or dismay in the way of virtue, and in accomplishing the will of God, whether it be the apprehension of poverty, or disgrace, of any pain, or infirmity, or whatsoever other like difficulty, and to fight valiantly against them all, in labouring to reduce them to the rule of reason through a fervent zeal for the glory of God, and of my own salvation, and to submit all my desires to the will of God, opposing myself against my inclinations, with a holy indignation conceived against them, even to the shedding of my blood in this holy combat.

2. Consider, secondly, the *great excess of our Saviour's love*, and *the liberality He showed in shedding His blood so willingly*, *for us*, for which cause He is compared, in the book of Canticles, to a myrrh tree,(5) which first, by the pores, distils the gum called myrrh, and then afterwards, being punctured, or burned, gives forth greater abundance. For even so our Lord would not stay until the cruel tormentors drew from Him His blood with whips, thorns, and nails, but chose rather that His own imagination and holy zeal should serve Him for executioners, by so lively a representation of those cruel torments which He was shortly to suffer in every part of His body; so that that alone sufficed to make Him sweat blood from His head, His face, His shoulders, His breast, and from the rest of His body. Insomuch that He then endured spiritually, and all at once, that which afterwards He was to suffer at divers times, no otherwise than if in spirit He had been taken, whipped, crowned with thorns, crucified, drenched with gall, and tormented with the pangs of death; to show thereby that He was more desirous to shed His blood for our good, than these blood-hounds were to draw it from Him to torment Him.

*Colloquy.*—O most blessed myrrh tree, who, before

(5) Cant. v. 13.

Thou art either pealed or punctured, dost of Thyself sweat myrrh, from the pores of Thy sacred body, I give Thee most humble thanks for this Thy liberal love, and so loving a liberality, which here Thou hast manifested to me; it had been enough, dear Lord, to have been tormented once only, but Thy great charity will show itself so liberal, to render thereby our redemption the more abundant, and the example Thou givest us to suffer more effectual. Oh that I could imitate Thee by making a "bundle of" this "choice myrrh," and placing it "between my breasts,"(6) that pondering with compassion, the bitterness which there Thou sufferedst, my hands might distil most approved and most chosen myrrh, chastising my flesh with penances, as Thou afflictedst Thine. Assist me, therefore, my best beloved, with Thy holy grace, stoutly to accomplish this my desire.

3. The third cause of this sweat was, *to declare the lively and tender feeling He had of our sins*, and of the mortal wounds which the whole mystical body of His Church receives by them, for the remedy of which He would, as our head, drink of the medicine of this inward "agony," with such a vehemency as caused Him even to sweat blood from every part of His natural body. And as sins are purged and pardoned by means of tears proceeding from the same sorrow, His sorrow was so excessive, that it made Him not only shed tears from His eyes like big water-drops, but also poured out from all the pores of His body "drops of blood," and that in such abundance, that the very "ground" was wet with it.

*Colloquy.*—O blood most precious, shed for my sins with infinite love, and with unspeakable pain! Oh that I had been that earth on which it fell, that being washed in such a bath, I might have remained clean

(6) Cant. i. 12, and v. 15.

and sanctified! Wash me, good Jesus, with this blood, apply to me one only drop, for one alone is sufficient for my salvation. What do I say?—for my salvation?—there needs but one drop to save the whole world, and why then, my sweet Saviour, dost Thou shed so many? O unmeasurable love! why do not I love Thee likewise without measure? Oh that all my members, and every particle of my body, were converted into tongues to praise Thy mercies, and into eyes, to bewail my sins with tears of blood.

4. The fourth cause was, to *manifest the lively feeling He had of those afflictions and torments,* which the mystical body of His elect were to endure, whose crosses and persecutions wounded Him so sore, that from mere compassion for them, He sweated blood; and so, as St. Laurence Justinian says,(7) He was then spiritually stoned with St. Stephen, crucified with St. Peter, racked with St. Andrew, flayed with St. Bartholomew, broiled on the gridiron with St. Lawrence, and devoured by wild beasts with St. Ignatius; in short, He suffered in spirit all that His martyrs afterwards suffered in body, for proof of which He sweated blood through His own.

*Colloquy.*—Thou dost merit, O Saviour of mankind, to be infinitely praised, served, and loved by all men, by reason of this love which Thou hast here manifested towards them. Oh that I might have given to me such a lively feeling of Thy pains, that in thinking only on them, I might sweat blood, for seeing that the head feels so sensibly the pains of the members, it is very reasonable that the members likewise should participate in the pains of their head.

5 Consider how *much this sweat weakened our sweet Redeemer, Jesus;* how He was all alone, having nothing in the

(7) Lib. de Spir. Christ. agon. c. xix. n. 40.

world to wipe or dry Him, nor anybody to comfort Him, only the angel, who was astonished at so strange a spectacle, encouraged Him anew, until it was now time to depart.

*Colloquy.*—O afflicted Jesus, that I had been present in the garden, to have accompanied Thee in this agony! Oh that I could have given Thee my soul and heart, to have served to wipe Thy sweat with some kind of comfort; permit, dear Lord, that I may assist in spirit at this Thy torment, and that I do with true compassion that which I would then have done to comfort Thee. Amen.

POINT III.

This conflict and bloody sweat being ended, our Lord Jesus rose from prayer, "and He cometh the third time" to His disciples, whom He found again asleep, and wakening them, He said to them:—"Sleep ye now, and take your rest. It is enough, the hour is come, behold, the Son of Man shall be betrayed into the hands of sinners. Rise up, let us go. Behold, he that will betray me, is at hand."(8)

1. Consider here the *force and courage which the humanity of our Saviour received by prayer*, in order to encounter the pains of His Passion; teaching us, by this example, the force and efficacy of holy prayer, for the fortifying of our feeble flesh, and to give it courage and heart to set on that which before it fled from and abhorred.

2. The *meekness of our Lord*, who, seeing Himself in the midst of such excessive grief, and His disciples so careless and sleepy, yet was not wrath with them, but taking compassion on them, said:—"Dormite et requiescite"—"Sleep, and take your rest."

*Colloquy.*—O good Jesus, how much more need

(8) Marc. xiv. 41.

hast Thou to refresh and rest Thyself than they; nevertheless, like a tender Father, Thou takest to Thyself the toil and labour, and wilt that Thy children be at their rest.

3. Some little space after He awakened them, and said to them:—"*Surgite, ecce qui me tradet prope est*"—"Rise up, let us go. Behold, he that will betray me is at hand." As it were sweetly reprehending them in these words: "You who are my friends sleep, and my enemies watch;" which thing ought to cause confusion in me, to see how the wicked are more diligent to persecute and offend Jesus Christ, than I am to serve Him, nevertheless, trusting in the power and virtue of our Lord, I will awake with the disciples, and will accompany Him in His afflictions, offering myself promptly to endure them all for the love of Him.

---

## MEDITATION XXIII.

### APPLICATION OF THE INTERIOR SENSES OF THE SOUL TO THE BLOOD WHICH OUR SAVIOUR SHED IN THE GARDEN.

Presupposing that which has been already said concerning this manner of prayer by application of the senses, this meditation will serve for any other time that our Lord shed His precious blood during the time of His Passion, as also for that which He began to shed at His circumcision.

#### POINT I.

Behold first, with the inward *sight* of the soul, the blood which our Lord Jesus sheds, pondering—*who it is* that sheds it,—*why* He sheds it,—*in what manner*,—and *with what affection*.

1. It is *God that sheds it* for my sins,—with infinite *love* and excessive pain,—accompanied with contempt and dis-

grace;—and it flows forth adorned with the lively colours of His virtues, humility, patience, and charity. Hence I will draw affections of admiration, of love, of thanksgiving, and of imitation in this manner:—

*Colloquy.*—What! Is it possible that a God of such an infinite majesty sheds blood so precious for so miserable a wretch as I, and that He procures my salvation at such great expense, making a medicine of His own blood for me, a sinner? O blessed be that unmeasurable bounty; what praises shall I give Thee, O Lord, for such a benefit? How shall I render Thee merited thanks? How shall I love Thee with all my heart, and how shall I imitate Thy glorious virtues? I purpose by the assistance of Thy holy grace to imitate them, although it be to shed my blood to practise them.

POINT II.

I will *hear with the ears of my soul the voices*, cries, and clamours which resound from this bloody sweat, and from the practice of so many virtues.—First, I will *hear this blood* that speaks and *cries aloud* to the eternal Father, not to demand vengeance, as did the blood of Abel,(1) but *craving pardon and mercy for men;* and obtaining all that it desires; for the eternal Father cannot refuse to hearken graciously to this cry. Hence I will draw great affections of confidence, to obtain by the means of this precious blood, pardon for my sins.

2. I will hearken to the cries *which our Lord addresses to me in this blood*, who speaks to me in this manner:—"Seeing that I give my most precious blood for thy profit, give me likewise thine, which is most vile, for my service, resisting sin, and shedding thy blood, if need be, rather than assent to it."

3. I will likewise hearken to *the words that our Lord*

(1) Heb. xii. 24.

*might use in offering up this blood* to His eternal Father for us. O how willingly would His Father give ear to them, accepting of the oblation, with promise to grant Him in return whatsoever He should demand of Him.

4. I will give ear to the sighings and groanings of our Saviour, and *to the noise that this blood made when it ran trickling* and streaming down from Him; heartily compassionating Him in sorrows and bitter pains, and feeling them in myself as if they were mine, bewailing my sins which have been the cause of them.

POINT III.

1. I will with the interior sense *smell the fragrance and most sweet odour of this blood,* which ascends to the eternal Father, appeasing by its sweetness His wrath and indignation, far better than did the bloody sacrifices of beasts, which were offered to Him by Noah.(2) O how sweet did that smell to Him which He saw shed with such flames of love, and which His Son offered to Him in sacrifice and oblation for our sins, delivering up Himself, as the apostle says, for us an oblation and sacrifice to God, in "an odour of sweetness."(3) Consider, likewise, how pleasing a scent this blood has when we offer it to Him in the sacrifice of the mass; drawing from the whole great affections of love and confidence.

2. I am besides to smell the fragrance of those *odoriferous virtues,* that accompany this effusion of the blood of our Lord Jesus, by the sweet odour of which I will encourage my heart to the imitation of them, by running after our Lord to overtake Him in these virtues, pondering that humility, patience, and obedience, being dyed in my blood mingled with the blood of our Blessed Saviour, on account of the resemblance they have with those vir-

(2) Gen. viii. 20. (3) Ephes. v. 2.

tues of His Son, are most sweet and agreeable to the eternal Father, which consideration will animate me to the practice of them with great fervour.

POINT IV.

With the interior *palate* of thy soul also taste how *savoury this blood is*, together with those virtues which, in the midst of this sweat, shine and show themselves, beholding the gust and contentment that our Lord had in the superior part of His spirit in shedding this blood, as also the great pleasure and liking He took in obeying His eternal Father for our salvation. Taste, moreover, the heavenly nectar of this blood, at what time it is drunk in the Blessed Sacrament of the Altar, exhilarating my soul with its sweetness, and earnestly desiring ever to be partaker of it. Taste also the unspeakable sweetness with which this blood sweetens all the bitterness of this life when dipped in it; making a generous resolution to take it as the sauce to those submissions, humiliations, crosses, and contempts that shall at any time befal me.

I ought, moreover, to taste the *bitter pains and agony*, which our Lord suffered in His sacred flesh, and to feel them in myself, according to that of S. Paul:—"For let this mind be in you which was also in Christ Jesus."(4)

*Colloquy.*—O most sweet Jesus, that I could feel that which Thou feltest, and taste that which Thou tastedst when Thou shedst for me Thy most precious blood! make me, I beseech Thee, to feel it, though it be most bitter to me, for it having first passed by Thee, I shall find it most sweet to me.

POINT V.

With the interior *touching* of the soul, I am to touch this blood, to kiss it, and to bathe myself in it, that by

(4) Phil. ii. 5.

the blood of this immaculate lamb, I may become white, pure, and unspotted. O that I had been the earth which was bathed with this precious blood! O that my heart were the reliquary in which this blood had been enclosed.

*Colloquy.*—O blood of Jesus, shed with an infinite love, inflame me with the love of Him that shed thee for my sake. O blood poured out with excessive sorrow and contempt, kindle in me a desire to suffer sorrow and contempt, for the sake of Him who shed thee. O blood of my Lord, which, in the Sacrament of the Altar enterest into my breast, let me touch, handle, taste, and embrace thee, incorporating and uniting myself to thee; grant that I may be always embraced by thee, and united to Him who has given thee to me, for ever and ever. Amen.

---

## MEDITATION XXIV.

### ON JUDAS' COMING WITH THE SOLDIERS TO APPREHEND CHRIST, AND OF THAT WHICH HAPPENED BEFORE HIS SEIZURE.

#### POINT I.

Our Lord being in the garden with His eleven apostles, Judas came thither with a band of soldiers under the conduct of their tribune, together with other magistrates and ancients of the people, accompanied with many officers and servants of the chief priests and Pharisees, to whom Judas had given a sign, saying: "Whomsoever I shall kiss that is He, hold Him fast. And forthwith coming to Jesus, he said: Hail, Rabbi. And he kissed Him, and Jesus said to him: Amice ad quid venisti? Friend, whereto art thou come?" what business has brought thee hither? "Dost thou betray the Son of Man with a kiss?"(1)

(1) Mat. xxvi. 48; Marc. xiv. 44; Luc. xxii. 48; Joan. xviii. 3.

1. First, consider the arts *and devices that Satan by his instrument Judas invented* to seize and lay hold of our Saviour Christ, as well by the violence of many graceless soldiers, as by cunning and wiliness, in covering and cloaking his treason with a kiss of peace. Moreover, consider the execrable villany of this traitor, who of an apostle of our Lord Jesus, made himself the captain and guide of that hellish crew, and the capital enemies of our Lord, whom he instructs and counsels what they must do to bring to pass their designs, and all for the lucre of the thirty pieces of silver promised him after he should have accomplished this inhuman treason. Behold the intolerable impudence, which he showed in taking advantage of the familiarity he had with Christ, and of the knowledge he had of the place, whither He retired to pray, for a means to betray Him, by coming and giving Him a kiss of love, as he was wont to do. This thing shall make me dread the judgments of Almighty God, and beseech Him that He forsake me not, lest that my malice transport me so far, as to draw evil out of good, and convert it to my utter ruin.

2. Consider the exceeding *charity and meekness of Christ* which He here declared many ways:—

i. First, in *receiving the kiss of this traitor*, though He well knew this to be the sign and watchward of his treason. O sweet Jesus, how does it not go against Thee, that this cursed mouth should kiss Thy divine face? How do not flames of fire issue thence and quite consume this miscreant? But Thy charity will not at this time cast forth any other fire than that of love, with desire to mollify this heart so greatly hardened.

Hence I will draw a great confidence in the mercy of this Lord, that He will not reject the kiss of sinners, who desire to reconcile themselves to Him, as Mary Magdalen, seeing that He does not refuse the kiss of Judas who betrayed Him.

ii. Secondly, He showed His meekness in *calling him "Friend,"* and in dissembling the matter in admitting his kiss, as if He had been utterly ignorant of his design, saying to him: "Amice, ad quid venisti?"—"Friend, what is the matter?" as if He would by this have admonished him, saying: "Remember thyself, that thou hast been heretofore my friend, and that as such one I have always used thee, desirous even yet at this present time to make thee of mine enemy, my friend; and of a feigned friend, a true friend; if this be the reason of thy coming hither, I willingly accept it, and freely pardon thee." O blessed be such a charity, which so gently invites him, who entreats Thee so cruelly.

iii. Our Lord *would lovingly reclaim and bring back Judas*, by manifesting to him that He knew well his purposes and intentions, and for this reason He said to him:—"Judas osculo filium hominis tradis?" "O Judas, dost thou betray the Son of Man with a kiss?" As if in great admiration He had said:—"O Judas, under the sign of friendship and amity, dost thou declare thyself my mortal enemy? under a kiss of peace dost thou make upon me so cruel a war?" Here we may observe that, although He calls this disciple *by his own name* in token of familiarity, and of the love He bare him, yet He calls Himself by no other than the common name of "Son of Man," as a mark of His humility, which He did to try, if by any possible means He might mollify that obstinate and hard heart, but, his obduracy was so great, that he profited nothing; for having given the sign of the kiss, as he had gone a little before the soldiers to discover Christ, so now he returned back to finish the treason he had begun.

POINT II.

Hereupon our Lord Jesus went Himself towards the soldiers, and asked them: "Quem quæritis?" Whom seek you? They answered him: "Jesus of Nazareth." They did not say: We seek Thyself: but Jesus of Nazareth, because they did not well know Him. "Jesus answered, I have told you that I am He;" and *presently they went backward and fell to the ground.*" (2)

1. Our Lord *would, in being apprehended, give certain marks of His omnipotency and divinity*, by working two miracles,—the one to discover the force of His *justice*,—the other to manifest the greatness of His *mercy.*

i. Concerning the first, think upon that magnanimity and omnipotence of our Lord, who went forth so courageously to meet His enemies, and *with one only word cast them all down to the earth*, and Judas himself together with them; whence they had never risen again had He not permitted them; which yet He did to show, as well to Judas as to the rest, that no frauds nor deceitful arts have any force against Him, any more than hostile arms and human powers, and that they could never have taken Him if He Himself had not been willing. Finally, that if He died, it was because He freely and willingly delivered Himself up to death. Hence I will infer, that what has no power against Jesus, will also have as little against those that are under His protection. So that I will rejoice in the omnipotence of my Lord, in which putting my confidence, I will encounter all sorts of labours.

ii. Consider the force of those words, "*Ego sum,*"—"I am He," which is *an exceeding consolation to the good*, who after they have sought Him and called upon Him in prayer, hear that which He said to His apostles:—"Ego sum, nolite timere"—"It is I, fear ye not." (3) That is:

(2) Joan. xviii. 4, 6, 8. (3) Mat. xiv. 27.

"I am your Father, your protector, your remedy, your rest, your joy, and your comfort; I am your wisdom, your justice, your sanctification, and redemption; I am your way, your truth, and your life." "Ego sum qui sum." "Qui est," &c.—"I am who am." "And by me you shall have a happy and blessed being, which shall participate in mine." But on the other side,—to the wicked who seek after Christ Jesus to injure and offend Him, this word, "Ego sum," will be terrible and fearful: "I am the omnipotent who will judge you; (4) I am the God of vengeance who will chastise you; I am He who by your own fault am to be your ruin and perdition." If then this word, pronounced by the mouth of our Lord Jesus when He was in such extreme affliction, had the force to overthrow His enemies to the earth, how much more powerful will that be which He shall speak when, judging as a king, He shall say to the wicked: "Ite maledicti"—"Depart from me ye cursed?" (5) This, no doubt, will be to them as a whirlwind, which will not only strike them to the earth, but will tumble them down headlong into the deepest pit of hell.

*Colloquy.*—Wherefore, O my soul, seek after Christ with humility, and thou wilt find Him to thy advantage; but if with pride thou searchest after Him, or for any vain intentions, thou wilt find Him to thy loss and destruction.

2. Consider why this troop of soldiers fell *rather backwards than upon their faces*, for this was not without mystery, to signify that the fall of the wicked is most perilous, who neither see where they fall, nor the fearful punishments that are prepared for them; in which they will find themselves involved, suddenly and unawares, when they shall least think of it.

(4) Exod. iii. 14. (5) Mat. xxv. 41.

*Colloquy.*—Preserve me, O my God, from such a fall, lest I turn back from the good I have done; or fall from Thy grace into the pit of sin. I will, sweet Lord, fall humbly upon my face, acknowledging my sins and my offences, together with the nothing that I am, and the dirt, of which I am framed, that after such a fall I may rise again, to enjoy Thy eternal glory. Amen.

POINT III.

Our Lord, having given leave to the soldiers to rise up, He asked them a second time: "Quem quæritis?"—"Whom seek ye?" They answered Him: "Jesum Nazarenum"—"We seek Jesus of Nazareth." And then He spake to them very imperiously, and with authority: "Dixi vobis, quia ego sum; si ergo me quæritis, sinite hos abire"—"I have told you that I am He; if, therefore, ye seek after me, let these go their way."

1. Consider here the *blindness and obstinacy of Judas and of these wretched soldiers,* who having seen this so manifest a miracle of the divinity and omnipotence of our Redeemer, Jesus, instead of acknowledging Him to be true God, and of submitting to Him, were so enchanted by the Devil, as to persist in their obstinacy; they, however, for all that, answered Him very pertinently, and to the purpose, viz: that they sought Jesus of Nazareth. The Holy Ghost declaring by their own mouths, though otherwise most wicked, that He whom they would take, and put to death, was Jesus, that is to say, the Saviour of the world,—a Nazarite,—that is, holy and consecrated to Almighty God, and flourishing in all heavenly virtues, such as He ought to be that should save us from death.

*Colloquy.*—O Jesus of Nazareth, if all men knew Thee, they would seek after Thee, not to put Thee to death, but to receive life from Thee. I will seek Thee,

O sweet Jesus, that Thou mayest be to me Jesus; I will seek Thee, O holy Nazarite, that I may become holy in Thee, and consecrated to Thy service.

2. But above all, ponder the *unmeasurable charity of our Lord* towards those that are His,—the care He has to provide for them, and, by His omnipotence, to defend them; for these words,—"Sinite hos abire"—"Let these go their way," were so powerful a commandment, and so efficacious, that His enemies could not possibly withstand the same, nor yet harm any of His apostles.

*Colloquy.*—O most loving Jesus, who dost not cease upon every occasion to express the love Thou bearest to us, Thou givest to Thy enemies full power against Thyself, but Thou deprivest them of it in what concerns Thy friends. Thou loadest the whole burden on Thy own shoulders, that Thou mayest ease the shoulders of Thine elect. Serve, O my soul, this our Lord with all thy heart, without whose permission nothing can hurt Thee, and who is so good, that if thou dost serve Him diligently, He will not permit anything to harm thee.

POINT IV.

The apostles perceiving that the soldiers began to lay hands upon their Lord, demanded of Him if they should defend themselves; but St. Peter, transported by his accustomed fervour, not expecting the answer, drew his sword, and smote the servant of the high priest named Malchus, "and cut off his right ear. But Jesus answering, said: Suffer ye thus far;" (6) and blamed St. Peter's indiscreet fervour with short and admirable sentences, mingled with severity and sweetness.

1. The first was:—"Converte gladium tuum in locum suum,"—"Put up again thy sword into its place, for all that

(6) Luc. xxii. 49

take the sword shall perish with the sword." (7) That is to say: "He that shall kill with a spirit of revenge is worthy of death." In which words we must consider how far off our Lord will have us to be from this spirit of revenge, in that which concerns our own particular, since He so sharply reprehends His disciple that would defend Him, being thereto induced by this spirit. The mildness also of our Saviour is here shown, in that He, being in the midst of so many enemies, who ill-treated Him, yet omitted not to give lessons of suffering, no otherwise than if He had been preaching to His disciples.

2. The second reprehension of St. Peter was in these words:—"*The chalice which my Father hath given me shall I not drink it?*" (8) In these words we may see with what kind of eye our Lord beheld the chalice of His Passion, and what reckoning He made of the drinking of it. He did not consider it as coming from the hand of His enemies, but as it was ordained by the will of His eternal Father, which He so earnestly desired to accomplish, that He was offended that any one would hinder Him from it; and although this chalice was very bitter, yet, because it was given by a Father so wise, and so full of love, this sufficed for the drinking it, in as willing a manner as if it had been most sweet and pleasant. With this eye, therefore, will I look upon all the crosses and tribulations that shall befal me; and if I chance to feel any interior temptation or thought that may withhold and divert me from the drinking of this cup cheerfully and willingly, I will say to this thought:—"Why wilt thou not that I drink off the cup that my Father gives me?"

*Colloquy.*—O most loving Father, I here offer myself to drink whatsoever it shall please Thee to send me, and to take such a medicine as Thou shalt pre-

(7) Mat. xxvi. 52. (8) Joan. xviii. 11.

scribe me, be it ever so bitter, or ever so distasteful; for, being ordained by Thy wisdom and providence, it will doubtless be very profitable and necessary to me.

3. The third was:—"Thinkest thou that I cannot ask my Father, and *He will give me presently more than twelve legions of angels*" for my defence? "How then shall the Scriptures be fulfilled, that so it must be done?" (9) In which words He teaches us, that it had been very easy to Him to defend Himself by the means of prayer, which would have obtained for Him many more troops of angels to defend Him than was there of soldiers to apprehend Him; yet that He would not make any such request of His Father, in order that the divine decree of His death, declared in the Holy Scriptures, might be fulfilled.

*Colloquy.*—O good Jesus, I give Thee humble thanks that Thou didst not demand of Thy Father that which would have been granted Thee, as being more mindful of the need we stood in of Thy death, than of the repose and ease of Thine own person.

4. Hence I will gather two instructions,—the one, of what force and efficacy prayer is, being made with a confidence in Almighty God, persuading myself that by the means of it, if so it be necessary, whole legions of angels shall defend me, and that what the prophet Eliseus said to his servant is true: "Plures enim nobiscum sunt, quam cum illis:" "Fear not, for there are more with us than with them." (10) The other instruction is, that when I am certain of the will of God, I ought not to crave of Him anything that is contrary to it, though otherwise I were sure to obtain it: for I ought to desire nothing so much as that His most holy will and decree be accomplished.

(9) Mat. xxvi. 53. (10) 4 Reg. vi. 16.

POINT V.

"*And when He had touched his ear, He healed him.*" (11) This is the second miracle that our Saviour wrought in His Passion, of both of which the motives were, *the accomplishing of the law of true and perfect love*, of doing good to His enemy, and one that sought to do Him so great an evil, as also to display His mercy, being afflicted to see any one in distress through His account; finally, *lest His enemies should thence* take an occasion of *molesting or persecuting His disciples*, in calumniating them as persons rebellious to the order of justice.

*Colloquy.*—O most sweet Jesus, who being able to work miracles to defend Thyself, wouldst not use Thy power, which, notwithstanding Thou didst employ to the help of him that offended Thee; impart, I beseech Thee, to me this spirit of love, which may make me rigorous to myself, and gentle to my enemies. Amen.

We may also examine the spirit and *mystery of this miracle:* for our Saviour, in healing the *right* ear, signifies to us that, by the merits of His Passion, *He will restore* us again the right ear of our soul, that is, *faith* and *obedience* to all that God reveals and commands. And it is probable that, inasmuch as the works of our Saviour were all perfect and complete, giving together with the health of the body the health of the soul, as we have deduced in the third part, this Malchus, in receiving this favour at His hands, amazed at the miracle, and at the omnipotence of our Lord Jesus, believed in Him, and so was healed also in his soul; and retiring from among this cursed crew, he went home to his house, much lamenting the injuries that were done to a man so holy and so powerful.

*Colloquy.*—O "mutatio dextræ excelsi;" O "change

(11) Luc. xxii. 51.

of the right hand of the most High!" Touch, dear Lord, the ear of my soul, and heal it entirely, that imitating the spirit of this servant, I may become a true Malchus, which signifies a king, serving Thee royally, with rule and dominion over my passions, for, to serve Thee, is to reign for ever and ever. Amen.

---

## MEDITATION XXV.

### ON THE APPREHENSION OF CHRIST.

#### POINT I.

Then did our Lord speak to the "chief priests and magistrates of the Temple and the ancients that were come unto Him: Are you come out as it were against a thief with swords and clubs? When I was daily with you in the Temple you did not lay hands upon me: but this is your hour, and the power of darkness." (1)

1. Our most innocent Lord was taken and *treated as if He had been a thief*, and as to such a one did they make towards Him; it being probable that the pagan soldiers went to apprehend Him.

*Colloquy.*—O good Jesus, how far off art Thou from stealing the goods of other men, seeing that Thou takest pleasure in giving away all Thine own? If it be theft to steal men's hearts, and to draw souls out of the power of Satan, it is true that Thou art then a thief, who dost call Thyself, "Accelera, spolia, detrahe, Festina prædari;" "Take away the spoils with speed. Quickly take the prey."(2) Make haste, and steal; but this stealing is no injury to any one, but an honour; it is not a crime worthy of prison, but it is an act that deserves eternal praise. Dear Lord, steal my heart, and take it to Thyself, for

(1) Luc. xxii. 52. (2) Is. viii. 1.

this shall not be to take away another man's goods, for it is truly Thine, and it belongs to Thee, and in doing this Thou shalt not do anything against the will of the owner, since I wish to be robbed in this manner.

2. Consider *the reproach* that our Lord made to this their outrage in these words:—"*I was daily with you in the Temple.*" As if He had said:—"Is this the payment that you return me for the continual pains I took in teaching you, to treat as a thief Him that has always been your master?"

*Colloquy.*—O heavenly master, we do indeed repay very ill the instruction and example Thou hast given us; pardon, I beseech Thee, our ingratitude, and take pity on our miseries, considering that however bad disciples we may be, Thou dost never cease to be a good master.

3. In these most tender words,—"*This is your hour, and the power of darkness,*"—our Lord gave all His enemies, and the Devil, whose ministers they were, power over His body, to take it and torment it at their own pleasure, and that not with limitation of reserving His life, as was given with respect to Job, (3) but with full power to take it from Him by force of torments. Which ought to move in me great affections of compassion and grief, beholding my Lord delivered to such cruel enemies, and that for my sake.

*Colloquy.*—I give Thee humble thanks, O most loving Jesus, for this great charity that Thou hast showed in abandoning and resigning Thy body and Thy life to the infernal powers for the freeing of my soul. It is I, it is I, dear Lord, that ought to be delivered into their hands, for it is I that have sinned; notwith-

(3) Job i. 12.

standing this, Thou of Thy charity, to free me from the fault, dost expose Thyself to this pain. I beseech Thee, O my God, to deliver me from their furies, that neither in this life, or in the next, I may fall into their darkness.

POINT II.

Leave being in this manner given by our Saviour, the whole squadron of soldiers *furiously assaulted and laid hands on Him*, and it is to be thought, that with this their impetuosity and violent fury, they threw Him down to the ground, trampling upon His belly, upon His face, and the rest of His sacred body, treading Him under their feet with an incredible rage and fury;—then setting Him up upon His feet, they beat Him down again with staves, and at the last, bound and fettered Him.(4) It is also very probable, that they bound Him by the wrists, very strait, with great cords, and put a halter about His neck, insulting and shouting as conquerors do, having taken their prey, (5) especially when they have desired it much, and seen themselves oftimes in danger of losing it.

In this fact, consider *the heroic virtues* of our Lord with a desire to imitate them, and take compassion of the torments which He endured.

1. The first virtue was, a most profound *humility*, since He who has His seat above all the Cherubim and Seraphim, (6) is here under the feet of men,—even of sinful and abominable men. Oh, what a tender feeling had our great Lord, beholding Himself thus trampled and trodden upon, upon which with the great prophet David, He cried out to His eternal Father in this manner:—"Have mercy on me, O God, for man hath trodden me underfoot: all the day he hath afflicted me, fighting against me. My

(4) Joan. xviii. 12. (5) Isa. ix. 3. (6) Is. vi. 2.

enemies have trodden upon me all the day long: for they are many that make war against me." (7)

*Colloquy.*—I give Thee thanks, most sweet Jesus, for this so profound humility which Thou hast here showed. It was no doubt a great humility in Thee, to prostrate Thyself at the feet of Thine apostles, and of Judas himself, to wash them; but that was very little in respect of this, where Thou permittest that traitor Judas, together with his cursed crew, to tread Thee under their filthy feet. Grant me, O most humble Redeemer, that I may take pleasure in being trodden upon, and being under the feet of all men, seeing I have justly deserved to be laid under the feet of Lucifer, and to be trampled upon by the devils in hell.

And here I will consider the difference there is between sinners and just men; for sinners, in sinning, tread upon the Son of God, and trample upon His holy law under their feet, (8) according to the apostle's words to the Hebrews; whereas the just, as the same apostle says to the Corinthians, glory and "bear God" (9) in their bodies, loading their heads and shoulders with His divine law. Reflecting therefore with myself upon my life past, I will bitterly bewail the times that I have trodden under my feet the Son of God, in contemning His blessed will, to accomplish my own.

2. Secondly, consider the invincible *patience* of this most meek lamb, who endures so many injuries and blows, without replying so much as a word, or even complaining or making any the least shew or motion of anger or indignation, however well He beheld the enraged hearts of His enemies, together with the acclamations and insults that they made, for having thus caught and entrapped Him, fulfilling by this what He Himself had long before

(7) Psal. lv. 2. (8) Hebr. x. 29. (9) 1 Cor. vi. 20.

spoken by the mouth of David, saying:—"Many calves have surrounded me; fat bulls have besieged me. They have opened their mouth against me, as a lion ravening and roaring," (10)

*Colloquy.*—O most patient lamb, what makest Thou here compassed about with so many ravenous "wolves" and cruel lions? Why dost Thou not open Thy mouth, and bleat against them? for by saying only, "Ego sum," "It is I," Thou art able to cast them all headlong to the earth. But, Lord, the time of speaking is now past, and Thou wilt permit Thyself to be trodden upon, suffering in silence, to give me that example of patience; help me, I beseech Thee, to suffer with silence all the outrages and indignities that shall at any time befal me. Amen.

3. But above all other virtues, the infinite *charity* of our most meek Saviour here shews itself, in giving His most blessed hands to be so cruelly bound and manacled, hands which had been ever occupied in doing good, even to those themselves who now tied them: and although He could have broken those cords far more easily than Samson broke his, (11) yet He would not do it, but Himself bound them with the cords of charity, in punishment of the lewd liberty and unrestrained dissolution of our hands; as also to deliver us thereby from that prison, into which we have deserved to be cast, bound and fettered hand and foot. Then was fulfilled that which He Himself had spoken by the prophet David:—"The cords of sinners have encompassed me: but I have not forgotten Thy law." (12) And what is this law, but that of charity, which our Lord Jesus did not forget,—loving sinners even when He Himself was bound by them, and desiring to draw and tie them to Himself, as the prophet says, "with the cords of Adam, with the bands of love?"(13)

(10) Psal. xxi. 13. (11) Judic. xv. 9. (12) Psal. cxviii. 61.
(13) Ose. xi. 4.

*Colloquy.*—O most beloved and most loving Jesus! Who had been able to have bound Thy hands, if Thy love had not first tied them? O most powerful and most liberal hands, which came but even now from distributing the bread of heaven to Thy family, and who were never bound when it was question of doing good to men, wherefore do you suffer yourselves to be bound with so great cruelty? O devilish presumption of men, who so ignominiously bind the hands of Almighty God. Permit not, dear Lord, that by my sins and ingratitude I bind Thy hands, and so hinder Thee from doing me good; on the contrary, I beseech Thee that Thou wilt bind my hands from committing even the least fault, and loosen them only to the exercise of all sorts of virtues. Amen.

POINT III.

"*Then the disciples all leaving Him fled.*" (14)

1. First, consider in the disciples, the *cowardice and fear* that possessed them; behold, how those who very lately had received so many favours, heard such wholesome counsels, and beheld so many miracles; who had vaunted that they were ready to die at His feet,—now, forgetting all this, were scandalized to see Him taken. Behold, how they forsake Him, and fly from Him, and that not only in body, but also in spirit, either quite losing their faith, or at least greatly staggering in it. Those feet that had just been washed at the last supper by the hands of Jesus, were now fouled and dirtied with the fault of this shameful flight; those hearts that had been fortified with the precious body and blood of Jesus Christ, now lost their strength through the fear of losing their lives;—the faith that had been so well rooted by the sight of so many miracles, was now obscured within the foggy mist that the fear of persecution had raised; all which

(14) Mat. xxvi. 56.

teaches me how little trust is to be put in man, whose property and condition is to accompany his friend during his life, and at his death to leave him; to follow him in time of prosperity, and to abandon him in his adversity. In the person of these disciples, I will consider myself who brag and presume in time of peace, but finding myself in war or contradiction, take my flight: who follow my Saviour as long as He gives me bread and cherishes me, but when it is question of drinking the cup of the Passion, or when I am afflicted, I retire and shrink away from Him, quite forgetting all the favours He has done me, as if I had never received them.

*Colloquy.*—O my sweet Saviour, deliver me, I beseech Thee, from committing such a scandal and so base a cowardice, and do not abandon me in time of temptation; for if Thou protectest me, I shall never forsake Thee.

2. Secondly, consider, on the part of our Saviour, the extreme *grief He had to see His flock dispersed and scandalized*, Himself remaining alone, abandoned by all His friends. Then might He well have said with the prophet David:—"Thou hast put away my acquaintance far from me, they have set me an abomination to themselves. I was delivered up and came not forth, my eyes languished through poverty."(15)

*Colloquy.*—O my well-beloved, that I had been so happy as to have accompanied Thee at that time, and so to have been Thy companion in prison, that the same cords might have bound Thy hands and mine; this had been a great honour to me, and God forbid that I should ever be so senseless, as to hold Him for an abomination, who is all my comfort and sanctification.

(15) Psal. lxxxvii. 9.

## (4.)—MEDITATIONS UPON THE MYSTERIES OF THE PASSION CONCERNING SUCH THINGS AS HAPPENED ON THE NIGHT OF OUR LORD'S APPREHENSION.

1. For the ground and foundation of the ensuing meditations, I will consider that our Lord, to endure the greater ignominies in His Passion, would be presented before *four* judgment seats or tribunals, composed of persons the best qualified that were in Jerusalem, of which *two* were *ecclesiastical* and *two secular*. (1)

i. The first tribunal was *of Annas*, prince and chief of the scribes and doctors of the law, whose custom was to assemble a council of seventy elders, for the discussion of causes and questions that concerned doctrine, preached and taught according to the Scriptures.—ii. The second was *of Caiphas*, the bishop and high priest, with whom were joined the other bishops, priests, and Pharisees, who were the Religious men of those times, to determine points of religion; and this was the ecclesiastical tribunal of the lawful judge of that time.—iii. The third was *of Pilate*, judge and president of Judea, to whose tribunal the sergeants, clerks, and other ministers of justice, as the manner was, repaired.—iv. The fourth was *of Herod*, king of Galilee, who was accompanied by courtiers and a great guard of soldiers. Before these four tribunals and councils was our Lord presented, and was contemptuously treated in all of them, so that He was scoffed at and des-

(1) Baron. Tom. 1, anno. 30 et 34, Christi.

pised by all those of Jerusalem, the best qualified in learning, religion, justice, law, and nobility.

2. And so He, who was the most eminent master in all sciences, would be despised by wise men and professors of sciences;—He that was the chief priest, and the pattern of all religion and of all sanctity, was contemned by priests, and even by those who professed sanctity;—He that was the most just judge of the quick and the dead, was scorned and mocked by judges and ministers of justice; and He that was the King of kings and Lord of lords, was trampled on by kings and courtiers, and all their troops of soldiers; to say nothing of the multitude of the common people, who co-operated with the rest in these contempts and indignities, His divine majesty permitting all this, to show us thereby an example of humility and patience, as also for the consolation of such as shall be despised in this world, by whatever persons; and lastly, for other ends which will be examined in the meditations following.

Here, by the way, it is to be observed, that I suppose the first interrogatory, or propounding of questions to our Saviour, when He received the blow on the face, to have been in the house of Annas, according to the opinion of many doctors, and so I follow the order of St. John's narration. Besides, I make a meditation of St. Peter's three denials, without respect to any order of places, whether he made them all in the house of Caiphas, or whether the two last only were made there, and the first in the house of Annas, as St. John seems to set them down; since as far as regards the subject or matter of these meditations, it does not much signify whether these things happened in one place or in another.

# MEDITATION XXVI.

ON THE SUFFERINGS THAT OUR LORD ENDURED FROM THE GARDEN TO THE HOUSE OF ANNAS, AND THAT WHICH HAPPENED TO HIM IN THE SAME HOUSE.

POINT I.

The band of soldiers with their tribune, and the officers of the Jews, as soon as they had taken Jesus, "led Him away to Annas, for he was father-in-law to Caiphas, who was the high priest of that year."(1)

1. Concerning this injury, consider the labours that our Lord endured all that long way.

i. First, great were the pains He suffered in being *cruelly forced onward by His enemies*, who dragged Him by the cords with which He was bound, striking and compelling Him to hasten His pace, so that He stumbled many times, and fell on His knees, as it chances to those who have no means to help themselves, either with arms or hands, but are yet forced to go a great pace. And now our Lord might call to mind the last time that He went to Jerusalem with His disciples, when He went a good way before them,(2) to testify the great desire He had to suffer.

*Colloquy.*—O most sweet Jesus, Thou goest indeed very hastily, pressed to it by Thy enemies, but much more by Thy charity, which permits them to do this! Oh how different was the company Thou hadst at present, from the company Thou hadst then! Where are Thy disciples, who then followed Thee? They are not able to follow so speedy and painful a pace, and therefore have they left Thee alone. Do not permit, dear Lord, that I cease to follow Thee, at least

(1) Joan. xviii. 13. (2) Marc. x. 32.

as well as I may, though Thou lead me a pace that is very painful. Amen.

ii. Consider the weariness which *the delicate body of Christ our Lord felt by reason of the bloody sweat*, which He had shed a little before. And it may very well be believed that being thus furiously led and haled along, His pores opened and He sweat again afresh, if not blood, at least a sweat of anguish and of faintness; likewise at the passage of the torrent of Cedron, most probably they made Him stumble at those stones and fall there: drinking,—not "de torrente in via," which David speaks, no· of "the torrent in the way,"(3)—but of the waters of weariness and afflictions that transfixed His heart.

*Colloquy.*—O most holy body, I give Thee humble thanks for the toils and weariness Thou didst sustain in this Thy journey. O most blessed feet, I glorify you for the speedy paces you were forced to make for the hasting of this journey. Now it is, O good Jesus, that Thy feet begin to pay for the sins that mine have committed, running hastily after evil. Restrain, dear Lord, and hold mine back from such steps, when at any time they would go astray: and make them light and swift, to follow and pursue that which is good. Amen.

iii. Our Lord endured very great disgrace in that journey, being *led like a thief*, with shouts and clamours; but especially when they entered in at the gate of the city, for then did these hellish ministers cry out and publish to the people the prize and booty they carried, with extreme pride and insolence.

*Colloquy.*—O my Redeemer, how different is this entry that Thou now makest into Jerusalem, from that which Thou didst make upon Sunday last! In that,

(3) Psal. cix. 7.

many bore in their hands boughs of palms in sign of victory; in this they march with weapons and lances, as triumphing over Thee. In that, every one sung Thy praises, saying:—"Blessed is he that cometh in the name of our Lord;"(4) in this they cry out in contempt and reproach of Thee, uttering many injurious speeches and blasphemies against Thee.—In that, for honour's sake, they strewed the way with their garments under the feet of the ass on which Thou wert mounted; in this they pull and hale Thee by Thy garments, and trail Thee with a rope on foot. O mutability of men against their God! O patience of God, that suffers such men! Deliver me, dear Lord, from such perverse mutability, and give me, I beseech Thee, so excellent a patience, that I may triumph over all sorts of inconstancy. Amen.

2. Lastly, consider *the spirit and affection* with which Christ our Lord made this journey, with so great patience and humility, offering up to His eternal Father with great charity those painful steps in satisfaction of those that we make to offend Him; and hence draw affections of gratitude and imitation, as will be shown hereafter.

POINT II.

"The high priest therefore asked Jesus of His disciples, and of His doctrine."(5)

1. First, consider, as touching this point, the *mockings and indignities*, that our Saviour endured at His entering *into the house of Annas*, where were assembled the ancients, the doctors, and masters of the law, as those to whom it belonged to examine the doctrine of Jesus, whom also the people reputed for a prophet. These men, then, since they were His enemies, and besides learned, proud, and skilful in the law, seeing our Lord Jesus come before them, began to laugh and to scoff at Him, declaring there-

(4) Mat. xxi. 9. (5) Joan. xviii. 19.

by the joy and content they had at His apprehension, and His being thus humbled; which thing may teach us that the "knowledge" which "puffeth up," leads a man even from his beginning and origin to contemn Jesus, in punishment of the sin of Adam, which had its origin in a desire of knowledge, and to know as God, both good and evil.(6)

*Colloquy.*—O most wise master, principle and author of all sciences, why do the wise rise up against Thee, and scoff at Thee, the author of their wisdom? My pride, O Lord, is the cause of this and the inflating knowledge stood in need of such a remedy, in order that, beholding Him who is wisdom itself, to be contemned by the wise of the world, I may take pleasure in being humbled by them, without respecting their erroneous judgments. My God, vouchsafe to give me humility in wisdom, for "the wisdom of the humble shall exalt his head, and shall make him sit in the midst of great men."(7)

2. Consider *the pride with which this high priest and his sages began to examine our Lord* with a mind to calumniate Him, asking Him:--i. What His doctrine was:--ii. Whether it was contrary to that of Moses or not.—iii. Whether it came from heaven.—iv. If He had received it by revelation.—v. How many disciples He had.—vi. Who they were.—vii. And where they were. To all which our Lord hearkened with great humility and meekness, although He was not ignorant of their wicked intention. Hence I will draw great affections, both of my own confusion, and of compassion for our Saviour, beholding Him in the midst of these His cruel enemies; they sitting in their seats like judges and controlers, and He standing on foot before them as a guilty person;—they in their habits and liveries of doctors, He fettered and tied like a malefactor.

(6) Gen. iii. 4. (7) Ecclus. xi. 1.

*Colloquy.*—O most excellent doctor, the Doctor of doctors, and of all nations, when Thou wert but twelve years of age, Thou didst sit in the midst of the doctors, "hearing them and asking them questions," (8) to the wonder and admiration of every one, and now Thou art standing on Thy feet, hearkening and answering them who laugh Thee to scorn! But if Thou didst manifest then an admirable wisdom in Thine answers, that which Thou dost manifest at present is no less admirable, suffering the ignominies and indignities that resulted from them. O that Thy most holy mother were now present; with what a tender feeling would she repeat again that affectionate rebuke of hers, used to Thee in the Gospel: "Fili, quid fecisti mihi sic?"—"Son, why hast Thou done so to me? Wherefore hast Thou left me all alone, and art come in the midst of these doctors, who are rather ravenous wolves than pious masters?" But, sweet Lord, Thou wouldst without doubt have answered her in the same manner as Thou didst before: "In his quæ Patris mei sunt oportet me esse."—"Mother, I must be about the things that are my Father's, whose will is that I pass through this examination." I give Thee humble thanks, most loving Redeemer, for the obedience that Thou performest to Thy Father, as also for the great humility that Thou dost show amongst men for the love of Him.

POINT III.

"Jesus answered him, I have spoken openly to the world: I have always taught in the synagogue, and in the Temple, whither all the Jews resort; and in private I have spoken nothing. Why askest thou me? *Ask them who have heard what I have spoken to them.*" (9)

1. Consider how our Lord, although He was a prisoner and in contempt amongst them, was *yet not any way terri-*

(8) Luc. ii. 47. (9) Joan. xviii. 20.

*fied or daunted* in this council, but on the contrary, *used great liberty of spirit*, which proceeds from the sanctity of His life, and from the verity of His doctrine, for a conscience that is grounded in truth and sanctity, is free and courageous to everything that is good, without either fear or any remissness, although it be before the wise and great of the world. I ought, therefore, to procure in myself such a conscience and holy liberty, as afterwards the apostles had, (10) in imitation of their master.

2. Ponder, secondly, *the great prudence of Christ* our Lord, *in not declaring in particular what this doctrine was*, knowing well how ill a true answer would be taken, but rather referring Himself to those that had heard Him, because He was so well assured of His own truth that He referred Himself even to His enemies themselves, who were there present, and to the testimony of those that had heard His sermons, which thing they themselves, by their behaviour, confessed to be true, for they were all presently dumb, not having a word to answer; nor was there any that could accuse Him of the least word spoken amiss.

*Colloquy.*—O purity of the doctrine of our Blessed Saviour, how powerful is Thy force, which not only givest generous liberty to him that preaches it, but also stops the mouth of the very enemy that hearkens to it. Grant me, my Saviour, light to understand it, liberty to publish it, and obedience to put the same in execution with perfection. Amen.

3. Consider *the reason why our Lord did not mention His disciples*, which was, because having left Him, He could give no good testimony, nor commend their fidelity; neither would He accuse nor publish their frailty; besides this, some are of opinion that Judas was present there, waiting for the payment that had been promised him for

(10) Act. v. 29.

the treason, which Annas was to pay to him. In consideration, therefore, that this miserable wretch was known to be the disciple of our Lord, his presence much blemished his master's reputation, with which our Saviour was very greatly afflicted.

*Colloquy.*—O most beloved master, do not permit that I should ever falsify the fidelity I owe to Thee as a loyal disciple, that so Thou mayest never be ashamed to acknowledge me for one of Thine, before Thy heavenly Father, and His angels.(11) Amen.

---

## MEDITATION XXVII.

### ON THE BLOW WHICH CHRIST RECEIVED ON THE FACE, AND HIS BEING SENT BACK TO CAIPHAS.

#### POINT I.

"One of the servants standing by *gave Jesus a blow*, saying: Answerest Thou the high priest so?" (1)

1. *This blow was the first injury* that our Lord received in the house of Annas the high priest, by the hands of one of his ministers, and this was so notorious an injury, that St. John would make particular mention of it, with the circumstances that accompanied it.

i. The first was, that it was *cruel*, as given by a caitiff, wholly inflamed with passion, and the desire of revenging the injury done to his master, intending thereby to get his good will, and to do a thing that should be grateful to all the company.—ii. It was *ignominious*, as done in the presence of such an assembly of nobles and persons of quality, and to a man that had always been till then honoured and respected by every one, from whose face issued forth a splendour that rendered Him venerable to all

(11) Luc. ix. 26. (1) Joan. xviii. 22.

those that looked upon Him without passion.—iii. It was *unjust*, being done out of revenge, for the sake of branding an answer pertinent and prudent, rashly condemning it for imprudent, and against the authority of the high priest.—iv. It was *with the approbation and applause of all that were present*, not any one either defending our Saviour, or reprehending this insolent fellow, and consequently it might serve for a warrant and an encouragement to others to do the like.

2. Behold, therefore, O my soul, the face of thy Lord marked with the blow of this furious wretch, blushing with a natural shame for so grievous an injury, and confounded at the insulting shouts and laughter of His enemies; *hast thou not compassion* to see buffeted that excellent face "on which the angels desire to look?" (2)

*Colloquy.*—O Son of the living God, "brightness" of the "glory" of the Father, and "the figure of His substance,"(3) who has imprinted on Thy divine face, the figure of so abominable a hand? O eternal Father, behold the face of Thy Son, marked with the hand of an infamous sinner, and seeing that He suffers this injury for the love of sinners, do Thou suffer them, and pardon them, in virtue of what He suffered for them.

POINT II.

"Jesus answered him: If I have spoken ill, give testimony of the evil: but if well, why strikest thou me?" (4)

1. Consider the great *patience and meekness* that our Lord preserved in His soul in receiving such an injury; for though this abominable wretch deserved to have been struck with lightning from heaven, or that the eart' should have opened and swallowed him alive, or that his

(2) 1 Pet. i. 12. (3) Heb. i. 3. (4) Joan. xviii. 23.

hand should have for ever withered up, as that of Jeroboam did, (5) when he would have laid hands upon a holy prophet,—though I say it would have been very easy for our Saviour to have punished this base miscreant with these or such like pains, yet instead of revenging this injury, He *suffered the same with such serenity*, that He showed Himself thereby to be ready to receive as much on the other cheek, even as many more as they would give Him.

*Colloquy.*—O most meek Jesus, true Prophet, who, for having said the truth, like another Micheas,(6) wert struck on the face, bearing this blow with patience and meekness most admirable, bestow upon me, I beseech Thee, the self-same virtues, that I may endure the injuries done to me, without disturbance of mind, or desire of revenge. Amen.

2. Our Saviour, who knew well how to hold His peace, and to overlook the disgraces and injuries done to Him, *would at that time quietly render an account of Himself*, lest otherwise they might have imagined that He had intended purposely to injure the high priest, and would also by the way rebuke and reprehend him that had offended, thereby to make him acknowledge his fault, saying to him:—"If I have spoken ill, give testimony of the evil: but if well, why strikest thou me?" seeing that thou art no judge, but only a witness; moreover, if I have spoken nothing but well, wherefore against reason dost thou strike me, making me guilty of incivility and irreverence?" But although His answer was very pertinent, yet it was not admitted, but served Him for nothing, not any one making any reckoning of His words, to teach me to behave myself patiently when I can neither be heard speak, nor my reasons be admitted, but rather contemned.

(5) 3 Reg. xiii. 4. (6) 3 Reg. xxii. 24.

*Colloquy.*—O most loving Jesus, whose property is ever to speak well, "neither was guile found in" Thy "mouth,"(7) and of whom it has been truly said:—"Never did man speak like this man;"(8) I give Thee humble thanks for the injuries and pains Thou didst endure for speaking well, in punishment of the faults that I have committed in speaking ill. Grant, dear Lord, that I may ever speak that which is pleasing to Thee, how displeasing soever it be to men, patiently enduring their calumnies. Amen.

POINT III.

"*And Annas sent Him bound to Caiphas the high priest.*" (9)

1. Consider *the resolution* that Annas, together with all the sages, took *of leading our Lord as a prisoner to the house of Caiphas*, who was the high priest and lawful judge in these cases, where were assembled the priests and Pharisees, together with the other ancients of the people, to treat of this affair. The Evangelist says, that "Annas sent Him bound," to signify that he held Him to be culpable, and it may be that they fettered and bound Him anew, and that they doubled the number of cords for fear He should escape, or that in passing along through the midst of the town He might be taken from them by force.

*Colloquy.*—O most meek lamb, although Thou goest from this first council more straitly bound to enter into the second, yet is not Thy charity, for all that, anything diminished; it is on the contrary, that which fetters and binds Thee with new desires of suffering, to unbind thereby from their enormous sins those that so straitly bound Thee with rough cords. Augment also in me, dear Lord, together with my crosses, a true desire and love of enduring them. Amen.

(8) Joan. vii. 46. (9) Joan. xviii. 24.

2. Consider the *weariness* as also the *ignominy* that our Lord endured in this second journey, *being led quite through the town*, with clamours of the soldiers and ministers, the people running out from their houses to see what was the matter, many also accompanying the soldiers, and helping them to injure our Saviour, quite forgetting all the good they had before received of Him. Notwithstanding all this, our meek Jesus did not lose one jot of His peace and charity, offering Himself to endure from many, that He might do good to all, which thing certainly renders Him worthy to be honoured and praised by all for ever and ever. Amen.

---

## MEDITATION XXVIII.

### ON ST. PETER'S TRIPLE DENIAL.

#### POINT I.

All the apostles having fled away, "Peter followed" our Lord "afar off," and with him there was another disciple, St. John, who having an acquaintance with the high priest, was admitted to enter into the court; St. Peter also having found means to get in, thrust himself amongst the servants of the house, who "stood at a fire of coals, because it was cold, and warmed themselves." (1)

1. Consider *the degrees by which St. Peter was brought to deny our Saviour*, in order that taking example by another, we may learn to avoid the like danger.—i. The first degree was, *a coldness of love*, arising from human fear; for the love of our Saviour invites him to follow, but worldly fear in such a manner cooled him that he followed afar off Him whom he had always before accompanied so near.—ii. The second was, *a forgetfulness of that which our Lord*

(1) Mat. xxvi. 58; Marc. xiv. 54; Luc. xxii. 54; Joan. xviii. 15.

*had foretold him*, namely, that he should that very night deny Him thrice; and, indeed, it is the property of those that presume too much of themselves to forget the warning of Almighty God, and the good admonitions that He gives them for the repressing of their pride, as though He had said nothing at all to them.—iii. The third was, under a colour of loving our Saviour to fall into the occasion of denying Him, *associating himself with bad company*, who provoked him to it, since he went to the fire, where there was a cluster of reptiles, breathing out nothing but dissolute discourses.

Nor is it without mystery what is here set down, "because it was cold," to signify thereby the frozen heart of St. Peter, together with the obscurity and darkness of his soul, all which originally proceeded from the secret presumption and confidence that he had of himself, which could not be cured by the warning which was given him by our blessed Saviour, but the same remaining still alive, in the end produced these pernicious fruits.

2. Hence I will draw three important resolutions:—i. Not to *presume anything of myself*, nor yet to trust to my own strength, being mindful of that which St. Paul says:—"But thou standest by faith, be not high-minded, but fear." (2) And to the Corinthians:—"Therefore he that thinketh himself to stand, let him take heed lest he fall." (3)

ii. The second purpose is, *to follow our Saviour*, not "afar off," but *near to Him*, and that with fervour, since he that follows our Lord "afar off," does not put his foot in the place where Jesus has put His, neither can he well mark the print of His feet, nor finally can he be protected by Him from perils.

iii. The third is, to *fly all occasions of falling*, and to

(2) Rom. xi. 20. (3) 1 Cor. x. 12.

avoid bad company, who may entice me to fall, remembering well that which the Wise man says:—"He that loveth danger shall perish in it." (4)

3. Consider, that if it be true, as many doctors hold, that *the disciple* who was known to the high priest was St. John the Evangelist, though he was placed in the same occasions of falling as St. Peter, yet he did not deny our Saviour, but was saved from that danger principally by the especial protection of the same Jesus, who kept and preserved him, and besides, because he was not infected with that secret presumption and pride of St. Peter.

*Colloquy.*—O Almighty God, deliver me, I beseech Thee, from all occasions of falling, and if at any time I do through my great misery light upon them, protect me with Thy divine mercy and compassion. "Deliver me, O Lord, and set me beside Thee, and let any man's hand fight against me;"(5) for if Thou dost give me Thy hand, who is able to overthrow me, or to pull me out of it?

POINT II.

Things standing in these terms with St. Peter, "there came a servant maid of"(6) the high priest, who was the portress of his house, and she, looking wistfully upon St. Peter, and knowing him to be one of our Lord's disciples, said to them that were standing by, Certainly this man is one of them that went with Jesus; and presently turning herself to St. Peter, she asked him, saying: Art not thou one of this man's disciples? without all question thou wert with Jesus of Nazareth. *To this St. Peter answered,* "*I am not.*" "I neither know nor understand what thou sayest."(7)

1. Concerning this point, first, consider the *cunning*

(4) Ecclus. iii. 27. (5) Job. xvii. 3. (6) Mat. xxvi. 29.
(7) Joan. xviii. 17; Marc. xiv. 67.

*craft of the Devil, who assailed St. Peter the first time by means of a woman*, as he had assailed Adam by means of Eve, in order to overthrow him; inasmuch as women, as the more insinuating sex, and more adventurous, throw down out of their places the very stones of God's Church, if they be not carefully fled from and avoided.

2. Ponder in the person of St. Peter *the weakness of man*, considering that he, who was the foundation of the Church, and to whom had been revealed the divinity of our Saviour, acknowledging Him to be "the Son of the living God," and offering himself to die for Him; now at the voice of a silly woman so trembles and fears, that he denies Him, says that he knows Him not, that he is none of His disciples, and makes no reckoning of Him.

By this example I will learn, not to presume anything of myself, seeing that I am neither rock nor stone, but mere dust and mud; deeply grounding myself in the true knowledge of myself, and the fear of my own mutability, for all the gold and silver of my virtues stands but upon feet of earth; and one little blow of a stone is enough to tumble them all down, and cast to the earth their whole frame and building.(8)

*Colloquy.*—O eternal God, give me, I beseech Thee, a profound knowledge of this dirt, whereof I am composed, to the end that I may not presume anything of myself, but rely wholly upon Thee, in whose virtue I may be able to resist the brunt of temptations, and preserve the gifts which I have received of Thee. Amen.

3. *How prejudicial is an immoderate apprehension*, either of *dishonour or death;* for that which overthrows me is not so much the night of adversity, as the fear of it, which oftentimes has made me deny my Saviour, if not in words,

(8) Dan. ii. 33.

at least in works, neglecting to accomplish some work of virtuous obligation, for fear of losing either a point of worldly honour, or some profit, or a sensual pleasure of the flesh. And, therefore, I will humbly beseech our Lord, that He will vouchsafe to encompass me with the shield of His protection, lest I be too much "afraid of the terror of the night,"(9) and that it seizes upon my heart.

4. Ponder the *great wrong that St. Peter did in this to his master*, together with the inward feeling which our Lord had when He saw His dear and well-beloved disdain to be His disciple, condemning by this fact the life of Him whom he disavowed to be his master. By the considera-tion of this I will move myself to compassion, beholding my Lord thus disowned and forsaken by His friends.

*Colloquy.*—O most sovereign master, I do not now wonder so much that lukewarm Judas through avarice betrays Thee, seeing that fervent Peter, out of pusil-lanimity, denies Thee. But, dear Lord, Thy wisdom permits this ignominy, the better to discover Thy patience in enduring, our frailty in sinning, and the power of Thy grace in converting him that has of-fended.

POINT III.

St. Peter, considering with himself what had passed, and the danger in which he stood, retired from the court to-wards the gate when the cock crowed the first time; not-withstanding he was so troubled, that he took no heed or notice of it, and so not long after he returned again to the place where the rest were warming themselves by the fire-side, who said to him: "Surely thou also art one of" the disciples of this man? And one of them swore that with-out all doubt he was one of them; but Peter took his oath to the contrary, that "*he knew not* the man." About an

(9) Psal. xc. 5.

hour after they pressed him again the third time that he was His disciple, giving him evident signs and marks of it, for one of them told him that he had seen him in the garden with Jesus; another, that he was a Galilean as appeared by his accent; then Peter denied Him *again*, and "began *to curse and swear that he knew not the man.*"(10)

1. First, upon this act of St. Peter, consider *the craft and fury that Satan used* in tempting him, doing in this that which our Lord had foretold, viz.,—that he had "desired" to "sift" St. Peter "like wheat,"(11) now by one temptation, now by another, never leaving off until he had overthrown him three several times; for he assails those that are the most strong with a greater fury, and if they be not firmly rooted in humility, he tumbles them down from the top of sanctity.

*Colloquy.*—O eternal God, "let not," I beseech Thee, "the foot of pride come to me; and let not the hand of a sinner move me,"(12) and cast me down from the place which I possess by Thy grace. Amen.

2. Consider *the danger that there is in remaining still in the occasion of sin,* without making any reckoning of the first fall, for that one sin commonly draws on another, and the lesser trains after it the greater, proceeding still from bad to worse, as we see in S. Peter; who, the first time did but simply deny our Saviour; the second time did it with an *oath;* but the third time: "Cœpit anathematizare et jurare,"—"he began to *curse and swear;*" whence we see that it is a very important thing to shake off at first all human fear, and to avoid the danger that threatens us, for by these pernicious plots the devils still cry out that

(10) Mat. xxvi. 71—3; Joan. xviii. 17; Marc. xiv. 70.
(11) Luc. xxii. 31. (12) Psal. xxxv. 12.

of the prophet: "Rase it, rase it, even to the foundation thereof."(13)

3. Consider, that as St. Peter had the night before presumed of himself three several times, saying that he was ready to die for our Saviour, that he would not be scandalized though all the world should be scandalized, and that he would not deny Him, though it should cost him his life;—even so, in punishment of these three presumptions, God permitted that he should *deny Him the same night three several times;* for pride is wont to draw incontinently after it humiliation, even in the same matter in which it had its nourishment. And, therefore, it very much imports me forthwith to deplore, and be sorry for the sin of pride, before the pain of humiliation falls upon me.

POINT IV.

"And immediately the cock crew again. And Peter remembered the word that Jesus had said to him: Before the cock crow twice, thou shalt deny me thrice." "And Peter going out, wept bitterly."(14)

Here is described to us the conversation of St. Peter, together with his penance.

1. In this is first to be pondered, *the infinite mercy and charity of our Lord* Jesus Christ, who, though He were environed and hemmed in with His enemies, and in the heat of terrible persecutions and calumnies, yet, forgetting His own afflictions, was mindful of His disciple, who by this injury augmented His pains. And, although He were far off from St. Peter, yet knew He well the sins he had committed, and instead of punishing him, took compassion on him, determining to incite him to repentance, that so He might pardon him; all which He performed with a great promptitude, in order to pluck

(13) Psal. cxxxvi. 7. (14) Marc. xiv. 72; Luc. xxii. 62.

His poor sheep speedily out of the jaws of the infernal wolf, who had devoured him. To this effect He hastened the crowing of the cock; yet this second crow had not done any more good than the first, if our Lord Jesus had not cast upon him the eyes of His mercy, illuminating those of St. Peter with a celestial light to make him see his faults, and mollifying his heart, that he might bewail them.

*Colloquy.*—O most loving Jesus, why should not I love Thee with all my heart, seeing that even when I am plotting to offend Thee, Thou dost interpose means to pardon me; and when Thou oughtest to manifest Thine ire in punishing, then Thou showest Thy mercy in pardoning. Dear Lord, take compassion on all sinners, look on them with the eyes of Thy mercy, unstop their ears, that they may understand the crow and voice of Thy preachers, who may touch them to the heart, even to the bewailing of their sins; and when at any time, through frailty, I shall offend Thee, forget not, I beseech Thee, to cast upon me the eyes of Thy mercy.

2. Consider, secondly, the *bitter tears of St. Peter*, which did not proceed from a fear of punishment, but from *love to his master;* for, calling to mind the favours and benefits he had received of Him, together with the ingratitude he had showed in denying Him on such an occasion, his eyes converted themselves into two fountains of tears, with an extreme bitterness and grief of heart, as one who felt that which the prophet Jeremiah says:—"Know thou and see, that it is an evil and a bitter thing for thee, to have left the Lord thy God."(15) "Alas," he said to himself, "how can I live, having renounced the author of life? Why does not the earth open and swallow me up, I who

(15) Jerem. ii. 19.

have injured its Creator? O mouth most abominable, how durst thou open thyself to swear that thou knowest not Him, who has done thee so great good? O most cursed tongue, how wast thou let loose to accuse thyself, if thou knewest Him who had showed thee so great love? O how just and reasonable would it have been that the same imprecation and malediction should have lighted on me, since I myself had made choice of it, and that it should have penetrated all my bones, seeing that I myself had desired the same? O that all the bitterness of the sea might be given to my heart, and a fountain of water to mine eyes, to bewail bitterly night and day the death of my soul, and the treason she has committed against her Creator! But, forasmuch as I already know His mercy, and that He desires not the death of a sinner, but rather that he be converted and live,(16) I will look upon Him, that looks on me, I will turn myself towards Him that has turned towards me, and with my heart I will draw near to Him, prostrating myself at His holy feet, and saying to Him as the prodigal child:—'Father, I have sinned against heaven and before Thee, I am not now worthy to be called Thy son,'(17) no nor yet Thy disciple. Receive me, I beseech Thee, into the rank of the hirelings of Thy house, for there can be no greater hell to me than to be chased from it."

In this manner did St. Peter deplore his sins, and yet found confidence of obtaining pardon, in the reflection he made on the words that our Lord had said to him;—viz., that He had prayed for him that his faith should not fail,(18) and that after his conversion he should confirm his brethren. In this manner did he also weep all the rest of his life, as often as he heard the cock crow; insomuch that it is said of him, that the multitude of scalding

(16) Ezech. xviii. 23. (17) Luc. xv. 21. (18) Ibid. xxii. 32.

tears, which he shed had made hollow furrows, like channels or gutters all along his cheeks.

3. Finally, consider *after what manner the divine illustration inspired and touched St. Peter, and converted him.* For, first, as soon as he had departed out of the place and occasion in which he fell, it made him remember the words of our Saviour, and then being remote from the rest and all alone, he *wept* bitterly; the like our Lord practises with us, when at any time He touches our hearts efficaciously. First, He moves us to fear, to confidence and love.—Secondly, He removes from us the impediments of true repentance;—and lastly, He makes us enjoy its fruit, which is the pardon of our sins, provided we have a will to confess them at the first opportunity.

*Colloquy.*—O my soul, as thou dost behold in St. Peter thy frailty and readiness to commit sin, so likewise behold in him the power of divine grace, to convert thee from sin; and as he wept, so do thou likewise weep for thy sins, that thou mayest obtain full pardon of them. Amen.

---

## MEDITATION XXIX.

ON THE FALSE WITNESSES BROUGHT BY THE JEWS AGAINST CHRIST IN THE HOUSE OF CAIPHAS, AND HIS ANSWER TO THEIR DEMANDS.

### POINT I.

"And the chief priests, and the whole counsel, sought false witness against Jesus, that they might put Him to death; and they found not, though many false witnesses had come in. And last of all, there came in two false witnesses; and they said: This man said, I am able to destroy the Temple of God, and in three days to build it."(1) But yet all these witnesses were insufficient, and our Lord made no answer at all to them.

1. Consider first, *the form of this judgment* which Caiphas attempted against our Lord Jesus. Consider who the *judges* are,—their wicked *intentions,—the pride and ambition* they covertly hatch in their judgment seats;—moreover, who the *accusers* and *witnesses* are;—their *multitude* and perverse *designs.*—On the other side, who the *prisoner is,*—and party accused;—His *divinity* and sovereignty, joined with such *modesty* and humility,—admitting that the Son of God, who is the judge of the quick and the dead, should appear in the quality of a guilty person, His hands bound, and hearing the calumnies that were uttered against Him before so accursed judges, who were His cruel persecutors, and who, under the cloak of justice, violated all the laws of justice, they themselves suborning false witnesses to condemn the innocent.

*Colloquy.*—O most innocent lamb, who has put Thee in the midst of these ravenous wolves? O most just judge, who has subjected Thee to the judgments of judges so unjust? The injustices that I have committed, dear Lord, are the cause of the calumnies Thou endurest, thereby to deliver me from my iniquities. "Redeem me, Lord," I beseech Thee, "from the calumnies of men, that I may keep" with quietness of mind "Thy commandments."(2) Amen.

2. The singular *innocence and purity which shone in our Saviour Jesus*, for His enemies passionately seeking after matter in which to accuse Him, whether by right or wrong, could yet find no apparent ground, of charging Him with aught worthy of the least punishment. By which we see how truly He said: "The prince of this world cometh, and in me he hath not anything."(3) For

(1) Mat. xxvi. 59; Marc. xiv. 9. (2) Psal. cxviii. 134.
(3) Joan. xiv. 30.

Satan, by means of his ministers, caused Him to be apprehended and to be condemned to death, and that under the pretext and form of justice; yet found he nothing of his in Him, that is, nothing that was sin, or which merited such a punishment.

*Colloquy.*—O most innocent and most pure Saviour, I humbly beseech Thee, by the innocency and purity of Thy most holy life, to grant me a life so pure and so innocent, that, when the prince of this world shall come at the hour of my death, he may find "nothing in me" that is his, of which to accuse me and condemn me. Amen.

3. The marvellous *silence of Christ* our Lord in all these calumnies, without so much as once defending or excusing Himself, or taking exceptions against the witnesses, or against their words, to discover their falsehoods, which had been very easy for His infinite wisdom to have done; but He would hold His peace, relying upon His innocency and on the force of the truth itself, fulfilling that which He had said by the mouth of holy king David:—"And those who sought evils to me spoke vain things, and studied deceits all the day long. But I, as a deaf man, heard not, and was as a dumb man not opening his mouth. And I became as a man who heareth not, and who hath not reproofs in his mouth."(4) All which our Saviour exercised to leave us an example of silence and suffrance in the like occurrences, committing our defence to Almighty God, and to the manifest truth. It is likewise a secret and most glorious means of triumph over our enemies, who often desire that we should speak, to get an opportunity of reprehending either our impatience, or indiscretion, or else of wresting and calumniating our answers. Caiphas, therefore, being much vexed to see such

(4) Psal. xxxvii. 13.

a silence in our Lord Jesus, rose up from his seat, and said to Him:—"Answerest Thou nothing to the things that are laid to Thy charge by these men? but He held His peace, and answered nothing."(5)

*Colloquy.*—O Word divine, Word eternal of the Father! Why dost not Thou allege some word in Thy justification? Remember Thyself well, that whoever holds his peace seems to consent, and take heed that Thou be not adjudged faulty, for want of sufficiently defending Thyself. Notwithstanding it is Thy great mercy, dear Lord, who wilt by Thy silence pay the price of my superfluous talking, and restrain my tongue, lest it should excuse its faults. Bridle it, good Lord, with Thy holy grace, that it may endure in silence what Thou endurest, and triumph over its enemies, as Thou triumphedst over Thine. Amen.

POINT II.

Caiphas, seeing that our Lord would not answer so much as a word, said to Him:—"I adjure Thee, by the living God, that Thou tell us if Thou be Christ, the Son of God. Jesus saith to him: *Thou hast said it.* Nevertheless, I say to you, *hereafter ye shall see the Son of Man* sitting on the right hand of the power of God, and coming in the clouds of heaven." (6)

1. Consider here, the great *reverence that our Saviour bore to the holy name of God,* who having held His peace so constantly, now seeing Himself conjured in the name of Almighty God, presently obeyed the high priest, and answered him, although He knew that this conjuring of Him proceeded from a mischievous intention, to draw from Him some word or other, on which He might be accused; and, besides, He could not be ignorant that His answer would cost Him His life, since they took it for the

(5) Marc. xiv. 60. (6) Mat. xxvi. 63; Marc. xiv. 62.

only subject of His condemnation; showing us in this an example of reverencing God's holy name, and of obeying for His sake the prelates of His Church, however perverse, without any opposition, and of not obstinately persisting in our resolution of being silent when they command us to speak, or bid us do any other lawful thing, although we had resolved the contrary with ourselves.

2. Consider, secondly, *the answer He made them: simply confessing the truth,—that He was Jesus Christ*, and, withal, drawing them out of the error in which they were concerning Him, because they saw Him so abased and contemned; intending also to impress them with a fear that might retain and divert them from their accursed intentions. As if He had said:—"I am Christ; and though at present you disown me, because you see me so humbled, yet a day will come when you shall see the Son of Man sitting at the right hand of the power of God and coming in the clouds of heaven," to judge the world, as has been prophecied of Christ; (7) be, therefore, well advised what you do.

*Colloquy.*—O Son of the living God, Son of Man, true God and true Man, humble and exalted, who art here standing on Thy feet like to a guilty person, to be judged by Caiphas, and shalt hereafter sit as judge upon the clouds of heaven, to be judge of the whole world, my soul burns with the fire of Thy love when I behold Thee so humbled to ransom me, and she trembles for fear when I consider Thee sitting on Thy throne to judge me. Let Thy love, dear Lord, be to me a spur to serve Thee, and Thy fear as a bridle that I do not offend Thee.

3. Consider, moreover, these words:—"*Hereafter you shall see the Son of Man.*" For, as the prophet, says—"A

(7) Psal. cix. 1; Dan. vii. 13.

thousand years before Thine eyes, are as yesterday, which is past."(8) And although it seems to us that the coming of Christ to judgment is long, *yet it will come speedily.* By which He would teach us, that when at any time we are humbled and afflicted, we should comfort ourselves by thinking that our exaltation will follow shortly after; and on the contrary, when we are puffed up and proud, it will be a good means of humbling ourselves, to remember that the day of judgment is at hand, at which time our pride will be pulled down; both in the one and in the other it will be expedient for us to consider what Caiphas will think, and all those of his council that were assembled against Jesus, when they shall see Him sit in so great glory, as judge, ready to give sentence of condemnation against them. Oh, what a change will there then be! for then they will weep and lament with an irremediable bitterness, for having been so rash as to have offended Him. Wherefore, choose to be humbled with Jesus in this life, that thou mayest be glorified by Him in the next.

POINT III.

The high priest, having understood this answer, "*rent his garments*, saying: He hath blasphemed: what further need have we of witnesses? Behold now ye have heard the blasphemy, what think ye? But they answering, said: He is guilty of death" (9)

1. Ponder first, the devilish *hypocrisy of this wicked high priest*, to incense all the assembly against our Saviour; on one side, he tears "his garments," in sign of grief, as one, forsooth, that had heard a horrible blasphemy against God; and on the other side, he is glad at heart to have found an occasion to condemn Him; insomuch, that in sign of victory, he says to them,—"Let us seek after no

(8) Psal. lxxxix. 4. (9) Mat. xxvi. 65.

more witnesses;" and so perverting all order of justice, he constitutes himself the accuser, and makes his assistants the judges, bidding them pronounce their sentence, and provoking them to condemn Him as a blasphemer, which they performed, crying out: "Reus est mortis"—He is guilty of death." By this I may learn, how erroneous the judgments of men are, especially when they proceed from passion, considering that they condemn to death the author of life, and adjudge for a blasphemer against God even God Himself.

2. Besides this, consider the *humiliation of our Lord* in this case, compassionating Him thus calumniated and oppressed for having answered nothing but the truth, and wonder with thyself to see the Son of God reduced into such contempt that they adjudge Him a blasphemer, and that His words, which are the words of eternal life, are reputed to be blasphemies, and to be worthy of eternal death. Draw also from this example motives of comfort, if ever thou shalt see thyself despised and condemned without thy own fault.

*Colloquy.*—O sweet Jesus, Thou hadst far more occasion given Thee to tear Thy garment, when Thou didst hear the words of Caiphas, as full of blasphemy against God, as thine were full of truth, and of the glory of the same God. Oh that my heart could break in pieces for grief at understanding the blasphemies they here breathe out against Thee. Blessed Lord, Thou wert not the blasphemer, but the blasphemed, who for the blasphemies that men utter against God, dost permit Thyself to be blasphemed by them, paying for their faults by Thine own pains.

3. Consider *with what affections our Lord hearkened to this sentence,*—"Reus est mortis"—"He is guilty of death;" for perceiving that they all pronounced it with

one consent, He was grieved to see this their injustice, that such persons as had received so many benefits from Him should so lightly sentence Him to death; and yet inwardly He accepted of it, offering Himself to die to give them life.

*Colloquy.*—O the immense charity of Jesus, who dost so much grieve Thyself for our faults, and for the damage that they bring to us, that Thou offerest Thyself to die, to deliver us from them; let all the angels praise Thee, O Lord, and let them all with one acclamation contradict this malignant council, crying out, "Dignus est vitæ"—"He is worthy of life, He is worthy of life; it is you that deserve death, and Jesus Christ alone who is worthy of eternal life."

---

## MEDITATION XXX.

### ON THE INJURY AND PAINS ENDURED BY OUR LORD IN THE PRESENCE OF CAIPHAS, OF HIS COUNCIL, AND THE REST, IN THAT NIGHT.

#### POINT I.

This sentence being given, those that held our Lord—for He was not only bound and fettered, but many held Him besides, for fear He should escape them—*began to injure and torment Him*, at Satan's instigating them to it, intermixing pains with their insults, thereby to redouble His torments; all which were of *five or six kinds.*

The first injury was, to "*spit in His face,*" (1) which was an ignominious and villanous torment; a thing that was in practice amongst the Jews, and reputed for an outrageous and a heinous injury. Now, as there were many officers and soldiers who spat upon Him, vieing, as it were, with one another, who could spit the most, the sacred face

(1) Mat. xxvi. 67; Marc. xiv. 65.

of our Lord Christ became all foul, covered over with filth, and greatly obscured.

1. Consider, therefore, with thyself, O my soul, who it is they spit upon,—who they are that spit—what face it is that is thus defiled,—and what mouths those are that thus defile Him, and thou shalt find that He who is so spit upon is the God of majesty, the Creator of heaven and earth; He that with His spittle made the blind to see, the dumb to speak, and the deaf to hear, (2) whose face the Seraphim are enamoured of,—which the angels are never satisfied to behold,—in which is contained the life of the whole world, and after which the Prophets long sighed, saying:—"Show us Thy face, and we shall be saved."(3) The same is here spit upon by worthless creatures, by most abominable sinners, by wretches who deserved that all the rest of the world should spit upon them, as in a place the most loathsome and most filthy that was to be found in the whole world; how then hast thou not compassion to see such a Lord spit upon by such slaves; so excellent a Creator by so vile creatures? O venerable face of my Lord Jesus, more bright than the sun, more fair than the moon, and more beautiful to behold than the stars of heaven, how comes it to pass that the loathsome spittings of earthly sinners have thus obscured and defiled Thee? Their sins are the cause of this, and Thou to cleanse them from them wilt Thyself be soiled! In former ages, it was the custom to spit upon him that refused to raise up the family of his brother deceased, without children,(4) but Thou, dear Lord, art spit upon because Thou dost raise up again the family of Adam, who killed himself and all his children.

*Colloquy.*—I give Thee humble thanks, gracious

(2) Joan. ix. 6; Marc. vii. 33.
(3) Psal. lxxix. 4. (4) Deut. xxv. 9.

Lord, for this inestimable charity, by which I heartily beseech Thee to raise up my poor soul, to wash it, and to adorn it with the beauty of Thy grace. Amen.

2. Then consider the *modesty, gravity, and serenity of our Lord*, who, with rare meekness and silence, endured that loathsome shower of spittings, without once turning away His face from those that spit upon Him, and, as the prophet Isaiah had foretold,(5) without showing any gesture, or the least sign of offence or displeasure, and without saying any one word against the spitters.

*Colloquy.*—O eternal God, if Thou didst spit upon the face of Mary, the sister of Aaron, because she had injured Moses, which was at the same instant covered over with leprosy,(6) why dost Thou not do the same now to these that spit upon Thee? why dost Thou not cover them over with leprosy, as their abominable licentiousness deserves? But Thou, O my God, art not come into the world to make lepers, but to heal them, taking upon Thee the pain of their leprosy, and the form of a leper;(7) Thou art not come to spit, and thereby to kill, but to heal and give life by Thy spittle to the sinner, who wants life; anoint me, sweet Lord, with this Thy spittle, rendering me thereby wise to know Thee, and whole and strong to love and serve Thee. Amen.

3. In order to obtain the spiritual fruit of what has been said, ponder within yourself, that *as often as you offend God* with any heinous sin, so often *do you spiritually spit in the face of Jesus*, and defile it with the spittle of your sin, cast out with a venomous tongue from a poisoned heart. You may also consider what a shower of these spittings has lighted, and does light upon Jesus, and how much greater feeling He has of faults above the rest, as

(5) Is. l. 6. (6) Num. xii. 10. (7) Is. liii. 4.

being more noisome and abominable before Almighty God; and finally, that to despise and spit at our *neighbour*, is to spit upon Christ Jesus, who takes this injury as done to Himself. From all which draw affections of grief and compassion, determining within yourself to fly from sin, seeing that our Lord esteems Himself to be spit upon by it.

POINT II.

1. The *second* injury was, to *blindfold the divine eyes*,(8) that they might more freely strike and scorn Him, as if He did not see them; for the serenity and gravity of the countenance of Christ, did as it were restrain them from scorning Him at their will, contrary to that which happened to Moses,(9) who himself covered his face with a veil when he spoke to the people, because the splendour that issued from his face, dazzled the eyes of such as beheld him; but our sweet Jesus, the splendour of the glory of the eternal Father, consents that His eyes be covered with another veil by the disciples of Moses, not intending that they may the more attentively hearken to Him, but that they may the more boldly abuse and contemn Him. Showing by this that His desire was as great of being dishonoured by them, as theirs was to dishonour Him; and it is very probable that the veil or cloth which they put before His eyes, was some old patched clout, or indecent rag, to make Him thereby the more ridiculous and contemptible.

2. *It is the custom of grievous sinners to desire that God should not see them*, or to imagine within themselves that He does not take any notice of them, that they may sin with the more liberty; saying that which is written in Job:—"The clouds are His covert, and He doth not con-

(8) Marc. xiv. 65; Luc. xxii. 64. (9) Exod. xxxiv. 35.

sider our things."(10) Even so did these miscreants blindfold the corporal eyes of our Lord Jesus, for fear He should see them; but that did not hinder Him from beholding them with the eyes of His soul, and of His divinity, so that they rather blindfolded their own eyes and sight, than hindered or deprived our Saviour of His. Wherefore I ought to consider when I commit sin, and forget myself to be in the sight of God, that this forgetting is as much as a veil, that I imagine to be put over the eyes of Almighty God, which is not over His, but over my own, for as the Wise man says:—"The eyes of our Lord in every place behold the good and the evil,"(11) and the good works and the evil that every one does.

*Colloquy.*—O eternal God, permit not, I beseech Thee, that I should ever cover Thine eyes, and Thy face, unless it be as the Seraphim cover them with their wings,(12) reverencing thereby the divinity, and confessing that they have no eyes able to comprehend it. But Thou, O Lord, hast most clear-sighted eyes to behold and comprehend me, which is sufficient to make me believe that Thou dost see my faults, and also to move me to lament them, with full resolution never to return again to them.

POINT III.

1. The *third* injury and torment was, *to strike Him with their hands.*

i. And that in *two ways*; some with their *fists* began to "buffet" Him upon the face, head, back, and arms, and all with great rage and fury, in such a manner that it is probable His divine face became swollen and discoloured, and His whole body much bruised by so many blows, as those who struck Him were many and cruel,

(10) Job. xxii. 14. (11) Prov. xv. 3. (12) Is. vi. 2.

incensed with rage and a show of zeal of revenging the blasphemy uttered, as they imagined, against God.

ii. Others there were that smote Him "*with the palms of their hands*," which manner of injury is esteemed amongst men more ignominious, than to be stricken with the fist. Here did our Lord fulfil according to the letter the counsel which He Himself had given in the Gospel:—"But if one strike thee on the right cheek, turn to him also the other." (13) For He did not here receive one blow, and no more, as in the house of Annas, but many; these ministers of the Devil vieing with one another, and striving who should strike Him most, thinking that in beating Him they should gain an indulgence for themselves; all which this most meek Saviour received, without once saying:—"Why do you strike me?" On the contrary, He said to them, in effect rather, than by word of mouth:—"If you will strike me, strike me and spare not, behold me here ready to endure blows and buffetings, my desire is to see myself fully loaden with such disgraces, in which was fulfilled that which the prophet Jeremiah had said:—'He shall give His cheek to him that striketh Him, He shall be filled with reproaches.'" (14)

iii. Consider here the mysteries of *these two kinds of blows* that our Lord received at the hands of sinners, of whom some strike Him with the *hand shut*, and these are avaricious and covetous, who fully occupy themselves in heaping up goods for themselves, and having gotten them, shut them up, without once opening their hand to distribute part to the poor;—others strike Him with the *palm of the hand open* and extended, and these are the proud and vain worldlings, the voluptuous and delicate towards their flesh, the prodigals who dissipate all they have in vanity and sensuality; and the faults of these latter are

(13) Mat. v. 39. (14) Thren. iii. 30.

more ignominious, because they affront our Lord Jesus, dishonouring Him to honour themselves. And in punishment of these two kinds of sins Christ our Lord would sustain these two different pains.

2. Therefore, I will consider within myself that it is I that "buffet" our Lord with my fist, when I offend Him through the covetousness of earthly goods; and that I "strike Him *with the palm of the hand* when I sin through vanity or sensuality, seeking to spread my fame, and to hunt after sensual delights.

*Colloquy.*—O most liberal giver of all good things, who dost so freely offer Thy cheek to him that strikes Thee, offering him also Thy heart for the love Thou bearest him; open, Lord, Thy most blessed hand, and touch them that strike Thee with theirs, that they may desist from striking Thee, and make them with the same to strike their own breasts, as did the publican,(15) confessing their enormous faults, to obtain forgiveness of them. Amen.

POINT IV.

The *fourth* pain and torment was, *to pluck off and tear away His beard*, and hair of His head, with excessive cruelty; for although the Evangelists make not any mention of this, notwithstanding, our Lord having foretold it by the prophet Isaiah, it is certain that the same was accomplished.—"I have," said He, "given my body to the strikers, and my cheeks to them that plucked them; I have not turned away my face from them that rebuked me, and spit upon me." (16)

*Colloquy.*—O sovereign high priest, much more noble than Aaron, whose unction ran from his head, all along his face to his beard, to signify his dignity and manly force, how dost Thou suffer Thy beard to

(15) Luc. xviii. 13. (16) Is. l. 6.

be torn away with such contumely and cruelty? O sacred Nazarite, whose hair was never to be shorn during the time of their consecration,(17) wherefore dost Thou suffer Thine to be thus pulled off, seeing that Thou ever remainest a Nazarite, that is to say, holy, yea, sanctity itself? But I acknowledge, O Lord, that my effeminate niceness is the cause that Thy beard is torn away, and from my inordinate excesses, the hairs of Thy head are plucked off. And seeing that the love that Thou bearest me, far other than that of Samson to Dalila—has permitted this; (18) I humbly beseech Thee that Thou wilt vouchsafe to pardon me my sins, that are the cause of so great pains, and to give me a manly courage to serve Thee, and well mortified, never more to offend Thee.

POINT V.

1. The *fifth* injury was, of *injurious words which they used against Him*, when having covered His face, striking and buffeting Him, they said:—"*Prophecy unto us, O Christ; Who is he that struck Thee?*" (19) As much as to say:—"Seeing that Thou dost vaunt Thyself to be the Christ and a prophet, prophecy to us" who has given Thee this blow; giving by this to understand, that they esteemed Him for a feigned Christ, and a counterfeit prophet. And St. Luke adds, that they uttered many other blasphemies against Him, (20) concerning which he leaves us to conjecture; to believe, therefore, that they were very many and enormous, it is sufficient to know that there were many impudent and insolent blasphemers full of choler and rancour, and besides, the hellish serpent "sharpened their tongues," (21) to vomit forth against Him injuries and blasphemies unheard of, that so they

(17) Num. vi. 5. (18) Judic. xvi. 4. (19) Mat. xxvi. 68.
(20) Luc. xxii. 65. (21) Psal. cxxxix. 4.

might provoke Him to impatience, and be the better revenged of Him.

2. And it is very likely that they repeated afresh all their former injurious words, calling Him "Samaritan," possessed with "a devil," glutton,(22) drunkard, "a friend of publicans," an infringer and violator of the feasts of Sabbaths, seditious, a stirrer up of the people, enchanter, necromancer, a blasphemer against God, and the like; in such a way, that they fully satisfied the longing they had to injure and abuse Him, accomplishing in our Lord Jesus that which holy Job said of himself:—"They have opened their mouths upon me, and reproaching me, they have struck me on the cheek, they are filled with my pains." (23)

3. And our Lord Himself, as the prophet Jeremiah said, was also satisfied even at the full with injuries, desirous, notwithstanding, to endure yet more enormous, which doubtless were not wanting to Him the rest of that night, for the longing desire of His enemies in this kind was like that disease which physicians call "appetitus caninus," a ravenous and unnatural greediness after meat, as also like to the insatiable thirst of the dropsy, both which are of that nature, that though the parties attainted do eat and drink till they burst again, yet are they still hungry and thirsty, even until death; nevertheless, the desire and appetite of our Lord Jesus was the hunger and thirst of an infinite charity, which can never be fully satisfied; and so though they desired to fill and press Him down with injuries, yet was He still ready to have endured more.

*Colloquy.*—O blessed be the insatiable charity, and the burning fire of so fervent a love, which could never say to them that injured Him, "It is enough."(24)

4. Finally, as touching those five sorts of injuries, the

(22) Joan. viii. 48. (23) Job. xvi. 11. (24) Prov. xxx. 15.

Evangelists did not disdain *to recount particularly the affronts and abuses of our Saviour*, because they well knew that it was a great glory to God, to our Saviour, and to us, that He should endure all this for our sakes; and consequently that we should not disdain to suffer the like, but rather that we should glory in them, and love with all our hearts Him that gave us such arguments and proof of His love towards us, praising Him without ceasing, and joining continual thanksgiving, with continual services, for all of which I may make as it were a litany in this or such like manner, saying:—

*Colloquy.*—I give Thee humble thanks, O most sweet Jesus, for having suffered with such an unspeakable patience and humility, that Thy enemies should spit upon Thy face, blindfold Thine eyes, buffet Thy cheeks, pluck off Thy beard, tear off Thy hair, beat Thee down to the ground with blows, and that they should fill Thine ears with innumerable blasphemies. And I heartily beseech Thee, dear Lord, by these most holy pains, to pardon me my sins which have been the cause of them, and to make me so happy as that I may endure for Thy sake in all patience and charity the pains that Thou hast endured for me. Amen.

POINT VI.

1. Consider, first, that which our Lord must have *suffered the rest of the night*, which is far more than we are able to conceive, for the high priest and others having gone away to take their rest, *our Lord remained still strongly bound in that hall* with many soldiers to guard Him, to whom ran also all the servants and the basest scullions of the house, who during the whole night made it their pastime to mock and scoff at Him in those five things before mentioned, besides many others which Satan suggested to them, to revenge himself by that means on Christ our

Lord, as also to soil His constancy; and whilst some through weariness went their way to sleep, others came in their places to prosecute these injuries, not giving Him one moment of rest or leisure to breathe all the night long, He serving them for a butt and mark to shoot at, according to that which Simeon had prophesied of Him when He said, that He should be put "for a sign which shall be contradicted." (25) And to that of the prophet David:—"But I am a worm and no man: the reproach of men, and the outcast of the people." (26)

2. But how did this sovereign Redeemer behave Himself then? Not as *man*, but as *more than* man, and the glory of all men; He showed a face of diamond and a body of steel, without being weary of enduring, or *once showing any sign of dislike or tediousness*, and inwardly He offered all these distresses to His heavenly Father for sinners, praying continually for them with exceeding fervour, so that we may truly say of Him, that which is in the Gospel:—"Et erat pernoctans in oratione Dei"—"He passed the whole night in the prayer of God;" (27) that is, in most high prayer worthy of God, neither the multitude of the injurious words which He heard, nor the extremity of the pains that He endured, being able to divert or weary Him. He had there with Him, present in His mind, His disciples, though they were dispersed one from another like sheep without a shepherd, for whom He prayed most earnestly, lest the infernal wolf should devour them; and I may likewise believe that He held me also as present in His memory, and that He offered up His prayer to His Father for me.

*Colloquy.*—O my Saviour, that I had been there to keep Thee company, and to temper in some sort the desolation of so long and doleful a night! Behold, I here

(25) Luc. ii. 34. (26) Psal. xxi. 7. (27) Luc. vi. 12.

offer myself in spirit before Thee, desirous to spend the night in the prayer of God, joining my prayer with Thine, that so I may obtain a good and speedy despatch.

POINT VII.

Consider, lastly, that *some one of the disciples*, peradventure St. John, *carried the news of our Lord's seizure to His mother, the most sacred Virgin*, who was at that time in Mary Magdalen's company, together with other holy women, where they had eaten their Paschal lamb.

1. Understanding, therefore, the heavy tidings, *her soul was presently pierced with the "sword" of sorrow*, and so violent a grief possessed her, that she might truly have pronounced her Son's words:—"My soul is sorrowful, even unto death;" that is, it is overwhelmed with mortal heaviness, with the sorrows and pangs of death; for as her love towards Him was most inflamed, and her faith most lively, with which she apprehended the injuries and pains that He was to endure, so understanding now that He was plunged into those torments, her soul was filled with bitter grief, and absorbed in a sea of marvellous compassion, inasmuch as we may well say of her with the prophet Jeremiah:—"Great as the sea is thy destruction: who shall heal thee?" (28)

2. Nevertheless, this Virgin, replenished by God, after the example of her son, *had recourse to prayer*, and casting herself upon her knees, her face prostrate upon the earth, she might say:—"Sovereign Father, if it be possible let not my son taste of this cup, or else season somewhat its excessive bitterness; nevertheless, Thy will be done, and not mine.—'Abba Father,' all things are possible to Thee, transfer this chalice of my son to me, and I will drink it, to exempt Him that He may not drink it, 'yet not my

(28) Thren. ii. 13.

will, but Thine be done.'" In this prayer did she insist a long while, exercising acts of confidence and resignation, and conforming her will to the will of God; and it is to be thought, that falling into an agony she prayed the longer, until the eternal Father, by an angel, or by Himself, sent her some internal comfort.

3. Then she rose up from her prayer, and after her son's example, like a good mother, she *began to comfort those that were in her company*, lest they should lose their faith; and the rest of the night she spent in thinking upon the afflictions that her son endured, according as she had read them in the books of the prophets, the consideration of which caused in her rivers of tears.

*Colloquy.*—O most sacred Virgin, who, like another Sion, dost weep and lament all night long, pouring down thy cheeks streams of tears, without receiving any jot of comfort from any of thy friends in this affliction,(29) thou hast certainly reason to weep, for "the breath" and life of our mouth, "Christ, is taken in our sins."(30) O my sins that are the cause of so great grief to Jesus, and to His mother, weep, mine eyes, all night long, weep and lament with an extreme sorrow, pouring down along your face great and abundant floods of tears, seeing that you cannot comfort them any other way than by bewailing your sins, which are the cause of their tears.

---

## MEDITATION XXXI.

### ON THE PRESENTATION OF OUR LORD BEFORE PILATE, AND THE UNHAPPY DEATH OF JUDAS.

#### POINT I.

"And as soon as it was day, the ancients of the people, and the chief priests and the scribes came together, and

(29) Thren. i. 2. (30) Thren. iv. 20.

they brought Him into their council 'the second time,' saying:—*If Thou be the Christ tell us.* And He said to them, If I shall tell you, you will not believe me. And if I shall also ask you, you will not answer me, nor let me go. But hereafter the Son of Man shall be sitting on the right hand of the power of God. Then said they all, Art Thou then the Son of God? Who said, You say that I am. And they said, What need we any further testimony? For we ourselves have heard it from His own mouth." (1)

1. Consider, first, *with what impatience they all*, as well our Lord as His enemies, though with different ends, *expected the appearing of the "day,"*—our Lord, because He intended that day to accomplish the redemption of the world, which He had expected the space of thirty and three years, reputing that day to be His, because it was entirely for our good.—His enemies longed that it were day, in order that they might bring to pass their damnable intent of putting Him to a cruel death; and for this reason they rose so early in the morning, to assemble themselves again together in council. Hence I will draw affections of gratitude to our Saviour, for the great desire He had to see this day; I will likewise draw forth affections of shame and confusion, considering how diligent the wicked are to do evil, and how early up to execute their own wills, I myself remaining so slothful to execute the will of Almighty God.

2. Consider *the malice and deceitful craftiness of those scribes, in the question* they proposed to our Lord, to entrap and take Him at an advantage, in what manner soever He should frame His answer; for if He had denied Himself to be Christ, they would have replied that He was contrary to Himself, and that He condemned Himself, for having procured that He should be taken and esteemed

(1) Luc. xxii. 66.

for Christ; but if He confessed it, according to His first interrogatory, then they would have sufficient matter of condemning Him.

3. *The answer of our Lord,* His admirable prudence, modesty, and meekness, accompanied with great liberty of spirit, adding this second time, that He should be sitting at the right hand of the power of God, thereby to make them fear; and to give us likewise to understand, that His humiliations were to end with an exaltation, as ours also will, if we follow in His footsteps.

4. Finally, with a spirit far different from that of these traitors, beholding our Lord, by reason of the grievous torments of this troublesome night, so disfigured, I will ask Him,—*Art Thou my Jesus, the Christ?* the Messiah? "the Son of the living God?" and the splendour of the eternal Father? and He that is "the figure of His substance," and the invisible image of Almighty God? If Thou be, as indeed Thou art, who has dared thus to disfigure Thy face? who has thus defiled it with spitting, who has thus darkened it with bruises? who has thus ill-treated Thee, without any respect at all of Thy venerable Person? *My sins*, dear Lord, *are the cause of this*, and Thy charity has taken upon Thee these marks, to testify thereby that Thou art indeed the Christ, the Son of the living God, who art come into the world to redeem the same, because none other but Jesus Christ could possibly have endured so cruel torments with so affectionate and loving an affection, and that in punishment of sins which He had not committed; and seeing that Thou hast suffered these pains, Thou art my Christ, my God, and my Saviour, to whom be all honour and glory, for ever and ever. Amen.

POINT II.

When they had understood His answer, "the whole

council binding Jesus anew, *led Him away, and delivered Him to Pilate.*" (2)

1. In this third station that our Lord made, the *ecclesiastical estate of the Jews*, open enemies to our Lord, by this sentence *gave Him over to the secular power of Pilate*, then president for the Romans, that by him He might be rigorously punished, judging that pain with which they could punish Him too little, because their intention was that He should die a cruel death, divine providence having so ordained it, to the end that both Jews and Gentiles should concur to the death of Him, who was to die for the salvation of all.

*Colloquy.*—O sweet Jesus, if those of Thine own nation, to whom Thou hast done so many favours, condemn Thee in this manner, what will strangers do, who know Thee not? And yet, notwithstanding this, dear Lord, Thou art prepared to be persecuted by all, in order to save all, for Thy death is our life, and Thy condemnation in this council of the wicked will be our salvation before God, for ever and ever. Amen.

2. Consider *with what cruelty they led our Lord through the streets of Jerusalem*, gathering together, with their clamours and shoutings, a great company of people; for there were at that time in the town very many assembled, for the feast of the Paschal lamb. Our good Jesus was led forth a great pace with His hands bound, but with a countenance very modest, grave, and mild, suffering Himself to be dragged on by these tigers, without making them any resistance at all, and enduring all the reproaches and ill-language that they used against Him, with a far greater disgrace than on the night before, for it being now open day, every one might behold and note Him, and under-

(2) Marc. xv. 1; Luc. xxiii. 1.

standing that this was done by command of the high priests, who closely followed Him there, no man dare gainsay them; nay, so far were they from that, that every one cried out and railed against the prisoner.

*Colloquy.*—I give Thee humble thanks, O good Jesus, for all the steps Thou madest from the house of Caiphas to that of Pilate, as also for all the disgrace Thou didst endure all the way long, by all which, I beseech Thee, that Thou wilt vouchsafe to pardon me the wicked steps I have made to offend Thee, and that it will please Thee to direct them in such manner hereafter, that they may be all employed in Thy service. Amen.

POINT III.

Judas seeing that our Saviour was condemned to die by the council of the high priests, and that they were now leading Him to Pilate for the confirming of the sentence, and to have it put in execution by him, began to repent himself of what he had done, and going to the Temple, where certain priests and ancients were busied in affairs of their office, said to them:—"Peccavi, tradens sanguinem justum"—"I have sinned in betraying innocent blood." But they said:—"Quid ad nos? Tu videris"—"What is that to us? Look thou to it." "And casting down the pieces of silver in the Temple, he departed; and went and hanged himself with a halter." (3)

1. Consider how the Devil *blinds the eyes of the sinner, when he commits sin*, for fear that, seeing the deformity of the offence, he should abstain from committing it, but after the sin is committed he takes off the blind, and makes the fault seem far greater than it is, representing it before them so ugly, that he drives them for very shame into despair, as it chanced to Cain, who in despair said to

(3) Mat. xxvii. 3.

God:—"My iniquity is greater than that I may deserve pardon." (4)

*Colloquy.*—I know well, O God, the greatness of my sin, but I acknowledge also that Thy mercy is yet far greater, in which I hope to obtain the pardon which I no way merit, because Thou desirest not the death of a sinner, but "rather that he should be converted from his ways, and live."(5)

2. Judas, indeed, *began to do penance*, and practised all its three parts, for he had an interior sorrow in that he was moved with repentance; he confessed his sin plainly before the priests, in that he said,—"I have sinned in betraying, innocent blood;" finally, he made *satisfaction*, restoring the money that he had received unjustly. Notwithstanding, *all this profited him nothing*, because neither was his repentance good, nor his sorrow true, nor was the confession made to whom it ought to have been made, nor, finally, with hope of obtaining pardon. Which thing shall serve me for a warning to procure that my penance be neither feigned nor deficient, for it is not enough to say as Judas did:—"Peccavi"—"I have sinned,"(6) but it must be said in the way that David did, to whom when he said "I have sinned," God forgave his sin, because he uttered those words with great contrition and confidence of obtaining pardon.

3. Consider *the obstinacy of these Jews*, together with the cruelty of the priests, who seeing the repentance of this disciple, and that he acknowledged the innocency of his master, notwithstanding, persisted still in their malice, saying to him:—"Quid ad nos? tu videris"—"What does thy master's innocence concern us, or that thou hast done wickedly in betraying Him? thou shouldest have looked to that before." Which froward answer of theirs drove

(4) Gen. iv. 13. (5) Ezech. xviii. 23. (6) 2 Reg. xii. 13.

him into despair; by which it is plain how perilous a thing it is not to show a good countenance to sinners, when they give any sign of repentance, which manner of proceeding is very far from the spirit of our Lord Jesus, of whom it is written:—"The smoking flax He shall not quench;" (7) that is, He does not put out the match of the lamp that has ever so little light in it, but on the contrary, He uses diligence to keep it in, and lights it again, that it may burn the brighter.

4. Fourthly, consider *the just judgment of God in abandoning this traitor*, as his sins deserved, and permitting that he should not find any consolation among men, nor contentment in his money, which, after he had accomplished his desire, served for his hangman, and even racked and tormented him, causing in him a greater anguish of mind to keep it than he had in the beginning to get it; insomuch that he cast down this money, without once having the heart to make recourse to God, or to crave pardon of his master, but tortured with his own conscience, and urged forward by Satan, not daring to expect the resurrection of Jesus, of which he had an assured knowledge, he resolved with himself to hang himself out of hand, which he did, to the end that all of us might, in this miserable wretch, consider the punishment of covetousness, which was, to lose both money, life, and eternal felicity, to die by his own hands, bursting "asunder in the midst," (8) and pouring out his very bowels, for not having had the bowels of compassion towards our Lord Jesus.

5. Consider, finally, the *feeling that our Lord had of the damnation of this disciple*, and how willingly He had received him to mercy, if, instead of going to the priests of the Temple, he had had recourse to Him with true repentance.

(7) Is. xlii. 3. (8) Act. i. 18.

*Colloquy.*—O most merciful Father, who dost not abandon a sinner, be he ever so much loaden with offences, seeing that Thou hast such a tender feeling of those that are Thine, do not, I pray, pluck Thy hand from me, for if Thou leavest to hold me, I shall with Judas fall into despair, forasmuch as there is no sin that one commits but another man may, if Thou givest him the bridle in his own hands, commit the same.

POINT IV.

The chief priest having received back the pieces of silver again, after they had consulted together what they should do with them, they would not "put them into the corbona," or common box of the Church, "quia pretium sanguinis erat,"—"because *it*" *was* "*the price of blood*, but they bought with them the potter's field, to be a burying place for strangers." (9)

1. Consider, on the one side, the *hypocrisy of these wicked priests*, and on the other side, the goodness of Almighty God, who by a secret instinct inspired them to do the same, to signify that the blood of Jesus Christ should be of no profit to the priests of the Temple and their followers, but that it was to be the price wherewith should be purchased eternal rest, to such as live in this world like poor pilgrims.

2. Moreover, consider how *our Lord showed the love which He bore to the poor*, in that He would that the price of His blood should give burial to them, stirring us up by this to works of mercy, though it should be with the price of our blood.

*Colloquy.*—O sweet Jesus, seeing that Thou dost so much love us, as to turn to our profit all that belongs to Thee, behold, I beseech Thee, my poverty,

(9) Mat. xxvii. 6, 7.

and relieve it with the price of Thy blood, to the end that I may pass as a pilgrim in this life, in such sort that I may diligently travel unto the happy rest of the life everlasting. Amen.

---

## MEDITATION XXXII.

### ON THE ACCUSATION OF CHRIST BEFORE PILATE, AND ON THE QUESTION HE ASKED HIM.

#### POINT I.

Our Lord being presented before Pilate in his place of judgment:—"Pilate therefore went out to them, and said, What accusation bring you against this man? They answered and said to him, If He were not a malefactor we should not have delivered Him up to thee." (1)

1. First, consider the bad entertainment, *and evil treatment that Pilate used towards our Lord*, when he saw Him thus led so straitly bound, with such a multitude, and upon so solemn a day, persuading himself that this must needs be some very abandoned fellow, seeing that He was brought thither by persons of such quality, and at that hour of the day. Take, therefore, compassion to see thy Lord so contemned, and call to mind that He received after another fashion the adulteress, that was brought by the Jews to Him to be judged of her act. (2)

*Colloquy.*—O most merciful judge, who dost receive with so great mildness accused persons, not only when they are innocent, but also when they are guilty, delivering them from their cruel accusers; how comes it to pass that Thou, being innocency itself, dost endure to be received of this proud judge with so great ignominy? Seeing that Thou confoundedst the accusers of her that was faulty, making them to drop away one

(1) Joan. xviii. 29, 30. (2) Joan. xxviii. 3.

after another by writing only their sins with Thy finger upon the earth, why dost Thou not write them out now, to the end that they, being confounded, may abandon Thee, and desist from accusing Thee? But Thy mercy is so great, that, having compassion of sinners, it will not have any on Thyself in enduring for them. Deliver me, sweet Lord, from my accusers, when I am presented before the tribunal of Thy justice, and receive me in mercy, that so being freed by Thy means, I may enjoy Thee for ever. Amen.

2. The pride and *extreme presumption of these accusers of our Lord*, in saying :—"If He were not a malefactor we would not" accuse Him before thee,—as if they would have said,—"It suffices that we, who are the high priests and the doctors of the law, do here present Him to thee, to assure thee that He is a malefactor." O sovereign humility, which humbles in this manner the sovereign benefactor! From this humility of our Lord Jesus, who being the benefactor to all, would, notwithstanding, be esteemed for a public malefactor, even by those themselves to whom He had done greatest good, I will draw a singular affection to humility, esteeming it a happy thing to do good to all, and that all esteem me for a malefactor, in imitation of my Saviour.

POINT II.

"Pilate therefore said to them, Take Him you, and judge Him according to your law. The Jews, therefore, said to him, It is not lawful for us to put any man to death." (3) that is to say, to punish Him with that kind of death which this man deserves, for we have only power to stone Him to death, which certainly would be a pain too easy for His misdeeds.

1. *Then did they frame His accusation* upon three heads:

(3) Joan. xviii. 31.

—i. That by His false doctrine *He stirred up the people* to sedition;—ii. That *He forbade to pay the tribute* that was due to Cæsar;—iii. That *He called Himself Christ*, the King,—that is to say,—that He claimed to be the Messiah promised, who was to be King of the Jews.

2. Consider here *the malice of these accusers*, and the calumnies that they forged against our Lord Jesus with a most venomous heart, for there was nothing so clear as that our Lord did not "stir up the people to sedition," but that He rather excited them to penance, and to all sorts of virtues, insomuch that He used these words to His disciples, saying:—"The scribes and Pharisees have sitten upon the chair of Moses. All things, therefore, whatsoever they shall say to you, observe and do." (4) And so far was He from "forbidding to give tribute to Cæsar," that He commanded, saying:—"Render, therefore, to Cæsar the things that are Cæsar's, and to God the things that are God's." (5) He even Himself paid the tribute for Himself and St. Peter, though He were not bound to do it. Neither yet had He ever named Himself temporal king, such as the Romans ordained; on the contrary, when they would have made Him a king He fled from them, and hid Himself in the mountain. As for naming Himself the Messiah, the works He did yielded sufficient testimony of it. But what could the malice of these false accusers do worse than to invent such calumnies? And what greater cruelty than not to satisfy their rage with that death which they could have put Him to, but to forge crimes against Him, with the intent of condemning Him to another more cruel death, viz., to the death of the cross?

*Colloquy.*—O sweet Jesus, I give Thee humble thanks for the silence with which Thou dost hearken

(4) Matt. xxiii. 2. (5) Luc. xx. 25.

to these calumnies, which Thou couldst most easily have overthrown; grant, I beseech Thee, that I imitate Thy patience, and deliver me from the vice of hatred, which forges such calumnies against those that it abhors.

POINT III.

Pilate having understood that which they had charged Him with, "went into the hall again, and called Jesus," to examine Him upon the crimes imputed to Him, beginning with the last, which he esteemed the most enormous, and said to Him:—"Tu es Rex Judeorum?"—"Art Thou the King of the Jews?" And our Lord perceiving that He asked Him simply, answered him:—"My Kingdom is not of this world. If my Kingdom were of this world, my servants would certainly strive that I should not be delivered to the Jews, *but now my Kingdom is not from hence.*" Pilate interrupting Him, said to Him:—"Art Thou a king then? Jesus answerd, Thou sayest *that I am a king;* For this was I born, and for this came I into the world; *that I should give testimony to the truth.* Every one *that is of the truth, heareth my voice.*" (6)

As concerning the interrogation that Pilate made to our Lord, consider the notable sentences that He uttered in His answers.

1. The first, that *His "Kingdom" was "not of this world,"* as are those on earth, and therefore He had neither warriors, nor a guard of soldiers, nor other officers, such as earthly kings ordinarily have in their kingdoms. And He did not content Himself with saying that He was not a king, but that least of all He pretended to be one, nor ever had pretended, as His accusers feigned.

2. The second was, *that He was truly a king*, but a celestial king, and that He had a kingdom, but that His King-

(6) Joan. xviii. 33—36.

dom was *of the other world*, which is the Kingdom of heaven, and the spiritual Kingdom of His Church, and consequently He had vassals and servants, yet celestial and spiritual, which are the angels, the just, and faithful, that believe in Him, for such as the king is, such are His vassals, and such as the Kingdom is, such are His citizens.

*Colloquy.*—O sovereign King, constituted by the eternal Father over the mount of Sion,(7) how justly did it appertain to Thy greatness to be also King of this world, and to have to Thy vassals and slaves all the kings of the earth. Nevertheless, Thy infinite charity renounced this worldly pomp, that Thou mightest thereby show us an example of humility, and to lift up my heart to aiming at the celestial Kingdom, in contempt of this earthly kingdom. Vouchsafe, O my gracious king, that I be a vassal worthy of Thy Kingdom, giving me courage to tread under my feet all that the world prizes and esteems.

3. The third sentence was, that He "was *born*" "*into this world*" *to* "*give testimony to the truth,*"—that is, to teach it and preach it, confirming it by miracles and works worthy of admiration, in which He had three particular excellencies:—i. That He never averred thing that was false or fabulous, but that which was the pure verity, and behoveful to attain to that Kingdom whereof He was King:—ii. That He published this truth with an invincible courage, although He were to lose His life by declaring the same:—iii. The last, that when it was a thing that turned to His glory, He spoke it not for His own honour, but for the accomplishing of His charge, which was to bear witness of the truth. In imitation of this our Lord, I will persuade myself that I am likewise born and am come into the world to bear witness to the truth, by my

(7) Psal. ii. 6.

works and words, endeavouring always to make appear in them the divine truth, without mingling either falsehood or fiction, though it should cost me my life.

4. The fourth sentence was, that *all those that are of the band of truth*, and love the same, *hearken to His "voice,"* and give credit to that which it says, obeying all that it commands. By this, therefore, shall I see whether I am of the band of Jesus, who is the truth itself, or else of the band of the Devil, who is the father of falsehood. (8) In all this that has been said, consider the authority of our Lord Jesus, and of the divinity that clearly shone in Him, who amidst so great contempts and disgraces, notwithstanding continued to execute the office of a master. And if this wretched judge would have hearkened to Him, He was ready to have taught him clearly this truth, but the unhappy wretch, although he had declared some desire to have known it, by demanding of our Lord:—"Quid est veritas?"—"What is truth?" did not wait for the answer, because, indeed, he did not deserve to understand it.

*Colloquy.*—O heavenly master, answer to my heart what truth is, and make me firmly to believe the same. Thou, O my God, art the truth itself, and all that proceeds from Thee is truth; Thy doctrine is truth, Thy precepts, Thy counsels, Thy miracles, and Thy sacraments are truth. Oh that my life conformed itself to this truth, and advanced itself every day more in this truth, until it should behold Thee clearly in Thy glory. Amen.

POINT IV.

From these answers of our Lord so exact and prudent, did Pilate gather His innocency, and leading Him after him out of the place of judgment into the sight of all the people, said to them:—"I find no cause in this man,"

(8) Joan. viii. 44.

worthy of death. The chief priests and the ancients hearing this, and fearing that Pilate should let Him go, began to propose new matter of accusations, to all which our Saviour answered not one word. Whereupon Pilate again asked Him—"Answerest Thou nothing? Behold in how many things they accuse Thee," and the proofs they bring against Thee; why dost Thou not return an answer? "*But Jesus answered nothing*: so that Pilate wondered."(9)

1. Consider, first, ***this admirable silence of our Lord*** Jesus, which, not without reason, caused in Pilate great amazement, as a thing altogether new and strange, and which had not as yet been seen in the world; for that there occurred many occasions, which, in all human judgment, ought to have made Him speak and answer for Himself. For there were many of the principal heads of their accusations evidently false, and that in matters very heinous, and of extreme dishonour to Him, proposed by personages of very great quality, and with intention to get Him condemned to a cruel and ignominious death; besides, the judge himself moved Him to answer, and to defend Himself, that he might have absolved Him, knowing well His innocency. Certainly the least of these things might have sufficed to make a man speak; nevertheless, our Lord Jesus being no way moved, either with the one or the other, would hold His peace without answering a single word; showing in this His grave meekness and patience, not only in that He would not revenge Himself of His calumniators, but that He would not so much as oppose their forgeries, which He could very easily have done. He likewise made manifest here His great fortitude, declaring by effect that He little feared either the dishonour or the torments of death, seeing that He would not so much as open His mouth to defend Himself, at which

(9) Luc. xxiii. 4; Marc. xv. 4.

Pilate so much marvelled, and at which I myself ought likewise to wonder.

*Colloquy.*—O good Jesus, with how great reason was the name of "admirable"(10) imposed upon Thee, since Thou art not only admirable in miracles and exaltations, but also in distresses and humiliations. Admirable is Thy meekness,—admirable Thy sufferings,—admirable Thy silence; Thy taciturnity before Caiphas was certainly admirable, yet this before Pilate was much more, in regard that the accusations were far more grievous, the peril much greater, and the judge better disposed to hearken to Thee. Such a silence, O Saviour, was needful to correct my babbling, and to give me an excellent example of holding my peace by enduring injuries patiently. "Set a watch, O Lord, before my mouth, and a door round about my lips."(11) Permit not my heart to decline itself into words of malice, to "make" vain "excuses in sins." I intend also, by the assistance of Thy holy grace, to "set a guard to my mouth,"(12) when the sinner shall stand against me, and to hold my peace and humble myself in suppressing that which I might lawfully utter in my defence, as Thou didst here keep in that which might have served for Thy justification.

2. I will also hence gather that such *a rare silence as this is cannot be found, but in those who have thoroughly mortified in themselves the love of honour* and of life, for such neither fear dishonour nor death, wholly relying upon the divine providence, as we have said before. And this is that which the Holy Ghost intends when He says:—"Melt down thy gold and silver, and make a balance for thy words, and a just bridle for thy mouth: and take heed lest thou slip with thy tongue:"(13) that is, assemble to-

(10) Is. ix. 6. (11) Psal. cxl. 3. (12) Psal. xxxviii. 2.
(13) Ecclus. xxviii. 29.

gether all the moral virtues with the virtue of charity, (figured by the gold,) and all the virtues of the understanding, with that of prudence, (figured by the silver,) forasmuch as all of them are requisite to know when to speak and when to hold one's peace; in regard that all vices join themselves together, to untie and set at liberty the tongue, and for this cause it is most needful, that all virtues conspire together to the sure tying of the same, and therefore, "If any man offend not in word, the same is a perfect man."(14)

---

## MEDITATION XXXIII.

### ON THE PRESENTATION OF CHRIST BEFORE HEROD, AND OF THE INJURIES THERE RECEIVED BY HIM.

#### POINT I.

The priests and the rest of the multitude persisting in accusing Christ, said to Pilate, "He *stirreth the people, teaching throughout all Judea, beginning from Galilee to this place.*"(1) From which speech Pilate gathered that Christ was a Galilean, and so to be of the jurisdiction of king Herod; understanding Him therefore to be of his jurisdiction, (who at that very time was in Jerusalem,) he sent to him this prisoner, that he might take notice of His cause.

1. Our Lord, of whom St. Peter says that He passed "from Galilee," throughout all Judea, "doing good" to all, and healing all that were oppressed of the Devil, is now accused to have seduced the people with His evil doctrine, from Galilee throughout all the parts of Judea; to declare hereby how much He would be humbled, permitting that all His journeys and preachings, which tended

(14) Jac. iii. 2. (1) Luc. xxiii. 5.

to no other end but to the profit of that people, should be calumniated with the title of their ruin.

2. Consider the *fatigue and ignominy that our Lord endured in this fourth station*, from the house of Pilate to the palace of king Herod, being led through the principal streets and public places of Jerusalem, with a vulgar crowd, it being now broad day: admire the charity and humility of the Son of God, who would be trailed before so many tribunals, of which every one was worse than the previous; and to come before the tribunal of a king most cruel and most unjust, who had incestuously taken to him the wife of his own brother, and had cut off the head of St. John Baptist, who reprehended him for the same, which was so ordained by His own providence, to the end that the more He endured for us, the more He might oblige us to His service, giving us herein most effectual examples of His patience.

POINT II.

"And Herod seeing Jesus, was very glad, for he was desirous of a long time to see Him, because he had heard many things of Him: and he hoped to see some sign wrought by Him. And he questioned Him in many words. But He answered him nothing. And the chief priests and the scribes stood by earnestly accusing Him." (2)

1. Consider here *the joy that Herod had seeing our Lord*, and the courteous entertainment he gave Him, not for charity, but of curiosity to see a man so renowned, and hoping to see some unwonted novelty. Nevertheless, all this afterwards turned to the greater disgrace of Christ our Lord, who, not respecting this His kind usage, would not reply a word to him, in answer to his questions, nor work any miracle in his presence.

(2) Luc. xxiii. 8.

i. In *detestation of his wickedness*, treating him as an excommunicated person, and one unworthy to see His marvels, and in this regard He termed him a "fox," declaring thereby the crafty malice with which he had cut off the principal sprigs of the vine of our Lord.

ii. Secondly, in *condemnation of his vain curiosity*, for Almighty God does not pronounce His divine words, nor work His wonderful works, only to content a curious desire; for whoever treats with Almighty God by prayer, having this vanity of spirit, will find Him both deaf and dumb in his behalf, and without feeling any inspirations, or his interior words, or good motions in matters of importance.

iii. To *show hereby the great desire He had to suffer and to die:* for He that had wrought miracles, to the end that He might be able to die for man, miraculously depriving Himself of the glory of His body that was due to it, being always blessed in His soul, would by no means be induced to work any miracles, to avoid torments and death itself, which thing confounds our tepidity, who crave miracles at God's hands, to be delivered from the pains or crosses that we will not endure.

*Colloquy.*—O good Jesus, who hast wrought so many miracles for relieving the necessities of others; why dost Thou not work at the least one for helping Thyself before Herod? I grant, indeed, that his curiosity does not deserve it, but necessity requires it; yet Thou wilt not hearken to the cries of Thine own necessities, to the end to hear the cries of our calamities, and wilt die to remedy them.

2. For the same cause, although the priests and scribes accused our Lord Jesus with might and main before Herod, *yet He held His peace* with a silence no less admirable, than that which He kept before Pilate; nay, in a certain

manner greater, for that He had already spoken to Pilate, being in the judgment hall, discovering the truth to him of what he demanded; but here He speaks not so much as one word to Herod, neither to defend Himself, nor by way of compliment or human respect, although He knew well that by this silence He incurred his indignation, teaching us hereby the holy liberty we ought to use of holding our peace before kings and princes, and not to do before them for any worldly consideration what they desire, though thereby we incur some danger and damage.

POINT III.

Herod, seeing that our Lord returned him not so much as a word, with his courtiers began to contemn Him, and all his army began to scoff at Him:—"*And putting on Him a white garment, sent Him back to Pilate.*"(3)

1. Consider here the *sentence of this unjust king against our Lord*, in esteeming Him to be a man without judgment, rude, clownish, and lacking good manners, who had, of doltishness and simplicity, held His peace, and desired to be a king; and for this cause he would not condemn Him to death, but would only disgrace Him, clothing Him by way of mockery with a white garment, after the fashion that the emperors wore, (saving that it was all ragged and torn,) to make Him the more ridiculous. In this plight he sent Him to Pilate, as if he had said:—"I send you here back this fool and simple dolt, who of mere simplicity would needs be a king." The whole army likewise, desirous to revenge the injury done their king, and to flatter him, hooted at our Lord, giving Him a thousand scoffing and taunting insults, calling Him idiot, impudent dolt, and fool, a petty king, and other infamous names and titles. And it is also very credible, that, by the instigation of the Devil, they forgot not to load Him as He passed through

(3) Luc. xxiii. 11.

them with that scurrilous kind of injury used in the courts of princes, all which our Lord endured with an admirable patience; to teach us to contemn vain honours of the world, and to make no reckoning of the scoffing judgments that men give of us, who use in this manner even God Himself.

*Colloquy.*—O divine Word, the Wisdom of the eternal Father, I give Thee thanks that Thou wouldst be so greatly humbled, as to be reputed of men for simple and senseless; such a humiliation was truly needful, to heal my extreme pride and my presumption. Oh how happy were he that could see himself clothed with this Thy livery, as to be accounted for a fool,—no just occasion being given of it on his part;—for certainly there is no greater prudence than to desire to be contemned by the world for the love of Thee, nor greater folly than to aspire after honours without Thee.

2. Consider, secondly, *the great disgrace that our Lord endured in the streets of Jerusalem*, these that lead Him continuing the scoffings begun by Herod's army, and calling Him aloud, that all the world might hear them,—fool, and fantastical king. O King of heaven, how far different are these cries from those that they sung but five days since, when they called Thee King of Israel, and the "blessed" of our Lord; but now it is time to suffer—to the end that Thou mayest shortly enter into Thy Kingdom, that which is written must be fulfilled:—"For the simplicity of the just man is laughed to scorn." "The lamp despised in the thoughts of the rich, is ready for the time appointed."(4)

*Colloquy.*—O most precious lamp, which illuminatest and burnest into doctrine, and brightness, which cast-

(4) Job. xii. 4.

est forth the beams of meekness and patience, suffering so great contempts for the love of us, the time will come that Thy worthiness will show itself, to the confusion of the rich and proud, who now contemn Thee. Confound them, dear Lord, in this life, by the examples of Thy humiliations, to the end that, reflecting upon themselves, they may love what they despised, and despise what before they so much loved and esteemed.

3. Our Lord returned again ashamed before Pilate with this new suit and livery, and was scoffed at afresh, and abused by His ministers and servants, the injuries of the most humble Jesus, still increasing, so that I be not wearied with those that happen to me by my demerit, blushing for shame at the care I have of being esteemed wise and prudent, not able to endure that one should call me fool, or ill-advised. To this effect I will call to mind that which the apostle says,—"If any man among you seem to be wise in this world, let him become a fool, that he may be wise. For the wisdom of this world, is foolishness with God."(5) As, on the contrary, the wisdom of God appears folly to the world.

4. And it is to be noted that *this white garment* with which our Lord was clothed for derision, *was a sign of the candour and purity* of His *soul*, and of the innocency of His life, which is ordinarily accompanied with contempts and humiliations: for it is a great point, as it is said in the Canticles,(6) to be pure and white in the interior, and to be sun-burnt and contemned in the exterior. And therefore I will crave of our Lord, that He clothe me with the garment of His innocency in soul, and also with the livery of His injuries in body, to the end that I may entirely resemble Him.

(5) 1 Cor. iii. 18. (6) Cant. i. 5.

*Colloquy.*—O Lamb without spot, in whose blood, although it be red, the saints wash themselves, and whiten their garments,(7) make me whiter than snow, in imitation of Thy purity, and dye me with Thy blood, in imitation of Thy Passion. Amen.

5. Consider, moreover, that "*Herod and Pilate,*" *who* "*before were enemies,*" "*from that time were made friends;*" to signify that the princes of the earth leagued themselves and conspired together against our Lord Jesus to persecute Him,(8) nevertheless our Saviour by His death linked them together in true friendship, uniting together the Jews and Gentiles in the union of charity, figured by the friendship that Herod and Pilate renewed between them, which thing shows that the least humility is of force to reconcile disagreeing hearts, considering that these two men, having become enemies by occasion of a competition about their jurisdictions, as soon as Pilate submitted himself to him, to send him this prisoner, who was one of his subjects, became presently friends, all at the cost of our Lord's humiliation, who, by His submission, purchased the union of charity that is between the elect, founded upon true humility.

6. To conclude, I may reflect upon the miserable ends of these two judges, who thus contemned our Lord Jesus, who, though He endures and dissembles His injuries, yet as He is a most just judge, a time will come in which He will chastise them according to their merits.

(7) Apoc. vii. 14. (8) Psal. ii. 2.

# MEDITATION XXXIV.

## THE JEWS' PREFERENCE OF BARABBAS, AND CONDEMNATION OF CHRIST.

### POINT I.

Pilate, desirous to deliver Christ our Lord from death, seeing that Herod had not condemned Him, resolved to use a means, as it seemed to him, very convenient for this effect; and it may be believed that it was by divine inspiration.

There was a custom that the president, at the feast of Easter, should propose two prisoners or more to the people, *giving them leave to choose one of the named*, and him they set at liberty. Pilate, taking advantage of this occasion, named with our Lord Jesus Christ one only prisoner, and he the most notorious malefactor that he held in prison, called "Barabbas," a man seditious, a thief, and a murderer, and for this cause detested and abhorred of every one, supposing that the people, not to set at liberty a man so wicked, would rather choose our Saviour Christ. He then asked them, "Whom will you that I release to you," according to the custom you have, "Barabbas or Jesus, that is called Christ?"(1)

1. In this thing is to be pondered *the humiliation of our Saviour Christ*, who, being so great, so holy, so wise, so universal a benefactor, enters into lots and competition touching His reputation with an infamous fellow, a thief, a rebel, a murderer, and a public malefactor, the controversy being of no less importance than liberty, honour, and life itself. Amongst us we esteem it for a great disgrace to be compared with a base fellow, or to dispute with

(1) Mat. xxvii. 17; Marc. xv. 6; Luc. xxiii. 17; Joan. xviii. 39.

one that has inferior parts, but our Lord Jesus is here put into the balance, with the most vile and abject wretch of all the people, to give us an example of humility in all occasions.

*Colloquy.*—O good Jesus, with how good reason mayest Thou complain, and say that which Thou saidst by Thy prophet :—" Cui assimilastis me, et adæquastis?"—" To whom have ye likened me, or made me equal?"(2) But I see well, dear Lord, that Thou dost yet expect a far greater injury, for that our pride is to be healed with a greater humility.

2. The people, as it were, standing doubtful whom to choose, the priests and ancients began to suborn them, and "*persuaded them that they should ask Barabbas.*" Here is to be considered the *great solicitude of these cursed priests to corrupt the people.* For it is very probable that they separated themselves into divers places, now speaking to one, now whispering to another, telling them a thousand evils of our Lord Jesus; as that He was more seditious, and a greater murderer than was Barabbas, seeing He made to revolt, not only one city, but the whole province and kingdom, in hazard to cause the death, not of one or two men only, but of all the people, if He escaped death; that He deserved death more than Barabbas, for that He was a more enormous sinner than he; that He was a blasphemer, an enchanter, an enemy to the law of Moses, &c. All this Christ our Lord understood, which caused Him in a manner even to break His heart, seeing how those false preachers deceived the simple people, taking from them the good opinion they had of Him.

3. Ponder likewise with a great grief and feeling of heart, how *Barabbas found so many supporters and advocates* in his cause, who excuse and favour him, suborning

(2) Isa. xl. 25.

the people, although his cause was so unjust; neither wanted he friends and spokesmen, who jointly with the priests speak for him. But our Lord Jesus is so left alone and abandoned, that He has not so much as one pleader, agent, or friend that undertakes His cause, informs the people, or speaks in His favour, His cause being so just, and the judge himself so inclined to favour Him; He has not one friend, neither of His disciples, nor of His kinsfolks, nor of any one of those to whom He had done so much good, that dares once to speak in His defence.

*Colloquy.*—O pleader and advocate of the poor, how is it that Thou findest no pleader, nor advocate to plead Thy cause? Make Thy complaint, O Lord, to Thy eternal Father, and say to Him:—"O my Father, Thou art the only protector of this poor and forlorn person, and the sole succour of this sorrowful orphan;(3) send down, I beseech Thee, from heaven above some one that may solicit for me, and that may serve me for a patron in a cause so weighty. But Thy infinite charity, my Saviour, willingly suffers to be thus forsaken of all, to deliver me from being forsaken by Thee, as my sin deserved.

### POINT II.

Pilate pressing the people to make election of one of the two proposed by him, said to them:—"Which will you have of the two to be released unto you?"—"Barabbas, or Jesus that is called Christ?"—"But the whole multitude cried out, saying: *Away with this man, and release unto us Barabbas.*"(4)

1. Here consider the extreme *humility and abasement of Christ* our Saviour, since, when in competition with a man so vile, and withal so abominable, He lost the precedence,

(3) Psal. ix. 14. (4) Mat. xxvii. 21; Luc. xxiii. 13.

and was rejected and judged more unworthy of liberty and life than wicked Barabbas.

*Colloquy.*—O most sweet Jesus, I now see with how great truth Thou saidst, "I am a worm, and no man, the reproach of men, and the outcast of the people,"(5) for all cast Thee out, and contemn Thee, preferring before Thee the most vile caitiff, and most despicable outcast amongst the people. O my pride, which presumest to ascend above all men, why dost thou not humble and abase thyself at this example, and deem thyself inferior to all the world? Dear Lord, confound and pull down, I beseech Thee, this my pride, since it is not reasonable that henceforward I should presume to lift up my head in the presence of so great humility.

2. *How erroneous are the judgments of men,* who, even in a case so clear, yet give their verdict against justice and truth itself, to the manifest prejudice of our Saviour Christ! and how powerful is the passion of envy and hatred to blind the understanding, and to cast it headlong into most intolerable errors! Moreover, how mutable are men, and how easily do they permit themselves to be seduced, since they who but a few days before, with loud voices proclaimed publicly that Christ was the Saviour and King of Israel, now proclaim Him worse than wicked Barabbas! From all this I will take counsel not to make any account of the judgments of men, nor to suffer myself to be guided by them, whether they praise or dispraise me. And I will comfort myself with this example of my Saviour Christ, when I shall see myself frustrated in my intentions, though what I desire be just, remembering well that life eternal is obtained only by the suffrage of that supreme judge who is exempt from all passion and deceit.

(5) Psal. xxi. 7.

*Colloquy.*—I give Thee thanks, O eternal God, that Thou hast not placed the liberty and life of my soul in the suffrages of men, nor wouldst that my salvation should depend upon opinions so erroneous and passionate as are theirs. So make me, O Lord, superior to them, that, despising their vain judgments, I may esteem none but Thine, for in very deed I am neither good nor bad for that which men shall speak of me, but for that I am indeed such in presence of Thee.

3. *As often as I offend Almighty God, there passes within my heart a perverse judgment*, like that of these Jews. For the temptation which incites and provokes me to sin, is nothing else but a demand that it proposes to me, which of the two I respect most, Christ or Barabbas?—God or the creature?—Heaven or earth?—The honour of God, or my own honour?—And when I doubt or stagger of which of these I am to make election, presently the Devil and the flesh endeavour to persuade me with their suggestions and reasons to relinquish Christ. And finally, when I give consent, it is as if I made election of Barabbas, of a creature, of a sensual delight, or of a vain honour, with great injury of Almighty God, with great contempt of Christ and His excellencies, and with notable ingratitude for so many benefits as He has done me. Of this I will be ashamed, reputing myself far more perverse than were the Jews, since retaining the true faith, as to what Almighty God is,—and who Jesus Christ is, I yet contemn Him and reject Him, for a thing more vile than vile Barabbas.

*Colloquy.*—O only Son of the celestial Father, who wast compared to Barabbas, which signifies, "son of the father," not heavenly, but earthly, and in comparison of him wast rejected by those who were the sons of the Devil, and did the will of this their "father;"(6) permit not, I beseech Thee, that ever I commit such treason as this within my soul, but that I always live as Thy true brother, and as son of Thy eternal Father, rejecting that which Thou rejectest, and approving what Thou approvest; esteeming Thee above all that is created, who art indeed infinitely to be more beloved than they all. Amen.

POINT III.

Pilate, much amazed that the people had made choice of Barabbas, said to them:—"What shall I do then with Jesus, who is called Christ? They all say, Let Him be crucified. The governor said to them: Why, what evil hath He done?"—"I find no cause of death in Him, I will chastise Him, therefore, and let Him go. But they were urgent with loud voices, requiring that He might be crucified."(7)

1. Here consider *the pusillanimity of this judge*, who, knowing the innocency of Christ our Lord, yet had not courage enough by virtue of his office to set Him free, but demanded of the frantic and enraged people, what should be done with Him, making them judges of Him, who abhorred Him, and who had for envy delivered Him to him; all which redounded to the greater ignominy of our Blessed Saviour.

2. *How grievous were those enraged*, and so often repeated *cries, of "crucify Him, crucify Him,"* to our Saviour Christ, in which He saw that they not only wished Hi death, but that He should die a death so cruel, as was to die upon the cross.

*Colloquy.*—O Saviour of the world, to how great extremity have my sins reduced Thee, for they are those which cry against Thee, saying:—"Crucify

(6) Joan. viii. 44. (7) Mat. xxvii. 21; Luc. xxiii. 22.

Him, crucify Him,"—for Thou, being crucified, they also remain dead and crucified with Thee upon the cross.(8) O my Lord, put them, I beseech Thee, so to death, that they never live again within my soul, that there never burst forth from her the like clamour, crucifying Thee again within my heart.(9)

---

## MEDITATION XXXV.

### OF THE WHIPPING OF CHRIST AT THE PILLAR.

#### POINT I.

Pilate seeing the perverseness of the people crying out to have our Saviour crucified, pronounced against Him for His first sentence, that He should be whipped, immediately delivering Him into the hands of the soldiers to put this sentence in execution.(1)

1. Upon this point is to be pondered, the *motives which* Pilate took to pronounce this sentence, which *were two.*

i. The one to try, if by means of this punishment, the *hearts of the people might be mollified,* that they might remain satisfied with it, and that so he might deliver Christ from death. Hence it is to be believed, that he commanded the soldiers that they should scourge Him soundly, and that they should handle Him so severely, as might move to compassion all who should behold Him.

ii. The other, that if he should be *crucified He should first be scourged,* according to the law of the Romans which so ordained, to the end that he, who was to be crucified, might not offend with his aspect the standers by which beheld him naked, but might move them to compassion to behold him so torn and wounded.(2) Whereupon some

(8) Rom. vi. 6. (9) Heb. vi. 6.

(1) Mat. xxvii. 26; Marc. xv. 15; Joan. xix. 1; Luc. xxiii. 16.

(2) S. Jer. in Mat. to. 9.

contemplate that Christ our Lord was scourged twice(3)—the first time, for the first motive before mentioned;—and the second for the second motive, when He was indeed condemned to the death of the cross. But howsoever it was, this sentence of Pilate was most unjust, most cruel, and most disgraceful, inasmuch as the judge knew right well that Christ was innocent, and yet without regard, or care of it, condemned Him to be scourged; which was a punishment most infamous, due only to thieves and slaves, a chastisement most cruel, shedding with terrible torments the blood of Him who was quite innocent, and confirming by this fact that election which the enraged people had made of Barabbas, and the condemnation of Christ; since that he treated Him in the self-same manner, that Barabbas was to have been treated for his thefts and villanies.

2. The sentence being such as we have seen, yet Christ our Lord so accepted it in His heart, that He appealed not from it, begged not any mitigation of it, uttered not the least word of complaint against it, nor made so much as any the least show of contradicting it; but on the contrary, *very willingly offered His body to the scourges*, in satisfaction of our sins, that with the wounds of His blessed body, as the prophet Isaiah said,(4) He might entirely heal the wounds of my soul, and so provoke me to love and serve Him. For discovering to me His holy bowels, so torn with scourges, He has obliged me that I should offer Him mine with all my affections. And it is very probable that at this present Christ our Lord lifted His eyes up to heaven, pronouncing to His eternal Father those words of the prophet David:—"Quoniam in flagella paratus sum;" My dear Father, "I am ready for scourges,"(5) because

(3) Gerson. in Monotes. cap. 146, rub. 6.
(4) Is. liii. 5.
(5) Psal. xxxvii. 18.

Thou, O Father, hast so ordained, my body ought by right to be "immortal" and "impassible" in such sort that "no evil" of pain might once "come to," nor the scourge come nigh the "dwelling" wherein my soul inhabits. But Thy providence has so ordained that I should assume a body apt to suffer and to be scourged, and even from that instant was I prepared to suffer the same, with desire "to pay that which I took away," not to deliver from pain those who had robbed Thee of Thine honour.(6)

*Colloquy.*—I give Thee thanks, O most sweet Redeemer, for having accepted of a sentence so cruel, so infamous, and so unjust. Behold me here ready for the love of Thee, to suffer scourges, and to accept the sentence which Thou shalt denounce against me, for neither is it unjust, since my sins have deserved it, nor yet infamous nor cruel, since it is the sentence of a Father who "chastiseth" "whom He loveth, and scourgeth every son which He receiveth,"(7) that he may amend.

POINT II.

This sentence being heard, the soldiers, with great insolence, forthwith ran upon Christ our Lord, and drawing Him into a hall, *stripped Him of all His clothes*, even to His garment without a seam.

1. In this fact we are to ponder,—first, *the great shame* which that beautiful young man and our excellent Lord sustained, to see Himself stark naked in the sight of so many soldiers, and the scoffs and laughter they burst into, perceiving Him to be ashamed. This disgrace, notwithstanding, would He suffer with singular patience, both in punishment of the shameless impudence with which I have

(6) Psal. xc. 10; Psal. xxxix. 7; Heb. x. 5; Psal. lxviii. 5.
(7) Prov. iii. 12; Heb. xii. 6.

stript myself naked of the garments of His grace, as also by that means, as a price, to buy for me the garment of grace with which my wretched nakedness might be covered.

*Colloquy.*—O most loving Lord, who invitest me to buy of Thee the pure gold(8) of burning charity, and the shining vestments of virtue, with which I may free myself from the eternal confusion, that by stripping myself naked of them, I have deserved; I offer Thee as recompense for the nakedness and shame which Thou didst suffer, a heart resolved to strip myself naked of all earthly things, beseeching Thee by the shame Thou sufferedst, so to clothe me with Thy celestial grace, that I come not to fall into eternal confusion. Amen.

2. That also which some say, may here be pondered,—how the soldiers *strongly tied and fastened Christ to a pillar* with His arms lifted up on high, that they might the better come at His body with their whips,(9) which was doubtless no small torment to Him, for they bound His feet below, and His hands above with great cruelty; who yet, although He had not been bound at all with those cruel cords, was most strongly bound with the cords of love, and prepared to suffer Himself to be flayed with scourges for our salvation.

*Colloquy.*—O immaculate lamb, who with admirable meekness sufferedst Thyself to be bound by these cruel shearers,(10) not only to take from Thee the wool of Thy sacred garments, but also to slay Thy delicate body with the shears of most cruel scourges, suffering this torment without once bleating or opening Thy mouth; bind me to Thee, I beseech Thee,

(8) Apoc. iii. 18.
(9) Hieron. in Epitaph. Paul ad Eustoch. tom. 1, et Gloss. in Luc. 23.
(10) Is. liii. 7.

so strongly with the "bonds of love,"(11) that no scourges, nor temporal torments be ever able to unloose me from Thee. Amen.

POINT III.

Christ our Lord being thus bound naked to the pillar, *those tormentors began to scourge Him* with extraordinary cruelty.

1. The *instruments* with which He was scourged, were, according to some,(12) of three different sorts, which different torturers employed, now one smiting Him, and then others. The first were, *green rods full of thorns.*—The second, *thongs of twisted leather*, made of the sinews of oxen, with sharp rowels of iron at their end.—The third were *little iron chains*, with which the flesh was so cruelly torn, that His very bones were discovered naked.

With these instruments did they smite the back and shoulders of our Saviour, so that first it became black and blue, next the delicate skin was all cut and mangled, and lastly, the flesh itself was so slashed and torn, that little channels of blood streamed down upon the ground. With the like cruelty did they rend and tear the rest of His body, without sparing either arms, breast, or shoulders, even to the discovering of the bones. In such a manner, that, as the whole mystical body of that people, as Isaiah says, was wounded "from the sole of the foot unto the top of the head,"(13) from the least to the greatest, with the wounds of sin; even so the body of Christ our Lord, "from the sole of the foot to the top of the head," had no part free from wounds, but like a leper, was wounded all over, whom the same Isaiah foresaw in spirit when he said:—"There is no beauty in Him, nor comeliness; and we have seen Him, and there was no sightliness that we should be desirous of Him; despised and the

(11) Osc. xi. 4. (12) Salmer. tom. x. tract. 29. (13) Is. i. 6.

most abject of men, a man of sorrows and acquainted with infirmity: and His look was, as it were, hid and despised, whereupon we have esteemed Him not. Surely He hath borne our infirmities, and carried our sorrows, and we have thought Him as it were a leper, struck by God, and afflicted. But He was wounded for our iniquities, He was bruised for our sins; the chastisement of our peace was upon Him, and by His bruises we are healed."(14).

O that I had light from heaven to contemplate, my dear Redeemer, the figure so disfigured which Thou hadst, being bound to this pillar! O that I had so enflamed a charity as might transform me into this figure through the force of compassion! O fairest of the children of men, who has deprived Thee of that comely figure, that before Thou hadst? O splendour of the glory of the Father, who has obscured the brightness of Thy divine face? O Man, above all men, most "desired" and expected "of all nations," who has tranformed Thee into "a man of sorrows," and made Thee the abomination of all men? O health of the lepers, who has made Thee like "a leper?" O eternal Father, why dost Thou suffer that Thy Son be treated like a thief, and reputed as a man, stricken and chastised of God Himself? If my sins be the cause of this, it is more just that I myself should be chastised for them. "I am he that have sinned,"(15) this innocent lamb has not offended. Turn, therefore, Thy hand against me, discharge Thy scourges upon my shoulders, that I may pay the pain, seeing it is I who have committed the fault.

*Colloquy.*—O immense charity of the Father, who so severely wilt chastise Thy Son to reconcile to Thyself so unworthy a slave! O infinite charity of the Son, who so wilt be chastised to reconcile a slave into

(14) Is. liii. 2. (15) 2 Reg. xxiv. 17.

grace with His Father! I give Thee thanks, O eternal Father, for this Thy immense charity. I give Thee thanks, Only-begotten Son Incarnate, for this Thy infinite love.

2. Secondly, to ponder the better the *cruelty of this punishment*, I may fix mine eyes upon *four things* that concurred to this.

i. The first, on the part *of the body of Christ* our Lord, which was *tender*, delicate, and wonderfully sensible,—and, on the other side, was exceedingly weakened by the bloody sweat which He had shed a little before, and with the fatigue of that night and of that day; and as the whips entered very deep into the flesh, even near to the bowels, so did they cause Him an excessive pain. And for this cause in the psalm where it is said:—"The wicked have wrought upon my back;" (16) another reading has:—"Have *ploughed* upon my back." For even as the plough cuts the earth, and makes it full of furrows, so did the whips plough His most sacred flesh, and furrow it, penetrating into the interior of it.

*Colloquy.*—O virginal earth, pure and white, little need hadst Thou to be ploughed or harrowed, if the compassion which Thou hast of the hardness of my heart had not moved Thee to it. Pierce it, O my God, with the coulter of compassion, that I may feel in my own flesh the pains and torments which Thou feltest in Thine. Amen.

ii. On the part of *the executioners*, who were by their very habits of life cruel, whom the president also had commanded that they should scourge Him with great cruelty, for the causes before mentioned. The Devil likewise instigated them to it, to move Christ our Lord to impatience; and the high priests and the Jews did not cease

(16) Psal. cxxviii. 3.

to enkindle the fire, and eagerly to incense them to it. And as the tormentors changed and succeeded each other by turns, so likewise laid they on Him with a new cruelty, especially seeing Christ to suffer so patiently without complaining, upon whom, peradventure, they employed all the violence they could in striking Him, to wrest out of Him some kind of exclamation or complaint.

iii. On the part of *the multitude of blows*, and of those who beat Him; for many affirm that they were more than five thousand in number; and of the cruelty of His enemies we may well presume, since there was not observed towards Christ that law which commands to give "forty stripes save one," (17) as St. Paul says of himself, but they gave Him many times forty, satisfying in this that penance which we had deserved for our sins.

iv. And this is the fourth circumstance,—on the part of *our own sins*, which were innumerable and most enormous, in regard of which the stripes with which the debt of sin was to be satisfied, were to be innumerable and most cruel.

3. With these considerations I ought to ponder the invincible *patience* of Christ our Lord, who was as it were *dumb*, without giving any exterior sign of complaint, trouble, or weariness, enduring those blows as if He had been an anvil, offering them up to His eternal Father in satisfaction of our sins, and that with a love so fervent and great, that the stripes were very many, yet had He a desire and a will to receive many more, and much more cruel, had it been necessary for our redemption, insomuch that He never said it was enough, until the rage of His enemies was fully glutted, and the justice of Almighty God fully satisfied. Hence I will conceive a most extreme horror of my sins, which were the cause of so severe a

(17) 2 Cor. xi. 24.

punishment, and a great desire to punish them myself with penance and disciplines. And, finally, I will prostrate myself at the feet of this our Lord, close by the pillar, beholding His solitude, having nobody to lament His case nor to condole with Him, and how while the blood spurts forth from all parts, He is greatly weakened. One time I will in spirit kiss the earth, bathed with the blood of my Lord and my Creator;—another time I will take up those whips dyed with His precious blood, and will apply them to my breast, beseeching Him to heal the wounds of my inordinate affections, and that He would wound me with His divine love;—other times I will embrace that holy pillar, and with great reverence will salute it saying:—

*Colloquy.*—O sovereign pillar, at which He was fastened and scourged, who is the pillar of the whole world, and the fortitude of all that is created! O blessed pillar,(18) wrought and enamelled with the blood of the Son of God, shed to make men strong pillars in the Temple of our living Lord! Oh that I were fast tied to Thee, so that being sprinkled with this blood, I might become a strong pillar in the service of Him, who endured so much as Thee for my redemption: O pillars of heaven, what do you, how tremble you not for fear, beholding your God scourged at this pillar! O most firm pillar, who dost support the whole world, take compassion on Thyself, invest Thee with Thine own fortitude! O arm of our Lord, how art Thou thus weakened and enfeebled, and brought to the point almost of fainting! But since Thou sufferest all this for my sins, vouchsafe to fortify me with Thy grace, that I may chastise myself for them, and may amend myself of them. Amen.

4. Lastly, I will ponder how this unjust and barbarous execution being ended, the *soldiers unloosed* Christ our Lord,

(18) Apoc. iii. 12.

who being over wearied with stripes, and debilitated through the abundance of blood that He had poured forth of His blessed wounds, it is very *probable that He fell to the ground.* And then seeing Himself to be stark naked, and that His garments were scattered here and there far asunder, He crawled after them upon the ground, wallowing Himself in His own blood, that was shed round about the pillar, and, as well as He was able, revested Himself, those hellish executioners, partly out of cruelty, and partly out of disdain, not vouchsafing to help Him. All this may I piously contemplate, taking compassion for the dereliction and great debility of our Lord.

*Colloquy.*—O King of heaven, who helpest every creature in their actions, forasmuch as without Thee they could do nothing, how is it that Thou hast none to assist Thee in this necessity? O sacred garments, which with your touch effected that the woman who touched the hem of you, immediately had the flux of her blood stopped, and healed as many infirm as touched you; heal the wounds of my Saviour, and stop the current of His blood, that He may be able to suffer, to give an end to our redemption. Oh that I had been there present to have assisted Him, although it had been requisite to have spent my blood to have eased him! My God, accept of this good will which Thou hast given me, and fortify me, that I may serve Thee in all that I am able, having a desire to do much more than I am able. Amen.

# MEDITATION XXXVI.

## ON THE CROWNING WITH THORNS, AND ON THE OTHER DERISIONS WHICH THEN SUCCEEDED.

### POINT I.

The soldiers who had whipped Christ our Lord, instigated to it by the suggestion of the Devil, invented new kinds of torments to afflict Him, (1) on the one side most painful, and on the other side most shameful, and in order that the shame might be so much the greater, *they called together the whole troop or band of soldiers* of the guard, *to be present at this spectacle*, and at the sport and mockery which they intended to make with Christ, to His great disquiet and disgrace, to which they all ran very willingly, as to their pastime and recreation.

In this fact consider:—

1. *The insatiable desire that Christ our Lord had to suffer torments for the love of us*, for hence it proceeded that He would have invented against Himself new sorts of injuries and torments, not contenting Himself with those which were common and ordinary to others, to manifest thereby the love He bore us, and the greatness of our sins; for even as men wholly transported with the love of themselves, invented new means to offend Almighty God, for their own honour and voluptuousness,—even so Christ our Lord, wholly transported with divine love, would that there should be invented new manners of punishments against such sins, and new manners of shedding forth His blood in expiation of them, like that which He invented in the garden.

(1) Mat. xxvii. 29; Marc. xv. 17; Joan. xix. 2.

*Colloquy.*—I give Thee thanks, O most sweet Jesus, for the excellency of this charity with which Thou hast loved us. Oh how does the name of "Just" beseem Thee, since Thou hast invented so many new means to attain justice, with which to justify us. I congratulate Thee for these inventions of Thy love, and I will say to Thee with the prophet Isaiah, that Thou art "Just" by excellency, that this name very well becomes Thee, and that Thou shalt "eat the fruit"(2) of Thine own "doings," purchasing and gaining by the means of them innumerable souls.

2. The *egregious malice of these wicked torturers*, set to work by Satan the Devil, to assemble the people and to make so great a concourse of set purpose to deride Christ, that so they might gaze and stare upon Him, whilst themselves despised Him; taking pity of the humiliation of this our Lord, who is made a laughing stock to men, and abhorred of those who solicited others to offend Christ, and to scoff and laugh at His mysteries; but I, my dear Saviour, desire to find myself present in spirit at this spectacle, not, like the soldiers, to deride Thee, but to meditate Thy marvellous works, and to exercise myself in the consideration of Thine inventions, and to take compassion on Thy pains and afflictions, and to obtain force to support my own.

3. With this spirit I will consider the torments which Christ our Lord endured in the same hall after His scourging, which may be reduced into *six*, all of them immediately succeeding one another.

POINT II.

1. *The first injury:*—They began their injuries to the person of Christ our Lord, by "*stripping Him*" *of His sacred clothes*, and it is to be believed that they did this in

(2) Is. iii. 10.

order that all the people might afterwards see His wounded body, so that they stripped Him even of His garment without a seam, leaving Him stark naked; hence He suffered great pain and great confusion,—pain, in that His clothes cleaved fast to His flesh, by reason of the fresh blood which stuck to them when He was clothed again; and it is to be believed that they pulled them off very boisterously, and without one spark of compassion at all. —The confusion was great, since He saw Himself naked in the sight of that band of soldiers, as we have meditated in the preceding meditation.

2. *The second injury:*—To this succeeded another, which was, that "*they put a scarlet cloak about Him,*" called "chlamys," which was a long garment of scarlet or purple, (3) with which kings are wont to be invested, but was put upon Christ our Lord for mockery sake, to make game and scoff at Him, as at a false and counterfeit king, so that that which with the world was held in honour, was converted to the dishonour of Christ, to make a spectacle of Him, or a counterfeit king upon a stage.

*Colloquy.*—O spouse of our souls, "white and ruddy, chosen out of thousands,"(4) Thou art enamoured of these colours, not for honour's sake, but for contempt, since in the house of Herod Thou wert clothed in white, and in the house of Pilate in purple colour, meriting for us by the means of these contumelies the white of innocency, and the purple of charity; assist me, dear Lord, that I may glory in this livery, and take a pride in this ignominious purple, esteeming for dishonour the vain honour of the world, and holding for true honour that which it holds for dishonour. Amen.

*This long purple garment signified our bloody sins*, which

(3) Mat. xxvii. 28. (4) Cant. v. 10.

more loaded and oppressed Christ our Lord, and more disgraced Him, than did the ignominy of the purple robe. And in particular it represented those works which are good and glorious in outward appearance, but in the eyes of Almighty God are most wicked and abominable, by reason of the worldly and earthly intention with which they are done, so that instead of honouring Christ with them, we despise Him and deride Him.

*Colloquy.*—O God of my soul, suffer not, I beseech Thee, that I put upon Thee such a garment, nor that I put it on myself. If I desire to make choice of purple, let it be the purple of burning charity, with which I may cover the uncleanness and "multitude of" my "sins,"(5) that so I may become pleasing to Thy divine eyes. Amen.

POINT III.

3. *The third injury:*—"*Platting a crown,*" not of gold, nor of silver, nor of roses, nor of flowers, but "*of*" *most sharp and pricking* "*thorns*, they put it upon His head," which, as they set it on with egregious fury, so the thorns pierced His sacred head and veins, insomuch that great abundance of blood flowed forth of His holy wounds.

Upon this point, first consider:—

i. The *shame and the pain of this coronation;* because this crown served for an instrument and sign of the one and other; for, first, they put it upon His head of mere mockery,—next, in resemblance of those crowns that kings wore, and of those that triumphed over their enemies,—and lastly, of such as were reputed and held for gods, to show hereby that He deserved to be mocked in these three respects,—in that He was a *petty king,*—a counterfeit God,—and that His triumph made upon the Sunday before was vain and idle. But besides this, they

(5) 1 Pet. iv. 8.

invented this crown to serve Him for a new and cruel torment, in that the multitude of sharp pricking thorns penetrated even to His skull, drawing out from the most noble part of the body that blood which the scourges had left untouched, and running down drop by drop all along His face and eyes, both caused great deformity, and tormented the forehead and brain with most grievous pain. Rise up, then, O my soul, in spirit, and as one of the daughters of Sion, "go forth" to contemplate this true "king Solomon," (6) with this cruel crown that has been given to Him by His mother, or rather His step-mother, the Synagogue, adorning Him with this for the spousals that He is to solemnize this day, upon the nuptial bed of the cross.

*Colloquy.*—O eternal King, who hast crowned man with a crown of "glory and honour,"(7) putting all things under his feet, as king and lord of them all, how comes it to pass that Thou art crowned by the hands of men, with a crown of ignominy and of torment? O ingratitude and inhuman cruelty of men against Almighty God! O goodness and ineffable meekness of God towards men! He crowns them with glory, and they crown Him with ignominy;—He out of the greatness of His mercy, and they from the savage barbarousness of their cruelty. How comes it to pass, O my soul, that these thorns do not pierce thy heart? Whence is it that they do not draw forth the abundance of water out of Thy head, and fountains of tears forth of Thine eyes, beholding the King of heaven to be thus pricked and pierced, to purchase for thee the crown of His eternal Kingdom? O true Solomon, who dost crown Thyself with thorns to celebrate Thy espousals with souls, crown likewise my soul with them, that it may merit to be partaker of Thy nuptial banquet. O sacred crown of my Lord Jesus,

(6) Cant. iii. 11. (7) Psal. viii. 6.

howsoever Thou art terrible to the world, I adore and reverence Thee, as the crown of my God: O sacred thorns, that I might be pricked with your sharp points, that your wounds might serve for a salve to heal my sores.

ii. *The great enormity of my sins*, especially those of pride and sensuality, which were *the cause of this cruel crowning.* These were the thorns which pierced deeper, and tormented this our Lord much more than did the others. Because I have crowned myself with roses (8) and flowers, in hunting after my pleasures, my Saviour was crowned with thorns;—because I sought after the "crown of pride," (9) in pursuing vain honours and preferments, my Lord chose to Himself the crown of humiliation, accompanied with great disgraces. Consider, therefore, O my soul, and seriously reflect upon all thy sins, which are the thorns that prick thy Redeemer, and prick thy heart with the thorns of penance and afflictions, for having committed them; seeing thy head, who is Jesus Christ, to be crowned with thorns, blush for shame that thou, a member of His body, art crowned with flowers, spending thy life in delights and vanities.

iii. *The mystery of this crown* of Christ our Lord, thus fixed on His head, which although it was put on in contempt, and for torment, yet *signified that Christ was an eternal king*, that His Kingdom was everlasting, and that His crown was stable,—not as those of earthly kings, that are put on very easily, and cast down with as great facility;—moreover, that He was vanquisher and perpetual triumpher over the devils, over hell, over the world, and over the flesh, although it cost Him the price of His blood shed by His crown, with the which He purchased for His elect innumerable crowns of victories, that they should

(8) Sap. ii. 8. (9) Is. xxviii. 1.

obtain in this life, and afterwards crowns of glory in the other. Consequently He teaches us, that with a crown of thorns is purchased the crown of heaven, and that it is better to embrace in this life the crown of pricking pains, than the crown of pleasures and delightful recreation, because, if during this life, after the custom of worldlings, I crown myself with roses, searching after vanities and delights, I shall be afterwards environed and pricked with the thorns of my sins, and with remorse of conscience, without it ever being possible for me to pluck them out.

*Colloquy.*—I give Thee humble thanks, O sovereign King, glorious vanquisher, and perpetual triumpher, for the manner Thou didst choose to gain the crown and triumph of glory; henceforth I offer myself to be crowned with thorns during this life, hoping that Thou wilt crown me one day with glory in the life to come.

POINT IV.

4. *The fourth injury:*—After they *had set upon* our Saviour's head the crown of thorns, "*they put a reed in His right hand,*" *instead of a sceptre, for derision*, to signify by this, that this His kingdom was hollow and without substance, that He was a king of rushes, more mutable than a reed, that He had a crazed brain, and wanted judgment in feigning Himself to be a king; finally, they did this in contempt of the palms and branches of trees that the people had borne, who solemnized His triumph and entry into Jerusalem a few days before.

i. Consider, first, the grievous injury that was done to our Lord Jesus, and *the base estimation which they made of His Kingdom*, of His doctrine, and of the perfection which He preached, all which they esteemed for a thing vain and empty, which disgrace, notwithstanding, our Saviour received with great humility; He resisted not to receive the reed, He did not forthwith cast it from Him, and so far even was He from this, that He took it into His most blessed hand, and held it most fast, as a mark of His contempt, who loved contempts, teaching me to accept the same, and to embrace them with hearty love.

*Colloquy.*—O venerable reed, O divine sceptre of my Lord, from whose hand thou receivest virtue to give life to whatsoever thou shalt touch far better than did the "golden sceptre"(10) of King Assuerus; touch me, O my King, with this royal rod, imprinting in my heart a great esteem of Thy contempts, for this touch will serve me as a sign of Thy clemency, and will be to me as the earnest-penny of eternal life.

ii. Hence I will also gather, *how erroneous the judgments of men are*, who take to themselves sceptres of massive gold, in sign of excellency and stability of their kingdom, being in truth but a wavering reed, that speedily passes away, and so frail, as the prophet Isaiah (11) says, one cannot lean upon it with security, and contrariwise they esteem it, according to the prophet Malachi, (12) a vain thing to serve God, and to keep "His ordinances." Hence I will learn to make small account of erroneous judgments, taking care not to follow them.

5. *The fifth injury:*—After this injury they added another, "bowing the knee before Him, they mocked Him, saying:—*Ave Rex Judeorum*—Hail, King of the Jews," (13) and all this salutation were of itself honourable, yet being spoken in mockery, it offended the ears of this our most excellent Lord, who was then in heaven hearing the praises of the angels, and is always delighted to hear our prayers.

*Colloquy.*—O sovereign King, after how different a manner art Thou adored by the angels in heaven, and

(10) Esther iv. 11. (11) Is. xxxvi. 6. (12) Mal. iii. 14.
(13) Marc. xv. 18; Mat. xxvii. 29; Joan. xix. 3.

by men on earth! The angels adore Thee as their God and true King, but men with feigned adoration here deride Thee as a false God, and as a counterfeit king: I, Lord, adore, Thee and salute Thee with the sincerest salutations that I possibly can, saying with my whole heart,—"Hail, King of the Jews," and of the Gentiles; hail King of angels and of men; hail King of heaven and of the earth.—Save me, O Lord, and admit me into Thy Kingdom, that I may enjoy Thee for ever and ever. Amen.

i. I may also consider that our Lord was *saluted twice in His Passion*,—once by the feigned secret hypocrisy of Judas, when he said to Him:—"Ave Rabbi"—"Hail Rabbi;"—the other time by feigned public hypocrisy by way of mockery, when the soldiers said:—"Ave Rex Judeorum"—"Hail, King of the Jews." In which we may note two kinds of sinners that offend Almighty God, —the one of hypocrites, who make show to love and honour Him, though otherwise they neither love nor reverence Him;—the others are public and scandalous sinners, who scoff and mock at holy things. And our Saviour endured all of them, that He might save all.

ii. Moreover, it is not void of mystery, that the Evangelist says:—"*Et genu flexo ante eum*," &c.—"And bowing *the* knee before Him," not *both the knees*, "they mocked Him;" (14) signifying by this, that worldlings do not give themselves entirely to God, but part to God, and part to the world, who with *one* knee adore their honours, their pleasures, and their riches, and with the other adore God; but this adoration little avails them, because Almighty God will not be served with a heart divided, nor to halves, but with a heart that is whole and entire.

(14) Mat. xxvii. 29.

POINT V.

6. *The sixth injury:*—To the injury of words, every soldier added some injuries of *works*, and such as were painful and ignominious to Him:—"And *spitting upon Him, they took the reed, and struck His head,*" twisting and forcing the thorns to enter further in;—others gave Him blows on the cheek,—others spit in His face, defiling Him with their filthy and loathsome spittles. These three sorts of injuries are related by the Evangelists, and it is also probable that others gave Him blows with their fists, and kicks with their feet, upon His body,—others villanously derided and abused Him by tearing off His beard, that so He might endure of the Gentiles in the house of Pilate the same that He had suffered before of the Jews in the house of Caiphas, except that the Gentiles did not blindfold His eyes, both for that they treated Him in the quality of a king all in mockery, as also because He being already so much disfigured, did not so well represent that majesty as to cause respect and fear in them, and hinder them from striking Him all open and discovered.

*Colloquy.*—O Saviour of the world, how often are Thy injuries iterated, and how are Thy cruel torments redoubled! It was sufficient, sweet Lord, to have been once buffetted, spit upon, and beaten by sinners, yet will Thy charity twice suffer these torments, at the hands both of the Jews and Gentiles, that suffering from all, Thou mightest satisfy for all, and obtain pardon for all. Lord, let all men bless and glorify Thee for this Thy charity, and seeing that Thou hast suffered for all, let all, I beseech Thee, enjoy the fruit of Thy Passion. Amen.

*Concluding remarks applicable to all the points of thi meditation.*

1. One may ponder in every one of these injuries that

which has been considered of in the thirtieth meditation, especially the invincible *patience* and humility of Christ our Lord in suffering them, although they were innumerable, for there were many soldiers that injured Him, and oftentimes reiterated their low scoffings in the way of pastime, sporting as it were, and making it their recreation to injure Him, who took pleasure to be injured, so as to give life, even to those that did Him the injury.

2. How *weary and over-toiled* our Lord Jesus remained with their mockeries of Him and tormentings! How weakened His head with the abundance of blood that ran down all along by reason of the thorns! How fouled His face with the spots of the blood, and with the great abundance of filthy spittings! How black and blue His cheeks with blows and buffets! Pondering that in all these torments He found nobody that had compassion on Him, or that spoke for Him, or that moderated the fury of this savage nation, until that they themselves grew even weary of tormenting Him. Nevertheless, the spirit of our good Jesus was not weary of being tormented, but prepared itself for new assaults, and for the new torments that attended Him. In regard for which I ought not to be wearied of casting myself at His holy feet, bewailing His pains and my own sins, that truly was the cause of them; adoring Him, therefore, with a true adoration, I will crave favours at His hands as of a true king, and yet these no other ones, than that He will vouchsafe to make me partaker of all His torments and derisions, together with the humility, patience, and charity with which He endured them.

# MEDITATION XXXVII.

## PILATE'S WORDS "ECCE HOMO," AND OF THE LAST EXAMINATION WHICH PILATE MADE OF CHRIST.

### POINT I.

Pilate coming into the place where our Saviour was, and seeing Him so pitifully treated and disfigured, by and by conceived a hope that he might now appease the people's fury, by showing Him to them in this wretched plight: and to this effect he commanded his soldiers to set Him in some eminent place, where He might be seen of every body; and, moreover, he himself going somewhat before them towards the people, said to them:—"Behold I bring Him forth unto you, that you may know that I find no cause in Him. *Jesus therefore came forth bearing the crown of thorns, and the purple garment.*"(1)

1. How *confounded and ashamed* our Lord was, seeing Himself before such a multitude of people in this habit and plight, so extenuated, and yet with what humility did He present Himself to their view, being in this pitiful figure!

*Colloquy.*—O my Redeemer, how far different is this figure from that which Thou hadst upon the mount Thabor, full of splendour and majesty! That Thou didst not discover, but to three of Thy disciples only, though Thou wert then upon the top of a mountain; but this Thou dost set out as a spectacle from an eminent place to all the people, that all the world may see Thine ignominies, and that by the sight of them Thy confusions may be redoubled. Give me, dear Lord, the eyes of a lively faith, to behold and

(1) Joan. xix. 4.

contemplate them, since I for my part will no less esteem this pitiful figure, than that other so surpassingly glorious.

2. Our Lord, therefore, being thus exposed to the view of all the people by Pilate, *He saith to them*, "*Ecce Homo*"—"*Behold the man.*" Consider these words spoken by Pilate, i. As proceeding from *his proper spirit;* and—ii., next as *uttered by the Holy Ghost, and*—iii., *the eternal* Father, by the mouth of Pilate:—and I will ponder the manner how I ought both to understand and speak them.

i. First, then, as they were *spoken by Pilate*, they signify, "Behold *this man that calls Himself King, Messiah, and the Son of God*, whom you see so punished and disfigured, that He scarcely appears to be a man, though otherwise He be truly a man; seeing, therefore, that He is a man as you all are, take compassion of your own human nature, and content yourself with the chastisements that this miserable man has already received." But thou, O my soul, behold in the exterior of this man that which may be able to move in thee a compassion of this His sad figure. Behold this man wounded with whips, covered over with spittle,—all swollen with buffets.—"Behold the man" clothed in mockery, and crowned with a crown of sorrow and contempt; behold Him well, and thou shalt find that to be true which is spoken of Him by the prophet,—"But I am a worm, and no man; the reproach of men, and the outcast of the people."(2) And He that was wont to be "Speciosus forma præ filiis hominum"—"beautiful above the sons of men,"(3) is now the very foulest of all. "There is no beauty in Him, nor comeliness; and we have seen Him, and there was no sightliness."(4)

*Colloquy.*—O Son of Man, true God and true Man, it was enough humbling of Thyself to take upon Thee

(2) Psal. xxi. 7. (3) Psal. xliv. 3. (4) Is. liii. 2.

the form of man: why dost Thou so much depress Thyself in this form as to come to be reputed for a worm and not a man, and for the very scorn of mankind? The pride with which I studied to make myself more than a man, equalling myself with God, is the cause that Thou, O my God, dost so humble Thyself, as to appear less than a man, because this my abominable pride stood in need of the medicine of so admirable an humility. Oh that my exterior man wholly resembled Thine in taking delight out of true humility to be trod upon like as a worm, and to be esteemed for less than man,—yea, the very refuse and outcast of men.

ii. Ponder, secondly, these words, as they were spoken *of the Holy Ghost by the mouth of Pilate*,—"Behold the man," who, though He appears to be but a man, is *more than a man*, because He is the Son of the living God, the Messiah promised in the law, the Head of men, and of angels, the Redeemer of mankind, and the sole repairer of all His miseries, whose charity has been such, that He has taken upon Him this wretched figure for the love of men, that He might pay the debts of their sins, and deliver them from these eternal pains they have deserved for them, for which He deserves that all should yield Him a million of thanks, acknowledging Him to be true Man and true God, praising Him, adoring Him, and serving Him, for ever and ever. Amen.

These and other excellencies ought I to consider in this Man, and imagining that these words are directed to me, I will break forth into the affections of admiration, of love, and of confidence, saying:—

*Colloquy.*—Is it possible that a man so divine should be thus abased? What shall not I hope of Him, who has borne to me so great a love? Ought I not to burn with the love of Him that hath done so much for me? O Man, more than man, and the honour of all mankind, I adore Thee and glorify Thee, both as man and eternal God, and beseech Thee that Thou wilt vouchsafe to accept me for Thy slave, branding my face with the same sorrowful figure that I behold on Thine.

iii. Thirdly, I will ponder these words as spoken *by the eternal Father.* "Ecce Homo"—"Behold the Man," whom I have sent into the world to be the master of men, and the pattern of all sanctity and perfection, who, to serve for an example of it, has taken upon Him this deformed figure. Behold His interior virtues, amidst such exterior occasions,—His humility in such contempts,—His poverty of spirit in such nakedness,—His meekness in so great injuries,—His patience in such terrible pains,—His modesty amidst so many blasphemers,—His obedience amongst so many persecutors,—and His charity in the midst of those that abhor Him. And seeing He has taken this figure for your example, behold it, and engrave it deeply in your souls.

*Colloquy.*—O eternal Father, is not this that man at whose baptism and transfiguration Thou didst say: "This is my well-beloved Son, in whom I am well pleased; hear ye Him?" If this be the very same, where is then the form of a dove that declares His innocency? —Where is the bright-shining cloud, that manifests His divinity?—Where is Moses and Elias, who approved and authorised Him by their presence?—I see Him here, abandoned of all, saving of His virtues, which only accompany Him, these preach His innocency, discover His divinity, and authorise His person. Seeing therefore Thou commandest me to behold Him, and to imitate Him, help, I beseech Thee, my weakness, that I may conform myself to the image of this celestial Man, blotting out of me the image of the earthly.

After this manner ought I to behold our Lord Jesus, both in the interior and exterior, considering that in the exterior He appeared less than man, and in the interior that He is more than man;—in the exterior He is all covered over with terrible wounds, and in the interior He is adorned with admirable virtues, endeavouring to obtain desires sincerely to imitate each of them.

3. Turning myself towards the eternal Father, to obtain of Him all I desire, *I will say to Him*:—"Ecce Homo," "Behold the Man." O most sovereign Father, behold this Man, wounded and disfigured for my sins: Thou commandest me that I behold Him to have compassion on Him, and I beseech Thee that Thou behold Him to have compassion on me. Thou desirest that I behold Him to imitate Him; *look upon Him, O Lord, and give me for the love of Him, force to follow Him.* O heavenly Father, whom all mankind have offended by their enormous sins, behold this Man tormented with most grievous pains, to satisfy for our offences, and appease Thy wrath in pardoning them. O Father of mercies, behold the Man that bears all men engraven in His heart, and who offers up His life for them; do not look upon me as I am alone, but look upon me as I am united to this Man, and that which I of myself do not deserve, grant me, I beseech Thee, for His holy merits. "Behold, O God, our protector, and look on the face of Thy Christ."(5) For it is not possible that Thou shouldst abandon those whom He has hidden in the secret of His face, thus afflicted and disfigured. Look, O my God, upon this glass, for in it Thou shalt acknowledge Thine own divine face, for that He is Thine image: look upon us through Him, and Thou shalt find that we are His image, and for the love that Thou bearest to Thy own image, pardon, reform, and sanctify all such as are created after

(5) Psal. lxxxiii. 10.

His image, and redeemed with the blood that He shed in this pitiful figure. Amen.

POINT II.

To these words of Pilate, the whole multitude of priests and people, with one voice, made answer, saying,—"*Crucifige, Crucifige*"—"*Crucify Him, crucify Him.*"(6)

1. Consider the devilish *cruelty of these priests*, of their ministers, and of the people seduced by them, who not only had no compassion of our Lord, so wounded and afflicted, but in whom out of an incredible hatred, the very sight of His misery increased the thirst of adding other torments that should exceed the former, crying out,—"Crucify Him, crucify Him;" as if they had said to Pilate:—"Thou hast given a good beginning in scourging Him, conclude what thou hast begun in crucifying Him, since scourging is to go before crucifying." O what a great feeling did these clamours cause in the ears of our Lord, beholding the perverseness of this people in demanding His death, with more cruelty than the very Gentiles, since those were weary and satisfied with tormenting Him, whereas, these desired still to add to Him new torments. Then did He remember the good that He had done to this nation, and seeing now the evil payment they rendered Him for the same, He deplored the punishment they deserved.

*Colloquy.*—O my soul, how dost thou not break with grief, beholding Him to be in this sort abhorred, who merited so exceedingly to be beloved? How is not thy face bathed with tears, beholding the face of thy Lord to be all bathed with blood, and His enemies yet thirsting to shed out the rest, even to the last drop? Love with a hearty love Him that so much loves thee, in recompense of this unjust hatred with which He is abhorred, and be thou more fervent

(6) Joan. xix. 6.

in loving Him, than His enemies were in abhorring Him.

2. Pilate, much displeased at the obstinacy of the high priests and ministers, said to them:—"Take Him you, and crucify Him, for I find no cause in Him. The Jews answered him, *We have a law, and according to that law He ought to die*, because He hath made Himself the Son of God."(7) In which words they accused our Lord Jesus of blasphemy, judging it for a blasphemy that He called Himself "the Son of God," not by adoption but by nature, and that therefore according to the law, He was to be punished with the pain of death. In this may be seen the abominable blindness of this nation, which held for a plasphemy, the verity itself of Almighty God approved by His word, which averred that the Messiah was the Son of God, and confirmed by so many miracles that our Lord Jesus had wrought in confirmation of it. Hence it plainly appears, that they themselves were blasphemers in censuring this for a blasphemy, and consequently most worthy of the punishment of the law; and yet notwithstanding the true blasphemy is pardoned, and the supposed is punished; because the Son of God would so far humble Himself, as to be punished as a blasphemer, to merit pardon by so doing for true blasphemers.

*Colloquy.*—O sovereign King, it is indeed an irrefragable truth that Thou art to die according to the law, not for having made Thyself the Son of God, but because Thou, being the Son of God, wouldst be made man, and wert to beget by Thy death many adopted sons for Almighty God. I humbly beseech Thee by the same death to make me Thy son, and that as such an one I may die to sin, to the world, and the flesh,

(7) Joan. xix. 6.

and so cease to live to myself, for to live entirely to Thee. Amen.

3. From that which has been said I will further infer, that it is the property of wicked and imperfect men, *to boast of the law, but not to fulfil it*, unless it be in that which is conformable to their taste and humour, for this effect they make use themselves of the law, desirous to dissemble and cover with it their damned designs. But detesting this perverse and obstinate custom, I will endeavour to boast of the law by the entire observation of the same; for otherwise the law will be my condemnation, by manifesting my disobedience against it.(8)

POINT III.

"When Pilate, therefore, had heard this saying, *he feared more.* And he entered into the palace again; and he said to Jesus, 'Unde es tu?'—'Whence art Thou?' But *Jesus gave him no answer.* Pilate, therefore, saith to Him: Speakest Thou not to me? Knowest Thou not that I have power to crucify Thee, and I have power to release Thee? Jesus answered, *Thou shouldst not have any power against me, unless* it were given thee *from above.*"(9)

1. In this let us consider first, the *reason of Pilate's fear*, when he understood that our Lord Jesus made Himself the Son of God. For doubtless the great virtues that shone in our Lord, were sufficient to induce him to believe that He spake the truth, and therefore feared much to condemn Him, not to incur the divine indignation. O how admirable was His meekness and patience, which was able, without other particular miracles, to make a Gentile judge believe, how perverse soever, that a man so afflicted and so evil treated, might be the Son of the living God.

*Colloquy.*—Grant me, O good Jesus, to imitate

(8) Rom. ii. 15. (9) Joan. xix. 8.

these Thy virtues, that Thou mayest be glorified in me by reason of them. Amen.

2. Ponder, secondly, the *pride with which this wicked judge was so* suddenly possessed in upbraiding, because our Lord gave him no answer to that he asked Him, as if he had felt himself touched in his authority;—as also his presumption, his inflated stateliness, together with the ostentation of his words, to make himself to be esteemed. All which is proper to worldlings, and ought to be very far from me, if I will follow the band of our Lord Jesus.

3. Thirdly, above all, ponder the *admirable prudence of Christ our* Redeemer, both in *holding His peace, and in speaking:*—He held His peace in this case where words *availed not for his defence;* but He spake when it was necessary for the *maintaining of the honour of God*, and for the correction of this insolent judge, who presumed so much upon his power; for then did He speak as freely as if He had not felt any misery at all; and that which He intended to say was this;—"Do not brag of the power thou hast, which is not of thee, but is from heaven, given to thee by my heavenly Father, without whose licence and permission thou couldst do nothing against me." In this the goodness of the eternal Father wonderfully shows itself, who gives this authority against His own Son, to so wicked a judge for our good.

*Colloquy.*—O sovereign judge, to whom the heavenly Father has given power to judge the quick and the dead; I give Thee thanks that Thou hast subjected Thyself to so proud a judge, who boasts of his power, whereas, on the other side, he is so fearful a coward, that he dares not use the same: deliver me, sweet Lord, from these two vicious extremes, that neither pride puff me up, nor pusillanimity depress me. Amen.

POINT IV.

By reason of this answer of our Saviour, Pilate was so much the more desirous to deliver Him, but the chief priests continued to urge him by threats, saying:—"*If thou release this man, thou art not Cæsar's friend;*"(10) as much as to say,—"If thou lettest this man go, we will accuse thee before Cæsar for having set at liberty his enemy, and Him that made Himself King to the prejudice of his empire." Pilate, terrified with this, brought our Saviour forth the second time, and said to them: "Ecce Rex vester"— "Behold your King."

1. These words may be considered,—i. as spoken by Pilate of his own motion; or—ii. as proceeding from the Holy Ghost, who moved him to speak them.

i. First, *Pilate spake them by way of scorn:*—"Behold, here this miserable wretch, whom you accuse of making Himself a king; see here that He is neither king, nor yet is any way able to aspire to such a dignity; He is but a painted king only, witness this crown, this sceptre, this purple with which He is adorned; take pity of Him, and do not believe that He is such a one as is able to oppose Himself against Cæsar, or to displace him of his kingdom."

*Colloquy.*—O King of heaven, how art Thou humbled amongst men in the figure of a counterfeit king, paying by this humiliation for the pride and ambition with which they desire to reign! A king of Israel entering into battle,(11) put off his royal robes, that so being disguised, he might escape the death his enemies intended against him alone, without making account of any other; but Thou, O my God, true King of Israel, dost take to Thee the marks and name of a king, on purpose to yield Thyself up to death, that by

(10) Joan. xix. 12. (11) 3 Reg. xxii. 30.

Thy death we might be delivered from death. Oh blessed be such a King who loves His subjects so much as to die to save their lives; let me die, O Lord, a thousand deaths, that Thou mayest live in me, and that I may ever live in Thee. Amen.

ii. Secondly, the *Holy Ghost likewise speaks these words to the Jews*, by the mouth of Pilate, to admonish them that they had there before them Him whom they had so much desired.—"Ecce Rex vester"—"Behold your King,"—whom you have expected so many ages; the King and the *Messiah* promised by the prophets for your salvation; the King that succeeds in the house of David with a sceptre of equity, whose Kingdom ought to be eternal; the King anointed of Almighty God to deliver you from the bondage of the Devil; here I present Him you, behold if you know Him, and desire to receive Him for your King."

2. Thirdly, with the same spirit I will imagine that the same words *are spoken to me* and to all the faithful, "*Ecce Rex vester*"—"Behold your *King*," holy and wise, meek and humble, liberal and magnificent, and so loving, that for your sakes He is in this pitiful state ill-treated and tormented. Behold here the King constituted by the eternal Father(12) over the Church militant and triumphant, King of heaven and earth, King of glory, and an eternal King, whose Kingdom shall be infinite. Consider, therefore, O my soul, whether thou wilt receive Him for thy King, and do the homage due to Him. Consider whether thou disdainest to have a king so outraged in outward show; behold if thou wilt wear His livery, and wait always upon His person, seeing this King is come hither for thy sake.

*Colloquy.*—I accept of Thee most willingly, O my King, and adore Thee for my King, and the more I

(12) Psal. ii. 6.

behold Thee depressed, so much the more do I esteem Thee. Clothe me, I beseech Thee, in Thy colours, since it is an exceedingly great honour for a vassal to be clothed like his king.

POINT V.

The high priests and people answered to this:—"Away with Him, away with Him, crucify Him. Pilate saith to them, Shall I crucify your king? The chief priests answered, *We have no king, but Cæsar.*"(13)

1. First, here consider the incredible *rage of this people*, who would not so much as look upon our Lord Jesus. And, therefore, they cried out,—"Away with Him out of our sight, Crucify Him that our eyes may never see Him more, make away with Him all at once, and do not make two labours of it;" in which they fulfilled that which the Wise man reports of them:—"Let us, therefore, lie in wait for the just, because he is not for our turn, as he is contrary to our doings, and upbraideth us with transgressions of the law, and divulgeth against us the sins of our way of life. He boasteth that He hath the knowledge of God, and calleth himself the Son of God. He is become a censurer of our thoughts. He is grievous unto us, even to behold, for his life is not like to other men's, and his ways are very different."(14)

*Colloquy.*—O the Just of the just, our most just Saviour—most behoveful and most profitable to us, since without Thee we all remained unprofitable and utterly lost for ever; Thy aspect is terrible to the wicked, and most grateful to the good; the rebellious sinners care not to behold Thee, but the just desire to contemplate Thee. Let me never, loving Saviour, lose the sight of Thy divine face, although it be in this sorrowful figure, which for my sake Thou hast

(13) Joan. xix. 15. (14) Sap. ii. 12.

taken; for in beholding Thee in this sorrowful condition, I shall encourage myself to imitate Thy labours, so to see and enjoy Thee afterwards in eternal rest. Amen.

2. Consider the *malice and blindness of this people*, in rejecting thus the true King, whom God had given them for their good, and to accept of a tyrant king, who deprived them both of goods and liberty,—things that they so much esteemed, they receiving him now whom they so abhorred before, out of the hatred they bore to our Lord Jesus, and with the intention of excluding Christ; in punishment of which wickedness God permitted that they should both lose their true King and their Messiah also, and besides, that the earthly king whom they had chosen, should band against them, and both raze their city and utterly ruin and destroy them.

3. All this ought I to apply to myself, reflecting with myself *how many times I leave the King of heaven* for the king of earth, and for some little points of fleeting honour, living in such a manner as if I had not, or that there were not, any other king than Cæsar, in which I commit an intolerable injury against God, as did this perverse and obstinate nation.

*Colloquy.*—O most sovereign King, I am infinitely sorry, and extremely repent having so often forsaken and offended Thee. When I was of the world, I confess that I said with the worldlings, "Non habeo regem nisi Cæsarem"—"I have no other king but Cæsar;" but henceforward, gracious Lord, I will say that for my part I will have no other king than Christ Jesus. Thou art my Cæsar and my King, whom I desire to obey and serve with all my heart, and if I obey the kings of the earth, it shall be in regard that Thou so commandest, and that only in such things as

Thou shalt like of, for, as for other matters that are in any way derogating from Thy holy love, "Non habeo regem nisi Cæsarem"—I acknowledge no other king but Thee, my Lord Jesus, to whom be all honour and glory, for ever and ever. Amen.

---

## MEDITATION XXXVIII.

### ON THE CONDEMNATION OF CHRIST TO THE DEATH OF THE CROSS.

#### POINT I.

"And as he was sitting in the place of judgment, his wife sent to him, saying: Have thou nothing to do with that just man. For I have suffered many things in a dream because of Him." (1)

Consider here that these visions which the wife of Pilate suffered in her sleep, might proceed either from *the Devil*, or else from a *good angel*, according as different saints contemplate, from both which ways I may draw out matter of profit for myself.

1. I may consider that *the Devil*, seeing the strange meekness of our Lord, and His invincible patience, amidst so many injuries and torments, *began now to suspect that this was the Messiah*, the Son of God, and He that was to destroy his kingdom; that for this reason by dreams he frightened the wife of Pilate, in order that she should use all means possible to hinder His death, imagining that by means of the wife he might persuade the husband whatsoever he wished. Here we may see how worthy of great consideration the invincible force of heroic virtue is, seeing that the very devils themselves stand amazed at it, who, as the apostle St. James says, both "believe and tremble;" (2) they *believe*, as forced through evident signs, and they

(1) Mat. xxvii. 19. (2) Jac. ii. 19.

*tremble* at the majesty and sanctity of that which they believe.

*Colloquy.*—O that all men so beheld the virtues of our Lord as to believe in Him, and to respect Him, but yet not contenting themselves with this alone as the devils do, they would also imitate and serve the same Lord.

2. Or, I may also consider that a *good angel*, by his inspiration, spoke in sleep to this woman, telling her that if her husband condemned Christ, *he himself should be condemned*, and should endure terrible calamities, and that *the Hebrew nation should be utterly destroyed;* besides this, the angel represented to her in her sleep certain fearful visions, so that she might the more earnestly persuade her husband to set Him free, and for this cause did she esteem Him to be a "just man," and intimated so much to her husband in her letter, saying:—"Nihil tibi, et justo illi"—"Have thou nothing to do with that just man."

*Colloquy.*—O just man, and the justifier of men, whose justice is very well known and proved, though for all this it be not received nor approved; justify me, I beseech Thee, with Thy justice, and give me part in it, for without Thy company I cannot live, neither will I ever forsake it.

POINT II.

"Pilate, seeing that he prevailed nothing, but that rather a tumult was made, taking water, washed his hands before the people saying: I am innocent of the blood of this just man, look you to it. And the whole people, answering, said: His blood be upon us, and upon our children." (3)

1. *The Evangelists often* in this history set *forth to us*

(3) Mat. xxvii. 24.

*the innocence of our Lord*, together with the testimony that Pilate himself gave of it, to make us remember by this, that every torment He endured was for our sins, inviting us by this to have the more compassion of our innocent Lord, as also to deplore our sins, by reason of which He suffered so grievous pains.

2. Consider the furious *malice of this Jewish nation*, who violently to deprive our Lord of His life, and to shed His *blood*, would *offer their own, together with their children's*, charging themselves with those punishments that the death of this just man, imposed so unjustly, deserved, all which indeed fell upon them, in regard that the blood of our Lord Jesus, which was able to give life even to those that shed it, was the occasion of their death, they persisting still obstinate in their rebellion. But I will say to the eternal Father, with another manner of spirit than these,—" O Lord, let the blood of Thy most innocent Son light upon me, and upon all the faithful, to cleanse and sanctify us. I do here offer Thee mine, my God, desirous to shed it for His sake, who has shed His own for me.

*Colloquy.*—O most precious blood of my Saviour, do not come upon me as upon these rebels to confound me, but come upon me with mercy, to wash and justify me. O my Redeemer, permit not, I beseech Thee, that I wash my hands with water as Pilate did, and leave my soul soiled with sin, nor that doing evil works, I seek to excuse them out of human fear, and to wash myself in outward appearance, imputing to others that which myself a sinner have committed.

POINT III.

" Then he released to them Barabbas, and having scourged Jesus, delivered Him unto them to be crucified." (4)

(4) Luc. xxiii. 24; Mat. xxvii. 26.

This was the sentence which the judge gave against our Lord Jesus, condemning Him to the death of the cross, concerning which sentence:—

1. Consider, first, how *unjust and cruel it was*, seeing that the judge himself acknowledged His innocency, testifying the same not only in words, but also with this exterior ceremony of washing his hands; and notwithstanding all this, moved with a worldly fear, that the Jews would accuse him to Cæsar, he pronounced this sentence, for human respect trampling justice under his feet. This sentence was likewise cruel, in regard that knowing well that the high priests accused our Lord out of *mere envy*, desiring for hatred to have Him crucified upon the cross, yet he would deliver Him over to their pleasure, following herein not reason, nor the laws of justice nor mercy, but the *will of the furious and malicious people*, that could no way content themselves with less than such a death.

*Colloquy.*—O sweet Jesus, I will not deliver Thee, nor anything that is Thine, into the hands of so cruel a tyrant as mine own self-will, but will that myself, and all mine, be wholly resigned unto Thine, since my proper will is so cruel, that it will not cease until it has crucified Thee once again in me by sin, but Thine is so merciful, that it will deliver me from death by Thy grace.

2. Consider *the great satisfaction of the people*, and the shouts they cast forth when they saw this sentence pronounced, congratulating one another that they had so well brought their intention to pass, which no doubt doubled the injury done to our Lord, who then gave ear to all this.

3. But above all, consider more devoutly how this sentence being intimated to our Lord Jesus, although He saw

well that it was most unjust on the judge's part, considering, notwithstanding, that it came from the ordination of the eternal Father, for the salvation of the world, *He presently accepted it most willingly,* without either appealing, supplicating, or else complaining of the outrageous wrong they did to Him, and without murmuring against the judge or his officers, but offered Himself freely to undergo the execution of it for our good and advantage, abandoning Himself by this His tender will to the enraged will of His enemies, that they should execute upon Him Pilate's sentence.

*Colloquy.*—I give Thee humble thanks, O most meek Redeemer, for this Thy frank heart, with which Thou didst accept a sentence so unjust and cruel, for the delivering of me from that just sentence of eternal condemnation that was pronounced against me. Dear Lord, with what shall I repay this good will? Behold here I give Thee my will for the entire fulfilling of Thine, and I am prepared to accept whatsoever sentence of torments, shall by Thy ordination or permission at any time be pronounced against me: help me, therefore, with Thy holy grace, that neither through fear nor pusillanimity I omit to accomplish that which Thou shalt command me, nor that I be defective in the office with which Thou hast encharged me. Amen.

4. Fourthly, I may, moreover, piously contemplate that some *one of the disciples* who was secretly there amongst the rest, *went with this news to our Blessed Lady,* recounting to her the pitiful condition in which he had seen her Blessed Son, whom he had left now condemned to the death of the cross; with which news her heart was pierced, wounded, and tormented, more than can be said or imagined; yet, notwithstanding, with rare resignation to

the divine will, she assented to the sentence, knowing well that her Son, to conform Himself to the will of His Father, would entirely accomplish it.

*Colloquy.*—O most sovereign Virgin, fortify thy heart, since thy presence is requisite at this sacrifice, to offer up to the eternal Father, that which thou hast received at His hands. And if the sorrowful tidings so much afflict thee which thou hearest with thine ears, much more afflictions will the sorrowful spectacle cause thee, which thou shalt behold with thine eyes.

---

## MEDITATION XXXIX.

### ON CHRIST'S CARRIAGE OF HIS CROSS UPON HIS SHOULDERS, AND THE OCCURRENCES UNTIL HE CAME TO THE MOUNT OF CALVARY.

#### POINT I.

The sentence being pronounced and accepted of, the soldiers did, by the commandment of the judge, three remarkable things to our Lord Jesus.

1. The first was, "*take off the cloak from Him, and put on Him His own garments,*"(1) that so He might be the better known; but we do not read that they took off the crown of thorns, but left it still fixed on, not to give Him any solace or assuagement.

*Colloquy.*—O sweet Jesus, how well hast Thou represented the person of a true king, and for this cause do they leave the crown still standing upon Thy head, which represents the perpetuity of Thy Kingdom. Now is it time that Thou represent the person of a thief and malefactor, though Thou be none, bearing the ensigns of true thieves and malefactors. Instead of the hollow reed that they take out of Thy hands,

(1) Mat. xxvii. 31; Marc. xv. 21.

Thou art to embrace the wood of the cross, and in company of thieves to go forth to die with them upon it.

We may also ponder, the injurious *words that* these cursed wretches gave to our Lord, as to a man condemned for heinous crimes, and the cruelty they used *in dragging and pulling Him* into the hall, where He had been scourged, to divest Him, giving Him back His bloody clothes that He might put them on again; which contained a mystery: for, as our Lord Jesus, to carry His cross, stripped Himself of those clothes that were none of His, and with which He had been clothed in the house of Herod and Pilate, and put on His own again;—so I, to carry my cross and imitate Him, will strip myself of all the vicious customs of the world and the flesh, and will clothe myself with those that are proper to our Lord Jesus, by which I shall be known and held for His disciple, especially with meekness, patience, mercy, and the bowels of charity.

2. The second thing they did was, *to drag to that place the wood of the cross,* being very great, and very weighty. Where I will ponder, *what our Lord said and thought in His heart* when He saw the same;—how He rejoiced in it interiorly, and said with much greater alacrity than afterwards did Blessed St. Andrew:—"Salve Crux preciosa, diu disiderata, solicite amata, sine intermissione quæsita, et aliquando cupienti animo preparata"—"Hail, noble cross, long desired, carefully loved, incessantly sought, and at the length prepared, for Him who desires to be fastened on thee; come, let me embrace thee in mine arms, seeing that thou art to receive me into thine. Come, and I will with my mouth give to thee a kiss of peace, for upon thee will I repose my head, and will sleep in peace the last slumber of death." O with what tenderness did our Lord embrace His cross, sanctifying the same with that first

embracement!—how joyfully did He take it into His hands and laid it upon His afflicted shoulders!

*Colloquy.*—O sweet Jesus, give me grace to behold Thy cross with the like eyes, and to embrace the same with the like love, and to search after it with this desire, glorying in the cross without ever reposing myself, until I die upon the same.

3. The third thing was, *to cause to be fetched out of prison two thieves*, that they should be joined with Him in the way to execution, as St. Luke says, and that they should die all three together: which thing redounded to the great disgrace of our Saviour, who thereby was reputed for a thief and malefactor. Oh with what different eyes did these thieves behold their crosses, trembling at the very sight of them, and shutting their eyes not to see them! These loved the fault, but abhorred the pain; but our loving Jesus loved the pain, and abhorred the fault;—these fled from the pains due to their own sins, but Christ accepted the pains which were due to other men's sins.

*Colloquy.*—I give Thee humble thanks, my sweet Saviour, for the willingness with which Thou didst embrace the pain of the cross, without the fault, to deliver me from it. Change my heart like, to Thine, that seeing I have with these thieves committed the crimes, I may accept with Thee of the pains I have deserved for them, and may offer myself with charity to support the pains due to others, suffering for the good of my neighbour, some little of that much which Thou hast suffered for them. Amen.

POINT II.

Our Lord Jesus "bearing His own cross," "went forth to that place which is called Calvary."(2)

(2) Joan. xix. 17.

1. Upon this touching passage consider, first, the *great shame that our Lord suffered in this* first issuing forth of the house of Pilate, laden with His cross between two notorious thieves, with the noise of serjeants and criers who proclaimed His misdeeds, with a great concourse of people, great numbers running to behold this spectacle.

O angels who behold this ignominious coming forth of our Lord, why do not you come forth of heaven to publish its cause, and to defend His reputation! O eternal Father, what dost Thou, beholding Thy Son issuing forth, laden with the wood of the cross, whereon He is to be crucified? Goest Thou forth like another Abraham with his son Isaac, bearing in Thy hands the fire and knife with which this sacrifice is to be offered?(3) O fire of love, who so burnest in the heart of the Father, that Thou dost make Him to unsheath the sword of His justice upon His Son, whom He sacrificed and put to death to give life to the sinner! inflame me, dear Lord, with this fire, that I may love Him who has so greatly loved me;—smite me with this sword, so that there may die in me that which is displeasing to Thee. But my God, what is the cause that Thou goest not forth with Thy Son by night, as Abraham did, and only with two of His own servants,—but in the midst of the day, with a great multitude of people to see this sacrifice? O fire of love, which dost burn and give light, and desirest that thy works enlighten and enflame, like the sun at noonday!

*Colloquy.*—Discover to me, Lord, I beseech Thee, the excessive charity of the Father, and the profound humility and obedience of the Son, that I may glory in their indignities, and embrace them with love, in the presence of all the world. Amen.

(3) Gen. xxii. 3.

2. Consider the intolerable *affliction and pain that the feeble body of our Lord Jesus endured*, bearing this so heavy burden,—how oft did He stumble and stoop to His knees with its weight, by reason that His body was greatly weakened with His former torments!—How did He sweat for anguish, overladen with the weight of this wood! how did He water the streets with the blood that ran trickling down from His wounds, oppressed and pressed out with this tree of the winepress, that so sore crushed them! O blood of the living God, blood of inestimable value, mingled with the dirt of the highways, and trodden under the feet of wretched men! O angels of heaven, why come you not to gather up this precious blood? How help you not this bloodless Lord, to support so painful a burden?

*Colloquy.*—O sweet Jesus, that I could bear the same upon my shoulders, that Thine might receive some kind of ease! But I perceive, O Lord, that it must needs be the shoulder(4) of God that must bear the same; upon it it is that Thou wilt, according to the words of the prophets, lay the principality and empire, which began by Thy cross, and the "key of the house of David,"(5) to open to us the gates of heaven, which had been until then fast locked against us.

3. Our Lord Jesus much more felt the *burden of our sins than the weight of the cross;* for if the prophet David said that his sins were insupportable, saying:—"Because my iniquities are gone over my head, and as a heavy burden are become heavy upon me;"(6)—how much heavier was the burden of the sins of all mankind, past, present, and to come, all borne by this our Lord, as the prophet Isaiah says,—"All we like sheep have gone astray; every

(4) Is. ix. 6. (5) Is. xxii. 22. (6) Psal. liii. 9; xxxvii. 5.

one hath turned aside into his own way, and the Lord hath laid upon Him the iniquity of us all."(7)

*Colloquy.*—My sins, O sweet Jesus, are that which makes Thee to bow down Thy shoulders;—I am the strayed sheep, and Thou art led like a sheep to the shambles of mount Calvary, there to be sacrificed for my sins. Oh that I had never committed them, to have lightened Thee by so much of this burden. But, seeing that by my fault I was the cause of it, it is only reasonable that I endure a part of the pain, and that I lay upon my back the cross that I have deserved. I here offer myself, dear Lord, to bear mine, as Thou hast borne Thine.

POINT III.

Our Lord Jesus, going now on His way, with His cross upon His shoulders, "They laid hold of one Simon, of Cyrene, coming from the country; and they laid the cross on him to carry after Jesus."(8)

1. Upon this passage consider, first, *the great weariness that our Lord endured in this way*, whence His enemies took an occasion of laughing at Him, for the weakness He there showed, as He that had formerly called Himself the Son of God, and who in the space of three days could erect that huge frame of the whole Temple; all which our Lord endured with admirable patience, till the chief priests, fearing lest He should die by the way, caused the cross to be taken from Him, not to ease Him by so doing, but out of a great desire that they had to have Him crucified on it. Hence I will take comfort in my fatigues, and in the cross that shall fall to my lot, be it ever so heavy, confiding in the mercy of our Lord Jesus, who will furnish me with strength to bear it, calling to mind for this purpose that which St. Paul says concerning our "tribulation, (as

(7) Is. liii. 6. (8) Luc. xxiii. 26.

his words are,) which came to us in Asia, that we were pressed out of measure above our strength. so that we were weary even of life. But we had in ourselves the answer of death, that we should not trust in ourselves, but in God, who raiseth the dead, who hath delivered, and doth deliver us out of so great dangers, in whom we hope that He will yet also deliver us." (9)

2. Consider, moreover, that although our Lord could have carried His cross alone to the mount Calvary, forcing His flesh miraculously, yet *He would not make use of this power*, but would rather that the cross should be given to another that should bear it after Him,—to signify, that the cross which He was to impart to His faithful, they were to bear, after His example, fulfilling that which He had said:—"If any man will come after me, let him deny himself, and take up his cross, and follow me." (10)

*Colloquy.*—O good Jesus, seeing that Thou goest before, and dost first carry so heavy a cross that makes Thee bend to Thy knees, is it much if I carry mine after Thee, assisted with the strength that Thou wilt give me to bear the same? Lord, the cross that I carry is Thine, and mine;—*Thine,* inasmuch as Thou hast borne it first, and that by Thy decree it comes upon us, and for Thy sake we carry it;—nevertheless it is also *mine,* because Thou hast hewed and adapted it to the proportion of my forces, and that it is for my advantage, for Thou wouldst never give me Thy cross but to make me partaker of the glorious fruits that proceed from it.

3. Consider that *there was nobody found who would bear the cross of our Lord Jesus*, nor assist Him in this labour, seeing that the Jews held it for a kind of malediction, and for an irregularity, so much as to touch the cross, because

(9) 2 Cor. i. 8.
(10) Mat. xvi. 24; Luc. ix. 23; Marc. viii. 34.

according to the law, whosoever died upon it was "accursed," (11) besides the Gentile soldiers reputed it an infamy, and among the disciples and friends of our Saviour nobody presented himself to bear the same, because they were stricken and daunted with fear, so that they were constrained to force a stranger that then passed by to bear the same.

In this is represented the different sorts of persons that fly from the cross of Christ, some because they believe not the virtue that God has placed in it, such are infidels,—others because they hold it for an infamy, and against their reputation, as the proud and ambitious,—others for fear of the pain there is in bearing it, against their sensuality, as the voluptuous and fleshly. Oh that He would give fountains of tears to mine eyes, to weep with St. Paul for so many in the world, who are "enemies of the cross of Christ, whose end is destruction, whose God is their belly, whose glory is in their shame." (12)

*Colloquy.*—O King of glory, permit not, I beseech Thee, that I be an enemy of the cross, lest by this I become Thine enemy also. I will not make a God of my belly, nor yet of worldly glory, but of Jesus Christ crucified; His cross shall be all my joy and my glory, and being a friend to the cross, I shall be likewise a friend to Him that died on it.

4. We all of us *naturally abhor the cross*, and there is none to be found to bear the same, if he be not in a manner forced to it, (13) like Simon of Cyrene, but after a different manner,—for some bear it with patience and without merit,—others with patience and merit, making a virtue of necessity, as this Cyrenean did,—but others there are that are sweetly forced by an efficacious inspira-

(11) Deut. xxi. 23. (12) Phil. iii. 18.
(13) S. Ber. ser. 34, in Cant. et infra medit. liii.

tion of God Himself, and of His grace, by which they surmount the repugnancy and inclination of the flesh, and with promptitude of spirit undergo the cross, glorying with St. Paul, and rejoicing in the bearing of the same at all times, and in all places.

*Colloquy.*—O sweet Saviour, who wilt not force any one to carry Thy cross against his will, and therefore hast said,—"If any man will come after me, let him deny himself, and take up his cross daily, and follow me," seeing that my flesh repines and murmurs to carry it, let Thy grace, I beseech Thee, prevent me to compel me to it, willingly to embrace Thy cross by following Thee, seeing that Thou hast so willingly carried it for the love of me. Amen.

POINT V.

Moreover, mark well the circumstance of this man that carried the cross of our Lord, and draw out thence the mystical sense, for they did not happen casually, or by chance.

1. The first is, that *this man's name was Simon*, which signifies "*obedient*,"—to show that the virtue of obedience consists in overcoming the repugnance of our proper will, in accepting the cross that God shall send us, after whatever manner it be, and that the obedient are those that ease our Saviour and His substitutes, but the disobedient are heavy upon them, and make, as the apostle says, that they carry their crosses sad and mourning. (14)

*Colloquy.*—O most sweet Jesus, who by obedience didst take to Thee Thy cross, and of Thyself, didst freely humble Thyself, becoming obedient even to die upon the same, seeing that Thou dost so much love obedient persons, that Thou wouldst not give Thy cross to any other than to him that bore the name of

(14) Heb. xiii. 17.

obedient: give me, I beseech Thee, this excellent virtue, with which I may submit myself wholly to Thy ordination, doing and enduring whatsoever shall proceed from the same, although it be a heavy cross to me. Amen.

2. The second circumstance is, that *he was a stranger, and "was coming out of the country" to Jerusalem,*—to signify, that those who are to meet with our Lord Jesus in their way, and be made worthy to carry His cross, ought to resolve with themselves to live like pilgrims, to forsake the world with her wild and savage customs, directing their steps and their works towards the heavenly Jerusalem; and, therefore, if I will live after this manner, I shall, when I think least of it, meet with our Lord Jesus, who will make me worthy to suffer with Him, and for Him. Oh, happy encounter to meet with Jesus carrying His cross! Oh that I were so happy as that He might meet me in the way thus laden, and that He would lay upon my shoulders the cross that He carried upon His own.—That apostle, likewise, was called Simon, who going out of Rome met with our Lord Jesus, and who as He then told him, went to that city, there to be crucified the second time.

*Colloquy.*—O my Saviour, let us go together, and let us both carry the cross; but yet let it not be as Simon of Cyrene did, who carried it only, but did not die upon it, but as Simon Peter, who was crucified with Thee, Thou being first crucified in him.

3. Finally, as the labour of Simon of Cyrene lasted but a little, yet *the memory both of him and his children remains in the Church* to this present day, as of persons so remarkable for their virtue, that St. Mark calls them by their names,—Alexander and Rufus;—even so they that bear the cross of our Saviour, however they begin to carry it

by constraint, yet undergoing the same patiently, and with a willing mind, their labour will speedily pass away, but their glory will endure for ever, because he that bears the cross with our Lord Jesus, will reign with Him in glory eternally.

POINT V.

"And there followed Him a great multitude of people, and of women, who bewailed and lamented Him. But Jesus turning to them, said: Daughters of Jerusalem, weep not over me, but weep for yourselves, and for your children. For behold, the days shall come wherein they will say: Blessed are the barren, and the wombs that have not borne, and the paps that have not given suck. Then shall they begin to say to the mountains: Fall upon us, and to the hills, Cover us. For if in the green wood they do such things, what shall be done in the dry?" (15)

1. Upon this passage consider, first, the *divers ends of those that followed Christ our Lord;*—some to crucify Him, as the soldiers and executioners,—others to mock Him and to rejoice at His death, as the priests and their officers,—others of curiosity to see so strange a spectacle,—and others for acquaintance sake, and of a kind of friendship they bore to our Lord, weeping of a natural compassion for the pains and torments He endured;—but none of all these followed Him to help Him to carry His cross, nor with any desire to die with Him, according to that which He had said:—"Si quis vult venire post me," &c.—"If any man will come after me, let him deny himself, and take up his cross daily and follow me."

*Colloquy.*—O good Jesus, give me grace to follow Thee, not as this troop of people, but in the same manner that Thou desirest to be followed, embracing Thy cross to die with Thee upon it.

(15) Luc. xxiii. 27.

2. Our Lord, even in the midst of such a troop of people, and in the heat of so great contempts and disgraces, still *preserved His divine authority;* and so turning Himself back towards the women that followed Him weeping, He taught them how to weep with more perfection, saying to them:—"Weep not over me, but weep for yourselves;" in which words He does not forbid to lament His Passion, because reason would that each one should bewail it, but the manner of bewailing it *only of a human compassion*, and forgetting the cause for which He suffers, which is our sins, as if He had said:—"Do not so much weep for me, and for what I endure, but for yourselves, and for your sins, and the sins of your children, which are the cause of this my Passion."

*Colloquy.*—O most excellent master, who amidst so many pains dost not forget to do Thy office, teach me, I beseech Thee, how to weep for Thee, and for myself, as also for my neighbour;—over *Thee*, bewailing the torments Thou dost suffer for my sake; for *myself*, lamenting for having so grievously offended Thee; for my *neighbours*, bewailing their sins, as Thou hast often bewailed them.

3. Ponder, thirdly, *the infinite charity of our Lord*, who forgetting His own pains, will that we lament ours, with those of our neighbours, especially the punishments of those that make not their benefit of His Passion and death, for the obtaining pardon of their sins, and for this cause it is that He pronounces that fearful sentence:—"If in the green wood they do these things, what shall be done in the dry?" That is, "if I that am a green and fruitful tree feel the terrible chastisements of the divine justice for other men's sins, how will the same justice punish the sinners themselves, who are dry and barren wood, for their own sins? If the innocent person has been scourged,

buffeted, crowned, and mocked, and that I go now to be nailed to this cross where I shall be fed with gall, what shall become of sinners? What whips, what thorns, what buffets, what scorns, what gall, and torments will fall upon them, when they shall have received their judgments?" O my soul, dost thou not tremble at the fearful punishment that is prepared for thee, if thou art a dry tree? If thou art not moved to bewail thy sins, behold what thy God has endured for them. Move thyself to see how much thou art to suffer, if thou dost not make thy benefit of that which He has suffered for thee. If thou art not awakened with the amiable voice of mercy, which the blood of our Lord Jesus sends forth shed with so great love, at least awake thyself with the cries of justice, which cries out against rebels from the same blood, poured forth with so great pain.

*Colloquy.*—O eternal Father, appease Thy wrath by the Passion of Thy innocent Son: let Thy justice be satisfied by the fruits that proceed from this tree of life; and although I deserve to be cut down like a dry tree, and to be cast into the fire of hell, I most humbly beseech Thee, by His mercies, that Thou wilt vouchsafe to graft me anew in Him, that so I may bring forth fruits worthy of eternal life. Amen.

POINT VI.

Consider, as a thing piously credible, how the most Blessed Virgin having understood the heavy news of the condemnation of her son, went out with St. John, St. Mary Magdalen, and the other devout women to find Him out, following Him with an unspeakable grief by the trace of His blood; and that when our Lord Jesus turned His face towards these women of Jerusalem, He also lifted up His eyes to look upon His mother, and *the mother likewise lifted up her eyes to see her son,* by reason of which encountering of eyes, their hearts were pierced with sorrow at the sight of one another.

1. *O what a sharp-pointed sword wounded the soul of the Blessed Virgin,* when she beheld her dear Son with this crown, with which His step-mother, the Synagogue, had crowned Him,—when she saw His divine face so disfigured, His whole body crouching down under the heavy burden of the cross, in the midst of two thieves, and environed about with innumerable hangmen, who tormented Him on every side! If the daughters of Jerusalem wept and had a tender feeling of the pains of our Lord Jesus, whom they reputed but for a holy man, how did she lament and feel them, whom she held for her Son and for her God?

2. Then she cast up the eyes of her soul towards the eternal Father, and seeing Him in spirit with the sword and the fire in His hands, *to sacrifice His Son,*(16) with deep sighs and hearty groanings, *she said to Him :*—"O fire of divine love, which never sayest it is enough,(17) say so now at least, since that which my Son has already endured, is more than enough for the redemption of the world. O sword of divine justice, enter again into thy scabbard, seeing that thou hast already drawn blood enough to pay the injury that has been done thee. O eternal Father, cease the rigour of Thy justice against Thy Son and mine, since He hath more than most abundantly paid for that which He owed, or else turn Thy sword against me also, that I may die with Him for sinners; for to live without Him is death to me, and to die with Him shall be my life, yet not my will be done, but Thine."

*Colloquy.*—O Father of mercies, since, according to

(16) Gen. xxii. 6. (17) Prov. xxx. 16.

Thine ordinance, Abraham went to sacrifice his son Isaac, without knowledge of his mother, wherefore wilt Thou that Thy Son be sacrificed, His mother knowing it, and assisting at this sacrifice? This is a new torment both of the Son and of the mother, why then wilt Thou increase the torments of the one, with the presence of the other? O my God, now know I well that it is Thy custom to torment much those whom Thou lovest much, in order that they may increase much in Thy love, or discover that which they bear Thee, setting more by Thy will than by their own, and offering themselves to die, to give life to those whom they love.

*Colloquy.*—O most sacred Virgin, seeing that thou dost so much love sinners, as to offer thyself, together with thy son, to die for them, show to me the love thou bearest me, in making me to feel the sorrows that thou didst feel, beholding thy son so afflicted, that I also may offer myself to die with Him unto all that is earthly, crucifying mine own flesh for the love of Him. Amen.

3. Our Lord, going on His way in the same manner that we have related, went out of the gate of the city, and so *came to the Mount of Calvary*, where we should ponder the inward feeling of Christ our Lord, when issuing out of the city of Jerusalem, with those marks and badges of a sinner. He remembered how that accursed city cast Him out of her gates, and for the same should be destroyed and left desolate, but His Passion should be profitable to others, who did not participate with her in her abominable treasons and wickedness.

*Colloquy.*—O good Jesus, who didst go "without the gate"(18) of the city, to the end that Thy sacred

(18) Heb. xiii, S. Tho. 3, p. q. xlvi. art. 10, ad. 2.

flesh, figured by the goats of the old law, might be offered in holocaust for my sins; help me, I beseech Thee, to go out of the pernicious city of this world, and from the perilous company of worldlings, bearing upon my back Thy contempts and disgraces, in which I may glory, embracing Thy torments with true love. Amen.

---

## MEDITATION XL.

### ON THAT WHICH PASSED UPON THE MOUNT OF CALVARY, BEFORE THE CRUCIFIXION.

#### POINT I.

Consider, first, the reason why our Lord would be crucified on mount Calvary at noon-day, and in the time of so great solemnity, since all this is not without mystery, inasmuch as, not by chance, but by His election and will, He chose to be crucified, as also the manner, the time, and the place, together with other circumstances of that sacrifice.(1)

i. The principal cause of this was, that His death and crucifying might be to Him on all parts, *the more painful, and to us more profitable*, for the rare examples of virtue, which by this occasion shines in it.—ii. He would die in *an open field*, that He might make His torments and ignominies the more *public*, and to be seen of all, as being for the good of all.—iii. He would that this should be upon the mount Calvary, *where malefactors were punished*, that He might make His death so much the more shameful; thus dying in a place where men were chastised for most heinous crimes; and, moreover, to give us to understand that He did not die so much by the sentence of human

(1) S. Tho. 3, p. q. xliv. art. 10.

justice, as by the sentence of the divine, in punishment of the sins of such as were truly malefactors, to satisfy for their pains, and to free them from their faults.—iv. He would that this place *should be called "Calvary,"* by reason of the bones and skulls of dead and executed persons, a place noisome, infectious, and full of horror and terror; to give us to understand that His blood was shed for the salvation both of the living and the dead, and to raise up the souls and the bodies also in their times.—v. He would be crucified *at noon-day*, that all might behold His nakedness and shame, and because He endured for all with excessive *fervour*, signified by the sun of mid-day; for which cause He also made choice to die upon the *solemn day* of Easter, at which time an immense multitude of people came to Jerusalem, that His torments might be so much the more ignominious, as they should be known of many and all the world might learn His heroic humility, patience, and charity; with which He suffered such things of such persecutors, and with such circumstances as never were seen before in the world.

*Colloquy.*—I give Thee humble thanks, most meek Redeemer, for having chosen to die in a place the most accursed and abject of the earth: to enter into the world Thou chosest a contemptible stable;—and to go out of the world, Thou madest choice of a contemptible Calvary.—To be born, Thou madest choice of a most loathsome place, and the abode of brute beasts;—and to die, Thou madest choice of another, full of malefactors' bones and skulls. When Thou wert born, many people assembled in Bethlehem, which was the cause Thou couldst not get a place to lie in;—and when Thou diedst, there flocked a great concourse of people to Jerusalem, to serve Thee for an occasion of greater disgrace. Thou wert born at midnight, and in a little town, thereby to hide Thy glorious birth; but Thou sufferest at noon-day, and in the chief town of the whole country, to notify to all Thy ignominious death. Seeing therefore that Thy election is always the most assured, grant, my sweet Saviour, that by Thy example I may choose for myself that which is the worst in the sight of the world, flying honours, embracing dishonours, and persevering in humiliation to death.

### POINT II.

Our Lord Jesus being now come to the mount Calvary: —"They gave Him wine to drink, mingled with gall. And when He had tasted, He would not drink."(2)

1. Consider the barbarous *cruelty of these torturers*, who being accustomed to give good wine to condemned persons, to comfort them in their torments, and our Lord being very sore afflicted, and pressed with thirst, having lost a great part of His blood, and withal having gone a good journey,—when they ought in all humanity to have given Him drink, they mingled gall in it, and most bitter myrrh, on purpose to torment His tongue, His mouth, and His stomach, whither neither the scourges nor the thorns had been able to penetrate. Nevertheless, our Lord, although He knew well what wine they gave Him, yet tasted of it without swallowing any down, willing to taste this bitterness, and to suffer this torment in His dry tongue and afflicted mouth, to satisfy by this for the sensual delights of our gluttony and drunkenness, giving us an example of patience, when in our greatest troubles and afflictions, we find instead of succours at the hands of men, only an augmentation of them; as also an example of suffering, when in our hunger and thirst we at any time want that which is necessary, or there be given to us anything of evil and unsavoury taste, seeing that to Him they gave gall.

(2) Matt. xxvii. 34; Marc. xv. 23.

*Colloquy.*—O sweet Jesus, how dear does our gluttonies cost Thee; it cannot be said of Thee, "The fathers have eaten a sour grape, and the teeth of the children are set on edge."(3) But contrarywise, we Thy children, have eaten the sour grapes, and the sourness of sins: and Thy teeth are set on edge, Thou suffering the torments that we deserved for them. Pardon, I beseech Thee, O my Redeemer, the excess I have committed in this sin, and let the sauce of my meat be the remembrance of Thy gall,(4) in such a manner, that I never trouble myself, or take any care for meat and drink, nor yet suffer myself to be overcome by dainty fare.

2. *How many there are at this day who give* as drink to our Lord Jesus *wine mingled with gall*, offering to Him works good of themselves with wicked intentions, and detestable circumstances. "Wine mingled with gall" is doctrine mingled with errors, faith with wicked works, zeal with revenge, alms for vain-glory, prayer with voluntary distractions, and all the works of hypocrisy. These are the grapes which Moses calls the "grapes of gall," and this is the wine that he names "the gall of dragons,"(5) with which sinners feast and banquet our Lord Jesus, which although He tasted, yet He did not swallow, but presently spit it out of His mouth, because such drink infinitely displeases Him.

*Colloquy.*—O most sovereign King, how different meat and drink dost Thou give me from that which I give to Thee! Thou givest me the bread of Thy most sacred body, and the wholesome wine of Thy most precious blood, mingled with the honey of most sweet consolations, and I in recompense of this, offer Thee bread and wine, mingled with most bitter gall. Par-

(3) Jer. xxxi. 29; Ezech. xviii. 2.
(4) Thr. iii. 19. (5) Deut. xxxii. 32.

don, sweet Lord, my ingratitude, and assist me, I beseech Thee, with Thy holy grace, whereby I may offer Thee henceforward the wine of good works, so pure and odoriferous, that Thou mayest take pleasure to taste of it, to "ruminate" (6) it, and swallow it down into Thy heart, joining me to it by the union of most perfect love. Amen.

3. Some contemplate how they gave our Saviour to drink *twice* upon the mount Calvary;—First, they gave Him most excellent wine, which St. Mark calls "*myrrhatum vinum*," "wine *mingled with myrrh*," (7) and compounded such as they were wont to give to those that were to be crucified, to bring as it were asleep His senses, and to render them in a manner insensible against the torments; and that it was of this wine that the Evangelist St. Mark says:—"Noluit accipere"—"He took it not," and that therefore the cruel soldiers offered Him the second time "wine *mingled with gall*," of which St. Matthew says that He tasted, but that He would not swallow it down: this being so, the charity of Christ our Lord shines in this,—that He would refuse the first wine not to receive the least consolation, but to suffer with His inward senses, and to endure the terribleness of those His torments,—yet tasted of the second wine, that so He might prove its bitterness, though He would not drink of it, for the reason before alleged.

POINT III.

To crucify our Lord they first despoiled Him of all His clothes, even of His inner garment, with extreme pain and ignominy.

Christ our Lord was *four times despoiled* in His Passion, in punishment of so many times that I have despoiled myself of the garment of grace, in offending Him by my sins.

(6) Cant. vii. 9. (7) Marc. xv. 23.

—i. The first time was, when *they whipped Him* at the pillar.—ii. The second, when they *crowned Him* with thorns, to clothe Him with purple.—iii. The third, when they *took off* from Him the same purple robe, *to put on Him again His own* clothes.—iv. The fourth, to *crucify Him*, which was the most painful and the most ignominious of all the rest, because it was very probable that His garment stuck fast to His flayed and bloody skin, insomuch that they were fain to tear it off by plain force, plucking away with them the flesh and skin, no otherwise than in shearing of sheep, the shears clip away morsels both of skin and flesh, together with the wool. The ignominy that He endured was unspeakable and above measure, seeing Himself all naked in an open field, full of innumerable people, who looking upon Him, scoffed and laughed at Him; yet our most patient lamb endured all this with an incomprehensible patience and humility, offering all this to the eternal Father for the confusion that our sins deserved, and giving us example to suffer, when at any time we shall want clothes, or any other thing necessary for our body, and exhorting us by this to the nakedness and evangelical poverty He had preached, and continually practised from the very hour of His birth.

*Colloquy.*—O my sweet Saviour, how punctually wilt Thou fulfil that which is written,—"Naked came I out of my mother's womb, and naked shall I return thither:" (8) Thou wast born naked into the world, and Thy mother did by and by wrap Thee in poor clothes and rags, and now going out of the world, Thou wast stripped of all the clothes that she had given Thee, it not being permitted her to cover Thee with any other. O second celestial Adam! how dearly dost Thou pay for the nakedness of the first terrestrial Adam,(9) proceeding from his disobedience, seeing

(8) Job. i. 21. (9) Gen. iii. 10.

that to cover him again with the robe of Thy grace, it was requisite that Thou shouldest be unclothed with so great confusion. O "wine" of celestial love, which has so inebriated this divine "Noah,"(10) the true restorer of the world, that thou hast left Him quite naked, scoffed at, and mocked by the people whom He had taken for His children, inebriate me also, that I may strip myself of all earthly things, and that naked I may follow our naked Lord Jesus, taking delight in His contempts. O my Saviour, "naked came I out of my mother's womb, and naked shall I return thither," like to Thee; Thy nakedness, therefore, shall be my clothing, Thy dishonour my livery, Thy poverty my riches, Thy confusion my glory, and Thy death my life, since dying with Thee, I shall rise again to a new life with Thee, to whom be honour and glory, for ever and ever. Amen.

---

## MEDITATION XLI.

### ON THE CRUCIFIXION OF OUR LORD.

#### POINT I.

Our Lord being now stripped naked, and the cross being laid upon the ground, the soldiers commanded Him to extend Himself on it, which He performed presently, stretching forth His arms and His feet that they might be nailed to the cross. (1)

1. Here is to be considered the excellent *obedience of our Lord*, which appeared in this,—that He hearkened to and punctually obeyed the voices of those cruel torturers, in a thing so sharp and terrible, as was to stretch Himself upon this hard bed of the cross, to be crucified on it,

(10) Gen. ix. 21.
(1) Mat. xxvii. 35; Marc. xv. 25; Luc. xxiii. 33; Joan. xix. 18.

giving me example to obey my superiors, howsoever wicked they be, and to subject myself "to every human creature," (2) for the love of Him, in all that is not contrary to His holy ordinance.

*Colloquy.*—O celestial Adam, who didst stretch forth Thy hands, not as the terrestrial Adam, to take the fruit of the tree of disobedience, but to the intent that Thou mightest be nailed upon another tree by obedience; give me grace that I may extend mine to the observing of Thy commandments, (3) stretching myself out, if need require, upon the bed of the cross, to die there for the love of Thee. Amen.

2. Afterwards I will ponder *what our Lord did, seeing Himself stretched out upon the cross*; without doubt He lifted up His eyes to heaven, giving thanks to His eternal Father for having brought Him to this, and offering Himself most willingly to be crucified upon this altar in a bloody sacrifice for our sins. And as the obedient Isaac offered himself to be found by his own father, and by his hand to be laid on high upon the altar of the wood, expecting the blow of the knife from the hand of his father, —even so our meek Jesus was now upon the tree of the cross, bound with the cords of love, expecting the blows of the hammer and the nails.

*Colloquy.*—O eternal Father, seeing that the submission and obedience of Isaac was so pleasing to Thee, that Thou didst send down an angel from heaven to hold the hand of Abraham, lest he should have smote him with the knife; content Thyself, if it be possible, with the submission of this most blessed Isaac, stretched out upon the altar of the cross, and send another angel that may hold the hands of these executioners, that they nail not those of Thy Son. He

(2) 1 Pet. ii. 13. (3) Psal. cxviii. 48.

has already given sufficient testimonies of His rare obedience; content Thyself with His generous will, without putting in execution anything further. But I perceive well, gracious Lord, that both Thy works and those of Thy Son are perfect works, and so both of You will that the sacrifice be perfect, that so our redemption be the more abundant. Blessed be Thy infinite charity, by which I beseech Thee to give me grace, that I may offer Thee a sacrifice of myself, entire, perfect, and pleasing to Thy majesty. Amen.

POINT II.

Our Lord thus extended upon the cross, the soldiers took one of His hands, and with a thick nail, driving the same with terrible blows, *nailed it to one part of the cross, and the other hand with another nail* on the other part; and in the same manner *they nailed His feet*, whether with one or two nails, with very great effusion of blood issuing forth from these four wounds.

1. Upon this passage consider *the intolerable pain* which Christ our Lord felt by these cruel blows, made in those parts of His body so full of sinews, and in a body *so exceedingly delicate.* If I so greatly feel the pricking of a needle, how much did this delicate Lord feel the piercing of these sharp nails, which passed through the veins, pierced the sinews, and bore away with them His tender flesh. O my God, how well agrees with Thee the name that the prophet Isaiah imposed upon Thee, calling Thee "Vir dolorum"—"A man of sorrows," (4) seeing that never were there in this life any sorrows like to Thine. O most sacred hands, in whom the strength of God is hid, (5) who has nailed you fast to the two arms of the cross, enamelled with the heads of these great nails? O most sacred feet, at whose presence the devils fly away and retire as vanquished, who

(4) Is. liii. 3. (5) Habac. iii. 4.

has fastened you to this hard wood? O sweet Jesus, "what are these wounds in the midst of thy hands" (6) and feet? Who has made the hammer and nails so hardy as to pierce these wounds, Thou being their Creator? Doubtless my sins are the cause of all this, which I have committed with the hands of my wicked works, and with the feet of my depraved affections, with which I wounded my soul, afflicting Thee much more with these wounds than with those which Thou receivedst in Thy body.

*Colloquy.*—O eternal Father, behold these wounds and sorrows of Thy Son, which He offers Thee in satisfaction of mine; accept His oblation, I beseech Thee, and heal me of them, since Thou hast ordained the wounds of Thy innocent Son, to give health to all those which were wounded through their own sins. (7)

2. Consider another terrible pain which our Lord endured in this crucifying,—that one hand being now nailed, *the sinews shrunk together*, insomuch that when they would have fastened the other it reached not to the mortice made to receive it, which that it might reach, they stretched it so forcibly, that the bones were almost thrust out of joint; and for this cause it is said of Him in the Psalm:—"They have dug my hands and my feet: they have numbered all my bones," (8) that is, they have so racked my members, and so stretched them upon the cross, and my flesh through torments is so consumed, that they may number all my bones. This pain was one of the most bitter that our Saviour endured in all His Passion, for although they did not *break any of His bones*, according as the Scripture says, (9) yet was this extending, racking, and disjointing exceedingly painful, which our Lord offered in satisfaction

(6) Zach. xiii. 6. (7) Is. liii. 5. (8) Psal. xxi. 7.
(9) Exod. xii. 46; Joan. xix. 36.

for the sins committed by the members of His Church in matter of disunion, want of concord, and of charity. O Saviour of my soul, I will now say with the prophet David:—"All my bones shall say, Lord, who is like to Thee?" (10) O that my bones were converted into so many tongues, to praise Thee for the pains and sorrows Thou enduredst in Thine. Whoever was like Thee in pains and torments, and in the ignominies and contempts that Thou sufferedst upon the cross? As none can equal Thee in the greatness of Thy divinity, so none can equal Thee in the humiliations of Thy humanity, wherein such admirable virtues are engrafted. O that I could number Thy bones, which are the interior virtues, covered with this lamentable figure, that Thou hadst upon the cross, to imitate them.

*Colloquy.*—Vouchsafe, I beseech Thee, O good Jesus, by this Thy sorrows, that the bones of Thy Church, which are the prelates and men of perfection, may live united among themselves, together with the rest of the weak people, which is the flesh of Thy mystical body, linked together in the union of charity, that we may all of us together glorify Thee, that our works may preach Thy greatness, saying:—"Lord, who is like to Thee in power, who dost so knit together such different wills, with such conjunction and union of love?

3. Consider the great *grief that the Blessed Virgin felt* when she heard the blows of the hammer in the nailing of her son, for one and the same blows pierced with the nail the hand or foot of the son, so also with a most pricking agony the heart of the mother.

*Colloquy.*—O sovereign Lady, if the name of a "man of sorrow," agrees with thy son, certainly the same name

(10) Psal. xxxiv. 10.

also agrees with thee, as being a woman of sorrows, for thou mightest truly say to all those that were there upon this mount, or that passed by that way:—"Attendite et videte si est dolor sicut dolor meus"—"Attend and see if there be any sorrow like to my sorrow." (11) O that these blows of the hammer did as deeply pierce my heart as they did thine! O that the ears of my soul were always open to hearken to the blows of God's hammer, which is His holy inspiration, breaking with sorrow my obdurate heart, for having offended Him, who with so cruel a hammer is nailed and clenched through my cause.

POINT III.

Our Saviour being nailed in this manner, the soldiers lifted up the cross on high, and it is to be believed that they let it fall into the mortice or hole, which was made for this purpose, with great violence, shaking the whole body with it with intolerable pains. Lift up thyself, O my soul, on high with thy Lord, and lift up the senses and affections of thy heart, to nail them with Him upon the cross.

1. First, then, consider the pain, shame, and affliction that thy sweet Lord Jesus felt when He saw Himself lifted up on high, *exposed to the shame and sight of so many people*,—naked, disgraced, and become the mark of all their ribaldry, and laden with intolerable pains throughout all the parts of His blessed body. Behold how His head has not whereon to repose itself, which if it incline against the cross the thorns are forced in farther;—the hands are torn with nails, by reason of their bearing all the weight of His body,—and the wounds of the feet open themselves wider, with the weight of the body which stays upon them; and beholding thy Lord thus torn with tor-

(11) Thren. i. 12.

ments for thy sins, rend thy heart with grief and sorrow for having committed them.

2. Behold these four rivers of blood that issue out of the four wounds, like the four rivers which flowed forth of Paradise, (12) to water and make fertile the earth of man's heart;—approach in spirit to these rivers, taste the sweetness of this blood, shed with so great love and pain, wash thyself with it to cleanse thee from thy faults, as those did that "have washed their robes, and made them white, in the blood of the Lamb." (13)

*Colloquy.*—O most precious blood, wash, purify, inflame, and inebriate me with the excess of the love with which Thou wast shed, and pierce me through with the excess of that sorrow with which Thou wast drawn forth of the veins of our Blessed Lord.

3. Open thy ears also to understand *the clamours and scornful shoutings of the enemies of Jesus,* who seeing Him lifted up upon the cross, they *cast out against Him,* glad at their very hearts to see Him so disfigured and afflicted, and past all hope of living any longer;—hearken in like manner to the plaints and pitiful cries of the daughters of Jerusalem, seeing this piteous spectacle, especially the weepings and sobbing of the devout women that were there present.

*Colloquy.*—O how were Thine ears, most sweet Jesus, tormented with the clamours of Thine enemies, and with Thy friends' bewailings! If the friends of Job, seeing him lie upon a dunghill covered over with sores and ulcers, lifting up their eyes to behold him and scarce knowing him, cried out and wept bitterly, tearing their garments, and putting ashes upon their heads, and in this plight remained by him the space of seven days together, not once speaking to

(12) Gen. ii. 10. (13) Apoc. vii. 14.

him:—"Videbant enim dolorem esse vehementem"—"For they saw that his grief was very great." (14) What shall Thy friends do, lifting up their eyes and beholding Thee upon this cruel bed, wounded from the head to the feet, with wounds so much more terrible and painful than those of Job? Thou wast so disfigured that they had much ado to know Thee,—they broke out into cries, mingled with sighs and tears,—they tore their very bowels by the force of sorrow, and covered themselves with the dust of shame for Thy nakedness,—they remained quite dumb and beside their senses, not being able to speak a word to Thee, seeing Thy intolerable pains and torments. O that I had a tender feeling like this of theirs, considering that I have far greater occasion of feeling Thy pains than had the friends of Job to feel his! For Job did not endure for the sins of his friends, and Thou, my Saviour, dost suffer for ours; if the pains of Job were vehement, Thine were without all comparison far more vehement, for he lost not his life with the force of his pains, but Thou didst lose Thine most cruelly with the excess of Thine. Weep then, O my soul, and bewail the torments of thy Lord; rend thy heart with sorrow, cover thy head with dust and ashes, by doing penance for thy sins, and although thy tongue be not able, nor knows how to speak, yet let thy heart meditate and ruminate upon His unspeakable pains and ignominies, not only seven days long, but all the days of thy life, sitting thee down at the foot of the cross.

4. Consider the sorrow that the most Blessed Virgin endured at this her first beholding of her son, for the eyes of our Lord Jesus and of His mother encountering one another, became both of them eclipsed and dazzled by the force of sorrow,—the mother remained spiritually crucified

(14) Job. ii. 13.

with the sight of the son, and the son was tormented anew by beholding His mother,—each of them holding their peace for very grief and pain, the heart of the one employed in feeling the torments of the other, sorrowing much more for them than for their own. Put, then, thyself, O my soul, between those two crucified ones, and lift up thine eyes to behold the son crucified with great nails of iron, then cast them down to look upon the mother, crucified with the sharp stings of sorrow and compassion. Beseech them both to divide their pains with thee in such sort that thou mayest be crucified with them by a true imitation.

(That which concerns this passage ought to be considered at leisure, according to the method we have set down in the fundamental meditation, eighth point.)

---

## MEDITATION XLII.

### ON THE MYSTERIES CONTAINED IN CHRIST CRUCIFED.

#### POINT I.

Having placed thyself at the foot of the cross, and lifting up the eyes of thy soul towards Him that is fastened on it, to know and penetrate all that there passes. (1) Thou art to consider:—

1. *Who is it* that is there crucified, pondering the *motives* which He had to it, which were on *His* part His bounty and mercy only, and on *ours* the remedy of our misery. Lift up, then, thy eyes, O my soul, from the cross to heaven, from this throne of ignominy which is on the mount Calvary, to the throne of glory which is in the imperial heaven, and consider the infinite majesty of this

(1) S. Tho. 3, p. xlvi. q. art. 6.

our crucified Lord, who is God, eternal and immense, who hath His "throne" in heaven, and "the earth" for His "footstool," who ascendeth "upon the Cherubim," and flieth upon "the wings of the wind," (2) who only is wise and omnipotent,—by whom all things in heaven and earth, both angels and men, have been created, and, as the prophet Isaiah says, who poiseth "with three fingers the bulk of the earth," (3) in that He conserves it by His bounty, wisdom, and omnipotence.

2. Having considered this, cast down thine eyes to behold the extreme *debasement and misery with which this divine Person is invested* upon the cross, pondering how His afflicted body is upheld by another triple support of three sharp nails, which hold Him fast clenched to this wood, without being able to move to one side or to the other, which so support the weight of His body, that withal they torment Him with exceeding pain, even so far as to deprive Him of His life. And making comparison of that which this divine Person has in these two thrones, thou wilt remain astonished and beside thyself, that such an exceeding greatness hath descended to such a baseness. And covering like the Seraphim, the height and lowness of thy Redeemer, which thou art not able to comprehend, say with all hearty affection:—"Holy, holy, holy, Lord God of Sabaoth." (4) Thou art thrice holy by the three fingers with which Thou dost support the world,—thrice holy by the three nails which support Thy body upon the cross,—and much more by other three, with which Thou Thyself hast fastened Thyself to the same,—the one of *the love of man*,—the other of *obedience to Thy eternal Father*,—and the third *the zeal of His glory and of our good*, which hold Thee much faster clenched to the cross than those of iron.

(2) Is. lxvi. 1; Psal. xvii. 11. (3) Is. xl. 12. (4) Is. vi. 3.

*Colloquy.*—I give Thee humble thanks, my gracious Redeemer, for this love, obedience, and zeal with which Thou wast nailed to the cross, and I beseech Thee that Thou wilt fasten me to it with the selfsame nails, in such a manner that I may ever love Thee more than myself, obey Thy will, without making any reckoning of my own, and that I be jealous of Thy honour, and of my own everlasting salvation, without esteeming any transitory thing. And if these nails be not sufficient to hold me fast, "pierce Thou," I beseech Thee, "my flesh, with Thy fear,"(5) making me to dread the secret judgments of Thy rigorous justice, and my eternal damnation, in such a manner that Thou deliver me from the same. Amen.

POINT II.

1. This our Lord upon the cross is that "*high priest for ever, according to the order of Melchisedech*," (6) chief pastor of the Church, elected and called by Almighty God, with much more excellency than was Aaron,—Prince of pastors, and the most vigilant "bishop of our souls,"(7) who ascended on the cross, to offer a bloody sacrifice, the most excellent, the most meritorious, that ever was offered in the world.

2. The marks and *ornaments of this high priest* are sorrowful and ignominious, but yet replenished with great mysteries;—for as *martyr* He carried a crown of thorns fastened to His head, because He is the perpetual head of the Church, and the eternal Priest who has no end;—the crosier, or pastoral staff, is the cross,—the rings are the nails in His hands,—the priestly robe of divers colours is His flesh, striped and marked all over with wounds of the lashes of whips; thus, then, attired did our good Jesus enter once only into the Holy of holies, to offer a sacrifice, not of beasts, but of Himself,—not for Himself, but for us,—not a common sacrifice, divided into parts, but a

(5) Psal. cxviii. 120. (6) Heb. vi. 20. (7) 1 Pet. ii. 25.

holocaust, that wholly burns with the fire of pain, and with the flames of love,—shedding out all His blood in remission of our sins, even until He remained dead and consummated upon the cross.

*Colloquy.*—O sovereign Priest, how dear does it cost Thee to appease the wrath of God against us, inasmuch as Thou dost not content Thyself to offer the flesh and the blood of beasts, but Thine own body and blood, united to Thy divinity, but now divided the one from the other with intolerable cruelty; such an oblation as Thine certainly was necessary for the just satisfaction of such an offence as was ours; it was requisite that both the priest and the sacrifice should be God, that so God might be entirely content and appeased; what shall I render Thee, O supreme bishop and pastor of my soul, for this sacrifice that Thou dost offer upon the cross for her salvation? I desire to assist at this bloody sacrifice, in offering to Thee the sacrifice of "a contrite and humble heart,"(8) *contrite* for the sins I have committed against Thee, and *humble* to behold the sorrows and disgraces that Thou dost suffer for me. And besides this, I will also offer Thee another sacrifice of praise and thanksgiving, for having done so much for my salvation, with full purpose to do whatsoever shall be possible for me in Thy service. Accept therefore, gracious Lord, these two sacrifices, invest me with the marks and ornaments of Thy priesthood, and make me like Thee in these things which Thou endurest for my sake. Amen.

POINT III.

1. Contemplate our Lord Jesus crucified, *as a doctor and master*, sent into the world by the eternal Father, to teach us the ways of truth and virtue, and to show us the paths of sanctity and perfection, all which He, having performed,

(8) Psal. l. 19.

both by word and work, for thirty-three years of His life, at the end of it ascended the chair of the cross, where He made an abridgment of all that He had before taught with an unexampled perfection. For even as when He first began to preach, "He went up into a mountain, and when He was set down, His disciples came unto Him, He, opening His mouth,"(9) He preached to them the eight beatitudes, which are the eight heroic acts of virtue, upon which the Evangelical perfection is founded; so does He now go up to the mount Calvary, and fastened to the cross, there practices the same virtues after a more excellent manner than ever as yet He had done before, as we have declared in the sixth point of the fundamental meditation.

2. Having, therefore, pondered His poverty, humility, and His other virtues, I will imagine that I hear God our Lord say to me what He said to Moses:—"Look, and make it according to the pattern that was shown thee in the mount,"(10) that is:—"Behold the example of virtues that my Son has given thee upon the mount of Calvary, and learning well the lesson that He has taught thee, work according to it." Place thyself, therefore, O my soul, at the foot of the cross, and hearken attentively to the lesson that Jesus Christ crucified reads to thee, and seeing that this lesson cost so much to read, be not negligent in often hearing and repeating the same, engrave it in thy heart, and put it in practice so seriously, that thou mayest glory with the apostle, saying:—"For I judged not myself to know anything among you, but Jesus Christ, and Him crucified."(11)

*Colloquy.*—O most excellent master, who didst say, "And I, if I be lifted up from the earth, will draw all things to myself,"(12) draw after Thee, I beseech

(9) Mat. v. 1. (10) Exod. xxv. 40.
(11) 1 Cor. ii. 2. (12) Joan. xii. 32.

Thee, my memory, that it ever think of that which Thou dost here teach me; draw my understanding, that it may comprehend it; draw my will, that it may affect and love it; finally, draw my whole spirit, that it may imitate and practise it. O most sacred Virgin, and thou, the well-beloved disciple of my Lord, who, being at the foot of the cross, didst learn this excellent lesson, and didst afterwards make your great profit of it; beseech your great master in my behalf, to imprint the same as deep in my heart, as He imprinted it in yours. Amen.

POINT IV.

1. Consider that He that is upon the cross *is the Lord of Hosts*, the God of battles, and of revenge, the valiant captain and strong warrior, who in the open field of the mount Calvary, gave battle to the infernal powers and princes of this world, against whom He fights, overcomes them, and utterly destroys the kingdom of sin.

2. The *arms* and weapons with which He combats, are the *cross*, the *nails*, the *thorns*, and other instruments of pain and ignominy, with which, breaking and tearing His own body, He breaks and "crushes the head" of the serpent,(13) who seduced our first parents, and by them brought original sin into the world, of which He obtained us pardon upon the cross. He did beside strike off the seven heads of the red dragon,(14) which are the seven capital sins, springing from original sins.—i. He threw to earth *pride*, by His ignominies and contempts, which He endured with a profound humility.—ii. He vanquished *gluttony*, by tasting of the gall and vinegar that was given Him to quench His thirst.—iii. He vanquished the pleasures of *luxury* by the intolerable pains He endured in all the members of His body.—iv. He destroyed *covetousness* by His extreme poverty and nakedness.—v. He subjected

(13) Gen. iii. 15. (14) Apoc. xii. 39.

*anger* by His heroic meekness and patience.—vi. He subdued *envy* by the excellent acts of charity which He practised for our profit.—vii. And, finally, He destroyed *sloth* by the fervour He showed in all the works of our redemption.

3. In this manner, therefore, our good Jesus, assuming to Him the form of a serpent upon the cross, fought like the serpent of Moses, against the serpents of the magicians, and devoured them all,(15) swallowing down all the sins that infect the world; and as Gideon, breaking "the pitcher" that he held in his hand, did by the light and splendour of the lamp hidden within, frighten and overcome the Midianites;(16) even so our noble captain, breaking in pieces His body by the pains of His Passion, by the brightness and splendour of virtues that thence He caused to shine, He vanquished vices, and destroyed the infernal powers. And this great God of vengeance, revenging in His own body the wrongs and injuries done to His Father, revenged Himself on His enemies, and trod them under His feet; teaching me by this example the manner of revenging upon myself the injuries that I have done to God, and also the way how to vanquish the Devil, the world, the flesh, and all vices, that make war against my spirit.

*Colloquy.*—O most valiant warrior, who, by shedding Thine own blood, dost subdue the devils, and destroy the kingdom of sin, and those vices that ruin the world; teach me, I beseech Thee, to fight as Thou hast fought, that so I may overcome as Thou didst overcome; give me a manly courage, that like the soldiers of Gideon, I break in pieces by penance "the pitcher" of my body, and that "the lamp of virtues may in such a manner shine in me, that my enemies

(15) Exod. vii. 12. (16) Judic. vii. 20; Is. ix. 4.

may fly, and I obtain the victory of them. O God of vengeance, teach me, I beseech Thee, to revenge myself upon myself for having so grievously offended Thee; for, revenging me upon myself, I shall triumph over mine enemies by the blood of Thy Son, to whom be all honour and glory, for ever and ever. Amen.

---

## MEDITATION XLIII.

### ON THE TITLE OF THE CROSS OF CHRIST, AND ON THE MYSTICAL CAUSES INCLOSED IN HIS PASSION.

#### POINT I.

"And Pilate wrote a title also, and he put it upon the cross. And the writing was, *Jesus of Nazareth, the King of the Jews.*"(1)

Concerning this title, consider the *four words* that it contains, in which, as St. Mark writes, was contained "*the cause*" of Jesus Christ, that is, the cause for which they crucified Him; not only the cause or reason that Pilate had, but principally and most of all that which moved the eternal Father to ordain and suffer it.

#### "JESUS."

1. The first word of the title was "*Jesus,*" which signifies "Saviour," because He came to save the world, and to deliver it from its sins, and from the pains that it deserved for them. This was the first cause why He was crucified, that by His death, and by the effusion of His blood, He should finish the work of our redemption. This name was imposed upon Him at His Circumcision, at which time He took possession of the office of Saviour by the little quantity of blood that He then shed; but now it is placed on high upon the cross, as the title of His Pas-

(1) Joan. xix. 19; Luc. xxiii. 38; Marc. xv. 26; Ma[illegible] 37.

sion, in sign that He finishes and perfectly performs all that belongs to this office, by the effusion of all His blood, with regard to which St. Paul says, "without the shedding of blood, there is no remission"(2) of sins, nor salvation.

*Colloquy.*—O most sweet Jesus, how dearly hast Thou bought this office of Saviour, seeing that to save us Thou dost pay the price of Thy precious blood, and that by shedding the same so liberally, not part, but all;—not by little and little, but by whole streams, gushing forth from the wounds of Thy hands and feet. O most sweet name of Jesus, how fitly does it now agree to Thee to be "tanquam oleum effusum," as "oil poured out,"(3) in the regard that, by pouring out Thy precious blood, Thou makest an oil that heals our wounds, and assuages the pain of our offences! O most liberal Jesus, be to me *Jesus,* and exercise upon me the office of Saviour,—be to me an "oil" to cure me, a medicine to heal me, and a most odoriferous ointment to comfort me, applying to me the fruits of Thy redemption. Amen.

"OF NAZARETH."

2. The second word was, "of Nazareth."

i. This is as much as to say "*flourishing;*" in which is declared the *second* cause why Jesus ascended the tree of the cross, to *bud forth thereon most excellent flowers of virtues,* which He there exercised for our instruction and example, which flowers were His poverty, His obedience, His meekness, humility, patience, and His charity.

*Colloquy.*—O Jesus of Nazareth, how flourishing art Thou on this cross! Thou hast continually blossomed all Thy life, but much more at its end; now mayest Thou very well say to Thy spouse the Church, "Lectulus noster floridus"—"Our bed is flourishing,"

(2) Heb. ix. 22. (3) Cant. i. 2.

(4) since the bed of the cross is replenished with the sweetness of flowers that Thou dost bud forth upon the same. Admit me, dear Lord, into this Thy "bed," though it be very "straitened"(5) and little, for there will be room enough for us both, considering that Thou hast said, "Where I am, there also shall my minister be."(6) Oh that he could be with Thee upon the cross, smelling the sweet flowers that Thou didst there bud forth, and animate himself by Thine example to do the like.

ii. "Nazarite" likewise signifies "Holy," which thing teaches us that this Lord, who is upon the cross, is the Holy of holies,(7) and consequently that He dies not for His own faults, but for other men's, to free men from their sins, and to make them holy, fulfilling that which is written, "By His knowledge shall this my just servant justify many, and He shall bear their iniquities."(8) Behold here the fruits that sprouted from these flowers, which our good Jesus produced in His death. "Amen, amen, I say to you, unless the grain of wheat falling to the ground, die, itself remains alone, but if it die, it bringeth forth much fruit."(9) O tree, full fraught with flowers and fruit, oh that I could sit under Thy shadow, and eat of Thy sweet fruit even to my full.(10)

*Colloquy.*—O sweet Jesus, who didst say, "I will go up into the palm-tree, and will take hold of the fruits thereof;" vouchsafe me the favour, I beseech Thee, that I may climb up with Thee upon "the palm-tree" of the cross, and enjoy "the fruits"(11) that Thou dost there produce, that imitating Thy virtues, I may obtain the palm of glory that they deserve. Amen.

(4) Cant. i. 16. (5) Is. xxviii. 20. (6) Joan. xii. 26.
(7) Dan. ix. 24. (8) Is. liii. 11. (9) Joan. xii. 24.
(10) Cant. ii. 3. (11) Cant. vii. 8.

"KING."

3. The third word of the title is "King," in which is declared the *cause why Pilate condemned our Lord Jesus to be crucified*, viz., because the Jews accused Him being their king. And it is true, indeed, that He was a king, not temporal, but celestial and eternal, whose Kingdom began to be established from the cross, according to that which is written:—"Quia Dominus regnabit a ligno," that "our Lord shall begin His reign from the wood;" (12) for even as the reign of sin had its beginning from the forbidden tree, and from the disobedience of our first father Adam,—so the reign of our King began from another tree, by the obedience of our Lord that died on it. Hence I will gather, that if I will reign with Jesus, my kingdom ought also to begin from the cross, on which I will crucify my old man, and will destroy the body of sin, since the kingdoms of the earth are indeed enjoyed by living, but the Kingdom of Jesus only by dying.

*Colloquy.*—O eternal King, whose crown and throne are eternal, for this a crown has pierced Thy head with pricking thorns, and for this Thou art fast nailed to Thy throne with rude nails, shedding Thy blood through the pain of these blows, to conquer thereby the Kingdom which Thou hast promised to Thy subjects. Seeing that Thou art so mighty, that sitting in Thy throne, Thou dost even with Thy very "look" destroy, and scatter away all evil,(13) destroy in me, I beseech Thee, all that is offensive to Thee, to the end I may enter with Thee to enjoy Thy Kingdom. Amen.

"OF THE JEWS."

4. The last word of the title was:—"*Of the Jews*,"— which, though they would not admit, and for *this cause*

(12) Hymn Eccles. (13) Prov. xx. 8.

crucified Him,—yet did He not for this *cease to be a king, sent by the eternal Father to reign in them,* and also in all those in whom should be found the signification of His name, which is,—to acknowledge with a true confession that which God has revealed, glorifying Him for the same, and for this cause was the name written in letters of Hebrew, Greek, and Latin, that all the nations of the world—comprehended under those three tongues—might know, and, as St. Paul says, "every tongue confess, that our Lord Jesus Christ is in the glory of God the Father." (14) O Son of the living God, I confess that this glorious title well agrees with Thee, since Thou only, and none other, art "Jesus of Nazareth, King of the Jews;" O that all the world would read this title and admit it, and that all would acknowledge Thee to be their King and Saviour.

*Colloquy.*—O sovereign title, in which is comprised all the means that I have for the purchasing of my salvation; by this title shall my praises be heard, my desires accomplished, and my necessities redressed. O eternal Father, acknowledge this title that is written upon the cross of Thy Son, and seeing that it is the title of the Kingdom that He acquired for me, receive me, I beseech Thee, into the same, there to reign with Thee in all eternity. Amen.

POINT II.

"This title, therefore, many of the Jews did read:"—"Then the chief priests of the Jews said to Pilate: Write not,—the king of the Jews,—but that He said,—I am king of the Jews." (15)

Concerning this point I may consider *three sorts of persons* that read this title of the cross of our Lord Jesus, upon mount Calvary.

1. The first was, of *priests and Pharisees,* with other ill-

(14) Phil. ii. 11. (15) Joan. xix. 20, 21.

affected persons, all enemies to our Lord, all which *held this title for false*, and would have had the same corrected. These are the figure of heretics and other infidels, who hear and read the holy Scripture, the titles and works of the divinity and humanity of our Lord Jesus, and yet deny the greatest part, and will correct them after their fancy, and according to their erroneous conceits.

2. Others there were that read this title *out of curiosity*, as the custom is in like occurrences, without either making any further account of it, or understanding it, or penetrating the mystery that it contained. These are a figure of those who hear and read the things belonging to Jesus Christ, and also believe them in the gross, but never found, nor search into the mysteries that are contained in them, and so they draw from thence no profit at all.

3. Besides these, there were yet others upon the mount Calvary, as the sacred Virgin and St. John the Evangelist, who "did read" this title *very devoutly*, and understood and penetrated the mysteries that it contained, reverencing them all with hearty affection. These are the figure of such as read devout books, and treatises containing the truths and mysteries of our holy Faith, upon which they *endeavour to meditate* and ruminate with devotion and spirit, out of a purpose to draw profit from them to themselves.

These, then, will I imitate, beseeching the most Blessed Virgin, together with the glorious St. John, that they will obtain for me the same light and spirit with which they read and penetrated this title, that I also with the same may read and penetrate the truths that faith teaches me concerning my Saviour Jesus, considering that my life everlasting consists in knowing Him, loving Him, and serving Him for ever.

POINT III.

Pilate made them this answer:—"Quod scripsi, scripsi" —"What I have written, I have written." (16)

These words did the president speak as inspired by the Holy Ghost, to give us to understand, *that what the title contained was true*, and that it was not to be changed for any human reason or persuasion. And it is most certain, that whatsoever is written either in this title, or in holy Scripture, will be for ever written without altering or changing any jot, let the enemies of our Faith do what they possibly can to the contrary. This thing also teaches me to remain constant in my good purposes and resolutions of following our Saviour, insomuch that if either the Devil, or the world, or the flesh would by temptations divert me from them, I will answer them:—"Quod scripsi, scripsi" —"That which I have written, I have written." "I have resolved what I will resolve, neither will I go back an inch from what I have said, nor blot out that which I have written, nor yet alter that which I have once resolved."

*Colloquy.*—O Saviour of the world, since Thou art so great a friend of stability, as not to consent that so much as one single letter of this Thy title should be changed; vouchsafe, I beseech Thee, to make me so stable in Thy service, that for no persuasion of my enemies, I be ever removed from it. Amen.

---

## MEDITATION XLIV.

ON THE PARTING OF CHRIST'S GARMENTS, AND ON THE MOCKERIES THAT HE ENDURED UPON THE CROSS.

POINT I.

"Then the soldiers, when they had crucified Him, took

(16) Joan. xix. 22.

His garments, and they made four parts, to every soldier a part." (1) Upon this parting is to be considered the *causes* and *mysteries* contained in it.

1. On the part of the four *soldiers*, which were the executioners that crucified our Lord, one cause was, *their own covetousness*, for being a company of base fellows, every one was desirous to have his share in these garments, casting lots which piece should fall to each of them, and that they might the more spite our Lord, they ripped and shared them asunder in His own sight, in mockery of Him, as if they had said to Him: "Thou hast now no more need of clothes." And some of them might, peradventure, while they cut them to pieces, say in His hearing: "Seeing that this blasphemer would not tear His own clothes, when He uttered His blasphemies against God, let us tear them for Him." And thus did they afflict both the eyes and ears of our good Jesus.

*Colloquy.*—O sacred garment, whence issued forth virtue to heal all sorts of diseases, of such as touched Thee,(2) how is it that Thou art fallen into the hands of these profane soldiers? The humility, no doubt, of Him that wore you is the cause of this your humiliation, to cure my pride in apparel. Grant me, dear Lord, this humility, to support and bear patiently all the injuries that may be offered to anything that belongs to me. Amen.

2. The second mysterious cause was, on the part *of our Saviour, who to show us an example of perfect Evangelical poverty,* did not only consent Himself to be stripped naked upon the cross, but would also be deprived of His garments, which was all the wealth He had to dispose of, insomuch that neither the use, dominion, nor propriety of them remained to Him, but was transported to those base

(1) Joan. xix. 23; Mat. xxvii. 35; Luc. xxiii. 34.
(2) Marc. vi. 56

soldiers, His cruel enemies. Hence ought I to conceive a most hearty desire of fulfilling in the best manner I possibly can that saying of our Lord:—"If thou wilt be perfect, go sell the things that thou hast, and give to the poor...and come, follow me."—"So, therefore, every one of you that doth not renounce all that he possesseth, cannot be my disciple." (3)

3. The third cause was, to declare His immense charity and liberality, *in giving to man all that He had*,—His body, blood, and all His substance, but especially to signify that all men, who from the four quarters of the world should come to Him, might be partakers of the garments of His grace, charity and virtues, with which to clothe and adorn them. And as these four soldiers who crucified Him had a right to these garments, which were died in His blood, even so sinners who crucify Him in themselves by their sins, have, notwithstanding, just title to demand these garments of His grace and virtues, not of any merits of theirs, but by the blood of the same Jesus to which these graces are conjoined.

*Colloquy.*—O most sweet Jesus, I give Thee thanks for Thine infinite liberality, in that Thou hast vouchsafed to invest with Thy precious garment, even him that so shamefully crucifies Thee; I am extremely sorry for having so much co-operated and participated in Thy crucifying; but seeing Thou art so passing liberal, give me, I beseech Thee, part in Thy sacred garments, by imparting to me Thy most sovereign virtues. Amen.

POINT II.

"Now, His coat was without seam, woven from the top throughout. They said then one to another, Let us not cut it, but *let us cast lots for it whose it shall be;* that the

(3) Mat. xix. 21; Luc. xiv. 33.

Scripture might be fulfilled, saying: They have parted my garments among them, and upon my vesture they have cast lots." (4)

1. Here is likewise to be considered the mysterious *causes of this fact*, since God would particularly that they should be foretold by His holy prophet.

i. First, on the part of the *soldiers*, the cause was, that if that garment had been cut in pieces, *none of them could have worn the same*, it being then whole, and of one entire piece, woven, as is believed, by the Blessed Virgin, who was not a little touched with tenderness to see that precious garment, bathed with the blood of her blessed son, in the hands and possession of those wretched miscreants.

*Colloquy.*—O sovereign Virgin, with how great reason mayest Thou say that which Jacob sometimes said:—" It is my son's coat, an evil wild beast hath eaten him, a beast hath devoured Joseph;"(5) with whose blood I behold dyed the same garment which I gave him. The fierce beast of envy has fastened Him upon the cross, and has dyed His garment, not with the blood of " a kid," but with the blood of His own veins, to deliver those from death who for envy had delivered Him to death! O fierce envy, how darest thou devour Him who is charity itself! O infinite charity, who slayest the furious beast which swallows thee, destroy in us this furious beast, that we may preserve entire the true garment of charity. Amen.

ii. The second cause of this fact was, that this garment *represented the humanity of Christ* our Lord, woven from the top throughout to the bottom, because from heaven, without the work of man, the same was woven in the womb of the Blessed Virgin, by the work of the Holy Ghost, being the most rich garment of the faithful, which

(4) Joan. xix. 23—24; Psal. xxi. 19.
(5) Gen. xxxvii. 33.

all put on when they are baptized, according to the saying of the apostle:—"For as many of you as are baptized in Christ, have put on Christ," (6) conforming their lives with His holy life, by the union of perfect charity, without admitting any division or separation, forasmuch as "Christ" cannot be "divided." (7) Blessed is he to whom the lot of this celestial garment falls, whereby himself comes to be the lot of God, and His inheritance.

iii. The same garment of Christ likewise represents *the Church His spouse*, in which He will not that there be any division, but that she preserve herself always one in the unity of faith and charity, and for this, in the book of Canticles, He says of her:—"One is my dove, my perfect one," (8) because the Holy Ghost is one, which also is figured by the "dove," and one the spirit of Christ, and of perfection which resides and dwells in her. He, therefore, who attempts to divide her, attempts to divide even Christ Himself, and His precious garment of one piece, and becomes herein much more cruel than those who crucified Him, since they attempt to rend and divide that which those others dared not divide, that to which this our Lord Himself would not give them any licence.

*Colloquy.*—O God of peace, and of love, suffer not that there be schisms in Thy Church, any discord in religion, or any division amongst Thy christian people; but keep them all in the unity of charity, that they may be all one in Thee, and that Thou mayest put them upon Thee as a most precious garment, to be placed in the Kingdom of Thy glory. Amen.

2. Finally, Christ our Lord had *two garments, one out ward*, which was divided amongst the soldiers, and another *inward*, which fell to the lot of *one alone;* for even so the

(6) Gal. iii. 27; Rom. xiii. 14.
(7) 1 Cor. i. 13. (8) Cant. vi. 8.

works, and the exterior ceremonies of Christianity, belong to all Christians, since all have their part in them, but the interior virtue, which is the grace, charity, devotion, and spirit included in them, is only given to one,—that is to say,—to very few, and these well united among themselves, by the union of the flesh with the spirit, and of the senses with reason, in all that which God commands. I, therefore, ought to endeavour to be of this little number, and to be this one to whom befel so happy a lot, as to receive this divine garment, so as to clothe myself with it.

POINT III.

The garments of Christ being now divided, the soldiers "*sat and watched Him.*" (9)

1. Here it is probable that the soldiers did this by the order of Pontius Pilate, *at the instance of the Jews*, whose evil and corrupted conscience caused them to fear, lest any should take Him down from the cross whilst He was alive, or it was to prohibit any to give Him any refreshment or ease, such as was wont to be given to others crucified, and which perhaps was given to the thieves, who then were crucified with our Lord, for this guard of soldiers was not placed there in respect of them.

*Colloquy.*—O King of heaven, whose soldiers are innumerable legions of Thy holy angels, who attend about the celestial throne, singing to Thee a thousand songs of celestial praises, how hast Thou so abased Thyself, as to be seated in this contemptible throne of the cross, and to have set over Thee to keep Thee, a guard of base and cruel soldiers, who never cease to dishonour Thee? I rejoice, O my Lord, for the glory Thou hast in Thy Kingdom of heaven, and am sorry for the dishonour and torment which Thou sustainest here in earth, for both which respects I laud and praise

(9) Mat. xxvii. 36.

Thee, desiring to have part in Thy disgrace, with hope hereafter to have part in Thy glory. Amen.

2. The enemies of Christ our Lord, after they had nailed Him to the cross, were not only moved to no compassion to see Him suffer so grievous torments and abuses, but with a devilish and damned cruelty studied to add yet other new, both with words, ghastly *looks, and shaking of their heads at Him*, uttering, by the instigation of the Devil, most grievous injuries and blasphemies against Him, intending by them to tempt Him, and to make Him fall,—one time into impatience,—another time into diffidence, and other times into inconstancy, of giving over what He had begun; but all these new afflictions this innocent lamb suffered and endured with admirable patience and humility, and with great constancy and magnanimity, without giving any kind of sign, either by word or even by countenance, of feeling the injuries, or of complaint against His blasphemers, nor of faintheartedness, or repentance for being so fastened to the cross, giving us thus a most heroic example, to suffer and vanquish such temptations as in this manner shall assail us.

All this will I ponder, discoursing *upon four sorts of persons*, that injured Christ upon the cross, as appears by the four sacred Evangelists of our Lord.

POINT IV.

1. *First sort.*—" *They that passed by blasphemed Him, wagging their heads*, saying: Vah, Thou that destroyest the Temple of God, and in three days dost rebuild it, save Thine own self; if Thou be the Son of God, come down from the cross." (10)

1. It is to be believed that they made with their mouths and with their lips various *mocks* and grimaces against

(10) Mat. xxvii. 40; Marc. xv. 29; Luc. xxiii. 35.

Him, as David insinuates in the Psalms, saying:—"All they that saw me have laughed me to scorn, they have spoken with the lips, and wagged the head." (11) To which the prophet Jeremiah, in his Lamentations, adds:—"All they that passed by the way have clapped their hands at Thee, they have hissed and wagged their heads," (12) for derision; which hissings our Redeemer endured, to heal the poison which the infernal serpent, by his poisoned hissings and accursed suggestions, had poured forth; and as He endured and made no count of his hissing when in the desert, he placed Him upon the pinnacle of the Temple, saying:—"If Thou be the Son of God, cast thyself down;" (13) so also made He no account of this hissing which he cast forth by the mouths of these blasphemers, saying:—"If Thou be the Son of God, come down from the cross;" but on the contrary, since He was the Son of God, He would not come down from the cross alive, but would die on it, to engender thereby many adoptive sons to Almighty God,—as also that I may understand that it is proper to the sons of Almighty God, not to come down from the cross by their own will, but to die on it, both to the world and sin, persevering in mortification even to the end.

*Colloquy.*—O Son of the living God, suffer not that the subtle serpent with his infernal hissings, deceive me, by persuading me to come down from the cross, which once I have ascended for the love of Thee; but grant me to persevere thereon, as it becomes the son of such a Father, lest I come to lose the dignity of a true son. Amen.

2. *Second sort*—"*The chief priests with the Scribes, and ancients,* mocking, said," aloud—"He saved others, Himself He cannot save: *if He be the king of Israel, let*

(11) Psal. xxi. 8. (12) Thren. ii. 15. (13) Mat. iv. 7.

*Him now come down from the cross*, and we will believe Him. He trusted in God, *let Him now deliver Him if He will* have Him, for He said, I am the Son of God."(14) In which words they scorned and upbraided Him in four things, in which our Lord chiefly gloried.—i. In His *power*, saying, that He who had power to save others, had not power to save Himself.—ii. In His *Kingdom*, saying,—"If He be the King of Israel, let Him now come down from the cross, and we will believe in Him;" as if they had said,—"so false is it that He is a king, as it is impossible for Him to come from the cross."—iii. In the *confidence which He had in Almighty God*, saying,—"If He vaunt Himself in His trust in God, that He loved Him, let Him ask of God that He deliver Him;"—as if they had said,—"He will not deliver Him, because He does not love Him."—iv. In the *dignity of the Son of God*, holding Him for false and counterfeit: in all which four things they mingled many falsehoods, because the Devil, the father of lies, spoke by their mouth to tempt Christ, and to know if He were the Son of God, and to make Him come down from the cross, under the pretext that people should believe in Him. But our good Jesus patiently endured these derisions, without answering them any word, nor making any reckoning of their reproaches, because He knew the perverse mind whence they proceeded.

*Colloquy.*—O most meek lamb, what shall I render to Thee for the patience with which Thou sufferedst so great scorns and blasphemies against Thy sovereign and divine virtues? That which I most desire to Thy glory is, to confess that those blasphemies took no effect in Thee, and to glory in this, that Thou didst contemn them. I confess that Thou hast saved many others, and that Thou couldst likewise have saved Thyself,

(14) Mat. xxvii. 41.

but wouldst not do it to save me, since my life wholly depends upon Thy death. I likewise confess that Thou art the true King of Israel, and for this cause wouldst not come down from the cross, whence Thy Kingdom takes its beginning, that Thou mayest draw all to Thee, to believe in Thee. I moreover confess that Thou hadst true confidence in God the Father, who loved Thee as His own Son, yet would not deliver Thee, because it is not an assured sign of the sons of God, to be delivered from their tribulations, but to persevere constantly in them, even to the death; grant me, Lord, this true confidence, resigned to Thy holy will, whereby I may persevere on the cross, even until I die on it. Amen.

3. *Third sort,—The soldiers* who were there also mocked Him, and reading the title of the cross, said:—"If Thou be the King of the Jews, save Thyself;" (15) as if they had said: "If Thou art so powerful a king, that Thou canst save and deliver the Jews, deliver Thyself from this cross on which Thou hangest." And in the selfsame manner, as St. Mark says, the two thieves who were crucified with Him blasphemed Him, as we shall by and by see.

In all these points we may consider the great *pain which the sacred Virgin endured*, hearing those execrable blasphemies which were uttered against her son, and those railings, hissings, and derisions with which they derided Him; for not having seen those things which He suffered in the house of Caiphas, and in the hall of Pilate, the divine providence ordained that she should hear these, in order that her ears should be tormented with those injuries and blasphemies, all which she felt more than if they had been spoken against herself; and it is probable that those fierce persecutors blaspheming her son, returned part upon the mother, who had brought forth such a son, yet she suffer-

(15) Luc. xxiii. 37.

ed the same with admirable patience and silence, beholding the example which her son gave her.

*Colloquy.*—O sacred Virgin, how many swords pierced through thine afflicted heart! The tongues of these blasphemers are sharpened swords,(16) and double-edged, which at one stroke strike thy son, and thee, who art His mother. Wherefore, O most holy mother, speakest thou not a word in the defence of thy son, since thou knowest His innocency and sanctity? But I see well that it is not now time for thee to speak, but to hold thy peace, since the greatness of sorrow has made thee speechless before men, although thou never ceasest to speak to Almighty God.

4. *Fourth sort,*—Finally,—"*The people stood beholding*" (17) Christ, to see the effects of His Passion, and that not of devotion, but *for derision,* and therefore Christ our Lord reckons it amongst His injuries, saying:—"They have looked and stared upon me." (18) O if these miserable men had beheld Christ as they ought to have beheld Him, what great good would they have received by this sight! If to behold the brazen serpent was sufficient to heal the deadly bitings of venomous serpents, how much more sufficient would it have been to have beheld their Saviour, figured by that serpent, fastened to the wood of the cross, bearing the figure of a sinner, to deliver them from the poisoned bitings of their sins.

*Colloquy.*—Grant me, O my Saviour, that I may behold and contemplate Thee with a lively faith, and with the spirit of love and devotion, that with this sight I may be made whole and strong, to praise Thee and serve Thee, world without end. Amen.

(16) Psal. lvi. 5. (17) Luc. xxiii. 35. (18) Psal. xxi. 18.

# MEDITATION XLV.

ON THE FIRST WORD SPOKEN BY CHRIST UPON THE CROSS, PRAYING FOR HIS ENEMIES.

Christ thus hanging on the cross, and suffering the ignominies which have been related, after long silence, *opened His most sacred mouth* to pronounce the first of "the seven words" which He there spoke, saying:— "*Father, forgive them, for they know not what they do.*" (1)

Open, O my soul, thine ears to hear, since thy celestial master opens His mouth in the chair of the cross to speak to thee; "Speak, Lord, for Thy servant heareth;" (2) and since Thou art the Word of the eternal Father, abridged by the mystery of Thy Incarnation and Passion, read to me some brief lesson, which I may retain in memory, ruminate with my understanding, and with my heart and my whole will embrace.

The first lesson, therefore, which this celestial master read, and the first word which He spoke upon the cross, was wholly *of love, praying for those that crucified Him*, and excusing them as well as He could, showing in this His infinite charity. Whence I will consider:—i. First, *the occasion* which moved Him to speak:—ii. *Each of the words* which He spoke:—iii. And, lastly, *the effects* which followed upon these words.

POINT I.

*The occasion.* First, therefore, I will consider Christ our Lord full of pains and torments in all the members of His body, without finding any place or repose *in that hard bed of the cross*, compassed all round about with His

(1) Luc. xxiii. 34. (2) 1 Reg. iii. 10.

enemies who nailed Him there, who even after that recreated themselves seeing Him so sore afflicted, adding further new afflictions, together with horrible injuries and blasphemies, as making mouths, moving their lips, and wagging their heads in contempt and scorn of Him. At this present, therefore, and upon this occasion, Christ our Lord lifted up His eyes to heaven, and shedding forth tears for them, opened His mouth, not to call fire from thence to consume them, as Elias did, nor to pour His maledictions upon them, as did Noah and Eliseus, (3) when they cursed those who derided them, but to pray His eternal Father to pardon them the sin which they committed in crucifying and scorning Him,—much more deploring the detriments which were to befal them for this sin, than the torments and injuries which He received of them, fulfilling by work that which before He had preached by word:—"Love your enemies...pray for them that persecute you;" (4) and that which was prophesied of Him,—that He prayed for the transgressors, namely, for those who had infringed and transgressed against Him, all the laws of charity and piety, of justice and gratitude, with the greatest cruelty and ingratitude that ever was seen in the whole world.

*Colloquy.*—O loving Jesus, how well hast Thou showed that Thou art the God of love and of charity itself, since the immense waters of such tribulations, and the furious floods of such great persecutions, were not sufficient to quench nor appease the fire of Thy charity, but have so much increased the same, as to lift up its flame as high as heaven, beseeching the celestial Father not to chastise those who had imposed upon Thee such terrible torments. Grant me, O Lord, such like charity, by which I also may love my enemies, and pray for them that persecute me, and persecute

(3) 4 Reg. i. 10; Gen. ix. 2.
(4) Mat. v. 44; Luc. vi. 27; Is. liii. 12. (5) Cant. viii. 7.

Thee, since Thy enemies are also mine, pardon all, O Father of mercies, that all may be partakers of Thy mercies. Amen.

POINT II.

*The several words of this prayer :*—Next I am to consider, *every word which this brief prayer comprehends.*

1. The first word was " Father," to whom He directed His petition; and however it pertained to Himself, as He was God, to pardon them, yet He would rather as man ask the same at the hands of His Father; for asking Him to pardon them, He clearly gave to understand that He on His part pardoned them, fulfilling in this His office of high priest, (6) offering Himself in sacrifice for the sins and ignorances of the people, and praying to God with much fervour for them; nor did He say, " *God* forgive them," but " *Father* forgive them;" to give us to understand that He had not lost the confidence which He had in Him, and to oblige Him with this affectionate title, the more to hear Him, and to pardon those His enemies, who as a father makes His sun to rise upon the good and bad, and raineth upon the just and unjust.

*Colloquy.*—O sovereign and merciful Father, whose charity was so great, that Thou wouldst the sun of justice, Thy Only-begotten Son, should be born into the world, to give light, heat, and the life of grace to mortal men, and that the dew of His doctrine should water the earth of sinners; behold this divine Sun set on the cross towards the east, ready to go down and to hide Himself, and notwithstanding casting forth beams of divine love, praying for His enemies;—hear His inflamed prayer, and for the same send down from heaven the dew of Thy grace upon all Thy people, that all may know Thee, and know Him, and may

(6) Heb. ix. 25.

imitate the rare example of His most excellent charity. Amen.

2. The second word was, "*forgive them.*" He says not, "forgive them *this injury* cr wrong they do me," but absolutely "*forgive* them," excepting none, since His desire was that all their sins should be forgiven universally, without excepting any; as also to show that He was not so much moved for His own injury, as for those which were done against His Father, whom, therefore, He prayed to pardon all. Nor did He say, "forgive those *that crucify me*," or "those that *injure me*," but—"*forgive* them," because He would not put in His prayer any word which might accuse them, or provoke the anger of His Father against them. Lastly, because He asked pardon not only for those who then actually crucified Him, but also for all those who through their sins were the cause of His crucifixion, all which He had present in His memory, and for the one and for the other said:—"Forgive them."

*Colloquy.*—O most liberal and ample charity of our Lord Jesus, which dost extend thyself to all sinners, without excluding any of those who desire pardon, penetrate their hearts, I beseech thee, that all may dispose themselves to receive the pardon which thou dost offer them, and to participate of the fruit of that prayer, which thou madest for them. Amen.

3. The third word was:—"*For they know not what they do;*" in which, as well as He could, He excused His enemies; for though the ignorance of them was very gross, affected, and notoriously culpable, yet the charity of this pious Redeemer sought to excuse it as much as He could, and to hide and cover the multitude and enormity of their sins. This excuse also, after a manner, extends itself to all sinners, for inasmuch as all are guilty in some degree of ignorance, not knowing as they ought who Almighty God is

whom they offend,—how grievous a thing it is to offend Him,—what great goods they lose by offending Him,—and what fearful evils they heap upon themselves; for if they knew all this, never would they sin against Him, and therefore that may be applied to them which St. Paul says:—"If they had known it," perfectly and as reason requires, "they would never have crucified," in themselves, "the Lord of glory."(7) This excuse did Christ our Lord add, not only to declare His infinite charity, and the desire that He had that His Father should pardon all sinners whatsoever, but for two other particular ends:—the one, to move us to great confidence in His mercy; for if He excuse us who shall accuse us, as St. Paul says:—"Who shall lay anything to the charge of the elect of God? God who justifieth. Who is he that shall condemn? Christ Jesus who died, yea, who rose also again, who is at the right hand of God, who also maketh intercession for us."(8) The other end was, to give us example how to excuse the faults of our neighbours, although our enemies, attributing them to ignorance, inadvertence, zeal, or to some other intention of less evil,—in such a way that not only we accuse them not, nor exaggerate the injury they have done us, nor wish that God would punish them for it, but, in the best manner we can, extenuate and excuse it, using also that excuse as a title and reason to move Almighty God to pardon them.

*Colloquy.*—O most sweet Saviour, how well hast Thou this day ascended "the mountain of myrrh, and to the hill of frankincense,"(9) conjoining on this mount of Calvary, the myrrh of most bitter mortification, and the incense of most inflamed devotion! Comfort, Lord, my heart with this holy myrrh, that it may embrace it, and with this incense, that it may offer it, always

(7) 1 Cor. ii. 8. (8) Rom. viii. 33. (9) Cant. iv. 6.

seeking Thy honour and glory, for ever and ever. Amen.

POINT III.

Last of all I will ponder *the effects* of this holy prayer of Christ our Lord, considering, first, how the eternal *Father heard it*, for if, as the Scripture says, "the prayer of the humble and meek hath always pleased" (10) Him, how much more pleasing was to Him the prayer of His meek and humble Son? who, as the apostle St. Paul says:—When He prayed on the cross with tears, "was heard for His reverence;" (11) that is to say,—for the respect that was due to the infinite dignity of His Person, and for the "reverence" with which humbling Himself, He honoured His Father.

1. And so in respect of this prayer of Christ our Lord, *many of the Jews* who were there present obtained pardon of their sins, whom St. Peter, upon the day of Pentecost, converted to the faith, not so much by his preaching as by the virtue of this prayer of Christ, by which also pardon is given to all sinners who ask and receive it.

*Colloquy.*—O eternal Father, hear the prayer of Thy Son, pardoning them those sins they have committed against Thee. Pardon me also, O Father of mercy, because I knew not what I did when I offended Thee; and although I am he who deserves not to be heard, yet Thy Son deserves to be heard, being who He is, and He who always has exhibited such reverence to Thee.

2. I may here likewise ponder the effect which this prayer wrought *in the sacred Virgin, in St. John*, and in other devout persons who were there present, who all *were astonished* to behold so great charity and humility of Christ

(10) Judith ix. 16. (11) Heb. v. 7.

our Lord, and lamented to see crucified with so unspeakable pain, Him who prayed for His enemies with so great love; the most holy Virgin especially, moved with the example of her son, presently exercised the same charity and love towards His enemies, and repeating the prayer she had heard from the mouth of her son, she said:—" Father, forgive them, for they know not what they do." O how acceptable was the prayer of this meek and humble Virgin to the eternal Father, more than the prayers of all other pure creatures! How acceptable was the same in heaven, which, joined together with that of her son, aided in obtaining the desired pardon!

*Colloquy.*—O advocate of sinners, plead my cause, I beseech Thee, before Almighty God, beseeching Him to pardon me, because I knew not what I did.

3. To this prayer also of Jesus Christ may be attributed the *conversion of the good* thief, *of the Centurion*, and *of other effects*, which shall be noted in the ensuing meditations.

---

## MEDITATION XLVI.

ON THE TWO THIEVES CRUCIFIED WITH CHRIST.—AND OF THE SECOND WORD SPOKEN BY CHRIST, IN WHICH HE PROMISED PARADISE TO ONE OF THEM.

### POINT I.

And " they crucified Him there *and the robbers, one on the right hand and the other on the left*, and Jesus in the midst."(1)

1. Upon this point is to be considered the rare humility of Christ our Lord, in that *He would be crucified in the midst of two thieves*, with so great contumely. And it is to be believed that His enemies made choice of the most infamous and most notorious in the whole prison, and such

(1) Luc. xxiii. 33; Joan. xix. 18.

as were like wicked Barabbas, that so might be fulfilled that which was prophesied, "And He was reputed with the wicked." (2)

2. To consider yet further this profound humility, I will lift up my eyes to behold His *infinite dignity*, considering how He it is who is the Word eternal, who is as in the midst of two divine Persons:—He who in the midst of Moses and Elias, was transfigured on the mount of Thabor;—He who is the corner-stone, in whom are conjoined together the two peoples;—viz., the Jews and Gentiles;—and He who at the day of judgment shall be set on a throne of Majesty, betwixt the good and the bad, the good placed on His right hand, and the bad on His left.—This Lord, I say is He, who on this mount of Calvary, and on this throne of the cross, in the midst between two thieves, is condemned and despised as if He were a very thief; but yet by this company no malice or infamy can any ways stain His honour, but rather He there represents to us the judgment He is to make between the righteous and the sinners.

In all this He gives us notable *example to comfort us*, when we see ourselves placed in any contemptible place, and reckoned in the number of notorious malefactors, persuading ourselves, that if their malice have not stained us, their infamy cannot hurt us.

*Colloquy.*—O King of glory, how well hast Thou shown that Thou camest into the world to give us an example of humility! For at Thine entrance into it, Thou wast placed in a manger between two beasts, and at Thy going forth Thou art placed on a cross between two thieves, that so the end might answer to the beginning, and humility increase by its degrees, even to the highest that it could attain. Grant me, dear Lord,

(2) S. Tho. 3, p. q. xlvi. art. 11; Is. lii. 12.

so to order my life in imitation of Thee, that the beginning, middle, and end of it may be true humility, embracing for Thy love all kind of humiliation.

POINT II.

"And one of those robbers who were hanging, blasphemed Him saying, If Thou be Christ, save Thyself and us. But the other answering, rebuked him, saying: Neither dost thou fear God, seeing thou art under the same condemnation. And we indeed justly, for we receive the due reward of our deeds; but this man hath done no evil."(3)

1. In this point is to be considered, the *difference between the wicked and the good;*—the ignominy which Christ receives from the one, and the glory He receives from the other.

i. First, one of the thieves, who is supposed to be on the left hand, representing the reprobate, *blasphemed Christ* our Lord as did the Pharisees, reproaching Him with the sin for which it was said He was there crucified; namely, for having made Himself Christ and the Messiah that was to come. This was a great ignominy to our Blessed Saviour, whose contempt came to that pass, that a man most vile, and who for his thefts and enormities, was condemned to die upon the cross, mocked and scorned Him, esteeming that he got the credit of dying well in deriding Him. Hence may be seen how proper it is to wicked men to be forgetful of their own sins, and to aggravate those of others, to murmur against them, and to contemn those that have committed such crimes; holding themselves as innocent, in comparison of them, as it happened to this wicked thief, who with this last sin filled up the measure of his own damnation, and gave occasion to our Saviour to demonstrate and exercise His admirable

(3) Luc. xxiii. 39.

patience, who held His peace without answering any word to him that injured Him, and who was so close and near to him.

ii. On the contrary, the other, who was upon the right hand of Christ, touched with the inspiration of the Holy Ghost, and assisted with the grace of the same Lord, whom he had so near him, *opposed himself against him that blasphemed*, so to defend the honour of our Lord Jesus, the divine providence so ordaining, that because Christ our Lord suffered with silence the injury offered to Him, there should not be wanting one who would answer for Him and defend Him.

In which answer he exercised certain heroic acts of virtue, especially of charity and humility.

(*a*) The first of which was publicly to *correct the blasphemer* with words grave and convincing, saying,--"Neither dost thou fear God, seeing thou art under the same condemnation" of death! As if he had said, "that those do not fear God who are in health, and out of danger of death, is no wonder;—but that thou dost not fear, being at the very point of death, is a thing most intolerable.—(*b*) The second was, to *confess his fault publicly*, and that he justly deserved the punishment which he suffered upon that cross, and of which he admonished his companion.—(*c*) The third was, to *confess the innocence of Christ* our Lord, saying:—"This man hath done no evil." So that he took courage to confess before that whole multitude of people, that the chief priests and scribes deceived themselves in accusing Christ, and that Pilate erred grossly in condemning Him, and that all did very ill in blaspheming Him, since in truth He had done no evil, nor committed any kind of sin.

*Colloquy.*—O admirable man, who was not ashamed to confess the innocency of Jesus Christ, when all the world condemned Him! The apostles fled,—the disciples hid themselves,—all His acquaintance held their peace, fearing the displeasure of the Jews;—and this thief alone, hanging on high upon the cross, with a loud voice published the innocency of Jesus Christ. It is but just, O my Saviour, that Thou accomplish the word which Thou hast said, "Whosoever shall confess me before men, him shall the Son of Man also confess before my Father, who is in heaven,"—and "before the angels of God."(4)

2. By this example I will learn, that as in the mount of Calvary, there were three on the cross, but after a different manner:—one guilty and impatient;—another guilty and patient;—another without guilt, and with admirable patience;—even so is it wont to happen to men in this life;—some for their sins are chastised of God, bearing their chastisement impatiently, and these will be condemned with the evil thief, descending from the cross down into hell:—others are chastised for their sins, bearing the pain with humility and patience, saying that of Micheas:—"I shall bear the wrath of the Lord, because I have sinned against Him,"(5) and these together with the good thief, obtaining pardon for their sins from that cross and temporal pain, will go to Paradise.—Others are afflicted without any fault of theirs, and this for their exercise and future crown, bearing their affliction with unspeakable patience, after the example of Christ our Lord, and these are more blessed, because, as St. Peter says in his canonical epistle, the most precious part of the cross and of affliction is to suffer the same without fault.(6) But I, wretched man, since I cannot attain to the felicity of these latter, because I am full of sins, for which I have deserved all kinds of punishments, I may and ought to say that which is written in

(4) Mat. x. 32; Luc. xii. 8.

(5) Mich. vii. 9.　　(6) 1 Pet. iii. 14.

the book of Job:—"I have sinned, and indeed I have offended, and I have not received what I have deserved."(7) and will endeavour at the last to be one of the second, imitating the example of the good thief, by which to obtain the mercy of Almighty God.

POINT III.

The good thief, turning himself to Jesus, said: "*Domine memento mei cum veneris in regnum tuum*"—"*Lord, remember me when Thou shall come into Thy Kingdom.*"(8)

1. In this heroic prayer and petition, is to be considered first, how this holy penitent, after he had exercised the works before-mentioned of charity and humility, confessing his own fault, and sanctity of Jesus Christ, presently *took heart and confidence both to pray* and to crave *pardon* of his sins, and *entrance into the Kingdom of Heaven*, with words short, but very devout and exceedingly full of faith and confidence. For,—i. with great reverence he called Him "Lord," honouring and respecting Him, who was despised of all, and reputed for "a worm," "and the outcast of the people."—ii. He *confessed that He was a King*, and that He had a true Kingdom, in the same sense that Himself had said:—"My Kingdom is not of this world,"(9) but of the other, of which eternal and celestial Kingdom He was to take possession by His cross and Passion.—iii. He craved of Him that He would "remember" him when He should "come into" His "Kingdom," as if he had said: "I do not beg that Thou save me here, delivering me from the death of the cross, as my companion desires; but that Thou save me after my death upon the cross, saving me with everlasting salvation. Neither do I ask that Thou lead me with Thee into Thy Kingdom, and that Thou assign me a throne and seat there, because a thief such as

(7) Job. xxxiii. 27. (8) Luc. xxiii. 42. (9) Joan. xviii. 36.

myself am, dare not ask so great a thing;—I only therefore ask of Thee that Thou wouldst "remember me," and this alone is sufficient for me, since if Thou rememberest me, Thou wilt bestow a good death upon me, and wilt place me in a seat of glory, as it shall seem expedient to Thee.

*Colloquy.*—O most prudent and most humble thief, how well hast thou learned to demand and purchase the Kingdom of heaven, which the violent carry away! That will not happen to thee which happened to Joseph with Pharaoh's baker, with whom he was detained in prison, and of whom he begged that when delivered from prison, and seeing himself in prosperity, he would remember him: who yet immediately forgot him.(10) No; this is not the condition of that Lord with whom thou art crucified; for the torment of the cross being passed, the time of His prosperity will approach; and He will be mindful of Thee, giving to thee a part of it.

2. I will consider the *causes whence proceeded the admirable conversion,* confession, and faith of this thief; for although the principal cause was "the change of the right hand of the Most high," (11) which wrought this change and alteration in his heart, yet the same "right hand" of that high God used certain means to illuminate him;—these were not principally miracles, for perhaps he had never seen the miracles which Christ wrought during His life, nor had those as yet their beginning which succeeded in His Passion and death. Neither were they sermons,—for he had never heard any sermon of Jesus Christ;—but instead of miracles, the heroic *patience and meekness* which he beheld in our Lord amidst such injuries, was that which moved him; and instead of His sermons, his heart was melted with the *example* of that His singular *charity,*

(10) Gen. xl. 14—23. (11) Psal. lxxvi. 11

when he had heard Him pray for His very enemies. From this celestial illustration he learned that this our Lord was most holy; (12) therefore since He affirmed that He was a King, the Messiah, and the Son of Almighty God, so out of doubt the same was true. Hence I will gather how much it imports to be truly patient, meek, charitable, and to give good example to others, as all these have the force and efficacy of miracles and sermons to convert sinners, although they be harder than the very stones.

*Colloquy.*—O most sweet Jesus, who, placed in the chair of the cross with Thy stupendous patience, and with the admirable example of Thy charity, didst so convert this thief to Thee; assist me, I beseech Thee, that in imitation of Thee I may do the like miracles, edifying my neighbours with the like examples, put the bad to silence, and inflame the good to greater perfection. Amen.

3. Lastly, in imitation of this good thief, prostrate at the feet of Christ crucified, *I will repeat* sundry times with great affection the selfsame prayer, saying:—"*Lord, remember me, when Thou shalt come into Thy Kingdom.*"

*Colloquy.*—O eternal King, I confess that for my sins I am justly nailed upon the cross of many troubles and temptations, be not, I beseech Thee, forgetful of me, nor suffer me not to perish; and since Thou now possessest Thy kingdom peaceably, vouchsafe to be mindful of me, a miserable man, beholding me with the eyes of Thy mercy. Amen.

POINT IV.

"And Jesus said to him: Amen, I say to thee, *this day shalt thou be with me in Paradise.*" (13)

Concerning this second word, which Christ our Lord

(12) Cass. coll. xii. c. 13. (13) Luc. xxiii. 43.

spoke on the cross, is to be considered the inestimable riches and *treasures of His liberality*, mercy, bounty, and charity.

1. Here is discovered *the efficacy of His prayer*, with which He prayed for sinners, gathering the first fruits of them in this great sinner, of whom some say, that at the beginning he blasphemed Christ, together with his companion, which St. Matthew and St. Mark insinuate, speaking in the plural number:—"The thieves also that were crucified with Him, reproached Him," (14) which being so, the virtue of Christ our Lord shines so much the more, in converting this blasphemer, as was afterwards showed in converting Saul, by the prayer of St. Stephen.

2. Here, likewise, shines the *efficacy of the blood of Christ* shed upon the cross, whose first fruits were manifested in this good thief, converting him after a wonderful manner, pardoning him his sins, both as to their guilt and pain, and promising and assuring him of his entrance into Paradise without delay.

*Colloquy.*—O good Jesus, how willingly dost Thou in every place exercise Thy office of justifying sinners! For in the womb of Thy mother Thou didst justify Thy precursor.—Lying in the manger Thou didst call the sages, illuminating them with Thy divine grace. And on the cross Thou calledst this thief, promising him life eternal immediately after this temporal life. I give Thee thanks for liberality so immense, and humbly beseech Thee to exercise in my behalf the office of a Saviour, to the end that I may reign with Thee everlastingly. Amen.

3. Consider the *liberality of this promise*, for the thief desired of Christ that He would only "remember" him *when He came to His Kingdom*, and Christ assured him

(14) Mat. xxvii. 44.

that *on that very day* he should be with Him in His Kingdom. O sovereign King, it would have sufficed to have promised him that he should after certain years enter into Thy Kingdom, but Thy charity will needs hasten the time which otherwise Thou hadst ordained, and instead of purgatory accept for payment the torments which he then suffered; and that he should not faint in those which he was yet to suffer, after his thighs were broken, He said to him:—"This day thou shalt be with me in Paradise;" this day shall thy lot and fortune be quite changed, and from this cross of torments thou shalt pass to a paradise of delights, where thou shalt be with me, as I have promised, saying:—"If any man minister to me, let him follow me; and where I am, there also shall my minister be;" (15) and as thou hast followed me upon the cross, thou shalt likewise follow me to glory, into which entering to-day thou shalt be with me.

*Colloquy.*—O King of glory, if Thou reward so liberally him that has followed Thee three or four hours of the day, how wilt Thou reward him who has followed Thee perfectly all the hours and ages of his life? If Thou show Thyself so grateful to a sinner, who has offended Thee such numberless times, for one time only that he honours Thee, what gratitude wilt Thou show to him who has employed his whole life in the worship and honour of Thee? O blessed thief, who having stood all the day idle, wentest into the vineyard, one hour only before night, where thou didst bestir thyself so industriously, that being the last, thou didst deserve to be the first, I say the first of all mortal men, who, departing forth of this life, immediately receivedst the wages of glory.(16) Hasten thy labour, my soul, since thou meritest more with the fervour of labour, than with the length of time, and if

(15) Joan. xii. 26. (16) Mat. xx. 8.

thou join them both together, thy reward shall be the more abundant.

POINT V.

1. Lastly, I am to consider *two sorts of men*, viz., *good* and *evil*, represented in these *two thieves*, of which one was reprobate and the other chosen; remembering that which Christ our Lord said, that in the day of judgment, of two which are "in the field," or "at the mill," or in bed, "one shall be taken, and one shall be left," (17) that is to say, of all states and manners of life, some will be received into heaven for the good work which they have done, prevented and assisted by divine grace, and others will be left for hell, for the sins they have committed with their free will; so that he that is in "the mill," in the state of matrimony, laden with cares and labours, ought not yet to lose the confidence of his salvation; he that is "in bed," with great rest in the state of continency, ought not to cast away the fear of his damnation; and he who labours "in the field" of the active life, and who reposes in the bed of the contemplate life, ought both to live with the same hope, joined with the fear of the judgments of God, whom I will beseech most humbly that I be not of the number of the rejected, but of the elected, leading a life so worthy that God be mindful of me, to place me with Him in His Paradise.

2. The blood of Jesus Christ was powerful to justify both the thieves, yet *it worked its effect only in one of them*, to give us motives both of fear against presumption, and of confidence against desperation. For this cause great sinners, when they see themselves at the point of death, should not despair, seeing a thief in that very hour doing penance to obtain mercy;—nor yet let any presume to live at his own liberty, deferring his penance till the hour of

(17) Mat. xxiv. 40.

his death, seeing that the other thief, although so near to Christ, dying without penance, to be chastised with the rigour of divine justice. And it is a sufficient motive of fear to see, that amongst so many evils as there were then on the mount of Calvary, it was only said to one thief:—"This day thou shalt be with me in Paradise."

3. I may ponder the deep *impression which all this success made in the heart of the holy Virgin*, as well the confession of the thief as the answer of her son; and how she did not a little comfort herself to see that there was not *altogether* wanting some one to defend the honour of her son; also how was she confirmed in faith, hearing made so excellent a promise, in which was declared that by the Passion of her son, the gates of heaven should be set open, which for so many thousand years had been shut before!

*Colloquy.*—O my soul, take breath a little amidst these tears, at the hearing of this joyful news, behold how this day the gates of Paradise are opened, and although it be at the cost of the blood of thy Redeemer, yet He comforts Himself in shedding it, that so the locks of these gates may be burst open with its virtue. O holy Abraham, I now nothing wonder that thou rejoicedst, when in spirit thou sawest this day,(18) since then Paradise was to be opened to thee, and to thy sons, imitators of thy faithful obedience. O Saviour of the world, in whose hands nailed upon the cross, is the "key of David," with which Thou openest, "and no man shutteth," shuttest, "and no man openeth;"(19) open to me the gates of heaven, which my sins have shut against me: and shut against me the gates of hell, which my sins have opened, that in the day of my death, I may, like this good thief, enter with Thee into Paradise. Amen.

(18) Joan. viii. 58. (19) Is. xxii. 22; Apoc. iii. 7.

# MEDITATION XLVII.

ON THE THIRD WORD SPOKEN BY CHRIST ON THE CROSS TO HIS MOTHER AND ST. JOHN.

POINT I.

"Now there stood *by the cross of Jesus His mother*, and *His mother's sister*, Mary of Cleophas, and *Mary Magdalen*," besides whom there was "*the disciple* standing whom He loved." (1)

1. Upon this point is to be considered how there approached near the cross of our Lord Jesus, *those persons who loved Him so remarkably*, for there is no greater mark of the love of Christ than to follow Him to the cross, taking compassion on His sorrows and contumelies, and making oneself partaker of them, so that the nearer we approach to it, and the more firmly and steadfastly, so much greater signs of this love do we demonstrate, like these four persons here expressed.

2. Among all which the *mistress and leader was the sacred Virgin*, for whose respect those others were with her in company, and without whom they would never have had the courage nor heart to have assisted at it. But she, as more firm in faith, and more inflamed in love, setting aside all human fear, and surmounting all difficulties and ignominies, which in that place might fall upon her, would find herself present at the Passion of her son, and placed herself upon her feet close to the cross, with great constancy and fortitude, approaching in body as near as she could be permitted, and in spirit so near, that she joined herself to the cross itself, and to her son, and stood there

(1) Joan. xix. 25, 26.

spiritually crucified together with Him, through the excess of love and sorrow, as has been pondered in the fundamental meditation; with three nails, therefore, was she there held crucified.—i. The first was, the vehement and lively apprehension of that which her son suffered.—ii. The second was, the inward love which she bore to Him, not only as her son, but as her God, and infinite benefactor, on which account all His pains she reputed hers.—iii. The third was, the compassion that such a Person should suffer so much for other men's sins, upon which so great sorrow invaded her soul, that it sufficed for a martyrdom, as if she had verily died upon the cross; for whilst she beheld the head of her son pierced with thorns, her own remained pierced with them;—whilst she beheld His hands fastened with nails, her own remained fastened with them;—whilst she beheld His bones, so loosened and disjointed, that they might all be numbered, all her own also trembled through fear; and in this manner, whatever her son suffered corporally, the same the mother suffered spiritually, but very grievously.

*Colloquy.*—O holy Virgin of virgins, with how great reason may we this day call thee the Martyr of martyrs! For, as thou surpassedst all virgins in the flower of virginity, so thou exceedest all martyrs in the fruit of martyrdom. Thou art a martyr in fervent desire, to suffer all the torments of death which thy son suffered. Thou art also a martyr on account of the terrible pains which thou sufferedst in beholding Him, which were fully sufficient to have procured thy death, had not thy son preserved thy life. Oh that I could accompany thee in this manner of martyrdom! Obtain for me, O Queen of martyrs, that I may some ways be partaker of it, martyring my flesh with penances, and my spirit with abnegations, approaching with fortitude of heart to the cross of thy blessed son, and crucifying myself on it, in imitation of thee.

POINT II.

"When Jesus, therefore, had seen His mother, and the disciple standing whom He loved, He saith to His mother: *Woman, behold, thy son.*" (2)

1. Here is to be pondered, first, *the charity of Christ* our Lord, together with the integrity and authority which He manifested amidst so many torments and contempts, so attending to the works of piety and mercy, and to the obligations of His office, *as if He had not been in the act of suffering;* for He prayed for His enemies as high priest,—He promised Paradise as Redeemer,—He beheld His mother as her son, and His disciple as a master; teaching us by this example that we ought not to fail in our obligation, though we see ourselves beset with sundry troubles.

*Colloquy.*—O sovereign priest Jesus, what difference is there between Thee and that other high priest Aaron, who said that he could not well discharge his office, nor please our Lord in ceremonies, "having a sorrowful heart;"(3) but Thou, O my Saviour, though encompassed with labours and afflicted with sorrows, yet dost perfectly discharge Thy function, praying for Thine enemies, pleasing Thy Father, and careful for the comfort of Thy mother. Give me, Lord, I beseech Thee, this integrity of heart, that I never omit to accomplish that which Thou hast charged me, though I see myself much oppressed with adversity. Amen.

2. *The words* which He spoke to the holy Virgin, saying:—"*Woman, behold, thy son;*" as if He had said:—"I am not forgetful of thee, nor of the obligation which I owe thee, as thy son; but because I depart out of this world, I bequeath to thee, instead of myself, John, for thy son, that

(2) Joan. xix. 26. (3) Levit. x. 19.

he may perform towards thee the duty of a son, serving thee, and doing to thee that which I myself was bound to do towards such a mother." Where He would not call her "mother," but "woman;"—first, not to torment her with a word so tender,—secondly, and principally, to show how little He attributed to flesh and blood, that He might wholly attend to the works of His celestial Father, for which cause we never read that He called her by the name of "mother," as we have meditated in another place. This word, nevertheless, caused an exceeding sorrow in the heart of the Blessed Virgin, both because she understood by it that her son took His last farewell of her to die, as also because she considered the great disparity and inequality of that change, which was, to change the Son of the living God for the son of a poor fisherman, and the master of heaven for an earthly disciple.

*Colloquy.*—O Saviour of the world, if beholding Thy disciple, Thou saidst to Thy mother, "behold, thy son,"—so likewise beholding Thyself, Thou mightest have said to her:—"Woman, behold, thy Son," behold Him whom Thou conceivedst by the work of the Holy Ghost, and broughtest forth without any pain.—Behold here Him whom thou reclinedst in the manger, in the midst of two silly beasts, and fedst Him with the milk of Thine own breast.—Behold here Him whom thou often barest in thine arms, rejoicing and delighting thee with His amiable looks.—Behold here thy Son hanging on the arms of a dreadful cross, and in the midst between two thieves, all disfigured and void of blood.—Behold, and see if thou canst know me for thy son, and, if thou hast anything to commend to me as a mother; but since thou holdest thy peace, and sayest nothing to me, in my place, I leave to thee my disciple.—"Ecce filius tuus"—"Behold thy son."

3. But the charity of our Lord in our behalf yet passed further in these words, and more enlightened the understanding of His mother in them, because He *not only bequeathed John* for a son to her, but also in him *all His other disciples*, which He then had, and which He was to have to the end of the world, and all which He delivered to her as her sons, and for all which He said:—"Woman, behold, thy son," take my disciple for thy son, and all those who shall be my disciples, for it is my will that thou be their mother, and they thy sons, and that thou have a care of them as of thy sons, procuring their good with all solicitude.

*Colloquy.*—I give Thee thanks, O most sweet Jesus, that Thou hast charged Thy mother, that she take us for her sons, making us by this means Thy own brethren. O Blessed Virgin, henceforth will I confidently say to thee, "Ecce filius tuus,"—"Behold thy son." O my Lady, "Behold, thy son." Remember what thine only son recommended to thee, that thou shouldst take me for an adopted son; acknowledge me, therefore, for thy son, and as a careful mother do thou provide what is necessary for me.

POINT III.

"After that He said to the disciple: *Behold, thy mother; and from that* hour the disciple took her to his own." (4)

1. As the words of Christ our Lord are effectual to make that which He speaks, and in the manner in which His will is to have it wrought, with this word *He imprinted in the Blessed Virgin the true spirit of a mother* towards St. John, and towards the other disciples; and likewise in St. John the true spirit of a son towards his mother, which spirit he communicated to all those which are his mother's true disciples; and since these words were not spoken

(4) Joan. xix. 27.

alone to St. John, but to all such as are like him, I am to imagine that Christ our Lord says unto me:—"Behold thy mother," love her, and reverence her as a mother, obey her, and serve her in all thou mayest, have recourse to her in all thy necessities; for as I have given my Father to thee as thine, so do I give my mother likewise to thee as thine, live, then, as it becomes the son of such a mother.

*Colloquy.*—O most sweet Jesus, "whence" "to me" so great a good, as to give to me Thy proper mother to be mine? Give me, therefore, the true spirit of a son, that I may so serve her, as the merits of so glorious a mother of due deserve. O most blessed mother, being assured that thou wast so obedient to thy son, as presently to accept the charge of a mother over me.

"Monstra te esse matrem,
Sumat per te preces,
Qui pro nobis natus
Tulit esse tuus." (5)

"Show thyself a mother,
Offer Him our sighs,
Who for us Incarnate
Did not us despise."(*)

2. Ponder the *causes* why Christ our Lord did this favour *to St. John*, which principally were two, and both of them together, disposed him to receive the same.

i. The first was, that *he was a virgin*, and it was convenient that the son of a virgin should not recommend the mother, a virgin, to any but to a virgin disciple, that so He might show to us the great esteem that He made of virginity, of body and soul.—ii. The second was, because he was *singular in the charity and love of Jesus Christ*, whom he followed even to the cross,—stood close by it,—breaking through all difficulties, which might withdraw him thence, as they

(5) Hymn:—"Ave Maria Stella." * Caswall's Lyra Catholica.

withdrew the other disciples; for inasmuch, therefore, as he manifested this love to Christ above the rest, he deserved to be favoured above all the rest.

Hence I will draw a great desire to imitate the glorious Virgin and St. John in chastity, and in the love of Christ, and of His cross, that I may be worthy that the Virgin accept me for her son, and I to hold her for my mother.

3. Finally, is to be considered, that which the Evangelist says, viz.—"*From that hour the disciple took her to his own.*" It is not said of the Virgin that from that hour she took the disciple for her son, because that was sufficiently insinuated when her son recommended that to her, who as she was most obedient to the beck of her son, so—any least sign being given of His divine will—most punctually accomplished the same; but of St. John it is said, that he "took her to his own," to exercise towards her diligently all the offices of a dutiful son towards such a mother, which he performed most exactly and with great punctuality, not only because his master had so commanded him, but because he held it for a most singular blessing to serve the son of such a mother.

*Colloquy.*—O glorious Evangelist, I rejoice for that good lot which befel thee on this day; beseech thy good master to impart to me the selfsame spirit of a son, which He imparted to thee towards His mother, that I may serve her as thou didst serve her. O my Saviour, since Thou shewest Thyself so liberal on the cross, as to bequeath Paradise to the thief that converted himself to Thee, and Thy mother to the disciples that loved Thee; use towards me this liberality, giving me in this life most inward devotion towards Thy mother, by whose mediation I hope to enter into heaven, where I shall reign with Thee and with her, world without end. Amen.

## MEDITATION XLVIII.

### ON THE DARKNESS WHICH WAS MADE OVER THE WHOLE EARTH, AND ON THE FOURTH WORD SPOKEN BY CHRIST ON THE CROSS.

#### POINT I.

"Christ being nailed to the cross, from the sixth hour," i. e. at noon-day, "there was a darkness over the whole earth, until the ninth hour," (1) (which is the third hour after noon.) Here is to be considered *the causes* for which Christ our Lord ordained *this prodigious darkness*, the sun eclipsing upon such an occasion, and for so long a space of time.

1. *To manifest His just anger* against that most ungrateful people, for that horrible offence which they committed against our Lord Christ, for they were not worthy to behold the light of the sun, who deprived the Sun of justice of His life. Moreover, by these exterior darknesses were signified the interior darknesses of that miserable people, and the eternal darknesses wherein they were to fall because of their obstinacy.

2. To manifest *the innocency and majesty of Christ* our Lord by means of this miracle, commanding that the sun should darken itself, and clothe the whole earth with mourning black, for the death of its Maker, and so well as it might, to show its compassion for His pains and ignominies, so that hiding its light, it took away the occasion from the persecutors of scorning Him, and from the blasphemers of adding new blasphemies, making them retire with this His obscurity.

(1) Mat. xxvii. 45; Marc. xv. 33; Luc. xxiii. 44; S. Th. 3, p. q. xliv. art. 2.

*Colloquy.*—O Sun of justice, it is most just that the material sun should obscure itself, Thou being obscured with so great sorrow, and upon the point of sitting, to transport Thyself to the hemisphere of the other life: but yet it had been more just, that I should become sorry for Thy death, because I am the cause of it. Suffer not, O my Lord, that I become so blind, as not to see the reason that I have to become sorry, nor yet so obdurate, as not to take compassion of Thy torments.

3. Christ our Lord ordained this darkness, that the night suddenly coming on them, those *cries and the noise of the people might cease*, that so He might with the more quiet spend those three hours in preparing Himself to die, and in praying for us with great fervour and tears; in the same manner as when He preached, He spent the day conversing with men, and the night coming, He retired Himself to the mountains to pray, doing all this not for His own necessity, but for our instruction and example. For even so being upon the mount of Calvary, with His hands extended upon the cross, having accomplished the offices of piety before repeated, He would in those three hours of darkness which succeeded, wholly exercise Himself in prayer, which He offered up for all the faithful, whom He then held present in His memory, of which number, since myself am one, He offered and applied the same also for me.

*Colloquy.*—O sweet Jesus, teach me how to pray with that quietness and spirit with which Thou prayedst in these three hours; and quicken my slothfulness, that I may make my profit of the time which is allotted me in this life, preparing myself with great fervour for my death.

4. I may likewise ponder how *the most holy Virgin spent*

*all this time in prayer*, with great fervour, elevating her spirit to a most sublime and most lofty contemplation, not of affections of joy, but of sorrow, after the imitation of her son. And the same is likewise to be believed of St. John, and of that good thief, inspired to it by the same Lord, who from the same cross used to them these interior words:—"Watch and pray" with me, "lest you fall into temptation."

POINT II.

"About the ninth hour, Jesus cried with a mighty voice, saying: Eli, Eli, Lamma sabacthani; that is, My God, my God, why hast Thou forsaken me?" (2)

1. This was the *fourth* word which Christ our Lord pronounced upon the cross, a little before He gave up the Ghost, which words He pronounced with a great voice, and with a strong cry, *that all might understand that He was yet alive*, and further, to declare the affection with which He spoke them, viz.—as most afflicted for the internal desolation which He endured,—which desolation consisted principally in two things:—

i. The first, in that the eternal Father suffered *His pains to last so long*, without delivering Him of those terrible torments which He endured, which kind of desolation Almighty God uses towards the just, for their greater profit, but in Christ our Lord the same was most terrible and most bitter, for He found no ease nor comfort in anything; for His divine head could not rest upon the cross without another new pain, His hands could not sustain or ease His body, but by tearing the holes to His greater grief; His feet could not support the weight and burden of His body without enlarging His wounds wider; wherefore, beholding Himself thus afflicted on all sides, He lifted up His

(2) Mat. xxvii. 46; Marc. xv. 34.

voice to heaven with a vehement cry, saying:—"My God, my God, why hast Thou forsaken me?"

ii. Secondly, this desolation appeared, in that *the divinity had left the humanity without any sensible comforts,* permitting the same to suffer extreme sorrow and anguish, as before in the garden of Gethsemani, which lasted even to the giving up of His life. And lest any think that His patience proceeded from insensibility, and that He showed Himself careful of others, because He felt not His pains, therefore He would declare by this word, how grievously He felt them, saying:—"My God, my God, why hast Thou forsaken me?" But that we should understand, that this complaint did not arise from desperation, but of love, for the reason aforesaid, He said not: "*God, God,* why hast Thou forsaken me?" "But, *my* God, *my* God, why hast Thou forsaken me?"—As if He had said, Thou art indeed the God of all, for that Thou givest to all the being they have, but much more art Thou *my* God, because Thy divine being, and lovest me with an especial love, and I Thee with the like love; wherefore then leavest Thou me in this tribulation?

O good Jesus, it is not now needful that another angel should come from heaven as in the garden, to comfort Thee in Thine affliction, and to insinuate to Thee the causes of this dereliction, because they are now very nigh to their last end: but I, Lord, will declare the cause to Thee.—viz., that Thy immense charity may be manifest in me. I have forsaken Thee, neglecting Thy will to accomplish my own, therefore Thou wilt be forsaken of Thy Father, meriting thereby that His mercy never forsake me; as also to give me an example of patience, when I shall feel the like dereliction, for it is not much if the disciple sometimes taste of that, which his Lord and master tasted before him.

*Colloquy.*—O most sweet master, "Ne me derelinquas usquequaque"—"Do not Thou utterly forsake me, when my strength shall fail me."(3) Amen.

2. Christ our Lord complained of another forsaking, which He felt much more than the former of which we have spoken; which was—that He saw Himself forsaken of His own disciples,—of that Hebrew people:—and those millions of men should forsake Him,—denying His faith, contemning His sacraments, and neglecting the fruits, which they might have drawn from His Passion.

*Colloquy.*—O most sweet Jesus, I do not wonder if Thou complainest of this forsaking, since Thy redemption being so ample, and Thy Passion so painful, yet are there scarcely any who do not make their profit of it. O our Protector, how forsaken do I see Thee in this world! For some nations will not receive Thy holy faith,—others, having received it, reject it,—others retain Thy faith, and embrace Thy law, but do not accomplish it,—others forsake one another, forsaking Thee in Thy little ones. O eternal Father, do not so forsake Thy Son, but since He has behaved Himself so valiantly in His Passion, procure that for this cause He be acknowledged and adored of all. Amen.

POINT III.

1. Although Christ our Lord only pronounced with a high voice the words before recited, which are the beginning of the 21st Psalm, which wholly treats of His Passion, it may be piously believed that *He repeated secretly the whole Psalm*, relating to His Father all the labours expressed therein, but chiefly and with great anxiety those words,—"Deliver, O God, my soul from the sword, my only one from the hand of the dog. Save me from the lion's mouth, and my lowliness from the horns of the

(3) Psal. cxviii. 8; lxx. 9.

unicorns." By the sword He means death, to which He was condemned by the Divine justice;—by "the dog," Caiphas, with his other persecutors which bite and bay at His good name;—by "the lion," Pilate with his other ministers and executioners, which afflicted and tore Him with those torments;—by "the unicorns," the powers of infernal darkness, which had stirred up His enemies against Him. These words our Lord pronounced with very great and inward feeling, conformable to that which the apostle St. Paul says of Him:—"Who in the days of His flesh, with a strong cry and tears, offering up prayers and supplications to Him that was able to save Him from death."(5)

2. Consider the *great feeling which the sacred Virgin had* when she heard her son utter these lamentable words, which entering at her ears penetrated even to her heart, and lifting up the same to the eternal Father, she besought Him that He would not forsake His afflicted Son. And as she was very skilful and ready in the Psalms of David, it is to be believed that when her son, that divine musician, with His doleful voice began that psalm upon the harp of the holy cross, she, together with Him, prosecuted the rest within her heart, deploring the torments related in that psalm of her blessed son, which actually she there beheld being accomplished in Him: with the same spirit, therefore, it becomes me to recite the same psalm, ruminating and devoutly pausing upon the particular words of it.

3. "And some that stood there heard these words, said: This man calleth Elias.(6)—And the others said, Let us see whether Elias with come to deliver Him." These things spoke those cursed persecutors to mock Christ, sporting with that word or expression "Heli," as if they

(4) Psal. xxi. 21. (5) Heb. v. 7. (6) Mat. xxvii. 47.

had said:—"This fellow is so miserable as that He cannot save Himself, and therefore laments and asks the help of Elias." After this manner did they distort and wrest the words of our Redeemer therewith to deride Him, His bounty permitting the same, that He might be tormented in all manners upon the cross.

*Colloquy.*—Dear Lord, permit not, I beseech Thee, that I distort or wrest Thy words, nor yet make use of them for other end, than to glorify and to serve Thee; and since they are words of everlasting life, vouchsafe to grant me that I may obtain the same by the means of them. Amen.

---

## MEDITATION XLIX.

### ON THE THIRST ENDURED BY CHRIST ON THE CROSS, AND ON THE FIFTH WORD SPOKEN BY HIM ON IT.

#### POINT I.

"Jesus, knowing that all things were now accomplished, that the Scripture might be fulfilled, said, "I thirst." (1)

Concerning this mystery, ponder, first, *the parching thirst* which Christ our Lord endured; for He had not drunk from the night before, and had suffered very grievous labours, going many journeys, and that enforced with great speediness; having likewise shed much blood by the whips and thorns, and by the nails which fastened Him to the cross, on which He remained about three hours: for which cause the same Lord said, in the 21st Psalm: "My strength is withered as a potsherd, and my tongue hath cleaved to my jaws, and Thou hast brought me down into the dust of death."(2) Which thirst, although it were

(1) Joan. xix. 28. (2) Psal. xxi. 16.

so exceeding great, yet did He suffer and dissemble it, even till He was ready to give up the ghost, but then He declared it: to give us to understand, what great pain He sustained for our gluttony, and our drunkenness, and that we might also be grateful to Him for the same, exciting ourselves patiently to endure the like thirst for the love of Him, if it chance to us to be afflicted with it.

*Colloquy.*—O most strong Samson, who after that Thou hadst slain with the jaw-bone of an ass a thousand Philistines, didst endure a mortal thirst, beseech Thy Father that from this cross with which Thou dost vanquish all Thine enemies, a fountain of water may spring forth, wherewith to quench Thy parching thirst. O living rock, and flint-stone of fiery love, since Thou wast struck with the rod of the cross, sprout forth like the rock which Moses struck, some fountain of water with which to refresh Thine afflicted tongue: (3) but I see, O my Lord, that Thy charity will not sprout forth fountains of water, but of blood, with which to wash my sins, for Thy refreshing is, to suffer much to deliver us from them. By this Thy thirst, dear Lord, I beseech Thee to grant to me patience and temperance, that neither the want of drink disturb me, nor the abundance of it disorder me. Amen.

POINT II.

Besides this *corporal* thirst, Christ our Lord had *another insatiable thirst of three things*, which we may collect from the cause which the Evangelist gives, for which He spoke this word, "sitio," "I thirst." For He saw that all His labours, foretold of Him by the prophets, were now accomplished, and that there wanted but only one, which was, that *they were to give Him "vinegar" in His thirst.*(4) To the end, therefore, that this prophecy might be accomplished, He said, "I thirst," provoking His enemies by

(3) Exod. xvii. 6. (4) Psal. lxviii. 22.

this word, that they should give Him the vinegar to drink they had there prepared.

1. In this fact was discovered three *most excellent virtues* of our most excellent Lord, founded on three sorts of thirsts, which afflicted Him.

i. An insatiable thirst *of obeying His eternal Father*, with which He desired to accomplish His holy will in all things, without omitting one jot or tittle, nor other thing how painful soever it should be to Him. Knowing, therefore, that the will of His eternal Father was, that in His thirst they should present Him "vinegar to drink," He would not omit to accomplish this point, and therefore said that He was athirst, not so much to drink water as that vinegar, for the love He bore to obedience.

*Colloquy.*—O most loving Jesus, whose meat and drink was "to do the will of Thy Father"(5) that sent Thee; give me, I beseech Thee, this thirst of fervent obedience, that I may take content in no other thing, but in the accomplishment of the same. Amen.

ii. The second was, a most inward *desire to suffer for the love of us;* for notwithstanding that He had suffered very much, yet did He desire to suffer much more, and without doubt would have suffered yet much more, had it been the will of His eternal Father. From whence it proceeded that, seeing how the drinking of that vinegar was yet unperformed, He said, "I thirst;" which He did not say to crave of them any kind of refreshment, but to suffer a new torment.

*Colloquy.*—O my Redeemer, I am ashamed of myself, for that the thirst which I have is not to suffer pains, but to swim in pleasures; take from me, I beseech Thee, so pernicious a thirst, and change the same into another thirst, like to Thine own, that I may

(5) Joan. iv. 34.

always thirst to suffer more and more, for the love of Thee. Amen.

(*a*) Of these two virtues it proceeded that Christ our Lord manifested His necessity with admirable sanctity, manifesting the same simply, *without alleging any reasons or causes to persuade them* to give Him drink, nor did He ask drink to be given Him expressly, but only said, "I thirst:" as if He had said: This necessity I endure, look you to it if you will remedy it, and how and when you will succour it.

(*b*) Wherein He taught us, especially such as are Religious, the manner how we are to represent our temporal necessities to God our Lord in holy prayer, and to our prelates, viz., with great resignation, contenting us only to declare our necessity to them, leaving the remedy of it to their providence, concerning the time, the manner, and other circumstances, prepared to endure even till the death, if Almighty God shall so dispose. And what great matter do I, if I do the same that my God, who is my Father, does, and my prelates, who are His ministers do, since Christ our Lord observed the same in His necessities towards the hangmen that were His torturers, of whom He expected no kind of remedy of His necessities? If I shall ask of God bread, will He peradventure proffer me a stone? And if I ask Him fish, will He give me a serpent? Or if an egg, will He present me a scorpion?(6) Or if I shall say to Him, "I thirst," will He offer to me gaul and vinegar? No, God is not so cruel a Father to me, as to deny me what is necessary for me, or to grant me that which may be hurtful to me; and since this is so, it will suffice me, only to propose Him my necessity, committing to Him with entire resignation, the whole care to redress them.

(6) Luc. xi. 11; Mat. vii. 9.

iii. The last thirst was, *of the salvation of souls*, which He redeemed by His Passion, for He thirsted that His blood might profit all, that all might serve His Father, and give Him that glory and worship which is due to God; for the ardent zeal of the house of God, continually ate His bowels, from which zeal proceeded this holy thirst,(7) which He sustained with so great anguish upon the cross. In particular I will ponder the thirst which there He had of my salvation, and that I serve Him with perfection, rendering Him worthy thanks for it, exciting myself to give Him drink with which to cool His burning thirst.

*Colloquy.*—O my soul, behold thy Saviour, saying, "Sitio"—"I thirst;" that thou become obedient, patient, humble, and charitable; give Him, therefore, to drink of what He asks thee, so to assuage and ease His travails. Take, O Lord, the vessel of my heart, wherein I offer to Thee that which Thou so thirstest after, viz., most fervent desires of serving Thee; drink as much as Thou desirest, admit me wholly to enter into Thy inward bowels, in such a manner that I never issue forth from them. Amen.

2. Hence I will gather, that if I desire to imitate Christ our Lord perfectly, I am to procure the thirst of these three things before recited, viz., of obedience to God, of suffering for God, and that many serve Almighty God; for after these follows another thirst,—of seeing God, the living fountain. And so shall be accomplished in me that which Christ our Lord said:—"Blessed are they that hunger and thirst after justice, for they shall have their fill."(8)

POINT III.

"Now, there was a vessel set there full of vinegar. And

(7) Psal. lxviii. 10. (8) Mat. v. 6.

they, putting a sponge full of vinegar about hyssop, put it to His mouth."(9)

1. Upon this passage is to be considered, first, *the cursed stinginess* and cruelty *of man towards God*, and the immense *liberality and bounty of God to man;* for greater liberality there cannot be, than for God to shed forth all the blood that is in His veins, without reserving one only drop, for the good of man; nor can there be greater stinginess and wretchedness than at that time for a man not to afford some refreshment to the thirst of Almighty God. But discussing this point more particularly, I am to consider first, the desolation of Christ our Lord in this His thirst, not having any to condole Him, nor give Him a draught of water to refresh Him, but vinegar, and that mingled with the bitter and distasteful herb of hyssop. Which affliction His majesty suffered with incomparable patience and silence, without complaining or giving any word or sign of indignation against the giver; to give us example of sufferance, and to deliver us from that eternal thirst which we had deserved for our sins in the fire of hell, where the damned beg with the covetous rich glutton one drop of water only, which, notwithstanding, is denied them.

*Colloquy.*—O sweet Jesus, I give Thee thanks for this desolation which Thou sufferedst almost like that of the very damned, not finding any to give Thee a drop of water, with which to mitigate Thy burning thirst. By the same thirst I humbly beseech Thee to deliver me from that thirst eternal, and to give me patience when means shall be wanting to assuage my temporal. Amen.

2. The like affliction of Christ our Lord in the *spiritual thirst* which there He endured when in that "sponge-full

(9) Joan. xix. 29; Mat. xxvii. 48; Marc. xv. 36.

of vinegar," put upon a reed, He considered, the drink which many sinners were to give to Him, exhibiting Him their hearts, empty of all good and virtue, and full of the vinegar of sin and vice, put upon the moveable reeds of vanity, and mutability of the flesh. O my soul, behold the drink which thou givest to thy Saviour, mingled with such a multitude of sins. Behold the vinegar which thou offerest Him, when thou afflictest with bitter words and injurious works thy neighbours, in whom He being, takes as done to Him, the injury which thou dost to them.

*Colloquy.*—O my Saviour, what a difference is there between the drink which Thou givest to me to quench my thirst, and that which I give to Thee to quench Thine. For the sponge full of vinegar upon the reed of hyssop, Thou givest me Thy most holy flesh mingled with the wine of Thy precious blood, crushed and squeezed forth upon this reed of the holy cross; vouchsafe to sprinkle me with it,(10) that I may be cleansed, and inebriate me with wine, that I may be filled with Thy love. I give Thee thanks for this so precious drink, and by the same, I beseech Thee, to pardon me the injuries I have committed against Thee, by the bitter drink which I have given Thee. Amen.

3. The great *grief which the most sacred Virgin felt* when she heard her sweet son say, "I thirst," and saw them give Him vinegar to drink, knowing withal the spiritual thirst which her son had, hers also increased wonderfully, thirsting that many souls might truly serve Him.

*Colloquy.*— O sovereign Virgin, how willingly wouldst thou have approached to have refreshed the corporal thirst of thy beloved Son, if this favour had been granted thee! And how much more willingly

(10) Psal. l. 9.

dost thou run now to quench His spiritual thirst, to the end that there may be many that may love Him, and enjoy the fruit of His holy Passion! Obtain, O mother, that my life may be such, that it may serve for a refreshment to thy thirsty son, serving Him sincerely, as He desires to be served, to the glory of His most holy name. Amen.

---

## MEDITATION L.

### ON THE SIXTH WORD SPOKEN BY CHRIST UPON THE CROSS.

"Jesus, therefore, when He had taken the vinegar, said, "Consummatum est," it "is consummated."(1)

This is the sixth word, which Christ our Lord spake upon the cross, after He had tasted a little of that vinegar, to give to understand that the end and cause why He said He was athirst, and tasted that drink, was to give an end to His torments, and therefore He said, "Consummatum est,"—"It is consummated." O brief, short, compendious, and most complete word! Who is able to understand completely the mysteries that are enclosed in thee, and to declare entirely what thou signifiest! For Christ our Lord fixed His eyes upon three things, when He pronounced this word, worthy of great consideration, of which, for this reason, we may add three several points.

#### POINT I.

1. First, He fixed His eyes upon all the toils and torments which His eternal Father would have Him suffer from the instant of His Incarnation, to this last point in which He was, which was the end of His Passion, and of His life; for He then called to mind the labours of His nativity and circumcision,—those of His flight into the

(1) Joan. xix. 30.

land of Egypt,—those of His preaching through Judea and Galilee, and lastly, all those which He suffered in His Passion; and seeing them all to be entirely accomplished without omitting so much as one, He comforted Himself exceedingly to see that He was at length arrived at the end of all His labours, according to the good pleasure of His eternal Father; and therefore, with an affection of acknowledgment and of gratitude, He said, "Consummatum est"—"*All is consummated" which my Father commanded me to suffer.* And it is to be believed that He repeated mentally the prayer which before He made in the supping chamber, thanking His Father for this work, saying, "Ego te clarificavi super terram, opus consummavi, quod dedisti mihi, ut faciam."—"I have glorified Thee on the earth, I have finished the work which Thou gavest me to do."(2) I give Thee thanks, O most sweet Father, that Thou hast brought me to this hour so much desired of me. I have glorified Thee upon the earth, I have consummated the work which Thou recommendest to me, which I offer to Thee for the redemption of all the world, and that all may be glorified by the means of Thee, O my Redeemer, who saidst:—"I am to be baptized with a baptism, and how am I straitened, until it be accomplished." Let Thy affliction now cease, since the baptism is now finished, and if "the hope that is deferred afflicts the soul," the accomplishment of Thy "desire" will be now to Thee "a tree of life."(3) Let it also be such to me, O my God, that I may gather the fruit which Thou hast budded forth upon the tree of the blessed cross. Amen.

2. Hence I will gather how contented I shall find myself in the hour of my death, if I have accomplished all that which God commands me, and have employed in it my whole life.

(2) Joan. xvii. 4. (3) Prov. xiii. 12.

POINT II.

Secondly, Christ our Lord fixed His eyes upon all the *ends of His coming into the world*, and upon the offices which His Father had given Him, calling to memory how His coming was to satisfy for the sin and offence of Adam, to break the head of the infernal serpent, to destroy death and hell itself, to open the gates of the Kingdom of heaven, to prescribe as master the doctrine of perfection, to give an heroic example of all virtues, to propose as in a table the Evangelical counsels, and to institute sacraments and sacrifices, meet and proper for the new law. Seeing therefore that He on His part had performed all that was necessary to attain these ends, and having accomplished entirely all His offices, with great contentment He said:—"Consummatum est"—I "have performed all my works ...in Jerusalem,"(4) for which I came into the world; I have concluded the consummation, and the abbreviation,(5) which was to be made in the midst of all the earth, whence may flow abundance of justice and sanctity into the world, consummating the indignation which He had against it.—I have likewise consummated the weeks of Daniel, wherein prevarication was to be consummated, and a final end imposed upon sin, iniquity to be blotted out, and sempiternal justice to succeed, and every vision and prophecy to be fulfilled.—Finally, I have accomplished on my part all that was necessary, that my elect might be "Consummati in unum," consummate in one, and perfectly united with the union of charity, "as I and my Father are one."(6)

*Colloquy.*—I give Thee thanks, most perfect Saviour of the world, that Thou hast so exactly fulfilled Thine office, and accomplished the work of our redemption; I beseech Thee, Lord, that Thou wouldst

(4) Is. x. 22. (5) Dan. ix. 24. (6) Joan. xvii. 23.

likewise perfect in me the work which Thou hast begun, consuming in me all my sins, communicating to me Thy full, complete, and consummate justice, that when my life shall have an end, I may be found in Thine eyes, consummate and perfect in all virtue. Amen.

### POINT III.

Thirdly, Christ our Lord fixed His eyes upon all *the shadows and figures of His coming*, which had succeeded from the beginning of the world until that instant, and principally upon the sacrifices and ceremonies of the ancient law, and upon those things which the prophets had foretold, to represent all that He was to do and suffer in the world, and seeing that all this was accomplished, He said:—"Consummatum est." All is consummated whatsoever was foreshadowed and prefigured, the sacrifices and ancient ceremonies are now consummated, the law of circumcision, with the intolerable burdens which it imposed upon men, is now consummated,—the law is also now consummated, and the *prophets*, which I come not to break, but to fulfil,—for "till heaven and earth pass, one jot or one tittle shall not pass of the law till all be fulfilled," (7) which is written therein. Verily, O Lord, Thou hast accomplished all that Thou saidst it should come to pass, for Thy word is more permanent than heaven itself, and more firm than is the earth, for which cause I desire that all the inhabitants both of heaven and earth may praise and glorify Thee for so great a work, as Thou hast consummated upon the cross. Amen.

The same Lord who upon the painful throne of the cross is now ready to give up the ghost, will return *at the day of judgment* on a throne of glory, and having separated the good from the wicked, and *pronounced sentence upon*

(7) Mat. v. 18.

*the one and the other*, conformably to their works, will likewise conclude with this word, saying:—"*Consummatum est.*" Now is the world consummated, and its vain glory,—now is consummated the *time to merit and demerit*, —*now are consummated* the delights of the wicked, and the labours of the good,—now is consummated the power and kingdom of the Devil, any more to tempt and deceive men,—now is consummated and accomplished the number of the elect for the Kingdom of heaven, and their measure is completely arrived to perfection,—and the same proportionably will He say to me in the hour of my death, when He shall come to judge me, for in that hour all these things shall be concluded on my behalf. With this consideration, therefore, I am to animate myself to live so well that I may say with the apostle St. Paul:—"I have finished my course, I have kept the faith" (8) and fidelity which I owe to my God, without defection or blame in it.

*Colloquy.*—O supreme judge of mortal men, whose justice will be as consummate and exact as Thy mercy was, accomplish now in me Thy mercy, that being now filled with Thy grace and merits, Thou mayest hereafter fill me with Thy justice, rendering me the crown due to them in Thy glory. Amen

---

## MEDITATION LI.

### ON THE SEVENTH WORD SPOKEN BY CHRIST UPON THE CROSS, AND ON HIS DEATH.

#### POINT I.

"Jesus crying with a loud voice, said:—*Father, into Thy hands I commend my spirit.*" (1)

(8) 2 Tim. iv. 7.

(1) Luc. xxiii. 46.

Upon these last words are to be considered, first, *the causes* why He pronounced them with *so loud a cry and sound.*

1. One was, to give to understand that He had force and vigour to lengthen His life, and to hinder death, *if so He had wished*, and that if He died it was because Himself would die, conformably to that which before He had said:—"No man taketh it away from me, but I lay it down of myself, and I have power to lay it down, and I have power to take it again." (2)

*Colloquy.*—I give Thee thanks, O sweet Jesus, for this will which Thou hadst to die, and to give Thy life for me; from henceforth I offer mine to Thee, ready to lose it where and when it shall be needful for Thy glory. Amen.

2. To declare the natural *feeling which the soul had in its separation from the body*, for it beheld how good company it had borne it for the space of three and thirty years, and how well it had served and aided it in all the works of our redemption; and since this body was united to the divinity as well as the soul, from thence resulted a vehement grief and natural sorrow to be separated from the same, which grief He signified by that cry, instead of the agonies and anxieties which other souls feel at the time they are separated from their bodies.

*Colloquy.*—O most holy soul of Jesus Christ, for that bitter sorrow which Thou feltest in Thy separation from Thy holy body, I humbly beseech Thee that Thou wouldst so vouchsafe to comfort mine, that I may not fear, or be dismayed to be separated from this of mine. Amen.

3. Christ our Lord cried out with a very high and sounding voice, in *sign of the victory which He had obtained over the Devil* and hell. For as Gideon, sounding the

(2) Joan. x. 18.

trumpets, and striking the pitchers one against another, and making a cry, overcame the Madianites, (3) even so our glorious captain, breaking His body by torments upon the cross, and crying out with His loud voice, overcame the devils by His death, striking fear and terror into the infernal powers; this voice also was miraculous, inasmuch as those that are crucified, in that they are without blood at the time they die, are exceedingly feeble; but our good Jesus then made use of His Almighty power, to show that His death was to overcome, and that His fortitude and victory lay hid therein.

*Colloquy.*—I give Thee thanks, O most powerful Saviour, for the notable victory which Thou hast got, not so much to Thyself as to us, who wouldst die to give us life. I beseech Thee, Lord, when my strength shall fail me, "not to forsake me," but to fortify me with Thine, that dying, I may obtain the victory which Thou hast obtained in my behalf. Amen.

POINT II.

Next are to be considered, *the words* which Christ our Lord pronounced with this cry, taken out of the thirtieth Psalm, for it is to be believed that as soon as He had said:—"Consummatum est"—"It is consummate," He began to recite interiorly this devout psalm, and coming to this verse, lifting up His voice on high, He said:—"Father, into Thy hands I commend my spirit;" (4) each word of which contains a particular mystery.

1. For He calls Him "Father," in sign of *love and confidence*, very necessary in the hour of death, that God may perform the office of a father in our behalf,—protecting and defending us, and admitting us to the inheritance promised to His beloved sons; and it is very necessary to this effect, that we, in our lives, perform towards Him the office

(3) Judic. vii. 19. (4) Psal. xxx. 6.

of good and dutiful sons, loving, honouring, and serving Him, as such a Father deserves.

*Colloquy.*—O most loving Father, grant me, during my whole life, to bear towards Thee the spirit of a son, that at the hour of my death I may confidently call Thee Father. Amen.

2. He *commended His "spirit" "into" "the hands" of His Father*, to signify, that in the hands of such a Father, and of no other, it could be secure. These "hands" were they which "formed" our spirit, and in them has He "graven" us, that He may not forget us. In these "hands" are our "lots," (5) for on them depend the happy lot of our salvation.

*Colloquy.*—O my soul, cast thyself "into the hands" of this thy Father, who, since He has written thee in them, will "not blot" thee out "of the book of life;"(6) and as thy lots are in His hands, He will cause that the happy lot of glory shall befal thee. O sweet Jesus, as Thou commendedst Thy spirit into the hands of Thy Father, so do I likewise commend my spirit into Thine, which Thou extendest abroad upon the cross, to embrace such sinners as fly to them. Here hast Thou written Thine elect with Thy blood, so fastened to Thee with Thy fortitude, that "no man shall pluck them out of" Thy "hand."(7) In my hands my own spirit is not secure, because they are exceedingly feeble; I resign it, therefore, into Thine, which are most mighty, with which, since Thou hast redeemed me, do Thou also glorify me. Amen.

3. He said that He commended *His* "*spirit*,"—not *His goods*, for He had none,—not His honour, for He did not regard it,—not His body, because He set *not* by it,—

(5) Psal. cxviii. 73; Is. xlix. 16; Psal. xxx. 16.

(6) Apoc. iii. 5.

(7) Joan. x. 28.

but His spirit, which is the principal part of man, upon whose good lot all the rest depends, instructing us by it of the care we ought to have in the hour of death, to commend our soul to Almighty God, committing the success of that which touches the body to His divine Providence, for, if my spirit come into the hands of Almighty God, that will suffice to make me blessed.

4. But the charity of Christ our Lord passed yet further, who not only commended His own spirit to His Father, delivering it into His hands, as it were, "in deposito," for a deposit, to resume it again after three days, and to conjoin it to the body, but in spirit He also commended *the spirit of all His elect*, which He held as His own; for, as the apostle St. Paul says:—"He who is joined to the Lord is one spirit" (8) with Him, so that here He recommended to His Father both my spirit and the spiritual life, which, of duty, I am to lead; beseeching Him that He would wholly take me under His safeguard and protection, and in the same sense I likewise may speak these words to our Lord, not only in the hour of death, but also in my life.

POINT III.

"And saying this," "bowing His head," "*He gave up the Ghost.*" (9)

1. As to "*this bowing*," or inclination of the "*head*," of our Lord, which, as it was voluntary, so was not without mystery,—*the causes* of it are to be considered.

i. The first was, to signify that He died *by obedience*,—"bowing His head" to the divine ordination.—ii. The second, to declare *the humility of His heart*, and His *poverty*, not having whereon to repose His head upon the cross.—iii. Thirdly, to show to us *the weighty burden of our sins*, which with their weight made Him to incline even to

(8) 1 Cor. vi. 17. (9) Luc. xxiii. 46; Jaon. xix. 30.

death.—iv. Fourthly, to *design the place of limbo*, to which His spirit directed the journey He was to make to despoil the same.

From these causes I am to draw affections both of *gratitude and imitation*, inclining my head and neck to the yoke of obedience, for the love of Christ, looking always upon the earth, of which I was formed, as also upon hell, which I have deserved, and to which the burden of my sins does depress me, beseeching Christ our Lord, that by the inclination of His head upon the cross, He would vouchsafe to give me true obedience, true humility, and true poverty, wherewith now inclining my head humbly, I may hereafter lift it up with great security.

2. Christ our Lord *rendered up His spirit* in such *a manner* that yet He verily died through the *force and asperity of the pains* which He suffered upon the cross, and for the want of blood, which drop by drop had flowed from His wounds, so that, as the veins began to be empty, and void of blood, so His countenance waxed pale, and the other members of His body became so feeble, that His forces failing, He gave up the ghost.

*Colloquy.*—O good pastor, how well hast Thou fulfilled Thine office, giving Thy life for Thy lost sheep! O sovereign priest, how acceptable a Sacrifice hast Thou offered of Thyself upon this altar of the cross! O most wise master, how high a lesson of justice and sanctity hast Thou read from this chair! O most liberal Redeemer, how copious a price hast Thou given for the redemption of Thy captives! O "Sun" of justice, who "as a giant" wentest forth of the orient, how admirably well hast Thou "run"(10) Thy course, illuminating and heating the whole earth, until Thy stay in the occident of death! I give Thee thanks for

(10) Psal. xviii. 6.

the labours Thou hast sustained for the love of me; it is now high time that Thou take Thy rest, putting an end to Thy pains, saying like another David, "In peace, in the selfsame I will sleep and I will rest."(11)

3. Although it is true that the body of Christ our Lord remained now void of pain, yet it was in such a state as to be a portraiture of sorrows to all those that beheld it; especially *to the sacred Virgin*, whose sorrows did not cease with the death of her son, but rather were renewed with it, seeing herself deprived of Him whom she loved so tenderly. Oh what tears did she shed forth of her eyes!—Oh what sighs and groanings did she breathe forth of her heart!—Oh what clamours of spirit did she send up to heaven!—Oh what lively desires had her soul to accompany that of her son's!—And what affectionate complaints did she pour forth before the eternal Father, that He left her alone in this vale of tears, though she suffered all with great conformity to the divine will; and as she had a most lively faith and assured hope of the resurrection, so she received some comfort to see Him out of pain, who had suffered so great torment, knowing that all His labours ended with death.

4. Finally, I may consider that which many saints ponder, that *the Devil was present on the one side* of the cross, expecting *if ought could be found in Jesus Christ that belonged to him*, to seize on it, but found "nothing," (12) as our Lord had said before. It is likewise to be believed, that since the angels were present at the death of the just, the eternal Father sent some of His Hierarchies to be present at the death of the supreme Just of all justs, not to help Him, but to honour and accompany Him.

*Colloquy.*—O good Jesus and sovereign priest, who,

(11) Psal. iv. 9. (12) Joan. xiv. 30.

in imitation of another priest of the same name, art "clothed with filthy garments,"(13) not with the spots of Thine own offences, but of others, and hast Satan beside Thee to be Thy adversary, although not on Thy right side as the other had, but on Thy left, because he could in nothing overcome Thee, and on the other side. hast not one angel, but many who assist to honour Thee; I humbly beseech Thee to remember me in the hour of my death, cleansing my soul from all filth of sin, so that Satan may not prevail against her, and vouchsafe to send me Thine holy angel, who may so defend me, that as soon as my soul shall be departed from my body, it may merit to be placed in Thy glory. Amen.

---

## A SUMMARY OR ABRIDGMENT OF THE PRECEDING MEDITATIONS, IN WHICH IS LAID DOWN A MANNER HOW TO LIVE WELL, AND A PREPARATION TO DIE WELL, AFTER THE IMITATION OF CHRIST CRUCIFIED.

1. As Christ our Lord was on the cross, stripped naked of His garments, and left them that the soldiers might divide them amongst them: even so ought I to endeavour *to strip my heart naked of the love of all the things of this life*, so that I remain entirely naked of the inordinate affections which before I had. Concerning the use of those things which I possess, I ought to be so moderate, that I take none but only those that are needful to me, stripping myself of those that are superfluous, and of those which are either for vanity or for delight;—and, as touching the propriety of them, I ought to strip myself

(13) Zach. iii. 3.

naked of some of them, so as to clothe the poor and needy; and, if I can, it will do much better to strip myself of all, renouncing them to follow naked Jesus, and to die all naked with Him, laying aside the cares of all things temporal, to attend to those that are eternal.

2. As Christ our Lord was on the cross, nailed hands and feet with three nails, without having liberty to move Himself on one side or other, His blood, by little and little running forth of His wounds, until such time as His veins were left empty:—even so I ought not to content myself to be stript of the exterior things which I possess, but to procure, as St. Paul says, to "*crucify my flesh with its vices and concupiscences*,"(1) upon the cross of Christ, in such a manner that I neither have my hands nor feet free, to desire or do aught which may decline from this cross, but that it be wholly subject to the spirit, and fastened with the nails of the fear of God, of His love, and of obedience to His holy word,(2) as has been pondered in the 44th Meditation. And in this manner ought it to persevere until it empty itself of all the evil blood of sins and imperfections it has. For, as he that is crucified, does not die all at one instant, but by little and little—so neither can I mortify all at once my passions and inordinate affections, but by little and little, with long patience of mortification, until I attain this perfect death. And, as he that is crucified does not crucify himself, but another crucifies and nails him—even so my flesh ought to be crucified by another, namely, by my spirit, with penances, and by denying it the appetites and desires thereof; likewise God Himself crucifies both the flesh and the spirit with afflictions, and men with persecutions, all which we ought to suffer patiently until we die this happy death.

3. As Christ our Lord had a special care to fulfil His

(1) Gal. v. 24. (2) Cass. lib. iv. 34, 25.

obligations and offices towards three persons,—namely, towards His Mother,—His disciple,—and the good thief, to whom He spoke, as has been said:—even so ought I to have a care to *accomplish the obligations of piety and justice*, belonging to my state and office, especially towards three sorts of persons.—i. Towards my *superiors*, signified by the mother.—ii. Towards *such as I live with*, signified by the disciple.—iii. Towards *other men*, signified by the good thief, giving to every one what in duty I owe, and helping all the best that I am able. Moreover, I am to fulfil the obligations of *perfect charity*, beseeching God in the behalf of my enemies and of His, that He would convert them, and excusing the defects of my neighbours, as the same Lord did, from this point first beginning to accomplish His office.

4. As Christ our Lord, after He had fulfilled these obligations for three hours that darkness lasted, applied Himself to prayer, as one that prepared himself to die: even so having fulfilled the obligations of my estate and office, I ought to reserve *some time and place of retirement*, to attend with quietness to the *service of God*, and to negociate *for* my salvation, and for *a happy death;* and in particular to excite in myself a great "thirst," like that which our Lord had, of obeying God and His ministers, of suffering much in His holy service, and of gaining many souls that may serve Him. And the more I shall approach to death, so much the more ought I to increase in the exercises of holy prayer, and in the effects which proceed from it, disposing myself to receive them, because, as St. Gregory says, "Quanto morti vicinior, tanto solicitior"—"The nearer I approach to death, so much more careful ought I to be that the same be good."(3)

5. To this end I must endeavour that all my works be

(3) Lib. 7, ep. 1.

so well done, that at the *end of every one I may say those words of Christ,* "*Consummatum est,*"—that is accomplished which God has commanded me in this work,—it is both perfect and complete: and in this manner I am so to spend the whole day, that, the night approaching, I may likewise say the same. And after the same manner ought I to ordain my life; to prepare me for its end, by means of the sacraments, of Confession, and of Communion, by making my will and by disposing of all my goods, so that I may say:—"Consummatum est."—"All is consummate and fulfilled which God has commanded me.

6. Lastly, both in life and death, with love and affection *to commend my spirit to Almighty God,* resigning it up into His hands, that He defend and keep it, govern and direct it to eternal blessedness, as has been pondered in the preceding meditation. But as Christ our Lord would die in the flower of His age, and at the three-and-thirty years of His life, at which time men apprehend death more vehemently: even so ought I to offer up myself with resignation into the hands of Almighty God, that He take me when it pleases Him, though it be in the very flower of my age, and in the height of my ambition, trusting that He will take me in that age, time, and place, which shall be most convenient for my salvation.

---

## MEDITATION LII.

### ON THE MIRACLES WHICH SUCCEEDED AT THE DEATH OF CHRIST.

After the death of Christ our Lord, besides the darkness which went before, there succeeded other miracles for three ends, that is to say, to declare the glory of Him that died:—the wickedness of those that crucified Him:—and to signify the admirable effects which should ensue after His death.

POINT I.

"And behold the veil of the temple was rent in two pieces, from the top even to the bottom."(1)

The *causes* of these rendings and divisions were two:

i. The first, because, as the high priest Caiphas, when he heard Christ affirm that He was the Son of God, judging the same to be blasphemy, rent his garments in sign of sorrow and grief;—even so the same God rent the veil of His temple, *in sign of the horrible blasphemy* and sacrilege which that people committed, in injuring and crucifying His only Son.

*Colloquy.*—O my soul, if thou be the Temple of the living God, rend thy heart with sorrow, for that which thy Saviour suffers on the cross, thou being the cause of it. O God of my heart, rend the same with Thy holy hand, imparting to me this sensible feeling, for I am of myself so weak, that I cannot by myself rend it as I desire.

ii. The second cause was, to signify, that by the death of Christ our Lord, the *way was "made manifest"*(2) *to know* the secrets and mysteries of Almighty God, which before lay hid, partly by the veil of the shadows and figures of the old law, partly by the veil of our sins, which made division betwixt us and God.(3)

*Colloquy.*—O my Saviour, rend in me this veil, whereby I am hindered from knowing Thee, give me divine light, that I may penetrate Thy divine mysteries, and discover to me the treasures of Thy celestial secrets, in such a degree as is expedient for me to serve Thee. Amen.

(1) Mat. xxvii. 51; Marc. xv. 36; Luc. xxiii. 45.
(2) Heb. ix. 8. (3) Is. lix. 2.

POINT II.

"And the earth quaked, and the rocks were rent, and the graves were opened."(4)

The *causes* of these miracles, were also two:

1. The first was, that *insensible creatures*, after their manner, *should demonstrate signs of sorrow* and feeling, for the death of our Saviour, in detestation of the hardness and obstinacy of that rebellious people, who put Him to death: as also to serve for a confusion to those, who have not compassion of the pains of Christ our Lord.

*Colloquy.*—O my soul, how dost thou not tremble and quake like the earth, seeing Jesus Christ to quake upon the cross? How dost thou not rend thyself in pieces, like the rocks, seeing Christ the living rock to be rent in pieces, separating His soul from His afflicted body! How dost thou not open for grief like the sepulchres of the dead, seeing thy Lord to be opened with so many wounds? O Saviour of the world, suffer not that I be more insensible than the earth, more obdurate than the rocks and sepulchres of the dead; for since I am he who has offended, I have more reason to feel that which Thou sufferest for my offences.

2. The second cause was, to signify, that in virtue of the Passion of Christ, *earthly hearts should tremble with the holy fear of Almighty God*, which is "the beginning" of justification: which although most hard, yet should be rent with contrition and sorrow for their sins, and should open themselves to discover in confession, their dead works which are the sins that slay their souls, that so they may rise again with Christ our Lord to newness of life; whence I will learn how fruitful it is to meditate these divine mysteries, with which are obtained in prayer the three effects aforesaid, as has been noted in the Introduction of this Fourth Part.

(4) Mat. xxvii. 51.

POINT III.

"The centurion, and they that were with him, watching Jesus, having seen the earthquake and the things that were done, were sore afraid, saying: Indeed this was "the Son of God,"(5) and "a just man. And all the multitude of them that were come together to that sight, and saw the things that were done, returned, striking their breasts."(6)

Here is to be considered, how those miracles beforesaid, *wrought the effects which they signified*, in virtue of the Passion of Christ,—moving the hearts of those that saw them, to believe that Christ was just and holy, and which is more, that He was the Son of God, smiting their breasts in sign of penance and of sorrow, for the injuries which they had done Him. And, although the centurion and the soldiers were both Gentiles, and that troop of Hebrew people had been so hard and perverse, in urging and craving the death of Christ, yet were they changed at this instant, convinced by the force of the truth, innocence, and sanctity of Him that died for them: as also in virtue of the prayer He offered upon the cross, praying for all those that persecuted Him; which prayer obtained this mutation and conversion of men so wicked.

In imitation, therefore, of this people, I will strike my breast for the sins which I have committed against our Lord, beseeching Him, by His holy Passion, to pardon them.

(5) Mat. xxvii. 54; Marc. xv. 39. (6) Luc. xxiii. 47.

# MEDITATION LIII.

ON THE OPENING OF CHRIST'S SIDE WITH A LANCE; AND ON HIS FIVE WOUNDS.

## POINT I.

The Jews, therefore, "besought Pilate that" *the* "*legs*" of those that were crucified "*might be broken*," and *their bodies* "*might be taken away*," that "they might not remain upon the cross on the Sabbath day, for that was a great Sabbath day."(1)

1. Here is to be pondered, first, the *iniquity of the chief priests*, who, under the pretext of feigned religion, covered their cruelty and their envy; for they intended to break the legs of Christ our Lord, to *add to Him a new torment, if in case He were yet alive;* or at the least that His body might receive this new injury, if He were dead. They desired, likewise, to take Him down from the cross, because they saw the people took compassion to behold Him, confessing Him for "just," and for "the Son of God," desirous to take Him out of their sight, so to obscure His glory. Whence I will draw a great fear of the judgments of Almighty God, concerning obstinate and obdurate sinners; who, instead of being moved with compassion at the sight of these miracles, as the more simple people were, hardened their hearts more than Pharaoh, adding and heaping sin upon sin, to advance their perverse intention.

*Colloquy.*—O most merciful God, suffer me not, I beseech Thee, to fall into such hardness of heart, as to convert to my hurt that which Thou hast ordained for my good. Amen.

2. The ancient law commanded that the "body" of the

(1) Joan. xix. 31.

crucified should, "the same day," be taken down from "the tree" and "be buried," *for that he was "accursed of God"* (2) *who died on it*, and to the end also he should not infect the earth with his filthy savour. By this law would Christ our Saviour pass, "being made," as St. Paul says, "a curse for us,"(3) to deliver us from the curse of sin, even the same day in which He died for the same.

*Colloquy.*—I give Thee thanks, O most sweet Saviour, that Thou hast so far humbled Thyself, as that Thy body should be counted as "accursed," and for the infection of the earth, which yet art the bliss of all nations, and the most sweet odour with which it is sanctified. Give us, Lord, this humility, that with its odour we may edify the holy Church, and deliver us from pride, whose evil savour contaminates the whole earth.

3. Pilate assenting to this petition of the Jews, "the soldiers, therefore, came, and they broke the legs of the first, and of the other who was crucified with Him. But after they were come to Jesus, *when they saw that He was already dead, they did not break His legs.*"(4) Concerning which is to be considered how the intentions of man can never prevail against those of Almighty God, which would not have the legs of Christ our Lord to be broken, so to accomplish the Scripture, which thus speaks of the Paschal lamb, the figure of Christ, saying,—"Os non comminuetis ex eo," "neither shall you break a bone"(5) of him, to signify that the torments of His Passion, although most terrible, yet should not break His fortitude and patience, nor diminish His charity nor His other solid virtues, signified by the bones, but should always preserve them whole and perfect, notwithstanding the Devil and his ene-

(2) Deut. xxi. 23. (3) Gal. iii. 13. (4) Joan. xix. 33.
(5) Exod. xii. 46.

mies might intend to break them; like as they now pretend to break those of the elect; but Christ Himself defends them, and animates them by His own example: to whom St. James afterwards said:—"Count it all joy, when you shall fall into divers temptations, knowing that the trying of your faith worketh patience; and patience hath a perfect work, that you may be perfect and entire, failing in nothing." (6)

*Colloquy.*—O eternal God, who deliverest the just from their manifold tribulations, and so keepest their bones, that "not one of them shall be broken;"(7) keep in me true fortitude in afflictions, and preserve the interior virtues of my soul, for unless Thou preserve these bones, they will immediately be broken by my enemies.

POINT II.

"*One of His soldiers with a spear opened His side.*" (8)

1. Upon this mystery is to be considered, first, *the cause of this stroke of the lance*, as it was given by the soldiers, which truly was no other than their cruelty and fury, so to be the more assured of the death of Christ, and to do some injury to the body being dead, whose legs they could not break alive. And although the body of Christ our Lord, which received this stroke, felt no pain because it was dead, yet the soul of the sacred Virgin felt the same exceedingly, who, for the greatness of her love, was much more in the body of her son than in her own.

*Colloquy.*—O sovereign Virgin, how truly mayest thou now say, that which the Apostle said, "I fill up those things that are wanting of the sufferings of Christ in my flesh, for His body, which is the Church."(9) There wanted to this wound sorrow in the body of Christ our

(6) Jac. i. 2. (7) Psal. xxxiii. 21.
(8) Joan. xix. 34. (9) Coloss. i. 24.

Lord, which, because it was dead, was devoid of feeling, and thou most afflicted Virgin suppliedst the default, suffering and feeling the pain which it was to feel, offering the same to the eternal Father for the mystical body of thy son, which is His Church. And since thou offeredst the same also for me, which am a member of this body, obtain me grace, that I may feel what thou feltest, and suffer somewhat of that much which thou sufferest; let this stroke pierce my heart, and torment it with great grief, for that by my sins I was the cause of this stroke which my Lord at this present did receive.

2. But much more worthy of consideration are the *causes* for which Christ our Lord contented not Himself, that His shoulders were torn and opened with whips, His head with thorns, His hands and feet with nails, but would also that His side should be opened with a lance, and that with a far greater aperture, *which should penetrate even to His heart*, ordaining this in punishment of the sins which the whole mystical body of mankind had committed in all their members, and in all their powers, both inward and outward, and most of all in the heart. Hence, as the same Lord says,—"come forth...those things" that "defile a man," (10) Therefore, to purge our heart from this poison, He would that His own should be opened, whence "life runneth out." (11)

*Colloquy.*—O my Saviour, by the aperture and wound of Thy precious side, I humbly beseech Thee to pardon the sins which have proceeded forth of my heart; and so shut the same, dear Lord, that there never issue forth of it works which may defile my soul; and open it so, that from thence may only proceed such works by which I may obtain life eternal. Amen.

(10) Mat. xv. 18. (11) Prov. iv. 23.

3. By this wound of His side, our good Jesus would also manifest the infinite *charity and love which He bears towards us*, and how all He had done and suffered for us unto that instant, He had done from, and with, pure love, as if He had said that of the Canticles:—"Thou hast wounded my heart, my sister, my spouse, thou hast wounded my heart." (12) Twice He says, "thou hast wounded,"—once with the wound of love, by my bounty and mercy alone, imparted my gifts to thee, to the end that they might incline thee to love me; and secondly, thou hast wounded it with the iron of the lance, since for thy sake it was wounded, that by the second wound thou mightest acknowledge the first, and thereby take notice how much I loved thee.

*Colloquy.*—O most loving Jesus, and my Redeemer, my brother, and the spouse of chaste souls, what shall I render Thee for the wounds Thou hast received for the love of me? Wound, dear Lord, my heart with the wounds of love and sorrow, that I may love Thee, for that Thou hast so greatly loved me, and may have compassion on Thee for the great pains Thou hast suffered for me. Give me leave, O my Lord, to enter at this opening of Thy side, that in this furnace of fire, which burns in Thy heart, I may be wholly inflamed in the love of Thee. Amen.

4. This sweet and tender-hearted lover would also that His feet and hands should be opened with nails, and His side with a spear, to the end that those *holes and caves of this living rock, should be a spiritual dwelling for all the faithful*, to what estate and degree of virtue soever they were come, so that sinners, and beginners, proficients, and perfect, entering by meditation into these wounds, might obtain their desired end. They are "rocks" of refuge "for the urchins," (13) which are sinners, full of prickles with

(12) Cant. iv. 9. (13) Psal. ciii. 18.

the thorns of their sins, and as a cave in which those may hide themselves from the wrath of God, who have offended Him. They are as rocks wherein the "weak people," figured by beginners, "maketh its bed," (14) into which retiring, they defend them from those visible and invisible enemies, who persecute them; who though of themselves they be fearful and pusillanimous, yet, inclosing themselves within these wounds, they become strong and invincible like to hills.(15) They are also as a spiritual solitude, to which those retire themselves who are tired and wearied with the tumult of the world, and like doves, desire to fly and build where they may take true rest. And, finally, they are as nests, in which those dwell in peace and security who heartily desire always to be united to Jesus Christ, whom Himself calls and invites, saying:—"Arise, make haste, my love, my dove, beautiful one, and come" and dwell "in the clifts of the rock, in the hollow places of the wall." (16)

*Colloquy.*—O beloved of my soul, since Thou openest Thy wounds, that I may dwell there, and dost withal invite me to it, I determine, with the help of Thy grace, to make to myself three tabernacles and habitations therein, not on the mount of Thabor, but on the mount of Calvary.(17)

5. Of these three tabernacles:—

i. One shall be in the wounds of Thy sacred *feet*, exercising myself in meditating upon Thy steps, to know by what way I must walk to attain eternal life, feeling withal the pains which Thou endurest in them.—ii. The second tabernacle shall be in the wounds of Thy *hands*, where I will always consider Thy works, and the torments which

(14) Prov. xxx. 26.

(16) Cant. ii. 10—14. (17) S. Bon. in Stim. div. am. c. 1.

(15) S. Aug. in manual, c. 22, 23; S. Ber. ser. 61, in Cant.

Thou sustainedst in them to do me good.—iii. But the third and most ample shall be the wound *of Thy side*, contemplating continually the insatiable charity with which Thou lovedst me, and offeredst up Thyself, to do and suffer all that was necessary for my salvation.

In these three tabernacles I will inhabit both day and night, here I will sleep, study, traffic, and contemplate, mingling whatsoever I shall do with the consideration of Thy affectionate and sorrowful wounds; but because I have not wings, with which I may fly to them, give to me, O my God, wings like a dove, which are pure cogitations and affections with which, like a dove, I may meditate and mourn for Thy pains, and for my own sins, mourning also and sighing, to be always united with Thee, with the union of perfect love.

*Colloquy.*—O most pure Virgin, who wast the first, who, like a dove, flew into the holes of these rocks, beg of thy blessed son that He admit me also to enter into them. O divine Noah, since in the side of the ark of Thy body Thou openedst a gate, through which those living things were to enter, which were to escape the furious deluge, give me leave to enter by this gate, to the end that the deluge of the sins of this world do not drown me. O sovereign pastor, since Thou art "the door" by which the sheep "enter in," and "find pastures"(18) of eternal life, make me, I beseech Thee, to enter by the gate of Thy side, whereby I may find the pastures of light and of love, in which I may feed my soul. O most strong David, who, with Thy five wounds, as with five pure stones, didst overthrow the giant Goliah,(19) i. e. the Devil, although one only was sufficient, overthrow, I beseech Thee, with these stones, the pride of my heart, pardon the sins of my five senses, and so bridle and restrain

(18) Joan. x. 9. (19) 1 Reg. xvii. 40.

them, that they may always be employed in Thy holy service. Amen.

6. These affections and purposes, with others like, which St. Bonaventure insinuates, (20) are to be deduced from the meditation of these wounds, beholding in them the infinite perfections of Almighty God, and the immense virtues of Christ our Lord, especially His ineffable charity, since, as St. Bernard says:—"Patet arcanum cordis per foramina corporis, quidni in viscera per vulnera pateant?" —"The secret of the heart appears through the holes of the body, why should not the bowels of His mercy appear through His wounds?" (21)

POINT III.

"And immediately there came out blood and water, and he that saw it, hath given testimony: and his testimony is true." (22)

1. The mystery of this "*blood and water,*" which flowed forth of the side of Christ our Lord, was *one of the principal ends* for which He would have it *opened with that lance.* The causes of this mystery were:—

i. First, to declare to us the immense bounty of His charity in *giving us all His blood,* without retaining so much as a drop; for that little modicum which remained in His heart, to which the thorns and nails could not approach, He would have drawn forth with the prick and wound of the lance.

*Colloquy.*—O Saviour, what shall I give to Thee, for this so prodigal a liberality, if yet I may be called prodigal, which was shed forth with such mature deliberation and providence! Take, O Lord, my heart, and all whatsoever is therein, take all the blood, and

(20) Stim. div. am. c. 1. (21) Ser. 61, in Cant.
(22) Joan. xix. 34.

all my vital spirits, that all may employ themselves in loving Thee, and that my blood may burn with desire of serving Thee. Amen.

ii. To declare to us *the efficacy of His Passion*, and of His death, to wash our sins, and to purify us in virtue of His blood, and with the water of His grace, as also to quench therewith our flames of covetousness, and to satisfy the thirst of our desire.

*Colloquy.*—O most sweet Saviour, now do I confess that Thou art the "fountain open to the house of David,"(23) forth of whose open side water and blood continually flows to wash the bloody spots of our offences; Thou art the living rock and the fiery flint, which, being struck on the side with the stroke of the lance, gushedst forth most abundant waters(24) to refresh those who in the desert of this world die for thirst. O fountains of our Saviour,(25) opened in to His feet, hands, and side, with great joy do I hasten your channels for the water of health, which may wash me, cleanse me, heal me, and finally save me. O my sweet Saviour, since Thou hast these open fountains, send forth through them water and blood, which may run down even to the inward of my heart, making the same the vessel in which to reserve it, that with so precious a liquor it may remain pure and holy, sound and safe. Amen.

iii. Hence proceeded the third cause, *to signify* that *from the side* of Jesus Christ dead on the cross with so great love, *should flow the sacraments of the new law*, with virtue to wash and sanctify souls, especially the sacrament of Baptism, and that of Penance, which is the drink of tears, shadowed by the water of His side, and the venerable Sacrament of the Altar, figured by the water and blood, in memory of which water is mingled with wine in the

(23) Zach. xiii. 1. (24) Num. xx. 11. (25) Is. xii. 3.

holy chalice. (26) Wherefore when I approach to receive these sacraments, but above all this most divine Sacrament, I am to imagine that I approach to the very side of Christ, to drink the water and blood which gushes thence, and to participate of the graces and gifts which flow from those fountains of our Saviour.

*Colloquy.*—O most loving Saviour, who hast by Thy pain merited those waters which I draw with great joy forth of Thy fountains; shut not from me, I beseech Thee, their channels, as my great ingratitude has deserved, for, from henceforth I purpose, assisted by Thy grace, to run to them, not slowly, but very joyfully, not with lukewarmness, but with great fervour, not seldom or lazily, but very frequently, endeavouring to draw from thence not water, but *waters*, filling my soul with the abundance of many graces and virtues, to Thy honour and glory. Amen.

iv. From all these causes is deduced one other cause, for which our Saviour would that His side should be opened, to signify, that *as of the rib* of Adam, being asleep, *Eve was formed;* (27) even so from *His side, sleeping* the sleep of death on the cross, *He would produce the Church* as another Eve, Mother of the truly living, "a glorious church, not having spot or wrinkle, or any such thing," (28) for being washed with the water and blood of the same side, she was to obtain this excellent beauty.

*Colloquy.*—I give Thee thanks, O celestial Adam, for the love which Thou bearest to Thy Church, exposing Thyself for her to so many troubles. But what marvel is it that Thou lovest her so much, whom Thyself hast drawn forth of Thine own side, and from the entrails of Thy heart? Preserve her, dear

(26) S. Tho. 3, p. q. lxxiv. art. 6.
(27) Gen. iii. 21. (28) Ephes. v. 27.

Lord, I beseech Thee, in peace and sanctity; cleanse her entirely from spot and wrinkle, that she may come with many children, to be truly glorious amongst the angels, beholding Thy divine essence, with the Father, and with the Holy Ghost, world without end. Amen.

2. Ponder, finally, that, as the Evangelist notes, these things were done *in accomplishment of the Scripture, which* says:—"*Videbunt in quem transfixerunt*"—"*They shall look upon me, whom they pierced,*" (29) to signify that we sinners, who with sins wound and pierce Christ, ought to behold and contemplate Him with a lively faith, to the end that by His stripes we may be healed, and by His wounds we may be delivered from our own, and by His lance our heart may be pierced, whence may flow a fountain of tears, making great lamentation for His death, and for the cause we gave to it. But if we neglect the same in this life, He does withal admonish us, the time will come in which we shall behold Him, not on the cross with these deformed wounds, but as judge on a throne of glory, with wounds of splendour, whence shall issue forth beams of anger and of vengeance against His persecutors, who lament bitterly without remedy for the injuries they have done to Him.

*Colloquy.*—O my soul, behold diligently the difference that there is between the one sight and the other, and between the one lamentation and the other; and since now thou mayest behold with devotion the wounds of Christ crucified, and mayest lament them to thy profit, do not neglect the time, in which Thou shalt behold them with trembling, and lament them in torments. Amen.

(29) Zach. xii. 10.

## MEDITATION LIV.

### ON THE TAKING DOWN FROM THE CROSS.

#### POINT I.

"And when it was evening, there came a certain rich man of Arimathea, named Joseph, who also himself was disciple of Jesus," although "in secrecy for fear of the Jews." He went in boldly to Pilate, and *begged the body of Jesus. And Pilate* understanding that He was now dead, "*commanded that the body should be delivered.*" (1)

1. Upon this passage consider, first, the providence and *care which God our Lord has of those that are His*, whether they be *living or departed.* The body of Christ our Lord hung nailed on the cross, to the great dishonour of His friends and acquaintance; and some devout women stood afar off from the cross, for fear of the Jews. His most holy mother, and His disciple St. John, with Mary Magdalen, stood near to the cross, but very mournful and afflicted for His death, and full of anxiety, because they knew not by what means to take Him down from the cross, with that decency which so precious a body of right deserved, fearing, moreover, if the soldiers took Him down, that they would do the same with great ignominy and irreverence. But in the midst of this anxiety, the divine providence was not wanting to provide for the honour of the son deceased, and of the mother so much afflicted, providing that it should be taken down with great reverence and devotion. For it is the property of our celestial Father to comfort the afflicted, and to honour the humbled, and so He decreed, that as the dishonour of His Son had

(1) Mat. xxvii. 57; Marc. xv. 43; Luc. xxiii. 50; Joan. xix. 38; S. Tho. 3, p. q. li. art. 1 et 2.

endured even to the death of the cross, so His honours should begin from the same cross, to the end that we should animate ourselves to suffer humiliations, since God so speedily hastens with exaltations.

2. Our Lord *inspired a certain man*, whose name was Joseph, *to undertake this pious office*, whose qualities were, to *be rich and noble*, for so it was convenient for him to be able to exercise this office; but he was withal "a good and a just man," (2) and who expected the Kingdom of God; for our Lord would not make use of a man evil, vicious, and of little charity. Nor made He any account of his nobility and riches, had not these qualities been accompanied with goodness and justice. This man, although he was a secret disciple of Christ our Lord, and somewhat timorous "for fear of the Jews," yet at that present manifested himself with great boldness, and took courage to go to Pilate, and to beg the body of his master; in which fact the virtue of the Passion of Christ shines exceedingly, and the efficacy of divine inspiration, who chasing away from the soul all timidity and pusillanimity, causes it to set upon the difficulties which before it feared, and to recover courage to undergo those things which before it abhorred.

*Colloquy.*—O most sweet Jesus, touch my heart, I beseech Thee, with the force of Thy divine inspiration, that, setting aside all human fear, I may undertake, with an invincible courage, whatsoever concerns Thy holy service. Amen.

3. Consider the humility and obedience which Christ our Lord would show to us after His death, and that *He would undergo the laws of malefactors which were crucified;* for it was not lawful to take down any such from the cross without the permission of the judge, and this permission

(2) Luc. xxiii. 50.

Christ would that it should be begged in His behalf, that as He ascended the cross by obedience of His celestial Father, even so being dead, He would descend from the same by obedience to the law which ordained it, and of the president, who being requested, granted it; that I may learn by this, not to descend from the cross on which God has put me, without permission of the same God.

POINT II.

License being obtained of Pontius Pilate, Joseph buying fine linen, and taking Him down, wrapped Him up in the fine linen. "Nicodemus also came...bringing a mixture of myrrh and aloes about an hundred (3) pounds weight," wherewith to anoint the body of Jesus.

1. Here consider the care which the divine providence had, to *adjoin to Joseph of Arimathea a companion*, who should help him in this pious work, and such a one as was equal to himself, being most noble and just, and a disciple of Jesus, although in secret; (4) for our Lord knows how much it imports for two that are virtuous to unite themselves in the works of charity, the one animating and urging on the other with his good example. Joseph cast off all fear by the company of Nicodemus, and he likewise by the company of his fellow Joseph, and both of them with great fortitude of mind set upon this work; for, as the Wise man says:—"Brother that is helped by his brother, is like a strong city." (5) And, as Christ our Lord, whilst He lived, sent His disciples two by two, so now being dead, He chose two other disciples to take His body down from the cross, willing that all His works should be done with charity.

2. But as either of those two brought something with

(3) Marc. xv. 46; Joan.. xix. 39

(4) Joan. iii. 1. (5) Prov. xviii. 10.

them to bury Christ, Joseph a winding sheet, in which to wrap the body, buying the same new out of the shop, for that he judged it not expedient to take a sheet that had served others; and Nicodemus a precious ointment, and in great quantity, wherewith to anoint Him; even so he who offers his heart to the service of Christ, always with the will annexes the works, which he is able to do according to his power, endeavouring that they be works clean, pure, precious, and many, and mingled with mortification and devotion, so that they be neither few because they be precious, nor of small price because they be many, but that we may conjoin all together in the best manner that we are able.

POINT III.

1. These two men, with great reverence and devotion, mingled with great compassion and tears, took the body of Christ down from the cross. They *unnailed the sacred feet and hands*, kissing them with great tenderness; they took off the crown of thorns from His head, adoring it with singular reverence; and when they had drawn forth the nails, they embraced the sacred body, to sustain with their shoulders that which before the nails had sustained, whose divine person sustained, with His only word, both heaven and earth, with all whatsoever is therein.

*Colloquy.*—O Son of the living God, united with a dead body, and reduced to that necessity that Thou standest in need to be sustained by Thine own creatures; I give Thee thanks for this humility, which here Thou showest full of great charity. O love strong as death! O zeal hard as hell! How hast thou vanquished Him that was invincible, subjecting Him to death, and causing Him to enclose Himself within a sepulchre? Vanquish me also, that I may die with my Redeemer, since to die with Him is gain to me, and to be overcome by thee is to get the victory.

2. The body being taken down from the cross, *the Blessed Virgin received the same upon her breasts*, embracing the same between her arms, but much more with those of her soul, which was quite and wholly pierced with sorrow, fulfilling to the very letter that which is said in the Canticles:—" A bundle of myrrh is my beloved to me, he shall abide between my breasts." (6) O sovereign Virgin, how unlike are these embraces from those which thou gavest Him in the stable of Bethlehem, and when thou walkedst with Him into Egypt. Then was He to thee a little bundle of myrrh, and like to a jewel set between thy sacred breasts, but now He is a great bundle of bitter myrrh, and which fills thee full of bitterness, so that thou mayest rightly repeat the lamentation of Jeremiah, saying:—" He hath filled me with bitterness, and hath inebriated me with wormwood," (7) exceedingly bitter; for she was truly filled with bitterness, when she sorrowfully beheld the body of her son, tormented in each of His members, from which she gathered the myrrh, of which she composed this bitter bundle. She beheld the bones disjointed, kissing the holes of the hands, and stretched forth the fingers that were shrunk and contracted together; then did she behold the wounds of His side and of His feet, her spirit remaining wounded with the sight of so many wounds, and inebriated with so many bitternesses.

3. *Mary Magdalen* likewise approached, *embracing those feet*, at which she had received the pardon of her sins, which, when she saw so cruelly wounded and disfigured, her heart remained wounded, and her eyes were turned into fountains of tears, with which she began to water them, wishing, if she might, to wipe them with her hair as she was wont to do. *The beloved disciple* addressed him-

(6) Cant. i. 12. (7) Thren. iii. 15.

self directly to that breast, on which he had leaned his head the night before, which seeing opened on the one side with the lance, he kissed that sacred wound, bathing it with the tears of his eyes, desiring also to enter in to sleep another slumber of contemplation, much more profound than was the former.

*Colloquy.*—O thrice blessed soul, to whom it was granted to touch and embrace this sacred body; grant me license, O my Saviour, that I may also in spirit embrace the same, transforming me wholly into Thy love, henceforth Thou shalt be to me "a bundle of myrrh," which shall always abide between my breasts, beholding the same with my eyes, and loving the same with all the affections of my heart.

---

## MEDITATION LV.

### ON THE FUNERAL AND BURIAL OF CHRIST.

#### POINT I.

1. The holy Virgin having had the body of her blessed son awhile in her lap, *gave it to Joseph and Nicodemus*, that they might perform towards it their office of piety, retaining to herself the crown of thorns and the nails, as brooches and jewels very precious.

2. These men, therefore, took to them that most holy body, and *anointed it*, spending on it *all the hundred pounds of myrrh and aloes*, so that the whole body was replete and embalmed with it; to signify that most sacred body, from His first conception even to the end of His life, lived always filled and replete with the myrrh of labours and mortifications, that the whole mystical body of His Church, and every member thereof being anointed with the like myrrh, may preserve itself from the corruption of sin; and

since the number of a hundred signifies perfection, by these "hundred pounds" are signified to us that our mortification ought to be most perfect, and most complete in all kind of virtue, as Christ was, according to that which the spouse says in the Canticles:—"My hands dropped myrrh, and my fingers were full of the choicest myrrh." (1)

*Colloquy.*—O my soul, call to mind seriously this myrrh of thy beloved, and anoint with it thine own body, "bearing" always therein, as the Apostle did, "the mortification of Jesus," that the life also of Jesus may be made manifest in our bodies."(2) Amen.

3. This unction being finished, they *wrapped the sacred body in a clean winding-sheet,* and the sacred head in a "napkin," "and bound it in linen cloths, with the spices, as the manner of the Jews is to bury."

*Colloquy.*—O sacred Virgin, what sorrow did thy heart feel when thou sawest wrapped up the face of thy son, on which thou desiredst more to look, than did the angels of heaven? O face more pure than the sun, who has covered thee with the cloud of this mortality? O celestial Adam, who has clothed Thee with the skins of dead beasts? Thy charity has done this, to deliver from death the earthly Adam, and to take away by this means the clouds of my sins, which hinder me to behold Thy divine countenance.

4. We may also ponder the love and affection which Christ our Lord had to poverty, who would that *the myrrh, the winding-sheet, and the napkin, should be given Him as an alms;* as also that the sepulchre should be another man's, and only be lent to Him; teaching us by this example to love that virtue which He Himself so greatly loved, and actually to exercise the same in our life, and in our death, according as Himself has done before us.

(1) Cant. v. 5 (2) 2 Cor. iv. 10.

POINT II.

1. The body being wrapped and bound up, it is piously to be believed that *it was laid upon a bier*, as the custom was to carry the dead, and all that company of devout women followed weeping, with the mother of the deceased, who wept, like the widow of Naim, for the death of her only son, who died in the flower of His age.

*Colloquy.*—O merciful God, why comest Thou not to meet this discomforted widow, saying to her,—"Noli flere"—"Weep not."(3) Why dost Thou not touch the coffin in which this blessed young man, her only son and Thine, lies enclosed, and say to Him:—"Adolescens tibi dico surge,"—"Young man, I say to thee, Arise," restoring "Him to His mother," who without Him remains so solitary and desolate? But I see, Lord, that the time is not yet come, for first Jonas is to enter into the belly of the whale, and the Son of Man to be "three days and three nights" "in the heart of the earth,"(4) to come from thence afterwards alive.

2. It is likewise piously to be believed, that the *choirs of angels* divided themselves into two parts, of which the *one accompanied the soul* of Christ our Lord, as we shall hereafter see,—*the other came to accompany this divine body*, united likewise with the divinity, to honour it as it beseemed, fulfilling that which was written:—"And His sepulchre shall be glorious," (5) for many things which concurred to honour the same, of which one was, this company of glorious angels, of whom we may say that which Isaias said:—"The angels of peace shall weep bitterly;" (6) not that they really wept, but that if they had been capable of tears, their charity would have constrained them to weep, where they saw there was so just a cause to weep.

(3) Luc. vii. 13. (4) Jonas. ii. 1; Mat. xii. 40.
(5) Is. xi. 10. (6) Ibid. xxxiii. 7.

*Colloquy.*—O angels of peace, obtain for me that I may bitterly weep for the death of my Lord, and with the tears of my heart, accompany those that weep, since I have been the cause that He has been so cruelly handled, as might move all even to weep.

POINT III.

And there was in the place were He was crucified a garden, and in the garden "a new monument" belonging to Joseph, "which he had hewed out of a rock," "in which no man yet had been laid." "And he rolled a great stone to the door of the monument, and went his way." (7)

1. Consider the *properties of this sepulchre*, which Christ our Lord chose for Himself taken of Joseph, who had hewed it.

i. The first property was, that it was in "*a garden*," because as the first Adam sinned in a garden, and there incurred the pain of death,—so the second Adam would deplore this sin in another garden, and in another sepulchre, to deliver him from sin and death.

ii. The second property is, that it was "*new*;" for our Lord being the new Adam, and a new Man, was not to choose for His body any other than a new sepulchre; as when He entered into the world He chose for His body the womb of the Virgin, which was as a sepulchre, but yet new, in which never any before had been laid, for that she was always a virgin, "a garden enclosed," (8) and the lodging of Christ alone, in whom her spouse Joseph had no part, as this other Joseph had no part in this sepulchre which he had hewed for himself.

iii. The third property was, that it was "*hewed out of a rock*," or mountain, hewn with the force and violence of iron tools;—to signify, that Christ the living rock, hewed with the tools of many distresses, was to be entombed

(7) Mat. xxvii. 60; Joan. xix. 41. (8) Cant. iv. 12.

there, of whom the eternal Father said:—"Behold, I will grave the graving thereof," and *will dig many ditches* therein, "I will take away the iniquity of that land in one day;" (9) for by virtue of the wounds which this divine stone received, the sins are pardoned with which the whole earth was infected.

*Colloquy.*—O lively rock, make me strong like a rock, hew me with the chisel and strokes of trials, that I may become a sepulchre, in which Thou mayest remain for ever. Amen.

2. In this sepulchre they laid the most holy body of our Lord Jesus, He humbling Himself *who sits above the heavens, to be placed amongst the dead* under the earth.—"They have laid me in the lower pit," says the prophet David, "in the dark places, and in the shadow of death." (10) This our Lord ordained that He might deliver us, by this His humiliation, from the lower lake of hell, from the darkness of ignorances, and from the shadow of death, which is sin,—for He buried with Himself all the vices of the world, that in virtue of His death they might remain for ever dead and buried.

*Colloquy.*—O glorious sepulchre of Almighty God, who enclosest within Thee Him who is the splendour of the eternal Father, the glory of the angels, the honour of the world, the health and life of mortal men; deliver me, O sacred sepulchre, from the obscure lake of hell, and from the mortal sleep of sin; admit me to enter into thee, that I may die, and be "buried together with Him"(11) who died, and was buried for me. Amen.

3. Consider, lastly, how in this mystery is proposed to us that due *preparation we are to make to receive the Blessed*

(9) Zach. iii. 9, Juxta Septuag. "Ego fodiam foveas in eo."
(10) Psal. lxxxvii. 7. (11) Rom. vi. 4.

*Sacrament*; for, as the consecration of the body and blood of Christ our Lord, in different species of bread and wine, signifies His death, as hath been said, in which the blood was separated from the body,—even so the sacred communion represents His burial. For this blessed body, with the five wounds, full of the merits which proceed from the myrrh of the same Passion, wrapped as in a napkin, under the veil of the species of bread, enters into our breast, as into a sepulchre, which, therefore, ought to be as "a garden," full of the odoriferous flowers of virtue, and "new" by the renovation of our life, casting forth all the filth of our old life, and to become so clean as if no dead thing had ever been laid there. It ought also to be "hewed out of a rock," for the great fortitude and constancy which it ought to have, in suffering the mortifications and tribulations of this life; it ought also to be near to the mount of Calvary, because it ought to be always exercised in thinking upon the afflictions of Christ crucified, and to imitate His excellent virtues.

4. By this preparation it will become a glorious sepulchre of Jesus Christ, who will delight to enter into it, and enrich it with the gifts of His grace; but, after I have communicated, I am to *roll* "*a great stone*" *against the door of the* "*sepulchre*," securely and strongly to keep the treasure hidden there, shutting the door of my heart and of my senses to all that may steal from me so precious a treasure, burying myself within myself, with the same Lord which I have within me, to discourse with Him, and to give Him thanks for the graces and favours which He has done me; for, as St. Gregory says, (12) contemplation is as the sepulchre of the spirit, in which it is enclosed and "hid with Christ in God." (13)

(12) Lib. Mor. c. v. (13) Col. iii. 3.

*Colloquy.*—O my soul, endeavour, with Joseph of Arimathea, to anoint thy Lord with the myrrh of most perfect mortifications, and to wrap Him in a "new and clean napkin" with great purity of life. Give to Him thine own sepulchre, which is thy heart, hewed with great firmness, and so shalt thou become another Joseph, that is to say, "*he that increaseth,*" since, at every time thou dost communicate, thou shalt increase in virtues, until thou shalt come to dwell in that celestial city, signified by Arimathea, which is interpreted high, and is placed on high, clearly seeing the God of gods, in His high tower of holy Sion, world without end. Amen.(14)

---

## MEDITATION LVI.

### ON THE SOLITUDE OF OUR LADY THE VIRGIN, AND ON THAT WHICH WAS DONE AFTER THE BURIAL OF HER SON.

#### POINT I.

1. The office of the burial being finished, the Virgin our Lady, full of new sorrow to see herself left all alone, and to be deprived, not only of her living son, but also of His dead body, determined *to return to her place of rest*, accompanied with those noble men, with Mary Magdalen, and with other devout women. Now, when they came to the mount of Calvary, the Virgin beholding *the cross of her son, adored it*, she being the very first of all that gave us example of this adoration. O what tender and devout words then spake she, cheering herself with the cross of Christ! She bowed herself upon her knees, and lifting up her hands on high, began to say:—"Hail, precious cross, upon whose arms died He whom I bore a little infant between mine; more happy was thy lot herein than mine, since between

(14) Jansen. c. 244, conc.

my arms He began the redemption of the world, but between thine He concluded and perfected it. Blessed art thou amongst all creatures, for that on thee is changed the malediction of guilt into the benediction of grace, for He died on thee that He might give life to the world. Hail, O noble tree of life, by whose fruits all men may obtain eternal life. I adore thee as His image, who is the image of the invisible God, and who extended His arms and feet hanging on thee, that He might renew the image which Adam had blotted out by his sin." With these or the like words the Blessed Virgin adored the holy cross, and those others which went with her did the same, in imitation of her.

2. Secondly, consider how in the way this Lady *walked with great care and wariness*, for fear of treading under her feet the blood of her son, which she knew to be the blood of Almighty God, united with His divinity, and she lamented grievously for those that trampled on the same, and deplored their sins, who, as the apostle St. Paul says:—"Hath trodden under foot the Son of God, and hath esteemed the blood of the Testament unclean." (1)

3. When she came to her lodging, the Blessed Virgin with great humility *rendered thanks to those two devout and noble gentlemen*, Joseph and Nicodemus, for that work of charity which they had performed towards her son, and so courteously took her leave of them; and peradventure she said to them, that which David said to the inhabitants of Galaad, when they buried Saul slain by the Philistines:—"Blessed be you to the Lord who have shown this mercy to your master Saul, and have buried him. And now the Lord surely will render you mercy and truth, and I also will requite you for this good turn, because you have done this thing." (2)

(1) Heb. x. 29. (2) 2 Reg. ii. 5.

POINT II.

1. The sacred Virgin being entered into her habitation, and recollecting herself in some secret closet, *began to deplore her solitude and desolation*, for she had her soul divided into many places, where the treasure of her heart was;—one part was in the sepulchre with the body of her son, meditating and ruminating the sorrows which He had suffered in His Passion;—another part was in limbo, with the soul of the same son, contemplating what He did with the fathers with whom He then conversed.—But much more at this present was her heart possessed with sorrows recalling them to memory, and deploring their causes, beseeching the eternal Father to apply the fruit of them to many, to the glory of Him that had endured them.

2. Another part of the night she spent in *discoursing with those that kept her company, of the labours of Jesus Christ*,—especially the Evangelist St. John, recounted to her the things which his master had done in the supping chamber;—as, how He had eaten with them the Paschal lamb, washed their feet, and instituted the most Blessed Sacrament of His body and blood, made to them a most divine sermon, and foretelling to them what was to come;—how He went to the garden of Gethsemani, and the sorrowful words which He spoke to them;—also how He withdrew Himself three times from them to offer His prayer.—Finally, how Judas came with a band of soldiers to apprehend Him,—the miracles which there He did, and how all His disciples fled and forsook Him. All these things the Virgin hearkened to with great devotion and spirit, and preserved them, revolving them inwardly in her heart; but when she turned herself to contemplate the pains which herself had seen, she was wholly melted into tears, and spent the residue of the night in meditation of them. O

sovereign Virgin, I heartily wish to weep with thee, as the prophet Jeremiah, and to say:—"How doth the city sit solitary that was full of people? How is the mistress of the Gentiles become as a widow? Weeping she hath wept in the night, and her tears are on her cheeks; there is none to comfort her among all them that were dear to her; all her friends have despised her, and are become her enemies." (3)

*Colloquy.*—Comfort thyself, O sovereign princess, let thy sighs and mournings cease, lest the stream of thy tears be stopped, because the grain of wheat, which thou hast hid and sowed in the sepulchre, within three days will rise up alive with most glorious fruit, to render thee a hundredfold of consolation, for this thy sorrow and desolation.

3. In the same time in which this good pastor had laid down His life for His sheep, although He descended as low as limbo, to give comfort and liberty to those that were detained in that fold, yet *was He not at all forgetful of those which were dispersed upon the earth*, "as sheep without a shepherd;" for, by the virtue of His omnipotence He inspired them even from limbo, that they should repair to the place where His mother was, that she might comfort and strengthen them in His absence. The first that came was St. Peter, weeping and lamenting for the triple denial of his master, and falling down before the Virgin, and before John his fellow disciple, he began afresh to renew his bitter tears, as well for those his denials, as for the torments of his master, and for the discomfort of the mother, and of those others which there lamented. But the Blessed Virgin gently comforted him, as one that knew full well the disposition of God, which is to comfort those that weep. By and by entered in the other apostles, whom the Virgin

(3) Thren. i. 1.

received with exceeding charity, as the hen gathers her chickens under her wings, when they fly to her for fear ot the kite. She exhorted them that they should keep their faith and hope of the Resurrection of her son; for, as that was fulfilled which He foretold of His death and Passion, so should that likewise be fulfilled which He had foretold of His Resurrection.

*Colloquy.*—O sacred Virgin, how well dost thou begin to perform that office of a Mother, with which thy son charged thee upon the cross; gather me also under thy wings, that the infernal fiends may not presume to hurt me. Amen.

4. Consider the feeling which the Blessed Virgin and the apostles had, when they observed that their number was diminished by the fall of Judas, and the infelicity of this miserable wretch, who if he had returned penitently to our Blessed Lady, as St. Peter did, out of doubt she would have received him, and have comforted him; but his offence had now brought him to that point where there was no peace, nor could be ever capable of consolation.

POINT III.

And the same day "Mary Magdalen, and Mary the mother of James and Salome," who had been to see the sepulchre, and the manner how the body of Jesus was entombed, "brought sweet spices, with which they might anoint Him," (4) the Sabbath day being past.

1. In this passage I will consider, first, the devotion and vigilance of these holy women, both in their attentive contemplation of that which passed at the sepulchre of Christ our Lord, and in observing the place and the manner they left Him, against the time when they should return again; as also in preparing speedily aromatic spices wherewith to

(4) Mat. xxvii. 62; Marc. xvi. 1.

anoint Him; for notwithstanding that there had been already employed a hundred pounds of myrrh in anointing Him, yet all that seemed little now to them, by reason of the desire which they had to honour and serve their beloved master, of whom they had received so much good.

2. And although this work of these pious women was mingled with some imperfection of faith, yet may I learn from thence two things, to be done by me during my whole life, especially after the holy communion.—i. The first is, quietly to contemplate for some time, not from curiosity, but charity, the manner in which Christ is crucified, dies, and is buried for me, and in which He enters into the sepulchre of living souls, who receive Him in the Sacrament, and what He afterwards works in them.—ii. The second is, not to content myself with meditation and contemplation only, but afterwards to proceed to gather the aromatic spices,—that is to say,—exercise the odoriferous virtues, to the glory of God, profit of my neighbours, and the edification of Christ's Church, which is His mystical body, and is anointed and sweetly embalmed with these works.

---

## MEDITATION LVII.

### ON THE GUARD SET AT THE SEPULCHRE OF CHRIST, AND ON THE INCORRUPTION OF HIS BODY.

#### POINT I.

"And the next day, which followed the day of preparation, the chief priests and the Pharisees came together to Pilate, saying:—"Sir, we have remembered that *that seducer said* whilst He was yet alive, After three days I will rise again. Command, therefore, the sepulchre to be guarded until the third day, lest perhaps His disciples come and steal Him away, and say to the people, He is risen from the dead, and *the last error shall be worse than the first.*"(1)

By this act is discovered *the fury of the enemies of Christ*, and how rightly David said, "The pride of them that hate Thee ascends continually."(2) For, notwithstanding that Sabbath day was so solemn, yet they went to Pilate early in the morning to accomplish their accursed persecution.

1. And first, these proud associates disdained to call Christ our Lord by His proper name, but like blasphemers, *called Him by a name belonging to the Devil, viz.*, "*seducer*," whereas in very truth He was the deliverer from all the seduction of the world, and the teacher, who detected all deceits, so that I may take comfort when I am loaded with ignominious names.

2. Secondly, these haters of Christ *became fearful and full of suspicion*, fearing where there was no cause to fear, suspecting that the disciples would steal away the body of their master, and then give out that He was risen from the dead, and that the people would credit this report; all which was without any grounds except that their own hatred blinded them and their own envy disturbed their judgment. So that those who called Christ a "seducer," did not perceive how they themselves were seduced; for the true seducer, who is the Devil, and the spirit of pride had indeed seduced them.

3. Moreover, those who counted it their happiness, to have deprived our Lord of His life, did not remain satisfied with this, *but troubled and unquiet* like a raging sea, endeavoured to obscure the glory of His Resurrection. This however, did not at all profit them, for the divine Providence turned their own inventions against themselves, and took

(1) Mat. xxvii. 62. (2) Psal. lxxiii. 23.

occasion from them to make the Resurrection of Christ more published and believed.

*Colloquy.*—O most sweet Jesus, who wast persecuted by Thine enemies, both in Thy life, and after Thy death, suffer me not to fall into such blindness, as to account seduction, that which is the detection of deceit, or to take the counsels of the just which follow Thine for frauds and impostures. If I am to be deceived, O my God, let it be by Thyself, who, with a holy deceit, art wont to deceive the flesh, and draw it on with delight to obey the spirit.(3)

POINT II.

"Pilate said to them:—You have a guard, go, guard it as you know. And they departing, *made the sepulchre sure,* sealing the stone, and setting guards."(4)

1. In this the Pharisees showed the anxiety of their execrable suspicion, *for they would not trust their own soldiers,* suspecting that the disciples of Christ might bribe them, and obtain leave to carry away the body secretly; and therefore they sealed the stone of the sepulchre with their own seal. But much better did the eternal Father seal it with the seal of His omnipotence, placing millions of angels to keep the body of His Son.

*Colloquy.*—O my Saviour, who, through the envy of Thine enemies, resemblest Daniel in the lions' den, the stone of which was sealed with the seal of king Darius,(5) Thou art secure in the den of Thy sepulchre, since neither lions, that is, the worms, dare approach to touch Thy body, nor enemies from without do it hurt; deliver me, O Lord, from those domestic enemies, my passions, lest they tear me with their teeth; and from my foreign enemies, the devils and

(3) Ose. ii. 14; Vide Ribera.
(4) Mat. xxvii. 65. (5) Dan. vi. 17.

their agents, lest they annoy me with their temptations and false charges. Amen.

2. From this example of diligence in the children of this world, I will learn to be no less diligent in keeping my soul, after it has been made the habitation and sepulchre of Christ our Lord *in the Holy Communion*, taking care to seal it up, and to guard it, lest any steal Christ and the spirit of devotion away from me; but what seal can I put upon it more secure, or what guard more powerful, than Christ Himself?

*Colloquy.*—O my beloved, who saidst, "Put me as a seal upon thy heart, as a seal upon thy arm, for love is strong as death, jealousy is hard as hell;"(6) seal, I beseech Thee, my heart, my senses, and my powers, with the seal of Thy charity, and of the imitation of Thy glorious virtues, that sealed with this seal, I may enjoy Thee for ever and ever. Amen.

POINT III.

1. The body of Christ our Lord remained in the sepulchre *three days and three nights*, counting a part for the whole, that is, strictly speaking, two nights and one entire day;(7) to signify, that by the death and burial of Christ, we are delivered from two deaths, that is, the death of both soul and body, by guilt and eternal punishment, represented by the two nights; and are restored to one life, expressed by the one day, the life of grace and charity.

2. All this time the body of Christ our Saviour was *preserved entire* and *free from corruption*, no part of it being resolved into dust, or anything else, as had been foretold by the prophet David, when he said:—"Because Thou wilt not leave my soul in hell, nor wilt give Thy Holy One to see corruption."(8) For, although Christ willingly

(6) Cant. viii. 6. (7) S. Tho. 3, p. q. li. art. 3.
(8) Psal. xv. 10; Act. ii. 31.

subjected Himself to the miseries of man, and to the penalty of death which He had incurred for His sin, yet He would not subject Himself to the penalty of corruption, and of being turned to dust, not willing to leave for any time, however short, either of the two parts of that nature, which He had united to Himself in unity of Person. For, if the body had been dissolved, this union also would have been dissolved, which His goodness and charity would not suffer, for He would never leave that which He had once assumed.

*Colloquy.*—O most loving Redeemer, I give Thee thanks for having delivered us from the two deaths of guilt and eternal pain, and for having procured for us by Thy death the life of grace, which is the beginning of everlasting life; dear Lord, apply to me the fruit of Thy Passion, deliver me from these two deaths, and grant me these two lives, which in Thee are but one. I rejoice, O my Saviour, that Thy body has always remained incorruptible, and that the union of Thy divine Person with it has never been interrupted. I beseech Thee, therefore, to deliver me from the corruption of sin, and so to unite me to Thyself, in the perfect union of perpetual charity, that I may persevere in it, even to life everlasting. Amen.

The descent of the soul of Christ into limbo will be considered in the Fifth Part which immediately follows; because it belongs to the glorious triumphs which Christ our Lord obtained by the merits of His Passion, for which He was glorified and honoured, both by men and angels, together with the Father and the Holy Ghost. Amen.

END OF VOL. IV.

---

RICHARDSON AND SON, DERBY.

Milton Keynes UK
Ingram Content Group UK Ltd.
UKHW041817211123
432980UK00001BB/2